Working Forests in the Neotropics

Biology and Resource Management Series

BIOLOGY AND RESOURCE MANAGEMENT SERIES

Edited by Michael J. Balick, Anthony B. Anderson, Charles M. Peters, and Kent H. Redford

Working Forests in the Neotropics

CONSERVATION THROUGH SUSTAINABLE MANAGEMENT?

Edited by Daniel J. Zarin, Janaki R. R. Alavalapati, Francis E. Putz, and Marianne Schmink

Columbia University Press
New York

Columbia University Press
Publishers Since 1893
New York   Chichester, West Sussex
Copyright © 2004 Columbia University Press
All rights reserved

Library of Congress Cataloging-in-Publication Data
Working forests in the neotropics—conservation through sustainable
 management? / edited by Daniel J. Zarin . . . [et al.].
     p. cm. — (Biology and resource management series)
   Includes bibliographical references and index.
   ISBN 0-231-12906-8 (alk. paper) — ISBN 0-231-12907-6
   (pbk. : alk. paper)
     1. Forests and forestry—Latin America. 2. Forest conservation—
   Latin America. 3. Forest management—Latin America. 4. Sustainable
   forestry—Latin America. I. Zarin, Daniel. II. Biology and resource
   management in the tropics series.

   SD153.W67 2004
   634.9'098—dc22
                                                        2004052789

Columbia University Press books are printed on permanent
and durable acid-free paper.

Printed in the United States of America

c 10 9 8 7 6 5 4 3 2 1
p 10 9 8 7 6 5 4 3 2 1

Contents

PART 3   **Working Forest Paradoxes**

PART 4   **Envisioning a Future for Sustainable Tropical Forest Management**

Contributors

Janaki R. R. Alavalapati, School of Forest Resources and Conservation, University of Florida, Gainesville, Florida, U.S.A.

Ane Alencar, Instituto de Pesquisa Ambiental da Amazônia (IPAM), Belém, Pará, Brazil

Keith Alger, Conservation International, Washington, D.C., U.S.A.

Arild Angelsen, Department of Economics and Resource Management, Agricultural University of Norway, Aas, Norway, and Center for International Forestry Research, Bogor, Indonesia.

Thomas T. Ankersen, Levin College of Law, University of Florida, Gainesville, Florida, U.S.A.

Gregory P. Asner, Department of Global Ecology, Carnegie Institution, Stanford University, Stanford, California, U.S.A.

Christopher Barber, Center for Global Change and Earth Observations, Michigan State University, East Lansing, Michigan, U.S.A.

Grenville Barnes, Geomatics Program, University of Florida, Gainesville, Florida, U.S.A.

Paulo Barreto, Instituto do Homem e Meio Ambiente da Amazônia (IMAZON), Belém, Pará, Brazil

Ana Cristina Barros, Instituto de Pesquisa Ambiental da Amazônia (IPAM), Belém, Pará, Brazil

Antonio Jose Mota Bentes, Instituto de Pesquisa Ambiental da Amazônia (IPAM), Belém, Pará, Brazil

David Barton Bray, Department of Environmental Studies, Florida International University, Miami, Florida, U.S.A.

Eduardo S. Brondízio, Department of Anthropology and Anthropological Center for Training and Research on Global Environmental Change (ACT), Indiana University, Bloomington, Indiana, U.S.A.

Aaron Bruner, Center for Applied Biodiversity Science at Conservation International, Washington, D.C., U.S.A

Walter Chomentowski, Center for Global Change and Earth Observations, Michigan State University, East Lansing, Michigan, U.S.A.

Mark A. Cochrane, Center for Global Change and Earth Observations, Michigan State University, East Lansing, Michigan, U.S.A.

Joshua C. Dickinson, The Forest Management Trust, Gainesville, Florida, U.S.A.

Gustavo A. B. da Fonseca, Center for Applied Biodiversity Science at Conservation International, Washington, D.C., U.S.A., and Departamento de Zoologia, Universidade Federal de Minas Gerais, Belo Horizonte, Minas Gerais, Brazil

John M. Forgach, A2R Ltd., São Paulo, Brazil.

Todd S. Fredericksen, Life Sciences, Ferrum College, Ferrum, Virginia, U.S.A.

Claude Gascon, Conservation International, Washington, D.C., U.S.A.

Bernardus H. J. de Jong, El Colegio de la Frontera Sur, Villahermosa, Tabasco, Mexico

David Kaimowitz, Center for International Forestry Research, Bogor, Indonesia

Michael Keller, International Institute of Tropical Forestry, U.S. Department of Agriculture, Forest Service, Río Piedras, Puerto Rico, U.S.A.

Paul Lefebvre, The Woods Hole Research Center, Woods Hole, Massachusetts, U.S.A.

Eirivelthon Lima, The Woods Hole Research Center, Woods Hole, Massachusetts, U.S.A., and Instituto de Pesquisa Ambiental da Amazônia (IPAM), Belém, Pará, Brazil

Martin K. Luckert, Department of Rural Economy, University of Alberta, Edmonton, Alberta, Canada

Ariel E. Lugo, International Institute of Tropical Forestry, U.S. Department of Agriculture, Forest Service, Río Piedras, Puerto Rico, U.S.A.

Eraldo A. T. Matricardi, Center for Global Change and Earth Observations, Michigan State University, East Lansing, Michigan, U.S.A.

David G. McGrath, Núcleo de Altos Estudos Amazônicos, Universidade Federal do Pará, Belém, Pará, Brazil

Elsa Mendoza, Instituto de Pesquisa Ambiental da Amazônia (IPAM), Belém, Pará, Brazil

Russell A. Mittermeier, Conservation International, Washington, D.C., U.S.A.

Daniel Nepstad, The Woods Hole Research Center, Woods Hole, Massachusetts, U.S.A., and Instituto de Pesquisa Ambiental da Amazônia (IPAM), Belém, Pará, Brazil

Michael Palace, Complex Systems Research Center, University of New Hampshire, New Hampshire, U.S.A.

Marielos Peña-Claros, Instituto Boliviano de Investigaciones Forestales, Santa Cruz, Bolivia

Charles M. Peters, New York Botanical Garden, Bronx, New York, U.S.A.

Michelle A. Pinard, Department of Agriculture and Forestry, University of Aberdeen, Aberdeen, United Kingdom

Miguel Pinedo-Vasquez, Center for Environmental Research and Conservation, Columbia University, New York, New York, U.S.A.

Francis E. Putz, Department of Botany, University of Florida, Gainesville, Florida, U.S.A.

Claudia Azevedo Ramos, Instituto de Pesquisa Ambiental da Amazônia (IPAM), Belém, Pará, Brazil, and Universidade Federal do Pará, Belém, Pará, Brazil

Richard E. Rice, Center for Applied Biodiversity Science at Conservation International, Washington, D.C., U.S.A.

Sara J. Scherr, Forest Trends, Washington, D.C., U.S.A.

Marianne Schmink, Center for Latin American Studies, University of Florida, Gainesville, Florida, U.S.A.

Robin R. Sears, Center for Environmental Research and Conservation, Columbia University, New York, and Institute of Economic

Botany, The New York Botanical Garden, Bronx, New York, U.S.A.

José Natalino Macedo Silva, Empresa Brasileira de Pesquisa Agropecuária (EMBRAPA) Amazônia Oriental, Belém, Pará, Brazil

David L. Skole, Center for Global Change and Earth Observations, Michigan State University, East Lansing, Michigan, U.S.A.

Catherine M. Tucker, Department of Anthropology, Indiana University, Bloomington, Indiana, U.S.A.

Adalberto Veríssimo, Instituto do Homem e Meio Ambiente da Amazônia (IMAZON), Belém, Pará, Brazil

Jorge Viana, Governor, State of Acre, Brazil

Andy White, Forest Trends, Washington, D.C., U.S.A.

Thomas E. Wilson, International Specialties, Inc., Germantown, Tennessee, U.S.A.

Daniel J. Zarin, School of Forest Resources and Conservation, University of Florida, Gainesville, Florida, U.S.A.

Foreword

The Honorable Jorge Viana, Governor of the State of Acre, Brazil

---

Acre is a unique state in Brazil. One hundred years ago the territory was part of Bolivia; on August 6, 2002, the state celebrated its hundredth anniversary. Of the state's 150,000 km^2, 90% is still forested. Most of the deforestation is located along the agricultural and cattle frontier in the east.

Migrants and entrepreneurs moved to Acre from southern Brazil beginning in the 1970s and began to clear the forests in the southeastern portion of the state where they could be reached by roads. The clearing of these forests took away the livelihoods of rubber tappers who had lived there for generations, since the rubber boom of the late nineteenth century that caused Peruvians, Bolivians, British, Americans, and Brazilians to take notice of this remote region, abundant in rubber trees.

But the rubber tappers organized to resist this onslaught on the forests on which they depended. During the 1970s, 1980s, and 1990s they developed a strong social movement in defense of the forest, whose best-known leader, Chico Mendes, was murdered in 1988 by a rancher. My "Forest Government," which has been in power since January of 1999, seeks to make reality of the dreams of Chico Mendes and the rubber tappers movement: proposals for development that improve the livelihoods of the state's peoples while preserving and using the state's forests.

The Acre we want is one whose development depends on wise use of the forest. We want to live and to raise our children, and them to do the same in an Acre where everyone has a decent life and all have the opportunity to prosper. We want an Acre with her natural riches conserved and her cultural diversity valued. We dream of Acre as a forested state, whose economy is based on solid and diversified competitive forest enterprises, both community-based and entrepreneurial, that generate certified environmental products and services with high value added.

Our actions seek to raise the level of sustainability in Acre according to the following principles:

- Social sustainability, by democratizing access to opportunities;
- Ecological sustainability, by using ecological indicators to govern use of natural resources;

- Economic sustainability, by stimulating and supporting competitive productive enterprises;
- Cultural sustainability, by respecting the values, traditions, and ways of living of traditional populations;
- Political sustainability, by promoting networks, linkages, partnerships, and participatory processes;
- Ethical sustainability, by insisting upon truth and honesty;
- Human sustainability, by respecting the sanctity of life.

The Acre we inherited was in institutional chaos parallel to the degradation of the state's deforested areas. The state government was financially insolvent, with a very bad reputation in Brazil; the public administration was practically inoperative and highly inefficient; there were severe deficits in the supply of public services for the population; and the institutional environment was anarchic. It has taken us three years to pay off the state's debts and reconstruct the government structure and infrastructure, and today the administrative structure is sound.

Some of our priorities, which constituted preconditions for our success, included the reconstruction of state and physical infrastructure and social services (24-hour electricity, roads), and absolute priority for education. We signed an agreement with the Federal University of Acre that expanded basic teaching as well as university training, now including 37 degree programs. We developed clear rules for resource use through the economic-ecological zonation of the state (a process that began 15 years ago and was completed within 6 months of our government taking power), and provided incentives to attract investments. We also developed partnerships with many local and outside organizations, including non-governmental organizations (NGOs), universities, unions, associations, and the federal government). An example of this strategy is the continuing strong collaboration with the University of Florida.

Our forest policy is based on a vision of integrated management of the forest, in which it is considered as a supplier of environmental products and services. I am a dreamer. For this reason I created Acre's Secretariat for Forests and Extractivism, the only one that exists in Brazil.

Acre's forest production is characterized by few products and low value. We are developing strategies to integrate the knowledge of local populations (Indians and rubber tappers) with scientific and technological advances and with market opportunities. The analytical process that we used to establish our forest policy consisted in the formulation of questions and the constitution of a strong network of partners focused on finding the answers most consistent with our reality. Our forest program, called "Sustainable Development Program for Forest Product Chains," works with all the specific actors in the product chains.

Some of the accomplishments achieved directly or indirectly by the program include

- Increase in rubber production by 200% since 1998;
- Development of management protocols for 21 nontimber forest products;
- Installation of two Brazil nut processing factories (in the towns of Xapuri and Brasiléia), increasing the capacity of adding value in the state from 5% to 50% for the Brazil nut harvest;
- Certification of the first community timber management project in Amazonia (Cachoeira Agro-Extractive Settlement Project, where Chico Mendes lived);
- Certification of the Porto Dias Agro-Extractive Settlement Project, supported by the Amazon Workers Center (CTA), a local NGO;
- Installation of the Aver Amazonia company in Xapuri, which specializes in products made from certified wood, such as furniture and high-quality and well-designed artifacts;
- A forest management demonstration project with a traditional timber company, following the Forest Stewardship Council certification guidelines;
- An Inter-American Development Bank Project with a total value of $132 million, which seeks to accelerate the process of creating and consolidating a strong forestry sector, including infrastructure to support forestry activities; creation of four production forests covering 1.5 million hectares; creation of three state parks covering 600,000 hectares; credit lines for communities and entrepreneurs to carry out timber and nontimber forest management projects; institutional strengthening for the Secretariat (office, vehicles, and equipment);
- A Forestry Law that establishes a state system of protected natural areas and institutes a regime of public concessions, a State Forestry Council, and a forestry fund;
- Additional new legislation which creates new mechanisms for privatization of services that can be delegated by the state to local NGOs, strengthening existing NGOs and stimulating the formation of new ones;
- Support for the creation and strengthening of the Cooperative of Rural Workers and Extractivists of Acre (COOPERACRE), the newest and most modern center for marketing of extractivist products;

- The Mahogany Project, in partnership with the Amazon Insititute of People and Environment (IMAZON), the United States Forest Service, the United States Agency for International Development, and World Wildlife Fund, which will carry out industrial-scale management and analysis of economic viability of mahogany management. Since extraction of mahogany is currently prohibited, this project can serve as an example of good management.
- Bioprospecting projects in Acre's forests, and research on drugs for neglected diseases (currently under discussion).

By 2006, our goal is to produce

- 10,000 tons of dry rubber/year (the same as 1984 production levels);
- 10,000 tons of processed Brazil nuts;
- 750,000 m³ of certified timber;
- 4,000 tons of oils (*copaiba, murumuru, andiroba, buriti*)
- 1,000 tons of barks (*unha-de-gato, ipê-roxo, jatobá*)

In a conservative scenario, we expect the following impacts:

- Increase of approximately 300% in income of extractivist families, generated through marketing of forest products;
- Involvement of most extractivist families;
- Direct and indirect generation of approximately 2,000 jobs;
- Insertion of approximately $60 million/year in the state's economy.

The challenges we face in implementing these plans in Acre depend upon the help and support of many partnerships with universities, research institutions, and scientists. The examples of states like Acre and Amapá have convinced the Brazilian government that these new approaches are necessary and viable. Many questions remain, and to answer them we need help. The challenge for scientists is to help make our dreams a reality by contributing your research to meet the needs of peoples and markets in Acre and other parts of the tropics. Acre's experiments in forest-based development offer a hopeful alternative to the steady deforestation observed in Brazilian Amazonia. Many long-term ecological, economic, cultural, and political challenges and opportunities remain for sustaining and adapting these policy initiatives. The contents of this book provide many insights that will inform efforts to overcome the challenges and seize the opportunities.

Acknowledgments

Many of the contributions to this volume grew out of an international conference held on the University of Florida campus in Gainesville, Florida, in February 2002. That event was co-sponsored by the university's School of Forest Resources and Conservation and by the Forest Management Trust. At the university, additional funding was provided by the Office of Research and Graduate Programs, the Office of International Programs, and the Dean for Research of the Institute of Food and Agricultural Sciences. External financial support was provided by the United States Forest Service, the United States Agency for International Development, and Forest Trends. We particularly thank Wayne Smith, former director of the School of Forest Resources and Conservation, and Jan Engert, of the United States Forest Service Office of International Programs, for their support of this project. We also thank Kelly Keefe, Patricia Sampaio, and Lucas Fortini for organizational and technical assistance with the manuscript text, tables, and figures. In addition to the editors, reviewers of the following chapters included Robert Buschbacher, Karen Kainer, and Mark Schulze.

Working Forests in the Neotropics

Chapter 1

NEOTROPICAL WORKING FORESTS
CONCEPTS AND REALITIES

Daniel J. Zarin

> The natural world does not organize itself into parables. Only people do that, because this is our peculiarly human method for making the world make sense. And because people differ in their beliefs, because their visions of the true, the good, and the beautiful are not always the same, they inevitably differ as well in their understanding of what nature means and how it should be used—because nature is so often the place where we go searching for the fulfillment of our desires.
> —Cronon 1995:50

In the past two decades, many scientists have measured rates of destruction and degradation of neotropical forests that are unprecedented in human history (e.g., Skole and Tucker 1993, Cochrane et al. 1999, Nepstad et al. 1999). In the same interval, others have increased our awareness of the intermingled history of humans and neotropical forests that stretches back millennia and, with the exception of the past few hundred years, is written not on paper or parchment but on the walls of caves and in the ashes of their hearths, in the shards and shells buried in middens and broken in the soil made black by the decayed wastes of human activities, in the layered silt of lakes and bogs, and in the very contours of the earth's surface (e.g., Roosevelt 1991, Denevan 1992, Roosevelt et al. 1996, Lentz 2000). With eyes fixed on both the present and the past, we are challenged to envision the future of neotropical forests and of the people who live in them.

What are working forests? The term has multiple meanings, a common problem for words or terms that express complex ideas (Williams 1980). We have a hard enough time with the word *forest,* for which a discussion group of the International Union of Forest Research Organizations found 624 definitions currently in use. Although all 624 consider forests to be areas with trees, they found 149 definitions of trees, varying with respect to inclusion of palms, bamboo, shrubs, vines, and coppice shoots, among others (Lund 2002).

What is a tree? What is not a tree? What is a forest? What is not a forest? This same issue of what to include and what to exclude challenges our definition of working forests.

Conceptually, the term *working forests* emerged as a way of distinguishing production forests from those set aside as wilderness. Broadly speaking, they are naturally regenerated forests used for economic purposes and so include places where logging and other extractive activities occur. Sometimes the term is used to suggest management for the sustained yield of forest products, but this is not always the case. Similarly, the term is sometimes used to identify forests outside parks, although legally protected areas certainly could include many that are managed, such as community forests, extractive reserves, or state or national production forests, not to mention private landholdings that may be limited to forest uses only, through regulation or deed restrictions.

In the United States, the concept of working forests resonates with that of working farms, as a bulwark against urbanization and suburbanization, particularly the spread of housing subdivisions and the sprawl of stripmalls—working forests and farms as places where the human footprint on the landscape is less destructive to its natural inhabitants. Uses of the term in the United States include reference to working forest easements, recreational areas, and wildlife habitat. There is also a rather specific use by the forest product industry to refer to industrial plantations as working forests. In 2002, the annual convention of the Society of American Foresters was titled "Forests at Work."

In Latin America, the working forest idea is part of a larger emphasis on the simultaneous promotion of conservation and rural development, which includes consideration of ecological, economic, and social sustainability, rather than the more narrowly characterized sustained yield (Uhl and Nepstad 2000). This multidimensional sustainability tends to focus on ecosystem services, financial competitiveness with respect to alternative land uses, and equitable distribution of costs and benefits among resident populations.

Is managing forests for the production of goods and services a viable strategy for achieving conservation and development objectives? Are conservation and rural development compatible or mutually exclusive goals? Both questions are too value laden to be answered by science alone, and they are subsumed within the larger philosophical question of whether we consider ourselves to be of nature or apart from it. For each of the questions in this widening frame of inquiry there are clearly more than just two possible answers arrayed in opposition to one another. I do not intend to explore the larger philosophical issue here but only to emphasize that one's response to it frames one's view of the more limited subject matter of this book, namely forest management as a neotropical conservation strategy, because managing neotropical forests is something people do either *in* nature or *to* nature, depending on the frame of reference through which one views human interaction with the natural world.

This book explores ideas and evidence about the efficacy of forest management as a strategy for neotropical conservation. As the varied contributions to this volume indicate, forest management encompasses many different kinds of activities and may mean very different things to different people; the same is true of forest conservation (Redford and Sanderson 2000). The extent to which forest management helps or hinders the achievement of conservation objectives certainly depends on the particulars of a specific management regime and the ecology of the specific forest in which it is implemented, but it also depends on what we mean by conservation or, perhaps more precisely, what we are worried about conserving.

The four parts of the book, briefly summarized here, are organized around key issues in neotropical working forests. Part I, "Industrial Forestry as a Tropical Conservation Strategy," describes where and how that strategy is being pursued, with an emphasis on Brazil and Bolivia. Part II, "Working Forests and Community Development in Latin America," provides case studies of community and smallholder forest management throughout the region. Part III, "Working Forest Paradoxes," focuses on the tension between forest management and conservation, and several of the contributions suggest reasons why working forests might not contribute effectively to tropical forest conservation. Part IV, "Envisioning a Future for Sustainable Tropical Forest Management," emphasizes the need for policies that ensure more equitable distribution of the costs and benefits of forest sector activities than has occurred in the past.

INDUSTRIAL FORESTRY AS A TROPICAL CONSERVATION STRATEGY

Heated debates often are framed as simple dichotomies: preservation versus people, wild versus managed, conservation versus development. In chapter 2, Francis Putz emphasizes that these dichotomies unnecessarily polarize debate. He points to an accumulating body of research that explores tradeoffs and complementarities between protection and production, timber and nontimber forest products or ecosystem services, corporate and community forest management, and legal and market incentives for conservation. Although simplicity has great emotive appeal, polarized debates can obscure more than they reveal of the rich detail of reality that should help guide the decisions about the futures of the varied forests of the neotropics. .

In the Brazilian Amazon, nearly all timber extraction still occurs in the absence of significant forest management, and much logging activity is actually illegal. In chapter 3, Adalberto Veríssimo and Paulo Barreto argue that Brazil's ambitious National Forest Program (PNF) has enormous potential for promoting good management, essential monitoring and enforcement, and critical land titling in a region where 45 percent of the territory is either unclaimed public land or under title dispute. Promulgated in 2000 by the Brazilian Ministry of the Environment, the PNF calls for the establishment of 500,000 km^2 of national forests throughout the Amazon by 2010. The effort is analogous to the establishment of the U.S. National Forest System by the Roosevelt administration in 1908 and to Brazil's prior establishment of vast indigenous and extractive reserves. The multiple objectives of the PNF are to contribute to frontier stabilization, capture income from the forest, encourage forest management, and conserve biodiversity. Veríssimo and Barreto place particular emphasis on the pressing need for adequate resources to develop and implement a concession model for the national forests that includes external auditing of forest management standards, accounting practices, and social impacts.

Along with its ambitious efforts in forest conservation, Brazil has also been a leader in tropical forest research. For the past five years, the Brazilian-led Large-Scale Biosphere–Atmosphere (LBA) Experiment in Amazonia has been investigating interactions between land use, carbon, and nutrient dynamics. In chapter 4, Michael Keller and colleagues report on a component of LBA that has focused on evaluating the sustainability of logging practices using remote sensing and modeling tools. They show that carefully planned reduced-impact logging can produce net increases in the forest carbon sink, consistent with earlier work in Malaysia (Putz and Pinard 1993). Using data from old-growth forests in the state of Pará, Keller and colleagues have calculated that a thirty-year rotation cycle based on extraction of up to 2 m^2 of basal area per hectare is sustainable out to 200 years. They also report on new analytical techniques that show great promise for monitoring logging activities and their impacts using remote sensing.

In neighboring Bolivia, another major research program has been in progress for the past ten years, under the auspices of the Bolivian Sustainable Forestry Project (BOLFOR), supported by the U.S. Agency for International Development (USAID) and counterpart environmental conservation funds (PL-480). In chapter 5, the succession of forest ecologists who have headed the research component of BOLFOR from its inception to the present share their collective experience. They focus on lessons learned, including the importance of basic species ecology for designing silvicultural systems; the role of land use history, which may date back hundreds of years, in shaping stand composition and structure; the impact of vines on regeneration and tree growth; the dominance of secondary effects of logging on biodiversity, especially faunal declines caused by increased hunting, when compared with the direct effects of selective harvesting; and the practical import of sociopolitical context, especially livelihood systems and land use practices in the larger landscape.

The BOLFOR effort has also brought the largest area of managed native forest in the tropics under third-party certification; in Bolivia, Forest Stewardship Council (FSC) certification fulfills newly instituted legal requirements for forest management. Third-party green certification of tropical forest management practices emerged in the 1990s as an alternative to consumer boycotts of tropical timber, and FSC has emerged as the principal third-party certifier in the neotropics. In chapter 6, Joshua Dickinson and colleagues, ardent supporters of the FSC certification system, describe the challenges facing the business of certified forestry in the contrasting contexts of Bolivia and Brazil.

WORKING FORESTS AND COMMUNITY DEVELOPMENT IN LATIN AMERICA

Unlike corporate firms, rural communities do not exist solely, or even primarily, for the purpose of optimizing net revenue from their activities. Can working forests contribute to community development? Can rural communities contribute to forest conservation? Part II contains five case studies that respond positively to those questions but begins with three chapters that provide an analysis of links between communities, forests, and markets; a set of strategies for promoting market access for community forest products and services; and a discussion of the complexity of community land and resource tenure systems underlying a varied array of forest resource uses in the neotropics.

In chapter 7, Marianne Schmink introduces part II by emphasizing the importance of understanding how forest management and marketing fit into and alter existing complex livelihood systems. Conducting what Schmink calls a social inventory before developing plans for community forests is essential for achieving that understanding. Planning a community forest enterprise necessitates information about the multiplicity of existing uses of forest resources, the variety of land and resource tenure forms, and the distribution of resources, as well as within-community institutional arrangements, cultural, ethnic, or religious divisions, gender issues, and demographic patterns. Such information is at least as critical to community forest management planning as the data on tree species composition and structure collected in a traditional forest inventory; its absence may be responsible for major failures.

In chapter 8, Sara Scherr and colleagues identify opportunities and needs for increasing market access for forest products from communities in developing countries. They suggest that market opportunities for communities are growing with increased community control over forest resources, along with increased overall scarcity of tropical hardwoods and the development of niche markets for forest products and environmental services. Realizing these opportunities requires strong producer organizations, strategic partnerships with industry and nongovernmental organizations, and technical assistance in all aspects of forest-based business management. Scherr and colleagues provide a set of policy guidelines to facilitate market development for community-based forest management.

Decentralization and transfer of control over forest resources from national governments to rural communities has been a significant trend in Latin America in the past fifteen years. But the meaning and complexity of that control differ markedly from place to place. In chapter 9, Tom Ankersen and Grenville Barnes discuss these differences through the prominent examples of a community concession in the Maya Biosphere Reserve in the Peten region of Guatemala, extractive reserve areas in the Brazilian Amazon, and the *ejido* system in Mexico. In each case, the tenure systems are fluid, and Ankersen and Barnes suggest that community-based information systems are needed to document and maintain critical information on a parcel-by-parcel basis.

Throughout Latin America, transfer of control over forests to rural communities has followed communal collective action against forest degradation or deforestation by outsiders, either corporations or wealthy individual landowners. In chapter 10, Catherine Tucker describes two such cases in Central American communities, one from Mexico, the other from Honduras; both began as protests against industrial logging concessions. For both cases, Tucker examines the factors that contributed to the success of their collective action and describes how their forests have fared in the aftermath.

In chapter 11, David McGrath and colleagues describe another circumstance in which transfer of control over the forest resource to rural communities occurred as a result of communal collective action. Their example comes from western Pará, Brazil, where the Tapajós-Arapiuns Extractive Reserve was created in 1998. For the past five years, members of three communities in the reserve have participated in a cooperative furniture-building enterprise. McGrath and colleagues report on the lessons learned from this experience, an example of what they call boutique capitalism, in which small-scale production of high-quality finished products is sold in green consumer markets.

In an influential article published in 1997, Richard Rice and colleagues at Conservation International (CI) made the case that, after two decades and hundreds of millions of dollars of investment, efforts to promote sustainable management of tropical forests had produced only trivial results (Rice et al. 1997). More recently, the CI group has elaborated their critique of forest management on both economic and ecological grounds (e.g., Bowles et al. 1998, Rice et al. 2001). Although several of the chapters in parts I and II take issue with their arguments, David Bray points out in chapter 12 that CI's case against the ecological and economic viability of sustainable forest management (SFM) relied almost exclusively on analyses of private sector logging in concessions on public land. Using the case of a Mexican *ejido,* Bray argues that extrapolation of the CI analyses to community forest enterprises is suspect because the nature of community interactions with communal forests differs dramatically from corporate interactions with public forest concessions.

In an astounding example of corporate–community linkage, Bernardus de Jong in chapter 13 reports on a project in southern Mexico in which the International Federation of Automobiles has been buying carbon storage in forests in and near rural communities to offset the carbon emissions from Formula 1 race events. Concern over global warming and the increases in atmospheric concentrations of greenhouse gases that are linked to it have led to a variety of similar initiatives to reduce or offset fossil fuel CO_2 emissions under the Clean Development Mechanism of the Kyoto Protocol (Smith and Scherr 2002). Many emitters have determined that forest-based carbon offsets are cheaper than reductions, and in many cases forestry-related activities in tropical countries are particularly attractive because of the low costs of land and labor. As de Jong notes, where the dominant agricultural land use is only marginally profitable, small payments can produce substantial changes in land use, from farms to forests.

In parts of the vast Amazon floodplain, forestry is already well integrated into the complex livelihood systems of rural smallholders. In chapter 14, Robin Sears and Miguel Pinedo-Vasquez compare small-holder management of one species, *Calycophyllum spruceanum* (Rubi-aceae), in three locales that differ in biophysical and socioeconomic characteristics. The smallholder management systems for *C. spruceanum* are characterized by rapid volume growth, market flexibility, and signif-icant technical prowess in silvicultural treatments and primary process-ing. Such systems are zoned into distinct land use areas on farms and are well integrated with agricultural production. Products include saw-timber, poles, and firewood, and production cycles may be adapted to market demands.

WORKING FOREST PARADOXES

Despite much guarded optimism in other chapters of this book about SFM as an effective strategy for neotropical conservation, most of the chapters in part III provide substantial rationales for skepticism. Janaki Alavalapati and I introduce this part in chapter 15 by focusing on the basic question raised by Clawson (1975): Forests for what and for whom? We highlight the complexities inherent in forest management for multi-ple products and multiple stakeholders and point out further challenges associated with the assessment of multidimensional sustainability in a changing world.

In chapter 16, Gustavo da Fonseca and colleagues suggest that rather than supporting working forests, conservation investors should allocate funds to subsidize keeping forests unemployed. Analogous to timber con-cessions, wherein loggers pay for extraction rights from public lands, in conservation concessions biodiversity investors pay to keep loggers and other resource users out of the concession area by providing a continuous stream of income to the concession grantor. This chapter builds on prior analyses of the importance of protected areas for biodiversity conserva-tion and the limitations and detrimental aspects of sustainable forest management as a conservation strategy (e.g., Bruner et al. 2001, Rice et al. 2001). Fonseca and colleagues also emphasize the need for landscape-scale corridor planning to link protected areas with uses that maintain forest cover, leaving open the possibility that forest management may have a role in conservation landscapes as an alternative land use that maintains forest cover, thereby contributing to landscape connectivity.

Unfortunately, deforestation and forest degradation have fragmented forested landscapes rather than connecting them. In chapter 17, Mark Cochrane and colleagues summarize the results of their work and that of others on the interactions between landscape fragmentation, selective logging, and fire in the Brazilian Amazon. Though apparently sympathetic to the working forest concept as a strategy for conservation and sustainable production, they emphasize that the efficacy of forest management depends on whether the landscape in which forests are embedded is fragmented and degraded, and therefore fire prone, or intact, and therefore fire resistant. Trends over the last two decades have resulted in the dominance of the former condition throughout large portions of Amazonia.

In chapter 18, Arild Angelsen and Martin Luckert take on the theoretical basis underpinning much of the investment in sustainable forest management: that enhancing production and prices of forest goods and services will stimulate conservation. They argue that the increasing marginal costs of production—for example, those associated with extracting forest products from increasingly inaccessible forest frontiers—are an exceptionally effective means of preventing forest exploitation and thereby serve as a passive means of achieving forest conservation. When forests become more valuable through increased production or higher prices, the effectiveness of that passive barrier to exploitation is reduced. They find no clear evidence to support the notion that the economic wants of resource users are fulfilled by incremental increases in production or price; such increases appear more likely to stimulate additional investment in resource exploitation.

The impact of market expansion on the ecology and socioeconomic organization of açaí palm fruit (*Euterpe oleracea*) production described by Eduardo Brondizio in chapter 19 illustrates the principles and processes articulated by Angelsen and Luckert. In some parts of Amazonia, cultivation of the native açaí has intensified to the point where it must be considered a plantation crop. Furthermore, successful marketing of this nontimber forest product has not yet resulted in proportionate benefits to traditional, smallholder producers, despite the marketing emphasis on açaí as a symbol of "sustainable development."

Concluding part III, Ariel Lugo provocatively suggests that the Caribbean island of Puerto Rico has already arrived at the future that may eventually characterize many of the world's tropical forests, a future in which quantitative measures of biodiversity can be high but where common invasives substitute for some of the rarer endemic flora. Not to fear, says Lugo; the aliens are compatible with most of the natives and often facilitate the reestablishment of native ecosystems on highly disturbed sites. Furthermore, the total number of species on the island has actually increased, even though endemism is somewhat reduced. These new forests are working forests, he argues, with significant conservation, ecotourism, and ecosystem service value. Whereas Lugo celebrates this new forest future, it seems clear that some of the authors contributing to this and other sections of the book might see Puerto Rico as "nature's end."

ENVISIONING A FUTURE FOR SUSTAINABLE TROPICAL FOREST MANAGEMENT

In the English language, ancient uses of the word *forest* did not necessarily connote tree cover but emphasized uncultivated land, outside settlements (from the Latin *foris;* Harrison 1992), claimed by the state, usually for the exclusive use of royalty. This older usage echoes the deep and widespread historical precedents for ongoing conflicts over forest resources between the state and allied powerful social and economic groups on one hand and marginalized rural populations on the other (Hecht and Cockburn 1989, Peluso 1992).

Growing frustration with forestry's limited fulfillment of its promise for tropical conservation has recently been matched by concern that forest management has little to offer as a development strategy because "natural forests lack comparative advantage for poverty alleviation" (Wunder 2001:1817). In chapter 21, David Kaimowitz suggests that such concerns should be met by wholesale refocusing of the forest sector from large-scale industrial concessions to smallholder and community forestry. He argues that policies have often subsidized industry's access to public forest resources at the expense of the rural poor.

Daniel Nepstad and colleagues make a related argument for the Brazilian Amazon in chapter 22, in which they highlight the role that good governance should play as defender of the full range of public interests embodied in the region's forests. Those interests include ecological, economic, and social concerns. Contrary to the position articulated by Veríssimo and Barreto in chapter 3, Nepstad and colleagues question whether the public's interests are well served by industrial concessions in remote national forests. Instead, they suggest that timber could be readily supplied from rural communities, in which landowners are legally required to maintain 80 percent of their holdings in forest cover. They argue that shifting timber production from the national forests to these community and family forests would result in lower ecological costs and more equitable distribution of social and economic benefits. To facilitate this process, they emphasize some of the same mechanisms highlighted by Scherr and colleagues in chapter 8: producer organizations, strategic partnerships with industry and nongovernmental organizations, and effective technical assistance programs.

One of the best examples of how governments can respond to the issues raised in these last two chapters is illustrated by the case of Acre, Brazil, described in the foreword to this volume by Acre's governor, Jorge Viana. In Acre, people engaged in nontimber forest product extraction for cash and subsistence economies precipitated grassroots initiatives for forest-based sustainable development, including establishment of the first communal extractive reserves. At a larger scale, the story is similar to the Central American cases discussed by Catherine Tucker in chapter 10, in which legal transfer of rights to forest resources to rural communities followed collective communal action (see also chapter 11). The difference in Acre is that the spirit of those collective actions is embodied in the state government. As articulated by the governor, Acre's forest policy is based on a view of the forest as a supplier of products and services, managed in the public's interest, with the explicit aim of improving indices of multidimensional sustainability.

Biodiversity conservation, sustainable development, sustainable forest management, working forests—these are all complex ideas, each representative of different beliefs about "what nature means and how it should be used" (Cronon 1995:90). The community of scientists, educators, managers, advocates, and policymakers involved in tropical forest conservation in Latin America is far from monolithic and speaks, often loudly, with many voices. We have gathered some of those varied voices here and hope that what they have to say will advance the cause of a more secure future for neotropical forests and for the people who inhabit them.

REFERENCES

Bowles, I. A., Rice, R. E., Mittermeir, R. A., and G. A. da Fonseca. 1998. Logging and tropical forest conservation. *Science* 280: 1899–1990.

Bruner, A. G., R. E. Gullison, R. E. Rice, and G. da Fonseca. 2001. Effectiveness of parks in protecting tropical biodiversity. *Science* 291: 125–128.

Clawson, M. 1975. *Forests for whom and for what?* Baltimore: John Hopkins University Press.

Cochrane, M. A., A. Alencar, M. D. Schulze, C. M. Souza Jr., D.C. Nepstad, P. A. Lefebvre, and E. A. Davidson. 1999. Positive feedbacks in the fire dynamic of closed canopy tropical forests. *Science* 284: 1832–1835.

Cronon, W. 1995. Introduction: In search of nature. In W. Cronon, ed., *Uncommon ground: Toward reinventing nature,* 23–56. New York: W. W. Norton.

Denevan, W. 1992. The pristine myth: The landscape of the Americas in 1492. *Annals of the Association of American Geographers* 82: 369–385.

Harrison, R. P. 1992. *Forests: The shadow of civilization.* Chicago: University of Chicago Press.

Hecht, S. B. and A. Cockburn. 1989. *The fate of the forest: Developers, destroyers, and defenders of the Amazon.* New York: Verso.

Lentz, D. L., ed. 2000. *Imperfect balance: Landscape transformations in the precolumbian Americas*. New York: Columbia University Press.

Lund, H. G. 2002. When is a forest not a forest? *Journal of Forestry* 100: 21–28.

Nepstad, D. C., A. Veríssimo, A. Alencar, C. A. Nobre, E. Lima, P. A. Lefebvre, P. Schlesinger, C. Potter, P. R. d. S. Moutinho, E. Mendoza, M. A. Cochrane, and V. Brooks. 1999. Large-scale impoverishment of Amazonian forests by logging and fire. *Nature* 398: 505–508.

Peluso, N. L. 1992. *Rich forests, poor people*. Berkeley: University of California Press.

Putz, F. E. and M. A. Pinard. 1993. Reduced-impact logging as a carbon offset method. *Conservation Biology* 7: 755–757.

Redford, K. H. and S. E. Sanderson. 2000. Extracting humans from nature. *Conservation Biology* 14: 1362.

Rice, R. E. R. E. Gullison, and J. W. Reid. 1997. Can sustainable management save tropical forests? *Scientific American* 276: 34–39.

Rice, R. E., C. A. Sugal, S. M. Ratay, and G. A. B. da Fonseca. 2001. *Sustainable forest management: A review of conventional wisdom*. Washington, DC: CABS/Conservation International.

Roosevelt, A. C. 1991. *Moundbuilders of the Amazon: Geophysical archaeology on Marajoara Island*. San Diego, Calif.: Academic Press.

Roosevelt, A. C., M. Lima da Costa, C. Lopes Machado, M. Michab, N. Mercier, H. Valladas, J. Feathers, W. Barnett, M. Imazio da Silveira, A. Henderson, J. Sliva, B. Chernoff, D. S. Reese, J. A. Holman, N. Toth, and K. Schick. 1996. Paleoindian cave dwellers in the Amazon: The peopling of the Americas. *Science* 272: 373–384.

Skole, D. and C. Tucker. 1993. Tropical deforestation and habitat fragmentation in the Amazon: Satellite data from 1978 to 1988. *Science* 260: 1905–1910.

Smith, J. and S. A. Scherr. 2002. *Forest carbon and local livelihoods: Assessment of opportunities and policy recommendations*. CIFOR Occasional Paper No. 37.

Uhl, C. and D. C. Nepstad. 2000. Amazonia at the millennium. *Interciencia* 25: 159–164.

Williams, R. 1980. *Problems in materialism and culture: Selected essays*. London: NLB.

Wunder, S. 2001. Poverty alleviation and tropical forests: What scope for synergies? *World Development* 29: 1817–1833.

PART I

Industrial Forestry as a Tropical Conservation Strategy

Chapter 2

ARE YOU A CONSERVATIONIST OR A LOGGING ADVOCATE?

Francis E. Putz

Progress toward resolving major conservation issues often is impeded by false dichotomies such as the question posed by the title of this chapter, inspired by an ecologist's recent critique of the World Bank's 2002 Forest Policy (Laurance 2002). A similarly irritating question—"Are you an environmentalist, or do you work for a living?"—was posed some years earlier in the title of a provocative essay by a well-known environmental historian (White 1995). In both cases the polarization may be politically expedient, but it seems unnecessary and even damaging. In any event, the points are compelling and relevant to the debate about industrial forest management as one of a variety of methods for promoting both nature conservation and rural development. Despite efforts to reconcile or at least clarify philosophical differences to further the cause of conservation (e.g., Callicott 1997, Callicott et al. 1999, Peterson 1999, Limerick 2002), dichotomizing or otherwise oversimplifying continuous and complex variables remains such a pervasive and destructive practice in discussions about the fates of forests that I use a series of them to frame this chapter.

NATURAL VERSUS CULTURAL

> Ecologists who seek out untouched nature—pristine forest—against which to assess human impact are drawing on and reaffirming this [nature vs. culture] divide; they may be disappointed, but not conceptually challenged, when they find pottery sherds in their soil pits beneath 'natural' vegetation.
>
> —Fairhead and Leach 1996:6

15

While battles about social constructionism of nature rage on in the humanities (e.g., Soper 1995, Eder 1996, Hacking 1999) and evidence accumulates that even forests of formerly unquestioned virginity might have been shaped by humans (e.g., Posey 1985, Denevan 1992, Fairhead and Leach 1996, Moran 1996, Foster et al. 1999), many conservation biologists seem to ignore the crumbling edifice of pristine nature (e.g., Struhsaker 1997, Oates 1999, Terborgh 1999). In contrast, patches of forest enriched with useful species by previous agriculturalists do not escape the notice of hunting and gathering groups, even if they do not recognize the origins of the rich patches. That environmentalists and even some ecologists often fail to recognize that many tropical forests are semidomesticated may result from the often subtle impacts of management, especially centuries after human interventions have ceased. On more philosophical grounds, reluctance to accept that a forest has not escaped human influences is understandable because once the "pristine myth" (Denevan 1992) is destroyed and both "nature" and "wilderness" are deconstructed by extreme postmodernists (e.g., Chase 1995, Cronon 1995), a Pandora's box of land use options seems to open.

Although nature–culture dualism has been fundamental to Western thought since the Enlightenment, North American environmentalists, in contrast to their European counterparts (e.g., Birks et al. 1988, Rackham 1980) and some Australians (e.g., Bowman 2001, Flannery 2001, Griffiths 2002), seem particularly unwilling to value "cultural landscapes" (e.g., Willers 2001). Nevertheless, reluctance to move beyond Cartesian ecology and accept that even the most altered landscapes, such as suburban neighborhoods, have environmental value is understandable where such alterations are common relative to more natural areas (but see Jackson 1984, Groth and Bressi 1997). *Nature* and *natural* may be social constructs, but they also represent a biophysical presence that should be recognized, even if it is difficult to draw the line between construct and reality (Peterson 1999). One might also reasonably argue that the few remaining tracts of old-growth forest in eastern North America are "natural" even though they lost their historically dominant tree species (chestnut) and vertebrate (passenger pigeon), both of which probably qualified as keystone species.

One way to avoid the polarizing question of whether an area is "natural" is to recognize that "naturalness" of ecosystems is actually a continuum from thoroughly domesticated (i.e., human dominated or artificial) to wild (i.e., natural, untrammeled, or self-willed; Foreman 1999, Angermeier 2000). The term *wild* has received less scrutiny than *natural*, which makes it less provocative. Furthermore, degrees of "wildness" have been quantitatively assigned using a variety of measures including, for example, road or human population densities (Sanderson et al. 2002, Rüters and Wickham 2003). That "wild" does not capture all of the values of "nature" (e.g., biodiversity richness, representativeness, or rarity) is perhaps advantageous insofar as it reminds us of the complexity of what is at stake.

Movement of species by humans, both intentional and accidental, has resulted in the breakdown of another dualism related to the nature versus culture dichotomy: that of whether a given species in a given location is native or exotic (i.e., introduced, alien, or naturalized). For many recently introduced species the distinction is straightforward, but how long does a species have to be in an area before it is considered native and not just naturalized? The question is not merely academic but could have important implications for conservation-oriented forest management. For example, some familiar commercial species may not be fully native to the forests in which they are currently common (e.g., *Spondias mombin, Brosimum utile, Ceiba pentandra, Durio zibenthus, Eusideroxylon zwagteri,* and *Shorea macroptera*). If these and other species were indeed favored by former forest cultivators, securing their sustained yields may entail silvicultural interventions that represent a substantial degree of forest domestication.

Another dichotomy closely related to the natural versus cultural split pits pristine (i.e., primary, virgin, or undisturbed) against despoiled (i.e., secondary, degraded, managed, domesticated, or disturbed) forest. Most modern ecologists are comfortable with the concept of ecosystems as shifting mosaics of patches in different stages of recovery after natural disturbances (e.g., Sprugel 1991), but humans are still often portrayed as defilers of the pristine. In light of the mounting evidence of human influences on the structure and composition of forests throughout the world, "pristine" should be invoked only with trepidation. Although there is much to do to increase the compatibility of forestry operations with conservation and development goals, it seems hard to justify fencing people out of forests that they and their ancestors helped to create (Slater in press). Furthermore, mimicking current "natural" disturbances may result in the loss of valued species and the disruption of ecosystem processes if these species and processes benefited from earlier cultural interventions.

PROTECTION VERSUS PRODUCTION

> We should dispel any notion that industrial forestry is bio-friendly. It should best be regarded as a form of agriculture.
> —Terborgh 2002:32

Depictions of deforestation can be gruesome, and recently logged forests can also look awful, especially in areas of concentrated timber harvesting, but there is plenty of room along the biodiversity protection to fiber farming continuum for compatibility. Actually, it is hard to generalize about the environmental dangers of production forestry with a timber focus in the tropics, given that logging intensities range over three orders of magnitude (Putz et al. 2001). Furthermore, knowing how a forest was logged is as important as knowing the logging intensity, given that studies on reduced-impact logging methods in many parts of the tropics including Southeast Asia (e.g., Pinard and Putz 1996) and Brazil (e.g., Johns et al. 1999) consistently reveal substantial reductions in collateral damage during selective logging when it is carried out in a planned manner by trained workers. That said, there are also plenty of instances in which timber industries have sorely abused the public's trust and plenty of forests that should remain roadless and unmanaged.

It may seem semantic, but it also seems critical that we not confuse the use of reduced-impact logging (RIL) techniques and the goal of ensuring sustained timber yields (STYs) with sustainable forest management (SFM). RIL is a necessary but mostly insufficient prerequisite for SFM and securing STYs (Poore et al. 1998). In forests with abundant advanced regeneration of commercial timber species, such as the lowland dipterocarp forests of Southeast Asia, following RIL guidelines is tantamount to STY as long as logging intensities remain below eight trees or 50 m^3/ha (Sist et al. 2003). In contrast, RIL contributes little to sustaining yields of the most valued commercial timber in Bolivia, where additional silvicultural treatments are generally needed (Fredericksen et al. 2003). Unfortunately, the silvicultural interventions needed for STY are difficult for many environmentalists to accept insofar as they involve purposeful forest domestication, such as the liberation of future crop trees by girdling noncommercial neighbors, vine cutting, and enrichment planting (Fredericksen and Putz 2003). We can never prove that a forest is sustainably managed, but SFM should always be held up as a goal to which managers should strive while they use RIL techniques and other necessary silvicultural treatments to achieve STY and other management goals (Putz 1994).

Despite ardent calls for protection before it is too late (see chapter 16), numerous studies have shown that selective harvesting of timber from tropical forests can have undetectable, short-term, or even positive effects on a range of ecosystem processes and taxa (Putz et al. 2001). Numerous studies of selective logging in the tropics have consistently revealed that the secondary effects of overhunting, increased susceptibility to fires, and uncontrolled colonization should be of most concern to environmentalists (e.g., Fimbel et al. 2001; see also chapter 17). The production versus protection debate is also rendered confusing in developed countries because most protected area managers accept that active management is needed in the face of the threat of invasive exotic species and the need to mimic historical disturbances, both natural and cultural.

The authors of chapters in this section of *Working Forests in the Tropics* probably would resent being called "logging advocates" and are at least as interested in protection as they are in production, but most accept forest management for timber production as a component of an overall tropical forest conservation strategy. Although none are focused solely or even primarily on timber yields, and forestry degrees are scarce among their many credentials, they are forging ways toward forest conservation that recognize that production and protection are not necessarily opposites. As large portions of the Brazilian Amazon are opened to logging (see chapter 3), working with loggers to improve their practices only increases in importance. Similarly, many indigenous groups and other rural communities with large tracts of forest are moving toward industrial models of forest management for timber as an alternative to forest conversion, presenting another suite of challenges to those who promote and teach environmentally sound logging techniques. Finally, at least some of the authors in this part of the volume accept intensive natural forest management or even the establishment of plantations in suitable areas as a means for reducing pressure on lands that are more appropriately left roadless and unlogged (Sedjo and Botkin 1997).

TIMBER VERSUS NONTIMBER FOREST PRODUCTS

The concept of extractive reserves attracted much attention in the 1980s and early 1990s from social welfare advocates, environmentalists, and policymakers (Spillsbury and Kaimowitz 2000). In this context, *extraction* referred to nontimber forest products (NTFPS, e.g., latex, nuts, vine stems, and fruits); timber extraction was explicitly not included. In fact, the revenues expected from the sustainable harvest of NTFPS often were contrasted with and shown to exceed substantially those from timber harvesting (Peters et al. 1989). After a flurry of articles purporting to demonstrate the high commercial value of NTFPS in tropical forests (e.g., Anderson and Ioris 1992), doubts were raised about both ecological sustainability (Hall and Bawa 1993, Peters 1996) and socioeconomic suitability (Browder 1992, Godoy and Bawa 1993, Southgate 1998, Sheil and Wunder 2002). Incompatibility between forest management for timber and NTFPS has been an underlying assumption in many of these studies.

Certainly the degree of compatibility varies with species and types of products harvested and with management methods, but the few studies conducted on this issue in the tropics have revealed few conflicts (Salick et al. 1995, Romero 1998, Anderson and Putz 2002).

FORESTS AS POVERTY TRAPS VERSUS SAFETY NETS

Tropical forests provide multitudes of products to a wide variety of people, but it is typically the poorest and least empowered people, often differentiated by age, caste, or gender, who depend on them the most (Arnold and Ruiz-Pérez 1998, Jodha 2000, but see Wickramasinghe et al. 1996). Forests can serve as safety nets for the rural poor by providing critical resources, especially when crops fail and in other periods of hardship. Under these conditions, biodiversity conservation is compatible with rural livelihoods. For people living at low population densities in extensive forests, in contrast, the forests may trap them in poverty by making it difficult for them to obtain medical care, educational opportunities, and other social services (Wunder 2001). And when they try to benefit financially from their timber resources, weak institutions, lack of capital, and lack of business acumen make them easy prey for predatory loggers and rapacious timber merchants (Colfer and Byron 2001). Within rural communities and even within households, therefore, forests may serve as both safety nets and poverty traps for different people, thus rendering the dichotomy problematic.

In forest-rich communities of subsistence farmers, household members are also differentially affected by forestry activities. Unless the communities simply sell stumpage, earning revenue from timber requires that some family members participate in inventory work, timber harvesting, and a variety of other tasks that remove them from the farming workforce. Their absence, even if temporary, necessitates substantial household-level workload adjustments and puts the entire family at risk if the enterprise fails (Cronkleton in press). Therefore it is reasonable for risk-averse families to refuse to jeopardize their subsistence activities to participate in for-profit forest management activities that, even under the best circumstances, are risky.

Progress toward making forests more than just safety nets while increasing the sustainability of forest use in the tropics is being enhanced through partnerships between foresters and social welfare advocates who see commercialization of timber as a way out of poverty for rural people. Recent strides toward making forestry effective for both conservation and poverty alleviation have been impressive, even while most tropical forests continue to be exploited for a few valuable timber species by a small group of wealthy loggers and their beneficiaries down the market chain, including purchasers of undervalued tropical hardwoods in industrialized countries.

The risks of physical injury associated with logging add a dimension to the concept of forests as safety nets. Even in developed countries with strong occupational and safety regulations, recent statistics indicate that the risks of injury and death in logging surpass those in all other industries (Myers and Fosbroke 1995, U.S. Bureau of Labor Statistics 1998). Perhaps the staggering number of logging injuries in the tropics (International Labour Organization 1990) should not be surprising given that there are plenty of poor people willing to do this high-risk work for low pay and take even greater risks for meager bonuses. Where inexperienced and untrained forest workers lacking even rudimentary personal safety gear fell, yard, load, and haul logs from large trees, often using old and marginally functional equipment, we can only expect that the frequency of injury and death will increase. Horribly, such conditions are the norm for most community-based and many industrial logging operations in tropical forest regions.

CORPORATE VERSUS COMMUNITY-BASED FOREST MANAGEMENT

Rapid development of community-based forest enterprises (see chapter 8) and the expanding range of company–community partnerships (Mayers and Vermeulen 2002) are making it difficult to differentiate between industrial and community forestry. For example, in lowland Guatemala (see chapter 9) and Bolivia (e.g., Pacheco and Kaimowitz 1998), community forestry operations are essentially rural enterprises, and the primary beneficiaries often are former participants in the "informal" logging sector (i.e., pirate loggers). There is nothing inherently wrong with this, but calling it community forestry conveys an impression of broad-based community involvement, which may not be the case. Communities that successfully use forests as revenue sources may assume many characteristics formerly associated with the corporate world, such as profit maximization at the expense of sustainability. This is not to suggest that there are not persistent and deep-seated differences between companies and communities but that by focusing on the extremes, we will miss many useful lessons. Furthermore, environmental watchdog organizations will have to remain vigilant lest rural communities with large tracts of forest start exploiting their resources as destructively as the worst of the industrial logging firms.

A divisive issue related to the corporate versus community management dichotomy concerns the issue of whether conservation interests are well served or threatened by empowerment of local people. While the debate rages in the United States (Limerick 2002), efforts are under way in the tropics to clarify the complex of social, economic, and political factors that determine which conservation solutions are appropriate from the wide range of possibilities (Wilshusen et al. 2002).

RULE OF LAW VERSUS MARKET INCENTIVES

With any positive discount rate, mining timber without regard to sustainability generally is more profitable than sustainable forest management (Rice et al. 1997, Pearce et al. 2002, but see Putz 2000). Although there are conditions under which RIL is more profitable than uncontrolled logging (Holmes et al. 2002), efforts to reduce harvesting rates or to introduce prelogging or postlogging silvicultural treatments are likely to be met with resistance from the logging industry. Is it better to control loggers through government regulation or to encourage changes in their practices with market incentives? In yet another publication titled with a provocative question—"Is market-oriented conservation a contradiction in terms?"—Crook and Clapp (1998) discuss this issue as if government regulation and market incentives were mutually exclusive options. In contrast, the substitutability of Forest Stewardship Council (FSC) certification for government regulation in Bolivia represents a good example of their compatibility.

Governments may be inefficient, ineffective, costly, and corrupt, but most markets have no conscience, and corruption within them is also rampant. Particularly when most environmental services and social benefits are treated as externalities in evaluations of different forest use options, there are problems when conservation success is monetarized. Markets for certified forest products, in contrast, were designed to have a conscience, but even the FSC can be criticized because most of the certified forests of the world are owned and managed by large corporations in the temperate zone, not rural communities in the tropics (Hardner and Rice 2002). In FSC's defense, the cost of doing business with small and poorly capitalized community-based forestry operations, which also often suffer other limitations in business practices and produce only limited volumes, is extremely high. Given that FSC's success is measured in hectares or millions of cubic meters (see chapter 6), the initial surge of industrial forest certifications is understandable.

The planned creation of millions of hectares of timber concessions in Amazonian Brazil (see chapter 3) indicates that despite failures at curbing illegal logging and at capturing the rents due from firms logging legally

(Repetto and Gillis 1988), decision makers in that country have faith in the government's capacity to control loggers. Perhaps if logging is legalized, the industry will be more controllable and timber prices will increase, but doubts persist, and synergies between market-based and command-and-control mechanisms for conservation merit further examination (see chapter 22). Even the most ineffective-seeming governments may actually control forest resource exploitation more than is apparent, as was revealed by the escalation of illegal logging from chronic to epidemic after the fall of the Suharto regime in Indonesia (Jepson et al. 2001, McCarthy 2002).

FOREST MANAGEMENT FOR TIMBER VERSUS ECOSYSTEM SERVICE PAYMENTS

Payments for forest-based carbon offsets, biodiversity protection, and maintenance of hydrologic functions and other ecosystem services often are portrayed as alternatives to forest management for timber, as though they were completely incompatible forest uses (e.g., Ferraro and Kiss 2002). There are certainly tradeoffs to be considered in any multiple-use approach to management, but there are also many cost-effective and otherwise attractive ways to combine uses. For example, although improved forest management is not being strongly supported in negotiations about the Kyoto Protocol, the cost-effectiveness of RIL as a carbon offset was demonstrated in Malaysia (Pinard and Putz 1996) and more recently in Brazil (see chapter 4). For political reasons, including the difficulty policymakers have with the idea of conservation with chainsaws, instead of improved forest management, "carbon forestry" has come to be closely associated not with improved forest management but with huge pulpwood plantations, reforestation, and the very questionable practice of planting trees in areas where they have not grown before, such as native grasslands. Although I formerly supported forest-based carbon offsets, I have recently become more skeptical as market forces and industrial interests seem to have pushed aside conservation and development concerns. I hope that links will be made between forest-based carbon offsets and the already well-established process of forest management certification by FSC, thus ensuring that environmental damage and social harm are not perpetrated in the name of carbon sequestration.

WORKING VERSUS UNEMPLOYED

I like the idea of working forests but nevertheless feel compelled to explore what is meant by the term, and I am determined that it not become synonymous with "exploited" forest (Trombulak 1998). In many senses, all forests "work" insofar as they all store carbon, circulate nutrients, harbor biodiversity, filter water, and have existence value. Although I have demonstrated my discomfort with many familiar dichotomies, I wonder whether a working forest might not best be defined by its opposite, which I assume is a forest that is unemployed by humans. Given that a forest can work by being an extractive reserve, an inviolate reserve for biodiversity conservation, an area dedicated to pharmaceutical exploration, a sacred grove, or a managed timber stand, then *working* is fairly broadly defined. Unfortunately, this dichotomy also fails to hold up under the scrutiny of anyone who has worked hard while ostensibly unemployed. For example, homemakers and primary child caregivers may work harder than their employed counterparts but are nevertheless considered unemployed. Although I like to work in forests, unemployed forests, if they exist, retain a certain appeal.

CONCLUSION

Ecologists have mostly accepted disturbance and rejected homeostatic mechanisms preserving equilibrium (e.g., Pickett and Ostfeld 1994), but many continue to disregard history in ways that have dangerous implications, both ecological and social. Failure to consider environmental history leads to forest managers, from forestry degree–holding employees of multinational vertically integrated, export-oriented forest product corporations to subsistence farmers tending their forest fallows, being portrayed either as ruthless destroyers or as caring stewards. Rewarding stewardship with, for example, FSC certification, and penalizing forest destroyers, as by criminalizing their activities (Peluso 1992), are both straightforward unless the interpretations of their activities and the landscapes they are managing are incorrect (Dove 1993, Denevan 2001). For example, according to anthropological studies in West Africa, for example, local farmers have been blamed and penalized for deforestation and savannization even though the savannas are the historical land cover and the forests are a more recent cultural artifact (Fairhead and Leach 1996).

As Fairhead and Leach point out, failure to incorporate history in ecology is more than an academic mistake insofar as there is great power associated with the predominant reading of the landscape. Furthermore, substantial errors are likely to be made in management decisions if forest histories are disregarded, as in Amazonian forests that appear to have regenerated on lands cleared for agriculture several centuries ago (see chapter 5). The debate over whose landscape interpretation is valid is made increasingly pertinent (and complicated) by the titling of extensive areas in the tropics to indigenous groups and other rural communities (White and Martin 2002), some of whom do not share the dominant constructs of nature held by more powerful interests in the nation-states that contain their lands.

In light of increasing evidence that much of the "nature" we cherish as environmentalists resulted from human interventions of which we were previously unaware, it is imperative that we stop interpreting all interventions as causing environmental degradation. I personally celebrate uninhabited wilderness areas and do not want people living in all parks, but I acknowledge that a multitude of approaches to conservation should be recognized. With the graying of populations of farmers and hunters, coupled with the urbanization of environmentalists, it is going to become increasingly difficult for people to accept active management as environmentally legitimate. At the same time, dangers inherent to the commodification of nature in conjunction with the excesses of some representatives of the "wise use" movement and industry render some approaches to active forest management environmentally deplorable. We also may not want environmental decisions to be made exclusively by extreme postmodern deconstructionists (e.g., Chase 1995), lest the best "sort-of" pristine forests and "seminatural" savannas we want to protect not be valued any more highly than suburban developments and the vegetation in sidewalk cracks. In part what is needed is a new paradigm for ecology that recognizes the importance of human history but in so doing does not diminish the intrinsic values of nonhuman "nature."

Extreme or oversimplified statements about what is good for forests might attract attention from some donors but generally stymie progress toward resolving complex conservation and development issues (Redford et al. 2003). Decisions about such issues demand consideration of a complex of factors that do not make good soundbites or headlines. Rather than continuing to simplify debates about forest fates by polarizing the arguments, we need to use conceptual models that capture the complexity of social, economic, political, and biological factors at play. Frumhoff and Losos (1998) proposed a three-dimensional model with continuous variables for guiding decision making about conservation strategies for tropical forests, but their composite variables (conversion pressure, biodiversity value, and incentives and enforcement capacity) obscure much of the underlying complexity that must be considered. Although portraying more than three dimensions is challenging, the decision-making models we use for determining the fates of tropical forests must have many more than three dimensions that are allowed to be nonorthogonal, nonlinear, interacting, continuous or discontinuous, and site and scale dependent. Straightforward solutions to forest conservation problems are needed, especially when we are trying to communicate to policymakers and the public, but let us not promote the use of overly simple models in which important factors are overlooked and viable approaches are disregarded.

REFERENCES

Anderson, A. B. and E. M. Ioris. 1992. The logic of extraction: Resource management and income generation by extractive producers in the Amazon estuary. In K. Redford and C. Padoch, eds., *Conservation of neotropical forests: Working from traditional resource use,* 175–199. New York: Columbia University Press.

Anderson, P. A. and F. E. Putz. 2002. Harvesting and conservation: Are both possible for the palm *Iriartea deltoidea? Forest Ecology and Management* 170: 271–283.

Angermeier, P. L. 2000. The natural imperative for biological conservation. *Conservation Biology* 14: 373–381.

Arnold, J. E. M. and M. Ruiz-Pérez. 1998. The role of non-timber forest products in conservation and development. In E. Wollenberg and A. Ingles, eds., *Incomes from the forest: methods for the development and conservation of forest products for local communities,* 17–41. Bogor, Indonesia: Center for International Forestry Research.

Birks, H. H., H. J. B. Birks, P. E. Kaland, and D. Moe, eds. 1988. *The cultural landscape: Past, present and future.* Cambridge, U.K.: Cambridge University Press.

Bowman, D. M. J. 2001. Future eating and country keeping: What role has environmental history in the management of biodiversity? *Journal of Biogeography* 28: 549–564.

Browder, J. O. 1992. The limits of extractivism: tropical forest strategies beyond extractive reserves. *BioScience* 42: 174–182.

Callicott, J. B. 1997. Conservation values and ethics. In G. K. Meffe and C. R. Carroll, eds., *Principles of conservation biology,* 29–55. Sunderland, Mass.: Sinauer Associates.

Callicott, J. B., L. B. Crowder, and K. Mumford. 1999. Current normative concepts in conservation. *Conservation Biology* 13: 22–35.

Chase, A. 1995. *In a dark wood: The fight over forests and the rising tyranny of ecology.* Boston: Houghton Mifflin.

Colfer, C. J. P. and I. Byron, eds. 2001. *People managing forests: The links between human well-being and sustainability.* Washington, D.C.: Resources for the Future; Bogor, Indonesia: Center for International Forestry Research.

Cronkleton, P. In press. Gender, participation and the strengthening of indigenous forestry management. In C. J. P. Colfer, ed., *No fair!: Enhancing equity in forest management.* Bogor, Indonesia: Center for International Forestry Research.

Cronon, W. 1995. The trouble with wilderness; or, getting back to the wrong nature. In W. Cronon, ed., *Uncommon ground: Rethinking the human place in nature,* 69–90. New York: W. W. Norton.

Crook, C. and R. Clapp. 1998. Is market-oriented forest conservation a contradiction in terms? *Environmental Conservation* 25: 131–145.

Denevan, W. M. 1992. The pristine myth: The landscape of the Americas in 1492. *Annals of the Association of American Geographers* 82: 369–385.

Denevan, W. M. 2001. *Cultivated landscapes of native Amazonia and the Andes.* Oxford, U.K.: Oxford University Press.

Dove, M. 1993. A revisionist view of tropical deforestation and development. *Environmental Conservation* 20: 17–24.

Eder, K. 1996. *The social construction of nature: A sociology of ecological enlightenment.* London: Sage.

Fairhead, J. and M. Leach. 1996. *Misreading the African landscape: Society and ecology in a forest–savanna mosaic.* Cambridge, U.K.: Cambridge University Press.

Ferraro, P. J. and A. Kiss. 2002. Direct payments to conserve biodiversity. *Science* 298: 1718–1719.

Fimbel, R. A., A. Grajal, and J. G. Robinson, eds. 2001. *The cutting edge: Conserving wildlife in logged tropical forests.* New York: Columbia University Press.

Flannery, T. 2001. *The eternal frontier.* New York: Atlantic Monthly Press.

Foreman, D. 1999. Will-of-the-land. *Wild Earth* 9: 1–4.

Foster, D. R., M. Fluet, and E. R. Boose. 1999. Human or natural disturbance: Landscape-scale dynamics of the tropical forests of Puerto Rico. *Ecological Applications* 9: 555–572.

Fredericksen, T. S. and F. E. Putz. 2003. Silvicultural intensification for tropical forest conservation. *Biodiversity and Conservation* 12: 1445–1453.

Fredericksen, T. S., F. E. Putz, P. Pattie, W. Pariona, and M. Peña-Claros. 2003. Tropical forestry in Bolivia: The next steps from planned logging towards sustainable forest management. *Journal of Forestry* 101: 37–40.

Frumhoff, P. C. and E. C. Losos. 1998. *Setting priorities for conserving biological diversity in tropical timber production forests.* Washington, D.C.: The Union of Concerned Scientists and the Center for Tropical Forest Studies, Smithsonian Institution.

Godoy, R. A. and K. S. Bawa. 1993. The economic value and sustainable harvest of plants and animals from the tropical forest: Assumptions, hypotheses and methods. *Economic Botany* 47: 215–219.

Griffiths, T. 2002. How many trees make a forest? Cultural debates about vegetation change in Australia. *Australian Journal of Botany* 50: 375–389.

Groth, P. and T. W. Bressi. 1997. *Understanding ordinary landscapes.* New Haven, Conn.: Yale University Press.

Hacking, I. 1999. *The social construction of what?* Cambridge, Mass.: Harvard University Press.

Hall, P. and K. S. Bawa. 1993. Methods to assess the impact of extraction of non-timber tropical forest products on plant populations. *Economic Botany* 47: 234–247.

Hardner, J. and R. E. Rice. 2002. Rethinking green consumerism. *Scientific American* 286: 89–95.

Holmes, T. P., G. M. Blate, J. C. Zweede, R. Periera, P. Barretto, F. Boltz, and R. Bauch. 2002. Financial and ecological indicators of reduced impact logging performance in the eastern Amazon. *Forest Ecology and Management* 163: 93–110.

International Labour Organization. 1990. *Occupational safety and health in forestry*. Geneva: International Labour Organization.

Jackson, J. B. 1984. *Discovering the vernacular landscape*. New Haven, Conn.: Yale University Press.

Jepson, P., J. K. Jarvie, K. MacKinnon, and K. A. Monk. 2001. The end for Indonesia's lowland forests? *Science* 292: 859–861.

Jodha, N. S. 2000. Common property resources and the dynamics of rural poverty: field evidence from the dry regions of India. In W. F. Hyde and G. S. Amacher, eds., *Economics of forestry and rural development: An empirical introduction from Asia*, 203–221. Ann Arbor, Mich.: University of Michigan Press.

Johns, J. S., P. Barreto, and C. Uhl. 1999. Logging damage during planned and unplanned logging operations in the eastern Amazon. *Forest Ecology and Management* 89: 59–77.

Laurance, W. F. 2002. Conservationists at loggerheads over World Bank plan. *BioMedNet*, October 29, 2002.

Limerick, P. N. 2002. Forestry and modern environmentalism: Ending the cold war. *Journal of Forestry* 100: 46–50.

Mayers, J. and S. Vermuelen. 2002. *Company–community forestry partnerships: From raw deals to mutual gains?* London: International Institute for Environment and Development.

McCarthy, J. F. 2002. Turning in circles: District governance, illegal logging, and environmental decline in Sumatra, Indonesia. *Society and Natural Resources* 15: 867–886.

Moran, E. 1996. Nuturing the forest: Strategies of native Amazonians. In R. Ellen and K. Fukui, eds., *Redefining nature: Ecology, culture, and domestication*, 531–555. Oxford, U.K.: Berg.

Myers, J. R. and D. E. Fosbroke. 1995. The Occupational and Health Administration logging standard: What it means for forest managers. *Journal of Forestry* 93: 34–37.

Oates, J. 1999. *Myth and reality in the rain forest: How conservation strategies are failing in West Africa*. Berkeley: University of California Press.

Pacheco, B. P. and D. Kaimowitz. 1998. *Municipios y gestión forestal en el trópico Boliviano*. Santa Cruz, Bolivia: BOLFOR.

Pearce, D., F. E. Putz, and J. Vanclay. 2002. Sustainable forestry: Panacea or pipedream? *Forest Ecology and Management* 172: 229–247.

Peluso, N. L. 1992. *Rich forests, poor people*. Berkeley: University of California Press.

Peters, C. M. 1996. *The ecology and management of non-timber forest resources*. World Bank Technical Paper No. 322. Washington, D.C.: The World Bank.

Peters, C. M., A. H. Gentry, and R. O. Mendelsohn. 1989. Valuation of an Amazonian rainforest. *Nature* 339: 655–656.

Peterson, A. 1999. Environmental ethics and the social construction of nature. *Environmental Ethics* 21: 339–357.

Pickett, S. T. A. and R. S. Ostfeld. 1994. The changing ecological paradigm and natural resource management. In R. L. Knight and S. F. Bates, eds., *A new century for resource management*. Washington, D.C.: Island Press.

Pinard, M. A. and F. E. Putz. 1996. Retaining forest biomass by reducing logging damage. *Biotropica* 28: 278–295.

Poore, D., J. Blaser, E. F. Bruening, P. Burgess, B. Cabarle, D. Cassells, J. Douglas, D. Gilmour, G. Hartshorn, D. Kaimowitz, N. Kishor, A. Leslie, J. Palmer, F. Putz, M. N. Salleh, N. Sizer, T. Synnott, F. Wadsworth, and T. Whitmore. 1998. No forests without management: Sustaining forest ecosystems under condition of uncertainty. *ITTO Update* 8: 10–12.

Posey, D. A. 1985. Indigenous management of tropical forest ecosystems: The case of the Kayapo Indians of the Brazilian Amazon. *Agroforestry Systems* 3: 139–158.

Putz, F. E. 1994. Towards a sustainable forests: How can forests be managed in a way that satisfies criteria of sustainability? *ITTO Tropical Forest Update* 4: 7–9.

Putz, F. E. 2000. Economics of home grown forestry. *Ecological Economics* 32: 9–14.

Putz, F. E., G. M. Blate, K. H. Redford, R. Fimbel, and J. G. Robinson. 2001. Biodiversity conservation in the context of tropical forest management. *Conservation Biology* 15: 7–20.

Rackham, O. 1980. *Ancient woodland: Its history, vegetation and uses in England.* London: Edward Arnold.

Redford, K. H., P. Coppolillo, E. W. Sanderson, G. A. B. da Fonseca, E. Dinerstein, C. Groves, G. Mace, S. Maginnis, R. A. Mittermeier, R. Noss, D. Olson, J. G. Robinson, A. Vedder, and M. Wright. 2003. Mapping the conservation landscape. *Conservation Biology* 17: 116–131.

Repetto, R. and M. Gillis, eds. 1988. *Public policies and the misuse of forest resources.* New York: Cambridge University Press.

Rice, R. E., R. E. Gullison, and J. W. Reid. 1997. Can sustainable management save tropical forests? *Scientific American* 276: 44–49.

Romero, C. 1998. Reduced-impact logging effects on commercial non-vascular pendant epiphyte biomass in a tropical montane forest in Costa Rica. *Forest Ecology and Management* 118: 117–125.

Rüters, K. H. and J. D. Wickham. 2003. How far to the nearest road? *Frontiers in Ecology and the Environment* 1: 125–129.

Salick, J., H. Mejia, and T. Anderson. 1995. Non-timber forest products integrated with natural forest management, Rio San Juan, Nicaragua. *Ecological Applications* 5: 878–895.

Sanderson, E. W., M. Jaiteh, M. A. Levy, K. H. Redford, A. V. Wannebo, and G. Woolmer. 2002. The human footprint and the last of the wild. *BioScience* 52: 891–904.

Sedjo, R. A. and D. Botkin. 1997. Using forest plantations to spare natural forests. *Environment* 39: 14–20.

Sheil, D. and S. Wunder. 2002. The value of tropical forests to local communities: Complications, caveats and cautions. *Conservation Ecology* 6: 9. Online: http://www.consecol.org.vol6/iss2/art9.

Sist, P., D. Sheil, K. Kartawinata, and H. Priyadi. 2003. Reduced-impact logging in Indonesian Borneo: Some results confirming the need for new silvicultural prescriptions. *Forest Ecology and Management* 179: 415–427.

Slater, C., ed. In press. *In search of the rain forest.* Durham, N.C.: Duke University Press.

Soper, K. 1995. *What is nature?* Oxford, U.K.: Blackwell.

Southgate, D. 1998. *Tropical forest conservation: An economic assessment of the alternatives in Latin America.* Oxford, U.K.: Oxford University Press.

Spillsbury, M. J. and D. Kaimowitz. 2000. The influence of research and publications on conventional wisdom and policies affecting forests. *Unasylva* 51: 3–10.

Sprugel, D. G. 1991. Disturbance, equilibrium, and environmental variability: What is "natural" vegetation in a changing environment? *Biological Conservation* 58: 1–18.

Struhsaker, T. T. 1997. *Ecology of an African rain forest: Logging in Kibale and the conflict between conservation and exploitation.* Gainesville: University of Florida Press.

Terborgh, J. 1999. *Requiem for nature.* Covelo, Calif.: Island Press.

Terborgh, J. 2002. The "working forest": Does it work for biodiversity? *WildEarth* 12: 29–35.

Trombulak, S. 1998. Wild forests are working forests. *Wild Earth* 8: 73–76.

U.S. Bureau of Labor Statistics. 1998. *Logging is perilous work.* Washington, D.C.: Bureau of Labor Statistics. Online: http://www.bls.gov.iif/oshwc/cfar0027.pdf.

White, A. and A. Martin. 2002. *Who owns the world's forests? Forest tenure and public forests in transition.* Washington, D.C.: Forest Trends.

White, R. 1995. Are you an environmentalist or do you work for a living? Work and nature. In W. Cronon, ed. *Uncommon ground: Toward reinventing nature,* 171–185. New York: W. W. Norton.

Wickramasinghe, A., M. Ruiz-Pérez, and J. M. Blochus. 1996. Non-timber forest products gathering in Ritigala forest (Sri Lanka): Household strategies and community differentiation. *Human Ecology* 24: 493–519.

Willers, B. 2001. The postmodern attack on wilderness. *Natural Areas Journal* 21: 259–265.

Wilshusen, P. R., S. R. Brechin, C. L. Fortwangler, and P. C. West. 2002. Reinventing the square wheel: Critique of a resurgent "protection paradigm" in international biodiversity conservation. *Society and Natural Resources* 15: 17–40.

Wunder, S. 2001. Poverty alleviation and tropical forests: What scope for synergies? *World Development* 29: 1817–1833.

Chapter 3

NATIONAL FORESTS IN THE BRAZILIAN AMAZON

OPPORTUNITIES AND CHALLENGES

Adalberto Veríssimo and Paulo Barreto

Forests cover approximately 65 percent of the 5 million km^2 that constitute the legal Brazilian Amazon, encompassing almost one-third of the world's remaining tropical forests (Uhl et al. 1997). These forests have important roles in hydrologic and carbon cycles that influence the global and regional climate (Salati and Vose 1984, Shukla et al. 1990, Skole and Tucker 1993, Houghton et al. 2000). Amazonian forests also contain tremendous biodiversity and have a great variety of tree species with timber value, of which about 350 are commercially harvested (Martini et al. 1994). The Brazilian Amazon ranks among the top three tropical timber producers in the world (with Malaysia and Indonesia). In 1998, timber production from the Amazon forest was about 28 million m^3 of roundwood (Veríssimo and Smeraldi 1999).

Roughly 95 percent of timber extraction in the Amazon is done without management, generating severe impacts on the structure of the forest and excessive pressure on high-value species and leaving areas susceptible to fires (Veríssimo et al. 2002b). Nonetheless, areas of managed forests in the region have increased in the last few years. In 2001, more than 1 million ha were managed, of which more than 0.35 million ha are certified by the Forest Stewardship Council (FSC) (Veríssimo et al. 2002b). With management, the negative impacts and the cycles of timber extraction can be reduced substantially, and profits can increase (Barreto et al. 1998, Holmes et al. 2002).

In the last three decades, a period characterized by a timber boom in the Amazon, predatory timber extraction resulted in the exhaustion of forest resources in the old logging centers in eastern Pará, north-central

Mato Grosso, and southern Rondônia. Scarcity in those places has forced lumber mills to relocate to new timber frontiers in north-central Pará (Pacajás and Anapu river regions), western Pará (along highway BR-163), and southwestern Amazonas. In these regions, loggers often occupy unclaimed public lands illegally and, in synergy with agriculture and cattle production, accelerate forest degradation and deforestation (Schneider et al. 2000). Roughly 45 percent of the territory of the legal Brazilian Amazon is either unclaimed public land or under title dispute.

To stabilize the timber sector in the region, three important objectives must be met. First, good management practices must be promoted. Second, enforcement and monitoring systems must become more efficient. Finally, land tenure must be regularized in private areas, and national and state forests must be established on unclaimed public lands.

In this chapter, we discuss national forest policy for the Brazilian Amazon. We review the status of national forests in the region, discuss the potential role of these conservation units in the promotion of sustainable use of forest resources, and evaluate advances and challenges in their creation.

NATIONAL FORESTS IN THE BRAZILIAN AMAZON

According to Brazilian legislation, "national forest" is a category of conservation unit covered by native forest species, the basic objective of which is the rational use of forest resources under a regime of sustainable, production-oriented management. Secondary objectives of national forests are to guarantee the protection of environmental services (especially water resources), offer recreation and tourism activities, and support scientific research. This type of conservation unit exists in other forested countries, including Canada, the United States, Malaysia, Indonesia, Peru, and Bolivia (Barreto and Arima 2002).

In Brazil, the concept of national forest as a conservation unit was established in federal code in 1965. However, only in 1974 did the federal government create the first unit of this type in the Amazon, the Tapajós National Forest. Although creation of national forests continued in the following decades—adding up to 83,000 km^2, or 1.6 percent of the Brazilian Amazon in 1999—their establishment was mainly for the purpose of protecting mineral reserves (Veríssimo et al. 2000). Only in 2000, with the launch of the National Forest Program by the Ministry of the Environment, did national forests gain political prominence in Brazil. According to the goals of the Brazilian government, national forests should represent a minimum of 500,000 km^2 of the Amazon (10 percent

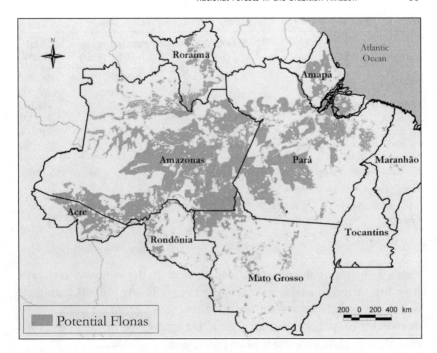

Figure 3.1   Potential areas for national forests (flonas) in the Brazilian Amazon.

of the territory) by 2010 (Veríssimo et al. 2002b). The scale of this initiative is equivalent to the establishment of the national forest system in the United States in 1908 by Theodore Roosevelt, and it does not have precedent elsewhere in the tropics (Veríssimo et al. 2002a).

To orient the decision-making process, the Brazilian government solicited a study to identify potential areas for the creation of national forests in the region (Veríssimo et al. 2002b). This study used an extensive method that incorporated information about protected areas already in existence, forest cover, infrastructure, human occupation, timber stocks, and biodiversity. Veríssimo et al. (2002b) identified an area of approximately 700,000 km^2 (14 percent of the legal Amazon) with potential for the establishment of national forests (figure 3.1). Those areas are located primarily in north-central and western Pará, a large part of Amazonas, and, secondarily, in Amapá, Acre, and northwestern Mato Grosso.

The areas with potential for national forests (700,000 km^2) have high commercial timber value and low human populations and are not within priority areas for the creation of parks and biological reserves (Veríssimo et al. 2002b). The establishment of national forests according to these criteria is politically possible, mainly because they avoid areas

Table 3.1　Established and Planned Protected Areas in the Brazilian Amazon

Category	Area in 2000 (km^2)	Planned to 2010–2012 (km^2)	Total (km^2)
Flonas	83,000	500,000	583,000
Resex, Redes[a]	97,000	90,000	187,000
Parks and reserves[b]	155,000	285,000	440,000
Indigenous lands[c]	1,040,000	*	1,040,000
Total	1,375,000	875,000	2,250,000
Percentage of legal Amazon (Brazil)	27.5	17.5	45

[a]Extractive reserves ("Resex"), sustainable development reserves ("Redes"), and security lands.
[b]Also includes ecological reserve stations.
[c]There is no specific plan to expand indigenous lands beyond those created in the last two decades.

where human populations were evident from national health census or from fires detectable by remote sensing, thus reducing potential conflicts with local populations. Additionally, these new national forests will be established on public lands that are either unclaimed or under disputed title, thus avoiding the costs of dispossession.

National forests can complement the units of integral protection of Amazonian forest cover. The newly approved Project of Protected Areas (ARPA), a collaboration of the Brazilian government, the World Wildlife Fund (WWF), and the World Bank, foresees the creation of 285,000 km^2 of parks and biological reserves and 90,000 km^2 communal extractive reserves by 2012. In combination with the national forest policy, these additions represent approximately 875,000 km^2 of new conservation units in the Amazon (table 3.1). When added to areas already in existence, this will enable the protection of 45 percent of the Amazon territory in the category of units of conservation (23 percent) and indigenous land (22 percent), placing Brazil among the leading countries in the conservation of natural resources.

THE ROLE OF NATIONAL FORESTS

In the Brazilian Amazon, stabilization of the timber sector entails adopting forest management in private areas and on public lands designated for sustainable forestry; these include national forests, state forests, and communal extractive reserves. The exhaustion of natural forests in the old frontiers (eastern Pará, north-central Mato Grosso) has motivated the migration of lumber mills to western Pará and southwestern Amazonas. In these regions, the government has an opportunity to avoid the predatory use of forest resources and the privatization of unclaimed public lands. The most promising alternative is the creation of national forests. Studies conducted by Schneider et al. (2000) and Veríssimo et al. (2002b) reveal that a forest policy based on a system of national forests can offer the following benefits:

- *Contribute to frontier stabilization.* The expansion of the national forest system can contribute to economic stability in the region by restricting predatory activities, limiting land availability, increasing land value, and promoting intensification of land use (Veríssimo et al. 2002a). In addition, the establishment of national forests can deter the disorderly expansion of the illegal occupation of unclaimed lands on the Amazon frontier. The negative impacts of development programs such as Avança Brasil (Forward Brazil) can also be reduced by the creation of national forests (e.g., along the highways to be paved). The government of Acre is already planning to establish a network of state forests along Highway 364, even before paving is completed. The same could be done in the case of Highway 163 (in Pará), which should be paved before 2005.

  The benefits of a national forest system in the region depend on adequate resources for implementation, which have not yet been committed. Key aspects of effective implementation include efficient monitoring and enforcement to reduce illegal logging; a concession model that includes external auditing of forest management standards, accounting practices, and social impacts; and dedicated institutional capacity to provide technical and managerial oversight.

- *Capture income from the forest.* Currently loggers extract timber illegally from unclaimed public lands without paying for it. In the national forests, the government will collect stumpage fees to strengthen the management, monitoring, and administration of the national forests. In addition, a portion of this fee could return to the communities in buffer zones and to the towns where these national forests are located. There are precedents in the Brazilian legislation (e.g., mineral royalties established by the constitution in 1998), which could serve as guidelines for elaborating the use of funds garnered from the stumpage fee (e.g., restricting the use of stumpage fees to initiatives for sustainable management, education, and local capacity building).

- *Encourage forest management.* In the Brazilian Amazon, one of the major obstacles to the adoption of forest management is the scarcity of regulated forest areas. According to Schneider et al. (2000), most loggers prefer to operate under defined rules, defined land tenure, and protection of timber supplies. For this reason, loggers have demonstrated strong support for the national forest policy in the Amazon. A recent study of 96 timber enterprises conducted by Barreto and Arima (2002) revealed that 80 percent of loggers interviewed support the national forest policy of the Brazilian government. The main reason for this support is the guarantee of access to managed and legalized raw material. In addition, the loggers would not need to invest in land acquisition.

- *Conserve biodiversity.* National forests are an essential complement to park protection in a global conservation strategy (Cabarle 1998, Veríssimo et al. 2002b). National forests were previously recommended as supplementary reserves for wildlife conservation (Frumhoff 1995). Wildlife conservation is also considered necessary for the long-term management of forests that regenerate naturally (Robinson et al. 1999). For this reason, integration between biodiversity conservation and good management practices is necessary for establishing sustainable production. Protecting areas of high biological importance entails the creation of a mosaic of conservation areas that combine national forests with parks and biological reserves. In this system, national forests serve as buffer zones for parks and reserves. National forests would also provide corridors for the movement of species between parks and reserves and private areas under sustainable management (Veríssimo et al. 2000b).

ADVANCES AND CHALLENGES OF NATIONAL FOREST POLICY

Establishment of National Forests

In 2001 and 2002 there were important advances, such as the establishment of five new national forests located in Pará, Amazonas, and Acre and encompassing 23,237 km² (table 3.2). Twelve additional national forests totaling 36,890 km² are being established, mainly in Amazonas and Pará (table 3.3).

State Forests

Acre has elaborated its strategy for establishing state forests, equivalent to the national forest strategy outlined earlier. The Acre state govern-

Table 3.2   National Forests Established in the Brazilian Amazon in 2001 and 2002

Name	State	Area (km^2)
Mulata	Pará	2,127
Pau Rosa	Amazonas	8,278
São Francisco	Acre	2,160
Santa Rosa do Purus	Acre	2,302
Jatuarana	Amazonas	8,370
Total		23,237

Source: Programa Nacional de Floresta, Ministério do Meio Ambiente, 2002.

Table 3.3   National Forests Being Established in the Brazilian Amazon, 2003

Name	State	Area (km^2)
Acari	Amazonas	5,182
Balata-Tufari	Amazonas	6,713
Pombal	Pará	930
Rio Novo	Pará	800
Crepori	Pará	2,502
Alalaú	Amazonas	2,650
Sucunduri	Amazonas	8,371
Roraima	Roraima	900
Jacundá	Rondônia	2,980
Anauá	Roraima	2,601
Paredão	Roraima	900
Jauaperi	Roraima	2,361
Total		36,890

Source: Programa Nacional de Floresta, Ministério do Meio Ambiente, 2002.

ment conducted a study similar to that of the federal government but at a more detailed scale. The study developed by Veríssimo et al. (2001) identified an area of approximately 36,000 km^2 (23 percent of the territory of Acre) with potential for establishing state forests. This area is sufficient to meet the government of Acre's goal of creating at least 15,000 km^2 (10 percent of the state) of state forests by 2006.

In other states in the Brazilian Amazon, the establishment of state forests has received increasing support. The government of Amapá has defined potential areas for establishing state forests. In Pará, the major timber producer in the Amazon, state forest regulation also foresees the expansion of state forests. In the state of Amazonas, the newly elected governor (2003–2006) has expressed a strong interest in an economy based on forests and state forest expansion.

Challenges

Although the strategy of establishing an extended network of national forests has made significant progress, the challenges of its implementation have just begun. An effective discussion about an appropriate concession system for Brazil should include issues such as national, state, and private sector rights and responsibilities, concession sizes and durations, taxes, and requirements for management plan development, approval, execution, and monitoring.

National forest establishment also faces resistance from some local stakeholders, particularly those whose livelihoods depend on agriculture and ranching. To overcome this resistance, the national forests must provide measurable benefits to rural people, including the provision of social services and equitable distribution of stumpage fees among communities and municipalities.

Concession Models

A study by Barreto and Arima (2002) revealed an array of preferences among loggers about concession models. Concerning concession duration, 69 percent of the loggers preferred long-term concessions, whereas 26 percent preferred short-term concessions and 3 percent had no preference (Barreto and Arima 2002). Concerning the role of the government, 56 percent of the loggers agreed that the government should be responsible for elaborating management plans, whereas the concessionaires retain responsibility for the actual management. Approximately 41 percent of the businesses thought that the management plans should be prepared and executed by the concessionaires, whereas the government should control and monitor the execution of the terms of the contract (Barreto and Arima 2002). The same opinion was shared by the majority of other stakeholders (54 percent) from the forest sector (academics, environmentalists, and technicians) interviewed by Barreto and Arima (2002), who also revealed a preference for a long-term concession model under the responsibility of the concessionaires.

Loggers and other stakeholders emphasized concerns about concession models and their implementation (Barreto and Arima 2002). The issues most discussed by stakeholders were the loggers' technical capacity, their reputation, and the transparency of the concession process. Stakeholders emphasize that concessions should guarantee opportunities to the local population and should avoid giving only a few businesses access to the national forests (Barreto and Arima 2002). Loggers also fear institutional instability in the public administration, the poor administrative capacity of the government, and the comparative advantage large timber companies may have in complying with bidding requirements (Barreto and Arima 2002).

CONCLUSION

National forests offer benefits to the local economy as well as to biodiversity conservation. The Amazon contains large areas of unclaimed forested land, currently without sufficient protection to establish a network of national forests, which could provide managed production capable of meeting the demand for timber production. The establishment of a national forest network is an important step toward a sustainable forest management system. It is also important that these national forests be established quickly, before economic and social factors make this initiative politically unfeasible.

There is a strong political support for expanding and consolidating a network of national forests in the Amazon. However, implementation of the national forest system in the Amazon will be surrounded by challenges and controversies. The success of this policy depends on the reduction of timber supply from predatory exploitation and deforestation. It is easier and cheaper for loggers to buy timber that comes from deforestation than to obtain timber that is harvested under a management plan. Implementing the national forest policy also entails contracting and training personnel to administer and monitor the concessions. Finally, to guarantee political support and social legitimacy it is essential that the Brazilian government open discussions of potential concession models to all stakeholders .

ACKNOWLEDGMENTS

The authors thank the Avina Foundation and William and Flora Hewlett Foundation for their support.

REFERENCES

Barreto, P., P. Amaral, E. Vidal, and C. Uhl. 1998. Costs and benefits of forest management for timber production in eastern Amazonia. *Forest Ecology and Management* 108: 9–26.

Barreto, P. and E. Arima. 2002. *Florestas nacionais na Amazônia: Consulta a empresários e atores afins à politica florestal.* Programa Nacional de Florestas. Brasília: Ministério do Meio Ambiente.

Cabarle, B. J. 1998. Logging in the rain forests. *Science* 281: 1453–1454.

Frumhoff, P. C. 1995. Conserving wildlife in tropical forests managed for timber. *BioScience* 45: 456–464.

Holmes, P. T., R. Pereira Jr., P. Barreto, F. Boltz, R. Bauch, M. G. Blate, and J. Zweed. 2002. Financial and ecological indicators of reduced impact logging performance in the eastern Amazon. *Forest Ecology and Management* 163: 93–110.

Houghton, R. A., D. L. Skole, C. A. Nobre, J. L. Hackler, K. T. Lawrence, and W. H. Chomentoswski. 2000. Annual fluxes of carbon from deforestation and regrowth in the Brazilian Amazon. *Nature* 403: 301–304.

Martini, A., N. Rosa, and C. Uhl. 1994. An attempt to predict which Amazonian tree species may be threatened by logging activities. *Environmental Conservation* 21: 152–162.

Robinson, J. G., K. H. Redford, and E. L. Bennett. 1999. Wildlife harvest in logged tropical forests. *Science* 284: 595–596.

Salati, E. and P. B. Vose. 1984. Amazon basin: A system in equilibrium. *Science* 225: 129–138.

Schneider, R., E. Arima, A. Veríssimo, P. Barreto, and C. Souza Jr. 2000. *Amazônia sustentável: Limitantes e oportunidades para o desenvolvimento rural*. Brasília: Banco Mundial and Instituto do Homem e Meio Ambiente da Amazônia.

Shukla, J., C. Nobre, and P. Sellers. 1990. Amazon deforestation and climate change. *Science* 247: 1322–1325.

Skole, D. and C. J. Tucker. 1993. Tropical deforestation and habitat fragmentation in the Amazon: Satellite data from 1978 to 1988. *Science* 260: 1905–1910.

Uhl, C., P. Barreto, A. Veríssimo, E. Vidal, P. Amaral, A. C. Barros, C. Souza Jr., J. Johns, and J. Gerwing. 1997. Natural resource management in the Brazilian Amazon. *BioScience* 47: 160–168.

Veríssimo, A., M. Cochrane, and C. Souza Jr. 2002a. National forests in the Amazon. *Science* 297: 1478.

Veríssimo, A., M. Cochrane, C. Souza Jr., and R. Salomão. 2002b. Priority areas for establishing national forests in the Brazilian Amazon. *Conservation Ecology* 6: 4. Online: http://www.consecol.org/vol6/iss1/art4.

Veríssimo, A. and R. Smeraldi. 1999. *Acertando o alvo: Consumo de madeira no mercado interno brasileiro e promoção da certificação florestal*. São Paulo: Amigos da Terra, Imaflora e Imazon.

Veríssimo, A., C. Souza Jr., and P. Amaral. 2000. *Identificação de áreas com potencial para a criação de florestas nacionais na Amazônia legal*. Brasília: Ministério do Meio Ambiente.

Veríssimo, A., C. Souza Jr., and R. Salomão. 2001. *Identificação de áreas com potencial para a criação de florestas estaduais no estado do Acre*. Belém: Imazon.

Chapter 4

SUSTAINABILITY OF SELECTIVE LOGGING OF UPLAND FORESTS IN THE BRAZILIAN AMAZON

CARBON BUDGETS AND REMOTE SENSING AS TOOLS FOR EVALUATING LOGGING EFFECTS

Michael Keller, Gregory P. Asner, Natalino Silva, and Michael Palace

Brazil has a strong internal market for wood and wood products. According to the Brazilian Institute for Geography and Statistics, the volume of roundwood production in the Brazilian Amazon between 1991 and 2000 was 35 million m^3 per year (http://www.igbe.br/, accessed August 2, 2002). Given a nominal harvest volume of 30 m^3/ha, this implies that in an average year approximately 1.2 million ha was affected by logging in the 1990s. Based on a survey of sawmills conducted in 1996 and 1997, Nepstad et al. (1999) estimated that approximately 1.0 to 1.5 million ha per year was logged. Although these numbers have been contested, no other published survey of logging activity covering the full Brazilian Amazon is available for estimating logging area.

The growth of demand for timber and road building in Brazil will expand the logging frontier in the Amazon. Production in older logging centers, such as Paragominas in Pará and Sinop in Mato Grosso, has already declined because of forest depletion in their vicinities. An emphasis on short-term profits rather than long-term productivity is the standard practice today on the Brazilian Amazonian frontier (Uhl et al. 1997), resulting in a boom-and-bust pattern of overexploitation of timber in a given region. Current logging practices in the Amazon, often called conventional logging (CL), cause enormous damage to the soil and the residual forest stands (Veríssimo et al. 1992, McNabb et al. 1997, Gerwing 2002). CL causes twice as much soil and canopy damage as reduced-impact logging (RIL) (Pereira et al. 2002). The cost of implementing RIL is reportedly no higher than that of cL (Holmes et al. 2002), although training and education at all levels—from the managers to the field personnel—is needed.

RIL is only part of a long-term system for sustainable forest management (SFM) (Wadsworth 2001). RIL is not a panacea because under some conditions, such as in some Asian forests dominated by dipterocarps, limitation of canopy opening under RIL may discourage the release of future desired species (Ashton and Peters, 1999). RIL is not synonymous with reduction of volume harvested. As Fredericksen (2000) pointed out, in forests of the Bolivian Amazon reducing harvest intensity may only spread damage over wider areas. Because logging damage is a nonlinear function of harvest volume, focused areas of intensive harvest may cause less overall damage than extensive areas of low-volume logging (Fredericksen 2000). Regardless of the management approach, some form of controlled harvest is needed under any imaginable SFM system.

Sustainable timber production from managed tropical forests should meet the definition of sustainable development coined by the Brundtland Commission as development that "meets the needs of the present without compromising the ability of future generations to meet their own needs" (World Commission on Environment and Development 1987). For forestry, this implies not only that economic production of timber must be sustained but also that forest ecosystems must continue to provide a host of services such as watershed and biodiversity protection (Daily et al. 2000). In a sustainable management system, timber output and the profits it generates should be equitably distributed and otherwise balanced with other societal needs. Any consideration of the social and economic sustainability of forestry operations necessarily includes the possibility of regulating forestry operations.

Consideration of all aspects of sustainable logging in the Amazon forests of Brazil is beyond the scope of this chapter. Furthermore, available data on logging in the Brazilian Amazon are limited to a few sites. We focus our discussion to consider an example of a potentially sustainable logging production system in the Tapajós National Forest (TNF), near Santarém, Pará. We also use data from the Fazenda Cauaxí, in the municipality of Paragominas, Pará. Consideration of this production system has implications for carbon budgets that we will discuss with respect to a simple ecosystem carbon model. Limitation of logging damage is critical both to sustainable production and for carbon budgets. Therefore we will consider approaches used to minimize and monitor damage.

STUDY SITES

The Tapajós National Forest is located south of the city of Santarém in the state of Pará. The logging demonstration site managed by the Brazilian Government Institute for the Environment and Renewable Resources is located near kilometer 83 on the BR-163 (Santarém-Cuiabá) Highway (3.04°S, 54.95°W). The region receives approximately 2000 mm of precipitation per year and has an annual mean temperature of 25° C. The terrain is nearly flat, and the soils are mainly well-drained clay-textured oxisol (80 percent clay, 18 percent sand, 2 percent silt) (Silver et al. 2000). Vegetation at the site is evergreen, tropical dense moist forest with a total biomass of about 372 Mg/ha (Keller et al. 2001). The most common timber species harvested in 2000 were *Manilkara huberi, Carapa guianensis, Couratari guianensis, Licaria brasiliensis,* and *Nectandra rubra.* The most common tree species (more than 35 cm diameter at breast height [dbh]) are *Pouteria* sp., *Manilkara huberi, Carapa guianensis, Eschweilera* sp., and *Sclerolobium melanocarpum.*

The Fazenda Cauaxí in the Paragominas Municipality, Pará, has hosted RIL demonstration and training by the Fundação de Floresta Tropical since 1995 in collaboration with the property owners CIKEL Brasil Verde S.A. A centrally located camp (3.73°S, 48.29°W) serves as a base for these activities. The climate at Fazenda Cauaxí is humid tropical. Total annual precipitation averages about 2200 mm (Costa and Foley 1998). Soils are mainly clay-textured dystrophic oxisols. The topography is flat to mildly undulating. The vegetation at Fazenda Cauaxí is evergreen tropical dense moist forest. The most common timber species that were harvested during five years of forest operations were *Manilkara huberi, Manilkara paraensis, Protium pernevatum, Dinizia excelsa,* and *Piptadenia suaveolens.* The most common tree species found are *Licania* sp., *Manilkara huberii, Astronium lecointei, Eschweilera odorata,* and *Parkia* spp. (Pereira et al. 2002).

A CASE STUDY OF LOGGING DAMAGE IN THE BRAZILIAN AMAZON

Forests in the Amazon region of Brazil are rich in tree species, but only a limited number of species are marketable for timber in the region. Therefore loggers practice selective logging. Most logging in the region is conducted by poorly trained workers with minimal planning. Waste and high levels of collateral damage are common (Veríssimo et al. 1992, Johns et al. 1996, Uhl et al. 1997, Pereira et al. 2002). RIL approaches recently have been introduced to the region primarily by the Fundação

1996

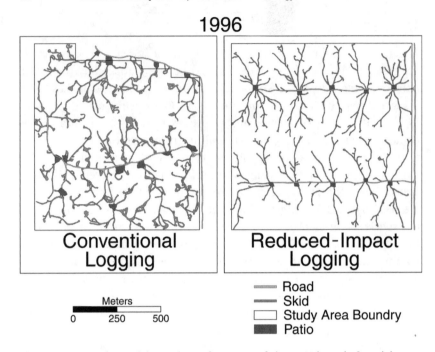

| Conventional Logging | Reduced-Impact Logging |

Meters
0   250   500

▬▬ Road
▬▬ Skid
☐ Study Area Boundry
■ Patio

Figure 4.1 Areas of ground damage in two forest areas of about 100 ha each. Ground damage indicates areas where soil has been compacted by mechanical disturbance. It includes log storage decks, skid trails, and roads. A total of 8.9% of the conventional logging block suffered ground damage, compared with 4.8% of the reduced-impact logging block in this example. (For color reproduction see Plate 1.) *Source:* Reprinted from Pereira et al. (2002), with permission.

Floresta Tropical (Holmes et al. 2002). Several medium and large companies that harvest, saw, and market lumber and other wood products have adopted RIL techniques in their harvest operations. In contrast to CL, RIL uses preharvest inventory and mapping and vine cutting. Inventory data are used to create harvest plans that incorporate directional felling. Skidding along planned trails uses wheeled skidders rather than crawler tractors. Comparisons of CL and RIL in eastern Pará, Brazil, show that RIL harvesting operations reduce ground and canopy damage by half compared with CL operations without any increase in cost (figures 4.1 and 4.2) (Pereira et al. 2002, Holmes et al. 2002).

To quantify logging damage, we have measured the amount of coarse woody debris (CWD) generated by CL and RIL operations in the vicinity of the Fazenda Cauaxí in eastern Pará (3.75°S, 48.37°W). We used line intercept sampling to survey CWD volume approximately one year after log-

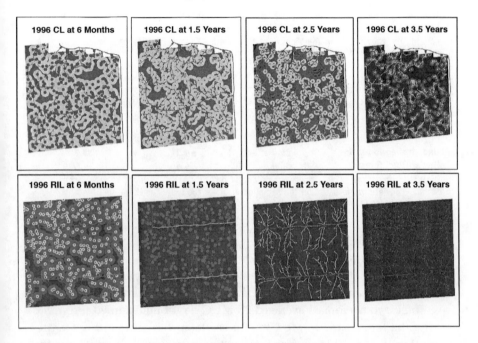

| 1996 CL at 6 Months | 1996 CL at 1.5 Years | 1996 CL at 2.5 Years | 1996 CL at 3.5 Years |
| 1996 RIL at 6 Months | 1996 RIL at 1.5 Years | 1996 RIL at 2.5 Years | 1996 RIL at 3.5 Years |

Figure 4.2 Canopy damage and recovery for two logged areas under conventional logging (CL) and reduced-impact logging (RIL). (For color reproduction and explanation see Plate 2.)

ging in two blocks each of CL, RIL, and unlogged forest (Brown 1974, De Vries 1986, Ringvall and Stahl 1999). Approximately 3000 m of survey line was sampled for each block. CWD included all dead woody material on the ground with diameter greater than 2 cm. We measured diameters for all wood on the line transect with diameter greater than 10 cm. We counted the number of intersections of wood on randomly selected subtransects (10 m out of each 50 m) in the classes 2–5 cm and 5–10 cm. CWD (diameter greater than 10 cm) was classified into five categories according to its physical appearance from freshly fallen (Class 1) to completely rotten material that could be broken easily by hand (Class 5) (Harmon et al. 1995).

CWD mass was calculated by multiplying the volume for each size and decay class by the relevant average wood density for the class. Density data for CWD were not available from the Fazenda Cauaxí; instead we used densities from a sample of logs (n = 448) from a similar forest near Santarém, Pará, in the TNF. We measured densities in each decay class by removing

Table 4.1 Coarse Woody Debris (cwd) Measured on Transects for Conventional Logging (cl), Reduced-Impact Logging (ril), and Undisturbed Forest Blocks Approximately One Year After Logging in Study Blocks in the Vicinity of the Fazenda Cauaxí, Paragominas, Brazil

	Mean cwd (Mg C/ha)	Standard Deviation	Number of Transects (n)
cl 1	58.7	5.8	6
cl 2	48.0	5.0	6
ril 1	36.8	7.1	4
ril 2	38.2	3.8	6
Undisturbed forest 1	25.6	4.2	6
Undisturbed forest 2	30.0	4.4	4

Standard deviations are based on the sampling error for the cwd volume. Transect lengths ranged from 260 to 960 m.

cylindrical plugs from radial sections of the dead logs. Plugs were oven dried at 60° C. Radial sections were photographed digitally and used to measure void space used to adjust the final density determinations.

Total cwd necromass averaged 28 Mg C/ha for undisturbed forest, 53 Mg C/ha for cl, and 38 Mg C/ha for ril (table 4.1). Accounting for the existing cwd in unlogged forest, the incremental damage as measured by necromass in cl was more than twice that found in ril. Standing dead trees were not considered in this measurement. Working in the same region using comparable methods, Gerwing (2002) found that intact forests contained about 17 Mg C/ha cwd more than 10 cm in diameter. CWD increased to 34 Mg C/ha at three "moderate intensity logging" sites sampled four to six years after harvest that had 28–48 m^3/ha of timber harvested using cl. Allowing for decomposition that occurred four to six years after logging, the excess cwd found at these sites is similar to our results at Cauaxí.

MODELED TIMBER PRODUCTION IN THE TAPAJÓS NATIONAL FOREST

Economic productivity is a sine qua non for any sustainable management system. Research on the selective logging system in the Brazilian Amazon is limited. We know of no published study of measurements that extend beyond a single harvest cycle for managed forest in Amazonia. Alder and Silva (2002) have modeled multiple harvest cycles. The existing published studies of timber harvest systems in Amazonian forest are limited to a few sites, mainly in the Eastern Brazilian Amazon, Bolivia, and the Guyanas (e.g., Gullison and Hardner 1993, Silva et al. 1995, Graaf 2000, Jackson et al. 2002). It is difficult to predict future production without detailed knowledge of the growth and response to logging of both the timber and nontimber tree species. In general, this requires detailed site-specific knowledge. Multiple measurements of harvested and undisturbed plots at the TNF (3.08°S, 54.94°W) and at Jari (0.86°S, 52.55°W) have been used to parameterize an empirical stand projection model, the Cpatu Amazon Forest Growth Model (CAFOGROM; Alder and Silva 2000). For this study, we used only the parameters determined for the TNF.

CAFOGROM accounts for growth, mortality, recruitment, harvest, damage during harvest, and potential silvicultural treatments. Tree species were classified into fifty-four groups that contain one to sixty species based on an ordination using five attributes: commercial value, diameter increment, annual mortality rate, proportion of dominant (as opposed to suppressed) trees, and largest diameter. Growth depends on canopy position (canopy and suppressed trees) that is allocated on a stand basis as a function of basal area. A large number of measurements (217,991 records for 52,320 trees) were used to fit growth functions of the form

$$i/d = a + b_1 C + b_2 \ln(d), \qquad (4.1)$$

where i is the annual diameter increment, d is the diameter, and C is a switch equal to zero for dominants and one for suppressed trees. Mortality was calculated for each species group for three categories of trees (canopy, suppressed, and defective or damaged). Recruitment, defined as ingrowth into the smallest model diameter class (5 cm), is modeled at the stand level and then partitioned to species group. For undisturbed stands, the recruitment rate is 0.5 and 0.7 m²/ha per year for stand basal area of 30 and 20 m²/ha, respectively. After logging, recruitment (I) is modeled as

$$I = 0.019L^{1.86}, \qquad (4.2)$$

where L represents basal area lost as a result of mortality of harvest trees and collateral damage.

Harvest is simulated in CAFOGROM according to selected limits both in basal area and in minimum diameter according to species groups. Total basal area for damage to trees and mortality during and after logging are modeled on a stand basis as a linear function of the number of trees removed. CAFOGROM was developed based on data from 64 ha of forest. In our initial runs of the model based on plots that had not been logged previously from the TNF, we found that the amount of damage generated by logging was inconsistent with our field observations of CWD from Tapajós (data not shown) and Cauaxí (table 4.1). The small size of the plots used in developing the model probably reflected minimal damage in these experimental units compared with commercial-scale harvest (D. Alder, pers. comm. 2002), where road building and skid trails are more prominent. We found that by doubling the slope of the relation of basal area damaged to the number of trees harvested, we accurately simulated the quantity of CWD generated in RIL harvests at TNF (Keller et al. 2004). Simulations discussed herein follow this modified parameterization.

We ran the modified CAFOGROM to simulate future timber harvests over multiple felling cycles to illustrate sustainable and unsustainable production levels. No silvicultural treatments were simulated. All species groups at Tapajós were divided into classes for currently commercial species, potentially commercial species, and those judged to have no commercial potential. The currently commercial species in CAFOGROM are marketable in the Brazilian Amazon, although they do not necessarily have a current market in Santarém, the nearest sawmill center to the TNF. We specified minimum diameter (as dbh) limits for harvest of 55 cm for the currently commercial species and 65 cm for the potentially commercial species. The felling cycle was set to thirty years. In two scenarios (figure 4.3) we varied the maximum basal area harvest limit. When harvest of 4 m^2/ha basal area was allowed (figure 4.3a), total harvest volume was about 55 m^3/ha in each of the first three cycles and declined precipitously thereafter. This simulation required that current potentially commercial species become marketable within thirty years. After the fourth cutting cycle, the simulated harvest did not exceed 20 m^3/ha because the initially heavy cuts of commercial species depleted stocks of those species. Simulated regeneration of the commercial species was crowded out by rapidly growing noncommercial trees.

Limitation of the basal area cut to 2 m^2/ha resulted in a simulated harvest of nearly 30 m^3/ha per felling cycle over a 200-year simulation (figure 4.3b). Currently commercial species would sustain the harvest volume through three cycles. The need to include potentially commercial species to sustain timber yields began only 120 years after the initial simulated cut. Yields continued at high levels through the seventh felling cycle. Thereafter, without any silvicultural intervention, simulated yields fell precipitously. Although not used on the industrial scale today in the Brazilian Amazon region, application of tested techniques, such as liberation thinning, could increase yields of commercial species and potentially extend the duration of productive forest use beyond those observed in this simulation (Wadsworth 2001).

Although neither scenario illustrated in figure 4.3 is infinitely sustainable, the time horizons considered are long from the perspective of

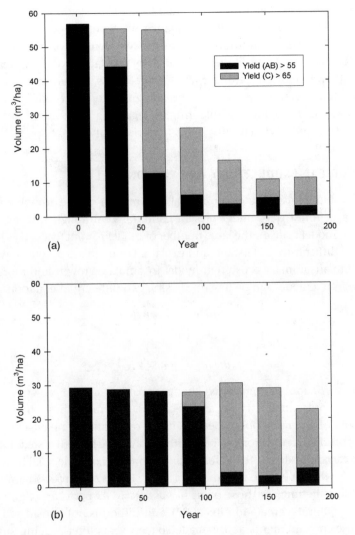

Figure 4.3 Roundwood geometric volume harvested over seven thirty-year felling cycles in two CAFOGROM simulations for the TNF. Wood categories A and B included the currently commercial species, and category C included potentially commercial species. Two scenarios are presented: **(a)** the maximum basal area of harvest is limited to 4 m²/ha; **(b)** the maximum basal area of harvest is limited to 2 m²/ha.

today's economy. Even the cut limited to 2 m²/ha would lead to considerable changes in tree species abundance and would depend on a major change in market conditions beyond the first century of management. The credibility of the model is limited by the lack of data to test the model over multiple felling cycles. Nonetheless, government policies and silvicultural systems must be designed today. Models such as CAFOGROM can provide valuable insights regarding current and potential harvesting and silvicultural systems (Alder and Silva 2002).

BIOLOGICAL PRODUCTIVITY AND CARBON CYCLING

CAFOGROM incorporates substantial information on the growth and behavior of forest trees under present conditions. Although this detail increases model realism, the large number of model parameters makes its behavior difficult to understand and explain. For heuristic purposes, we use a minimal summary ecosystem model to simulate growth and mortality. This simple model can be described using two differential equations:

$$dB_i/dt = G_i + \mu_i B_i \qquad (4.3)$$

and

$$dN_i/dt = -\mu_i B_i + k_i N_i. \qquad (4.4)$$

Biomass (B) and necromass (N) change according a fixed growth rate (G) and first-order mortality (μ) and decay (k). The model may follow any number of separate pools (i), each with its own rates. We have chosen to focus on the woody biomass pool only because we are interested in long-term carbon budgets. To evaluate carbon budgets over decadal or longer periods, we can ignore the fine pools (e.g., leaves, fine roots) because of the short lifetimes of those pools ($\mu \sim k \sim -1$ to -3 per year) (e.g., Smith et al. 1998, Kitayama and Aiba 2002). Soil carbon is not considered here because measurements at TNF made sixteen years after logging suggest minimal changes in total soil carbon (McNabb et al. 1997).

Whether carbon in old-growth Amazonian forest is at or near steady state is a matter of debate (Chambers et al. 2001a). Because we focus on the logging perturbation to forest carbon storage, we assume steady state ($G_i = -\mu_i B_i$) for undisturbed forest as a first approximation. As our initial biomass value, we take our best estimate for the biomass of the TNF of 186 Mg C/ha (Keller et al. 2001), nearly all of which is woody tissue. We use this approximation and a range of mortality rates for tropical forests found in the literature to set a range of parameters for growth of woody tissue. Phillips and Gentry (1994) found that annual mortality rates for 38

Table 4.2 Coarse Woody Debris (CWD) Decay Constant (k) and Instantaneous Mortality Rate (μ) for the Simple Model and the Calculated Steady State Woody Tissue Annual Growth Rate and Steady State CWD

k (per yr)	μ (per yr)	Growth (Mg C/ha/yr)	CWD (Mg C/ha)
−0.13	−0.032	6.0	46
−0.17	−0.032	6.0	35
−0.13	−0.010	1.9	14
−0.17	−0.010	1.9	11

tropical forest plots ranged from 0.7 to 3.3 percent per year. To simulate a realistic range of mortality, we selected exponential mortality coefficients (*sensu* Sheil et al. 1995) from 0.01 per year to 0.032 per year. The latter is the average mortality for all species groups at Tapajós (Alder and Silva 2000) weighted by the number of observations per group. For the decay rate of CWD, we used the range determined by Chambers et al. (2000, 2001b) of 0.13 to 0.17 per year. The range of parameters and the steady state CWD predicted for unlogged forest are shown in table 4.2. The range of estimates in table 4.2 brackets the mass of CWD (25 Mg C/ha) that we measured for undisturbed forest at the TNF (Keller et al. 2004).

How does this simple model compare with the behavior of CAFOGROM in a simulation of logging? We simulated logging in the simple model by removing biomass from the live pool and adding to the necromass pool after subtracting the mass of roundwood removed from the site. Using the high mortality rate and associated rapid growth rate for the Tapajós forest and a thirty-year felling cycle with a removal of 30 m³/ha, we compared the biomass estimates of the simple model with the results of the CAFOGROM simulation with a 2-m²/ha basal area cut limit per felling cycle (figure 4.3b). The resulting comparison (figure 4.4) showed reasonable agreement. The average total biomass for 200 years in these simulations is nearly identical (162 and 163 Mg C/ha for CAFOGROM and the simple model, respectively). We note that initially, CAFOGROM showed slower rates of biomass recovery than the simple model, and later in the simulations the relative rates shifted. In the simple model growth rates were fixed, whereas in CAFOGROM growth rates shifted with tree diameter, species composition, and canopy position of the trees. As larger, slow-growing commercial trees were harvested, the species composition in the CAFOGROM simulation shifted toward smaller, more rapidly growing noncommercial trees.

The response of the simple model to simulated CL and RIL at 30 m³/ha on a thirty-year felling cycle under two bounding scenarios for growth

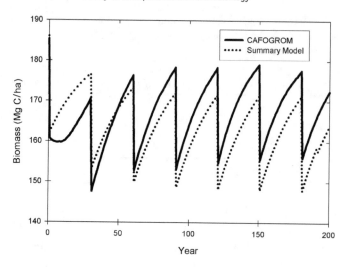

Figure 4.4 A comparison of total forest biomass simulated by CAFOGROM (equations 4.1 and 4.2) and the simple model (equations 4.3 and 4.4). The conditions of the simulations are detailed in the text.

rate is shown in figure 4.5. The simple model does not distinguish species, so it is impossible to determine whether selective logging would be sustainable under these conditions. However, it is apparent that for the slow-growth scenarios biomass declined substantially over 200 years of simulated logging. Therefore, it is unlikely that logging conducted in forests that maintain this growth rate would be sustainable. Under the high growth rates, growth was nearly sufficient to maintain biomass at undisturbed forest levels.

Forests with high growth rates may be able to sustain timber harvests for long periods. What is the carbon balance for these forests under different harvest and decay rate scenarios? We simulated both CL and RIL for rapid growth rates (G = 5.95 Mg C/ha per year) and both slow and fast decay rates (k = –0.13 to –0.17 per year). Long-lived wood products are an important part of the net ecosystem exchange calculation. We added an additional compartment to the model to account for long-lived wood products. We assumed that roundwood is sawn within one year of harvest. Based on currently inefficient sawmill production, we assumed that only 33 percent of the roundwood ends up in long-lived products (Jenkins and Smith 1999). This constant efficiency would lead to an underestimate of future net ecosystem exchange (NEE) if sawmill efficiency improves with time. Even long-lived wood products have a finite lifetime. We followed Houghton and Hackler (2001) and conservatively estimat-

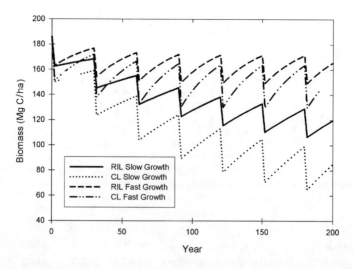

Figure 4.5 Total forest biomass for two woody tissue growth rates and two logging approaches as simulated by the simple model (equations 4.3 and 4.4).

ed that wood products decay at an instantaneous rate of 0.01 per year. More rapid decay of products would tend to decrease NEE.

We integrated NEE over simulation periods of thirty years (a single felling cycle) and 200 years assuming for each year of the first thirty-year felling cycle that new areas are opened for logging and thereafter logging continues in those same areas. Results in table 4.3 show that the decay rate has a minor influence on the carbon balance at time scales of thirty years and more. In contrast, the logging practice, CL versus RIL, has a major influence. RIL saves approximately 7 Mg C/ha over thirty years and approximately 13 Mg C/ha over 200 years. Pinard and Putz (1996) analyzed carbon losses in RIL and CL in Sabah, Malaysia. They concluded that RIL represented an opportunity for a greater carbon offset than CL.

NUTRIENT LIMITATION TO TIMBER PRODUCTION

Soils of the Amazon Basin are dominated by highly weathered oxisols and ultisols (Uehara and Gilman 1981, Sanchez et al. 1982). Agricultural production and secondary forest regeneration on cleared sites can be limited by nutrient availability. In some cases, logging tropical forests has caused significant nutrient losses (Brouwer 1996, McNabb et al. 1997). Is it likely that timber production in logged forests of the Brazilian Amazon would become limited by nutrient availability? As a first approximation, we as-

Table 4.3 Integration of Net Ecosystem Exchange (NEE) Including Long-Lived Products for Four Logging Scenarios Simulated by the Simple Model

Coarse Woody Debris Decay Rate	Harvesting Regime	NEE 30-yr Integration (Mg C/ha)	NEE 200-yr Integration (Mg C/ha)
Slow	Conventional logging	−19.1	−29.7
Fast	Conventional logging	−19.4	−28.8
Slow	Reduced-impact logging	−12.3	−16.7
Fast	Reduced-impact logging	−12.2	−15.8

Slow and fast decay for coarse woody debris correspond to $k = 0.13$ per year and $k = 0.17$ per year, respectively. Negative NEE indicates a loss of carbon from the forest ecosystem and finished products to the atmosphere.

sume that forests cycle nutrients tightly and that the only significant loss pathway is through the timber removed. As a case study, we look again at the TNF, where we have detailed knowledge of soil nutrient stocks (Silver et al. 2000). We used measured data for the total stocks of nitrogen (N) and phosphorus (P) in the upper meter of soil and the exchangeable stocks of calcium (Ca), magnesium (Mg), and potassium (K). Nutrient exports from logging were calculated based on the nutrient content of logs from an experimental logging project (Biomassa e Nutrientes Florestais, BIONTE) in forest near Manaus, Brazil (Fernandes et al. 1997). We assumed a harvest of 30 m^3/ha and an average density for the timber species at Tapajós of 0.75 Mg/m^2 (Fearnside 1997).

We compared the nutrients removed in timber harvest with the total stocks in the top meter of soil and with the likely inputs of nutrients in rainfall. Lacking rainfall nutrient content for the TNF, we used data from Williams and Fisher (1997) from a remote site in the state of Amazonas for comparison. Soil stocks of N and P (table 4.4) are far greater than the nutrients removed in timber harvest. The calculated time to deplete the stocks of these elements based on a thirty-year felling cycle, assuming no nutrient replacement, is well over 1000 years in both cases. Even given limited availability of P, the likelihood of N and P availability limiting timber production at this site seems remote. For K, Mg, and Ca, the amounts of nutrients removed in timber harvest are quite similar to those in the exchangeable pools of the top meter of soil. The removal of timber could lead to nutrient limitation on forest growth in 250 years or less assuming no replacement of these nutrients and no additional losses. The situation is most critical for Mg, where the figures for soil Mg in table 4.4 are upper bounds based on the detection limit quoted by Silver et al. (2000).

The rainfall inputs of nutrients measured by Williams and Fisher (1997) exceed the hypothetical losses in timber by at least a factor of two

Table 4.4 Nutrient Stocks and Fluxes Based on a Hypothetical Timber Harvest of 30 m³/ha on a 30-Year Felling Cycle

Element	Nutrient Stock in Soil to 1 m Depth (kg/ha)	Nutrient in Harvest per 30 yr (kg/ha)	Time to Depletion (yr)	Nutrient Removed (kg/ha/yr)	Rainfall Input (kg/ha/yr)
N	9,010	56	4,805	1.88	4.16
P	1,676	1	44,701	0.04	0.34
K	111	14	246	0.45	0.90
Mg	43	9	143	0.30	0.30
Ca	63	18	105	0.60	1.32

Magnesium values for soil are an upper bound calculated based on the limits of detection used by Silver et al. (2000). Rainfall inputs are based on data from Williams and Fisher (1997).

for N, P, K, and Ca. However, these inputs are barely sufficient to balance the loss of Mg exported in timber harvest (table 4.4). Given site-to-site variability in rainfall composition and soil chemistry and admitting the existence of other loss pathways for base cations besides log removal, it is possible that K, Ca, and especially Mg could limit timber productivity under multiple harvests in Amazonian forests.

We recognize that for a variety of reasons our calculations here may be far from the true nature of nutrient cycling after timber harvest. Logging disturbs soil organic matter (SOM) in log decks, roads, skid trails, and treefall gaps. SOM contains many of the available nutrients found in tropical soils (Vitousek and Sanford 1986, Silver et al. 2000), and disturbance to the SOM layer can mobilize these nutrients (Brouwer 1996). Mobilization of P and base cations in particular can lead to their subsequent immobilization in the underlying mineral soil or loss from the system entirely, as has been documented in deforested lands in the vicinity of the TNF (Asner et al. 1999, Townsend et al. 2002). Our calculation here should be considered a very conservative estimate of nutrients lost from plant available forms; we treat only off-site removal of nutrients and not in situ changes to available nutrients critical to forest regrowth after logging.

MONITORING LOGGING DAMAGE

Limiting logging damage is a first step in implementing sustainable production systems in natural forest management in the Brazilian Amazon. Changing the current wasteful system of logging to a more sustainable system includes educating forest owners and training foresters and forest workers in good forest management practices, including proper harvest planning. Some combination of incentives and controls must be instituted to catalyze the change in current practices. To determine whether incentives or controls are effective, governments, nongovernmental organizations, and businesses need cost-effective means to monitor logging operations. The vast distances and difficulties in transportation in the Amazon region make on-site monitoring costly and difficult. Satellite remote sensing may provide an alternative to on-site monitoring. Multispectral remote sensing has been used to detect the general location of selective logging operations (Stone and Lefebvre 1998, Souza and Barreto 2000). Unfortunately, common techniques such as the interpretation of band reflectances and textural analyses most commonly used to identify the presence or absence of logging do not provide accurate estimates of the canopy damage caused by logging (Asner et al. 2002). However, new spectral mixture analysis (SMA) techniques demonstrate high precision in the quantification of canopy damage caused by logging when compared to ground based data (Asner et al. in press).

The new SMA approach uses Landsat ETM+ satellite imagery. These images are readily available, and the cost of a scene that covers approximately 34,000 km^2 is about $600. Although cloudiness presents a barrier to acquiring these optical images, there is a probability of nearly 100 percent that a scene with less than 10 percent cloudiness can be acquired for nearly any location in the Brazilian Amazon south of the Amazon River in a given year (Asner 2001). The spectral unmixing technique developed by Asner and Lobell (2000) and modified for use in tropical forests (Asner et al. 2003, in press) decomposes the reflectance for each pixel of remotely sensed data into a linear combination of three endmember reflectances: photosynthetic vegetation or canopy cover, nonphotosynthetic vegetation (e.g., litter, dead wood, bark), and soil. Figure 4.6 displays an analysis of an area of logged and unlogged forests and pastures in the Municipality of Paragominas, Pará. Most of the image shows the signal (green) of the photosynthetic vegetation. Bare soil (red) is clearly visible in the roads and senescent pastures of this dry season scene. Nonphotosynthetic vegetation (blue) is obvious in areas of heavy logging damage with large quantities of logging debris on the surface.

A comparison of the forest canopy cover fraction obtained from the spectral unmixing to ground-based forest canopy gap fraction showed excellent correlation (r^2 = 0.96) between the satellite-based and ground-based estimations at about six months to one year after logging (figure 4.7). The strength of the correlations declined somewhat after regrowth but remained high in comparison to more traditional remote sensing techniques (Asner et al. 2002). These correlations may be used to estimate the degree of logging damage based on the analysis of a satellite image, particularly if annual images are available.

1999   2000

Figure 4.6 Composite images of the automated Monte Carlo unmixing output for 1999 and 2000 in the vicinity of the Fazenda Cauaxi. (For color reproduction and explanation see Plate 3.) *Source:* Reprinted from *Remote Sensing of Environment,* Vol. 87, G. P. Asner, M. M. C. Bustamante, and A. R. Townsend, "Scale dependence of biophysical structure in deforested lands bordering the Tapajós National Forest, Central Amazon," pages 507–520, Copyright 2003, with permission from Elsevier.

These early results show promise for monitoring the degree of canopy damage after timber harvest and the rate of canopy closure in subsequent years. It is plausible that the spectral mixture modeling approach could be applied to many images throughout the Amazon each year. Routine use of such techniques takes automation and attention to techniques for handling the large data volumes needed for regional monitoring. Furthermore, although our approach shows promise, we recognize that the accurate broad-scale use of this approach first requires additional ground-based studies incorporating a wider range of forest structural characteristics, topographic and edaphic conditions, and types of logging practices.

CONCLUSION

Our studies clearly indicated that selective logging as it is currently practiced may release substantial carbon to the atmosphere. Under CL management in highly productive forest, a simple summary model suggested that in a single thirty-year felling cycle with industrial harvests of 30

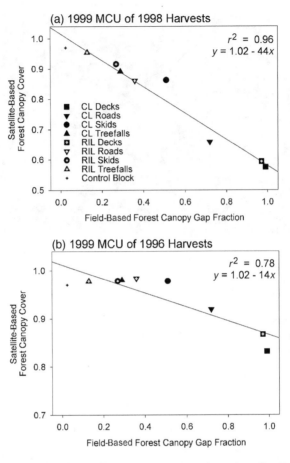

Figure 4.7   Correlation between field-based canopy gap fraction and satellite-based canopy cover for **(a)** 1998 harvests and **(b)** 1996 harvests, as imaged in 1999. CL, conventional logging; MCU, Monte Carlo unmixing; RIL, reduced-input logging. *Source:* Reprinted from *Remote Sensing of Environment,* Vol. 87, G. P. Asner, M. M. C. Bustamante, and A. R. Townsend, "Scale dependence of biophysical structure in deforested lands bordering the Tapajós National Forest, Central Amazon," Pages 507–520, Copyright 2003, with permission from Elsevier.

m^3/ha more than 10 percent of the forest biomass will be released to the atmosphere, even accounting for rapid regeneration and slow degradation of long-lived wood products. Over 200 years, the modeled carbon loss was nearly 30 Mg C/ha, more than 15 percent of the biomass of the intact forest. It should be noted that the growth rates for these optimistic simulations are at the high end of the expected range based on field data. Carbon losses for forests with less rapid regeneration would be far greater. Modeled management of the forests using RIL techniques suggested that the carbon loss could be reduced by half. Results of field investigations of the debris creation by logging in forests of the eastern Amazon confirmed that carbon loss is nearly twice as high with CL management as with RIL management. This result agrees with pioneering work by Pinard and Putz (1996), who demonstrated that RIL management of harvests in dipterocarp forests of Malaysia could halve carbon losses compared with CL management despite very high logging intensities.

Simulations using the CAFOGROM stand projection model, carefully calibrated with field data from the TNF, showed that under RIL harvesting practices, with a felling cycle of thirty years and a basal area cut limit of 2 m²/ha, log production could be sustained for about 200 years. Sustainability of this simulated production depended on market acceptance of currently noncommercial species after about three cutting cycles. This is a reasonable assumption given that far more species are commercial in locations such as Paragominas that are close to Brazilian internal markets than in Santarém, where much production goes to the more selective international market.

Sustained production simulated in the stand projection model does not guarantee sustainability of actual harvests. First, this model assumes that all growth conditions of the forest will follow current trends. Second, the model does not consider limitations to regeneration such as soil compaction, organic matter removal, or nutrient limitation. Nutrient limitations and other biological limitations may limit the long-term sustainability of forest production. A preliminary inspection of nutrient budgets suggested that base cations such as Ca, Mg, and K may become limiting to forest production on highly weathered soils over a few felling cycles. The potential of base cations to limit forest productivity in the Amazon scarcely has been investigated and deserves greater attention. Long-term biological productivity probably depends on the maintenance of biological diversity in the ecosystem, especially for key organisms such as pollinators and seed dispersers. Maintenance of the gene pool for the harvested timber trees is also an important concern given the relative rarity of these species in the ecosystem.

Long-term forest production will depend as much on social and economic concerns as on biological limitations. Development of favorable conditions for sustainable management of forests may require some combination of incentives and controls. Monitoring will be needed to ensure that controls and incentives function as planned. Given that the Amazon is a vast area with difficult access, remote sensing probably will play a role in any practical monitoring scheme. We presented recent results on a linear unmixing technique for Landsat ETM+ data that offers a potentially economical pathway for development of remote sensing monitoring of logging damage to forest canopies. When this research tool is translated into an operational tool, such monitoring could be used by governments, nongovernmental organizations, and industries in the Amazon region to ensure that logging is managed using best practices.

The examples we have presented derive mainly from a limited set of data in the eastern Amazon region in the state of Pará. Although these examples may point to some important trends and research directions, it would be imprudent to make conclusions for the entire Brazilian Amazon based on such a spatially limited data set. Data on forest production and regeneration in both intact and logged forests are very scarce in the Amazon region of Brazil. Planning for sustainable forestry in the Amazon necessitates more data that are geographically distributed across the forest areas most likely to be managed for timber production.

ACKNOWLEDGMENTS

We thank Tom Holmes and Dennis Alder for their advice. Lorena Brewster provided valuable bibliographic support. We are grateful to the Brazilian Ministry of Science and Technology for their leadership of the Large-Scale Biosphere–Atmosphere Experiment in Amazonia and to Brazil's Center for Weather Prediction and Climate Studies for their management of that program. Johan Zweede and the staff of the Fundação de Floresta Tropical provided critical support for our field studies. We are grateful to the National Aeronautics and Space Administration (NCC5-225, NCC5-357, and NAG5-8709), the U.S. Forest Service, the U.S. Agency for International Development , and the Department for International Development for financial support.

REFERENCES

Alder, D. and J. N. M. Silva. 2000. An empirical cohort model for management of Terra Firme forests in the Brazilian Amazon. *Forest Ecology and Management* 130: 141–157.

Alder, D. and J. N. M. Silva. 2002. Sustentabilidade da producao volumetrica: Um estudo de caso na Floresta Nacional do Tapajós com o auxilio do modelo de crescimento CAFOGROM. In J. N. M. Silva, J. O. P. de Carvalho, and J. Yared, eds., *Silvicultura na Amazônia oriental: Resultados do projeto EMBRAPA/DFID*, 325–337. Belém: EMBRAPA Amazônia Oriental.

Ashton, P. M. S. and C. Peters. 1999. Even aged silviculture in tropical rain forests of Asia: Lessons learned and myths perpetuated. *Journal of Forestry* 97: 14–19.

Asner, G. P. 2001. Cloud cover in Landsat observations of the Brazilian Amazon. *International Journal of Remote Sensing* 22: 3855–3862.

Asner, G. P., M. M. C. Bustamante, and A. R. Townsend. 2003. Scale dependence of biophysical structure in deforested lands bordering the Tapajós National Forest, Central Amazon. *Remote Sensing of Environment.* 87: 507–520.

Asner, G. P., M. Keller, R. Pereira, and J. Zweede. 2002. Remote sensing of selective logging in Amazonia: Assessing limitations based on detailed field measurements, Landsat ETM+ and textural analysis. *Remote Sensing of Environment* 80: 483–496.

Asner, G. P., M. Keller, R. Pereira, and J. Zweede. In press. Forest canopy damage and closure following selective logging in Amazonia: Landsat ETM+ and spectral mixture modeling. *Ecological Applications.*

Asner, G. P. and D. B. Lobell. 2000. AutoSWIR: A spectral unmixing algorithm using 2000–2400 nm endmembers and Monte Carlo analysis. In R. O. Green, ed., *Proceedings of the 9th Annual JPL Airborne Earth Science Workshop,* 29–38. Pasadena, Calif.: Jet Propulsion Laboratory.

Asner, G. P., A. R. Townsend, and M. C. M. Bustamante. 1999. Spectrometry of pasture condition and biogeochemistry in the central Amazon. *Geophysical Research Letters* 26: 2769–2772.

Brouwer, C. 1996. *Nutrient cycling in pristine and logged tropical rain forest. A study in Guyana.* Utrecht, The Netherlands: Elinkwijk.

Brown, J. K. 1974. Handbook for inventorying downed woody material. *General Technical Report, Int-16,* 1–24. Ogden, Utah: USDA Forest Service.

Chambers, J. Q., N. Higuchi, E. S. Tribuzy, and S. E. Trumbore. 2001a. Carbon sink for a century. *Nature* 410: 429.

Chambers, J. Q., H. Niro, J. P. Schimel, L. V. Ferreira, and M. J. Melack. 2000. Decomposition and carbon cycling of dead trees in tropical forests of the central Amazon. *Oecologia* 122: 380–388.

Chambers, J. Q., J. P. Schimel, and A. D. Nobre. 2001b. Respiration from coarse wood litter in central Amazon forests. *Biogeochemistry* 52: 115–131.

Costa, M. H. and J. A. Foley. 1998. A comparison of precipitation datasets for the Amazon basin. *Geophysical Research Letters* 25: 155–158.

Daily, G. C., T. Soderqvist, S. Anuyar, K. Arrow, P. Dasgupta, P. R. Ehrlich, C. Folke, A. Jansson, B. Jansson, N. Kautsky, S. Levin, J. Lubchenco, K. Maler, D. Simpsom, D. Starrett, D. Tilman, and B. Walker. 2000. The value of nature and the nature of value. *Science* 289: 395–396.

De Vries, P. G. 1986. *Sampling theory for forest inventory. A teach-yourself course.* Berlin: Wageningen Agricultural University; Heidelberg: Springer-Verlag.

Fearnside, P. M. 1997. Wood density for estimating forest biomass in Brazilian Amazonia. *Forest Ecology and Management* 90: 59–87.

Fernandes, E. C. M., Y. Biot, C. Castilla, A. C. Canto, J. C. Matos, S. Garcia, R. Perin, and E. Wanderli. 1997. The impact of selective logging and forest conversion for subsistence agriculture and pastures on terrestrial nutrient dynamics in the Amazon. *Ciencia e Cultura: Journal of the Brazilian Association for the Advancement of Science* 49: 34–47.

Fredericksen, T. S. 2000. Logging and conservation of tropical forests in Bolivia. *International Forestry Review* 2: 271–278.

Gerwing, J. J. 2002. Degradation of forests through logging and fire in the eastern Brazilian Amazon. *Forest Ecology and Management* 157: 131–141.

Graaf, N. R. D. 2000. Reduced impact logging as part of the domestication of neotropical rainforest. *International Forestry Review* 2: 40–44.

Gullison, R. E. and J. J. Hardner. 1993. The effects of road design and harvest intensity on forest damage caused by selective logging: Empirical results and a simulation model from the Bosques Chimanes, Bolivia. *Forest Ecology and Management* 59: 1–14.

Harmon, M. E., D. F. Whigham, J. Sexton, and I. Olmsted. 1995. Decomposition and mass of woody detritus in the dry tropical forest of the northeastern Yucatan Peninsula, Mexico. *Biotropica* 27: 305–316.

Holmes, T. P., G. M. Blate, J. C. Zweede, R. Pereira, P. Barreto, F. Boltz, and R. Bauch. 2002. Financial and ecological indicators of reduced impact logging performance in the eastern Amazon. *Forest Ecology and Management* 163: 93–110.

Houghton, R. A., and J. L. Hackler. 2001. *Carbon flux to the atmosphere from land-use changes: 1850 to 1990*. ORNL/CDIAC-131, NDP-050/R1. Oak Ridge, Tenn.: Carbon Dioxide Information Analysis Center, U.S. Department of Energy, Oak Ridge National Laboratory.

Jackson, S. M., T. S. Fredericksen, and J. R. Malcolm. 2002. Area disturbed and residual stand damage following logging in a Bolivian tropical forest. *Forest Ecology and Management* 166: 271–283.

Jenkins, M. B. and E. T. Smith. 1999. *The business of sustainable forestry: Strategies for an industry in transition*. Washington, D.C.: Island Press.

Johns, J. S., P. Barreto, and C. Uhl. 1996. Logging damage during planned and unplanned logging operations in the eastern Amazon. *Forest Ecology and Management* 89: 59–77.

Keller, M., M. Palace, G. P. Asner, R. Pereira Jr., and J. N. M. Silva. 2004. Coarse woody debris in undisturbed and logged forests in the eastern Brazilian Amazon. *Global Change Biology* 10: 784–795.

Keller, M., M. Palace, and G. E. Hurtt. 2001. Biomass in the Tapajós National Forest, Brazil: Examination of sampling and allometric uncertainties. *Forest Ecology and Management* 154: 371–382.

Kitayama, K. and S. I. Aiba. 2002. Ecosystem structure and productivity of tropical rain forests along altitudinal gradients with contrasting soil phosphorus pools on Mount Kinabalu, Borneo. *Journal of Ecology* 90: 37–51.

McNabb, K. L., M. S. Miller, B. G. Lockaby, B. J. Stokes, R. G. Clawson, J. A. Stanturf, and J. N. M. Silva. 1997. Selection harvests in Amazonian rainforests: Long-term impacts on soil properties. *Forest Ecology and Management* 93: 153–160.

Nepstad, D. C., A. Veríssimo, A. Alencar, C. Nobre, E. Lima, P. Lefebvre, P. Schlesinger, C. Potter, P. Moutinho, E. Mendoza, M. Cochrane, and V. Brooks. 1999. Large-scale impoverishment of Amazonian forests by logging and fire. *Nature* 398: 505–508.

Pereira, R., J. C. Zweede, G. P. Asner, and M. Keller. 2002. Forest canopy damage and recovery in reduced impact and conventional selective logging in eastern Pará, Brazil. *Forest Ecology and Management* 168: 77–89.

Phillips, O. L. and A. H. Gentry. 1994. Increasing turnover through time in tropical forests. *Science* 263: 954–958.

Pinard, M. A. and F. E. Putz. 1996. Retaining forest biomass by reducing logging damage. *Biotropica* 28: 278–295.

Ringvall, A. and G. Stahl. 1999. Field aspects of line intersect sampling for assessing coarse woody debris. *Forest Ecology and Management* 119: 163–170.

Sanchez, P. A., D. E. Bandy, J. H. Villachica, and J. J. Nicholaides. 1982. Amazon basin soils: Management for continuous crop production. *Science* 216: 821–827.

Sheil D., D. F. R. P. Burslem, and D. Alder. 1995. The interpretation and misinterpretation of mortality-rate measures. *Journal of Ecology* 83: 331–333.

Silva, J. N. M., J. P. O. Carvalho, J. do C. A. de Lopes, B. F. Almeida, D. H. M. Costa, L. C. Oliveira, J. K. Vanclay, and J. P. Skovsgard. 1995. Growth and yield of a tropical rainforest 13 years after logging. *Forest Ecology and Management* 71: 267–274.

Silver W., J. C. Neff, M. McGroddy, E. Veldkamp, M. Keller, and R. C. Oliveira Jr. 2000. Effects of soil texture on belowground carbon and nutrient storage in a lowland Amazonian forest ecosystem. *Ecosystems* 3: 193–209.

Smith, K., H. L. Gholza, and F. D. Oliveira. 1998. Litterfall and nitrogen-use efficiency of plantations and primary forest in the eastern Brazilian Amazon. *Forest Ecology and Management* 109: 209–220.

Souza, C. and P. Barreto. 2000. An alternative approach for detecting and monitoring selectively logged forests in the Amazon. *International Journal of Remote Sensing* 21: 173–179.

Stone, T. A., and P. Lefebvre. 1998. Using multi-temporal satellite data to evaluate selective logging in Pará, Brazil. *International Journal of Remote Sensing* 19: 2517–2526.

Townsend, A. R., G. P. Asner, C. C. Cleveland, M. Lefer, and M. C. C. Bustamante. 2002. Unexpected changes in soil phosphorus dynamics following forest conversion in the humid tropics. *Journal of Geophysical Research* 107(8067).

Uehara, G. and G. Gilman. 1981. *The mineralogy, chemistry and physics of tropical soils with variable charge clays.* Boulder, Colo.: Westview Press.

Uhl, C., P. Barreto, A. Veríssimo, E. Vidal, P. Amaral, A. C. Barros, C. Souza Jr., J. Johns, and J. Gerwing. 1997. Natural resource management in the Brazilian Amazon. *BioScience* 47: 160–168.

Veríssimo, A., P. Barreto, M. Mattos, R. Tarifa, and C. Uhl. 1992. Logging impacts and prospects for sustainable forest management in an old Amazonian frontier: The case of Paragominas. *Forest Ecology and Management* 55: 169–199.

Vitousek, P. M. and R. L. Sanford. 1986. Nutrient cycling in moist tropical forest. *Annual Review of Ecology and Systematics* 17: 137–167.

Wadsworth, F. H. 2001. Not just reduced but productive logging impacts. *International Forestry Review* 3: 51–53.

Williams, M. R. and T. R. Fisher. 1997. Chemical composition and deposition of rain in the central Amazon, Brazil. *Atmospheric Environment* 31: 207–217.

World Commission on Environment and Development. 1987. *Our common future.* Oxford, U.K.: Oxford University Press.

Chapter 5

FOREST SCIENCE AND THE BOLFOR EXPERIENCE

LESSONS LEARNED ABOUT NATURAL FOREST MANAGEMENT IN BOLIVIA

Francis E. Putz, Michelle A. Pinard, Todd S. Fredericksen, and Marielos Peña-Claros

Bolivia, one of the poorest nations in the Americas, is a world leader in ecologically sound and socially just management of natural tropical forest, as certified by the Forest Stewardship Council (FSC; Nittler and Nash 1999, Fredericksen et al. 2003). Of the many conditions favorable to forest management in Bolivia, low population density, poor access to extensive forests, and high costs of transportation to world markets outside this landlocked country figure prominently. Applied research and training in forestry under the auspices of the Bolivian Sustainable Forestry Project (Proyecto de Manejo Forestal Sostenible de Bolivia, BOLFOR) also contributed to better forestry in Bolivia. In this chapter we review some of the lessons learned from our successes and failures as the sequential leaders of the BOLFOR research program over the nearly ten years of the project (1994–2003).

In the early 1990s, when BOLFOR was planned, forestry activities in lowland Bolivia generally consisted of extensive harvesting of a few valuable species by untrained and poorly supervised crews. Annual cutting areas were not designated, and many concessionaires had logging crews dispersed over areas of more than 400,000 ha. Although logging intensities were generally low (Gullison et al. 1996), and the primary impacts were consequently minor, field crews were expected to hunt for a good portion of their sustenance, which greatly increased their overall impacts on biodiversity (Rumíz et al. 2001). In the absence of operational timber harvesting plans or designated annual cutting areas, logged stands were reentered whenever they could be harvested at a profit, such as when markets developed for species other than mahogany (*Swietenia macrophylla*), Spanish cedar (*Cedrela* spp.), or tropical oak (*Amburana cearensis*). Almost nothing was done to secure regeneration of the commercially valuable species or to otherwise sustain timber yields (Gullison et al. 1997). The government agency responsible for regulating logging and collecting fees (Centro de Desarollo Forestal) was judged so inefficient and corrupt that it was disbanded. These were the conditions in 1994 when funds from the U.S. Agency for International Development (USAID) and counterpart environmental conservation funds (PL-480) were used to start BOLFOR.

Radical political reforms in the mid-1990s created what has been called a textbook model of forest administration (Contreras-Hermosilla and Vargas Rios 2002). The reformation process was broadly participatory and culminated in the Forestry Law of 1996, which promoted sustainable forest management, installed a new forest fee system, and instituted methods for combating illegal logging and corruption. The law set minimum cutting cycles at twenty years, provided incentives to promote reforestation, and required establishment of permanent sample plots to monitor growth and yield. As a result of the 1996 Forestry Law, combined with the 1994 Law of Popular Participation, control over huge areas of forest in lowland Bolivia were officially transferred to indigenous groups and other rural communities (Kaimowitz et al. 1998, Pacheco and Kaimowitz 1998). BOLFOR provided technical support for implementing this legislation and thereby acquired a broad set of research partners, some of whom were new to the forestry sector.

To foster accountability and as a verifiable indicator of the project's success, BOLFOR planners set the goal of having 25 percent of the production forest in the Department of Santa Cruz certified as well managed by the FSC by 2001. Voluntary third-party certification was viewed as a mechanism for promoting better forestry and a quantitative measure of progress toward the goal of sustainable forest management. Setting this goal was risky because at the time of project initiation, the FSC was in its early stages of development, and the current Bolivian forest authority and the Superintendencia Forestal were only in the planning stage. In retrospect, this area-based goal may have initially caused the BOLFOR research team to focus more on large forest industries than fledgling community forestry initiatives, but this emphasis changed substantially during the final phase of the project. Increased emphasis on rural industries was motivated by concerns about social justice. Also, after legislation passed in the mid-1990s, indigenous groups and other rural communities controlled a substantial portion of the production forests in Bolivia. Emphasis on large corporations was not completely misplaced given that over the course of the project it became clear that the financial success of community-based forest enterprises depends on a vibrant forestry sector. Most of the research sponsored by BOLFOR that we will discuss was directed toward developing approaches to forest management that were ecologically sound, socially just, and economically viable, as detailed in the FSC principles and criteria.

Organization of research activities evolved over the ten years of BOLFOR. In the first few years, research was administered by the forest management division and was coordinated by a postdoctoral associate. The desire to reduce competition between BOLFOR's forest management division and the research group, coupled with growth of the latter, stimulated the creation of a separate research division. It is perhaps telling that throughout the project the chief researchers were forest ecologists (F.E.P., M.A.P., T.S.F., and M.P.-C. in succession), but they supervised social scientists as well as others with a biophysical orientation.

Dissemination of the results of BOLFOR-sponsored research was always among the project's explicit objectives. To meet this challenge, all researchers were required to file reports that were published in Spanish and also loaded on an active Web site (http://bolfor.chemonics.net). BOLFOR also published a free newsletter in Spanish that was mailed to about 400 people and institutions in Bolivia and around the world. A series of books on topics ranging from directional felling to interpretation of the 1996 Forestry Law and a series of silvicultural guides were published by the project (e.g., Mostacedo et al. 2001b). To reach international audiences and to ensure research quality, BOLFOR researchers were also encouraged to publish in peer-reviewed journals; in the project's ten years, nearly 100 articles appeared in regional and international journals.

The purpose of this chapter is to summarize some of the successes and failures of research on natural forest management supported by BOLFOR. Our hope is that this retrospective analysis will serve as a basis on which to continue building toward sustainable forest management in Bolivia and in working forests elsewhere in the tropics. After providing a bit of context for the project, we provide overviews of the principal results from each of our main study sites. The sites are presented in chronological order of the inception of the research, much of which continues at the time of this writing.

MODUS OPERANDI OF THE BOLFOR RESEARCH PROGRAM AND CONTEXT OF THE PROJECT

BOLFOR was an integrated conservation and development project (ICDP) dedicated to reducing degradation of Bolivia's lowland forests and protecting biodiversity by fostering natural forest management as both a source of income and a conservation strategy. The project was planned and then implemented by Chemonics International, a Washington, D.C.–based environmental consulting company, with the participation of Tropical Research and Development, Conservation International, and Wildlife Conservation Society, with later participation by the Forest Management Trust, the University of Florida, and the Center for International Forestry Research (CIFOR). Over the project's nearly ten years of operation, BOLFOR staff, which included a mixture of Bolivians, other Latin Americans, and North Americans, were involved in a wide range of issues related to forestry. For example, BOLFOR assisted in the formulation and implementation of the 1996 Forestry Law, provided extension services to rural communities and forest industries, granted fellowships to Bolivians for postgraduate study, and supported applied research. BOLFOR also helped to create the Bolivian Council for Voluntary Certification, a local office of the FSC, and the Amazonian Center for Forest Enterprise Development, an organization dedicated to improving the entrepreneurial capacity of the forest sector in Amazonia. BOLFOR was far too large and multifaceted to be summarized here. Instead, in this chapter we focus on some of the lessons learned from forest research sponsored by BOLFOR, especially as these results relate to forest management as a conservation strategy.

From its inception, the philosophy of BOLFOR's research division was to assist in the development of a solid forest industry sector by building research capacity while solving practical problems related to forest management as a conservation and livelihood strategy. Training in research methods therefore was an integral part of the overall project. This training involved funding and supervising Bolivian university students pursuing thesis projects, sending Bolivians abroad to obtain graduate degrees, teaching short courses and hosting workshops on selected topics in forestry, and producing publications on research techniques. During the project, about 150 undergraduate students received stipends to complete their undergraduate degrees in forestry and related disciplines. Undergraduate students and natural resource professionals were also assisted through BOLFOR short courses on topics including silviculture, harvesting, biodiversity protection, research methods, dendrology, statistics, and experimental design. Fifteen Bolivians were also fully funded to attend graduate school abroad in various disciplines including forest economics, ecology, wildlife, and forest management. It is noteworthy that to date all recipients of fellowships to study abroad returned to Bolivia when their studies were completed and now occupy prominent positions in government and nongovernmental organizations; many are still involved in research. As a result of BOLFOR training programs, it is difficult to find professionals in the Bolivian forestry sector who are not BOLFOR alumni. International students

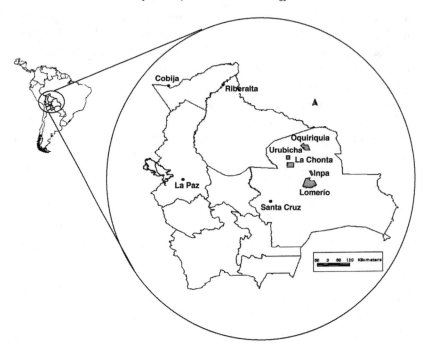

Figure 5.1   The main study sites used by BOLFOR researchers.

have also benefited from BOLFOR research grants. A competitive grant program invested nearly $400,000 in research stipends for work in Bolivia to interns, graduate students, and postdoctoral researchers from fifteen institutions in twelve countries. In addition to conducting their own research, BOLFOR research grant recipients served as mentors to Bolivian undergraduate students, many of whom worked on parallel projects of their own. Researchers from CIFOR became more actively involved in BOLFOR in its final years, which strengthened the social science research program and gave the project a broader international scope.

BOLFOR supported applied research in dry, moist, and wet forests on timber concessions, private lands, and areas titled to indigenous groups and other rural communities (figure 5.1). Researchers were supplied with modest stipends, transportation, and basic research equipment. At the field sites, researchers camped, provisioned, and cooked for themselves, often under conditions made difficult by seasonal scarcity of water. Toward the end of the project, after several field workers contracted leishmaniasis, modest screened field stations and sanitary facilities were constructed at the main research sites.

Following guidelines from USAID, BOLFOR researchers were prohibited from making silvicultural recommendations without first determining their biodiversity impacts. Our initial approach to this challenge was to conduct research in forests that were as close to pristine as possible and thus an appropriate source of baseline data for assessing management impacts. Although it was difficult to find forest in lowland Bolivia that had not been exploited, one site that met many of the criteria for selection was identified in the Bajo Paraguá Forest Reserve.

Although the forests of Bolivia are vast, as are the numbers of research sites and potential research partners, we chose to concentrate our efforts at the few sites that are described in the next sections. We made this decision because the Bolivian research community is small and is likely to remain so in at least the near future. Our hope, which was realized to a moderate extent, was that having researchers concentrated in a few sites with access to basic infrastructure and baseline data would foster collaboration and increase research capacity.

THE BAJO PARAGUÁ EXPERIENCE: PROGRESS DESPITE FUNDAMENTAL MISTAKES

From the half-dozen large privately held timber concessions in the Bajo Paraguá region, we settled on Oquiriquia (200 m a.s.l.), which is in the northern part of Santa Cruz Department on the San Martin River. The semievergreen forest (precipitation, 1500 mm/year) of the 600,000-ha Oquiriquia Concession is part of an extensive forest tract, and when we arrived in 1994 it had been uninhabited for at least 10 years and was accessible only in the dry season on dirt roads (Rumíz et al. 2001). In addition to the twenty-four or more hours needed to haul forest products from Oquiriquia to Santa Cruz, the forest was mostly intact because much of it is flooded during the wet season, which limits forestry activities to eight months per year. Because of its isolation and the huge populations of stingless and Africanized bees, coupled with scarcity of surface water in the latter part of the dry season, the name *Tierra Prometida* (Promised Land) was facetiously bequeathed on our research camp in Oquiriquia.

When we initiated our research, the more accessible portions of the concession were already high-graded for *Swietenia macrophylla, Cedrela odorata,* and *Amburana caerensis* at least once in the previous twenty years. The area around the Tierra Prometida camp was one of the least accessible portions of the concession, and wildlife was abundant, which made it suitable for studies on the "before-logging" condition. The timber harvested in the region was transported to a modern mill near the small village of Florida, less than 100 km from most of the felling areas. Quite remarkably for such a remote site, the mill produced sliced veneer in addition to more familiar sawn-timber products.

Another attraction of the Oquiriquia Timber Concession was that its owner appeared to enthusiastically support our efforts, at least at the outset. Our initial impressions proved incorrect because lack of support from the concessionaire and his field manager became extremely problematic. In fact, the field manager condoned or at least ignored logging in areas that had been set aside for research, including our erstwhile "permanent" plots. In retrospect, our emphasis on negotiations with the concessionaire appear misplaced. The project's goals might have been better served had we paid more attention to the field manager, making sure that he could perceive (and perhaps enjoy) some benefits from our presence. Ironically, although he was reported to be on the brink of shutting down his logging operations and declaring bankruptcy, this concessionaire was the principal beneficiary of the carbon offset project in the buffer zone of the Noel Kempff Mercado Park (Asquith et al. 2002).

After four years of frustration at Oquiriquia, BOLFOR suspended research at the site. The remoteness of the site, which initially made it attractive, also meant that the logistics of access, communication, and protection were very difficult. By the time of our departure from Oquiriquia, the 1996 Forestry Law had passed, and a number of other concessionaires had requested assistance from BOLFOR in complying with the new legal regulations and FSC guidelines. Although we had invested nothing in buildings or other infrastructure in Oquiriquia, it was intellectually costly to abandon our ongoing research, but the work we did there formed the basis for studies in more logistically promising areas with more supportive owners and operators.

Our initial research was focused on establishing baseline conditions and exploring the conventional timber harvesting practices in the concession. Along with establishment of permanent sample plots for growth and yield studies, diagnostic sampling was conducted in forest logged two to ten years previously to determine stocking levels and to establish priorities for silvicultural interventions. In the process, we helped develop the mensuration methods that were later adopted under the implementation guidelines of the 1996 Forestry Law. In Oquiriquia, average extraction levels were only 8 m^3/ha (Gonzales Paniagua 1997). The very low harvestable volumes of high-value species recorded in our sample plots, coupled with the scarcity of regeneration of these species, highlighted the need to focus on management of a greater number of species and on methods for promoting regeneration.

Our (F.E.P. and M.A.P.) experience with forest management in Southeast Asia, where reducing logging damage is an absolute prerequisite for sustainable forest management (Pinard et al. 1995, 2000, Pinard and Putz 1996), coupled with general concern about the deleterious impacts of logging, caused us to initially focus on timber harvesting practices in Bolivia. In Bajo Paraguá, as elsewhere in the world, the majority of logging damage was associated with roads, skid trails, and log landings; harvest planning effectively reduced the ratio of road density to volume extracted and reduced the amount of waste wood left in the forest (Santillan Dávalos 1996). To some extent this emphasis on reduced-impact logging (RIL) was justified, but over time it became apparent that it might be less important in the dry forests of Bolivia, on level terrain, than in the wet, steep, and intensively harvested forests of Southeast Asia. We discovered later that the restriction on mineral soil exposure, which was a component of the set of RIL methods we were promoting, might not have been appropriate in lowland Bolivia, given the regeneration needs of many of the commercial timber species. Although some RIL guidelines are universally applicable, such as those pertaining to worker safety and protection of watercourses, we learned that RIL guidelines should not be transferred between forests without due consideration of local conditions, especially the silvics of the species for which the forest is being managed. Furthermore, it became clear that silvicultural interventions in addition to logging often are needed to regenerate many commercial tree species in Bolivia (Fredericksen et al. 2003, Fredericksen and Putz 2003).

Lianas are a severe silvicultural nuisance in Oquiriquia. With an estimated 2471 climbing lianas more than 2 cm dbh per hectare, Oquiriquia has the dubious honor of holding the world record for liana density (Pérez-Salicrup et al. 2001a). Fully 86 percent of trees more than 10 cm dbh were liana laden. Examination of the distribution of lianas on trees revealed no evidence of tree species preferences, but proximity to smaller trees that serve as trellises helped explain why some individual trees were so heavily liana infested (Pérez-Salicrup et al. 2001b). Our studies on interactions between trees and lianas suggested that lianas interfere with water availability to some host tree species (Pérez-Salicrup and Barker 2000) but not others (Barker and Pérez-Salicrup 2000). Generally, liana cutting resulted in increased growth rates of formerly infested trees and of uninfested tree seedlings in the understory (Pérez-Salicrup 2001). While studying the effects of lianas on tree growth and survival, we conducted studies on liana cutting, recording costs and monitoring the duration of treatment benefits over two years. Mostly because of their abundance, cutting all lianas in Oquiriquia was expensive (about $15/ha) but kept trees mostly liana-free for at least two years (Pérez-Salicrup et al. 2001a). We doubt that there were any long-term impacts of liana cutting on liana species diversity in the treated areas because most species sprouted prolifically (Sanchez Acebo 1997).

One study carried out on the biodiversity impacts of silvicultural treatments focused on densities of two bird species in 1-ha plots in which all the lianas had been cut two years previously (Merry 2001). As has been repeatedly observed in studies on the effects of forestry activities on a variety of species around the world (Putz et al. 2001a), the responses of the bird species we studied varied. Chestnut-tailed antbirds (*Myrmeciza hemimelaena*) apparently were favored because liana cutting increased the woody debris on the forest floor, which this species preferentially forages. In contrast, ringed antpipits (*Corythopsos torquata*) were common in control areas but absent in liana-cut plots, presumably because they avoid open-canopied forests. Based on these and related results, as well as costs, we never again chose to cut all lianas in a management area, focusing instead on liberation of trees to be harvested and future crop trees.

Numerous studies on wildlife conducted elsewhere in the tropics (e.g., Johns 1985) indicated that the impacts of even the most severe silvicultural interventions, including the direct effects of tree cutting and road building, pale in comparison with the impacts of hunting. For this reason, soon after arriving in Oquiriquia we commenced studies on the hunting activities of tree finders, road crews, and millworkers and their bushmeat suppliers. The harvest rates of wildlife in areas recently opened to logging far exceeded those estimated to be sustainable, and many of the species being killed by hunters (e.g., giant armadillos, tapirs, cracids, and monkeys) were priorities for conservation (Rumíz et al. 2001). The quantities of bushmeat recorded in the logging camps obviously were higher than what might be expected for local consumption, suggesting that some of it was shipped out of the region for sale (Rumíz et al. 2001). This work also highlighted the importance of implementing sustained yield hunting regulations, so we recommended that companies provide their crews with domestic meat and prohibit hunting by field crews. By the end of the project, hunting in many concessions had declined because of a combination of enforcement of the new forestry law, including the restriction of logging to one-twentieth or less of the management area each year, coupled with interest in FSC certification.

The vision of the research team evolved substantially in the first few years of BOLFOR. The initial emphasis on making comparisons with undisturbed control plots began to seem misplaced or even naive. As our ecological knowledge of the lowland forests of Bolivia grew, we became aware of the complexities of disentangling factors related to hunting, land use, and fire history. It also became increasingly difficult to disregard the abundant pottery shards and charcoal that we encountered in Oquiriquia and at all of our other study sites; perhaps these forests were not as pristine as we initially thought, and the goal of establishing pristine "control" areas was misdirected.

One of the studies that might have benefited from more attention to forest history concerned the population consequences of palm heart harvesting in Bajo Paraguá (Peña-Claros 1996). In contrast to its more easily managed multiple-stemmed congener, *Euterpe oleraceae* (Pollack et al. 1995), the palm species that is commonly harvested in Bajo Paraguá, *Euterpe precatoria,* is single-stemmed. Harvesting the terminal bud in this species therefore kills the individual. Peña-Claros's matrix-based population study revealed that harvesting was far too intensive unless harvesters were willing to wait nearly a century to reenter a stand or were willing to apply silvicultural treatments to increase growth rates and seedling recruitment. Although representatives of the modern palm heart industry were not interested in managing the resource, we strongly suspect that the dense monospecific stands of Bajo Paraguá benefited from such interventions in the past, which would be in keeping with accumulating evidence of extensive but often subtle stand management treatments applied to forests all over the Amazon for millennia (Denevan 2002). Perhaps by understanding stand histories and particularly the management interventions responsible for their creation, socially attractive silvicultural interventions can be developed.

THE LOMERÍO EXPERIENCE: CHALLENGES OF COMMUNITY-BASED FOREST MANAGEMENT

In keeping with the BOLFOR design, while we were establishing our research program in the Oquiriquia Concession we were also working with the Chiquitano indigenous group of Lomerío, a region of dry forests and savannas near the town of Concepción. Before BOLFOR's involvement in this region, the communities of Lomerío were provided technical forestry assistance by a local nongovernmental organization (NGO) called Apoyo para Campesino Indígena del Oriente Boliviano (APCOB). The Chiquitanos, as represented by their organization Central Indígena de Communidades Originarias de Lomerío and APCOB, expressed interest in working with BOLFOR on forest management.

Lomerío is in a transitional zone between the humid forests of Amazonia to the north and the dry scrub areas of the Chaco to the southeast.

The seasonally deciduous forests of the region receive about 1100 mm/year of precipitation and occur in a mosaic of savanna, agricultural clearings, and granitic outcrops; even the "mature" forest is short (12–18 m) and quite open, except in riparian areas. The area was high-graded for *Macherium scleroxylon* in the 1970s and 1980s and perhaps witnessed some earlier logging for *Schinopsis brasiliensis* and *Astronium urundeuva*, species used to carve columns for the Jesuit missions built in the region in the early 1700s. There was no written or oral evidence that the area dedicated to forest management was ever cleared for agriculture.

The twenty-eight communities of Lomerío, with a total population of 5000–6000, are scattered through the approximately 290,000 ha of which 61,000 ha was included in forest management plans by 2001. Most of the people are subsistence farmers, but wage employment was intermittently available in one of the communities (Puquío) that had a sawmill purchased with funds from other donors.

As in Bajo Paraguá, our early priorities in Lomerío were to collect baseline information and initiate impact studies. At the same time, we expended much effort assisting the communities with mapping and delimiting their boundaries and building local institutional capacity. While commencing wildlife censuses and establishing permanent sample plots, we characterized vegetation types in the region (Navarro 1995) and cataloged vascular plant species (Killeen et al. 1998). We also funded a study on nontimber forest products used by the Chiquitano people (Centurión and Kraljevic 1996). As with our other research partners, we assisted our Chiquitano hosts in preparing management plans that, in the Lomerío case, resulted in FSC certification in 1995.

Timber harvesting did not evoke major environmental concerns in Lomerío because logging intensities were low (1.8 m³/ha), felling gaps were small, averaging only 72 m², and impacts on residual stands were even lighter than in Bajo Paraguá (5.9 percent of the area; Camacho Mercado 1996). We therefore focused on improving timber harvesting efficiency and on using harvesting to promote regeneration of the commercial timber species. We also dedicated substantial resources to improving operations at their sawmill, which was plagued by mismanagement only partially because it was too large for their needs. For these reasons and others that are more difficult to fathom but worth investigating (McDaniel 2002), the sawmill was seldom run at a profit. We learned that owning a sawmill is only one small component of a broader strategy for capturing the added value of semiprocessed timber.

From our early inventory work and permanent sample plot data, it was clear that the twelve to fifteen commercial timber species in the forests of Lomerío vary tremendously in their ecology, distribution, and abundance (Pinard et al. 1999b). Many of the species being exploited were not represented as advanced regeneration across large tracts of the forest. Furthermore, after logging about 38 percent of the trees in the residual stand had vine loads that were considered detrimental to growth (Antelo Paz 1997). In addition to vines, a terrestrial bromeliad (*Pseudananas sagenarius*) dominates much of the understory and constrains tree regeneration (Fredericksen et al. 1999b). These results raised questions about the suitability of a polycyclic harvesting system characterized by RIL without the use of other silvicultural treatments, especially after we found that most commercial species fail to regenerate in felling gaps. It also became clear that in predicting changes in these open-canopied forests in response to logging and other silvicultural treatments, lianas and ground bromeliads must be considered because these nonarboreal growth forms often control the processes and rates of canopy gap regeneration.

To promote regeneration of light-demanding and commercially valuable tree species, we tested various treatments in felling gaps including mechanical soil scarification, controlled burns, and chopping of vines, shrubs, and noncommercial trees with machetes. We also felled additional trees on the margins of felling gaps to enlarge the canopy openings. In general, these treatments proved ineffective at increasing the establishment of the light-demanding trees that were being harvested (Pinard et al. 1997). Instead, despite our best efforts, shade-bearing noncommercial species that were abundant in the understory remained abundant in the gaps four years after treatment. Furthermore, even after harsh treatment, many gaps became dominated by lianas and herbaceous vines. Subsequent experiments with higher-intensity controlled burns in large gaps showed some promise, but such burns would be expensive and dangerous to implement on a large scale (Kennard et al. 2001).

To support the development of appropriate silvicultural systems, we characterized tree species with particular attention to their regeneration needs (Guzman Gutierrez 1997, Pinard et al. 1999b). Given the variability in regeneration needs we found in the commercial species in Lomerío, it became clear that no single silvicultural system would be appropriate for the full complement of species. Although we found that aggregating tree species into guilds was useful for predicting the impacts of various silvicultural interventions with which we were experimenting, our initial efforts were based on too few variables (light needs for establishment, fire susceptibility, capacity for propagule dispersal). In this forest, seed bed needs (i.e., access to exposed mineral soil), sprouting capacity, and competition from nonarboreal vegetation (e.g., lianas and ground bromeliads) also proved to be important.

We increased our attention to fire ecology and the use of fire as a silvicultural tool in Lomerío as evidence accumulated from oral histories, studies of tree responses to fire, dendrochronological studies, and patterns of tree establishment in abandoned agricultural plots that fires and small-scale forest clearing influenced the development and composition of the upland forests. Although wildfires in Lomerío promoted the regeneration of *Cedrela odorata, Anadenanthera colubrina,* and several other commercial timber species (Gould et al. 2002), the forest is not purely fire maintained. Instead, the forest contains a baffling mixture of both thick-barked species that are very resistant to fire damage and thin-barked species that are vulnerable to cambial death from even low-intensity fires (Pinard and Huffman 1997). Tree species also vary in their capacity to heal wounds to the stem caused by fire or logging (Schoonenberg et al. 2003). Later we found that some of the species that fail to regenerate in the understory or in canopy gaps are abundant in fallowed agricultural fields (Gould and Quiviquivi 2000, Kennard 2002). Based on vegetation surveys in forest fallows up to fifty years old, Kennard (2002) predicted that the species composition and volume of the forest being harvested for timber would be recovered in 80–100 years after cessation of agricultural activities.

As in Bajo Paraguá, the direct impacts of logging on mammal populations in Lomerío were negligible, but hunting pressures often exceeded levels considered sustainable (Guinart Sureda 1997, Rumíz et al. 2001). Nevertheless, our Chiquitano research partners emphasized that hunting is an important part of their culture, and bushmeat is a critical source of protein. Our wildlife research in Lomerío therefore focused on building a basis for management, which included describing wildlife community composition, estimating population sizes and growth rates, determining patterns of habitat use, and identifying keystone resources and their availability. We conducted this research in a participatory manner with a core group of hunters from several communities in Lomerío. We found that animal densities were very low in Lomerío, perhaps because of hunting but probably also because of low ecosystem-level productivity. Maintenance of the populations of many hunted species apparently depends to a great extent on the riparian forests that make up a small proportion of the area, presumably because they provide better cover, year-long access to water, and greater fleshy fruit production during the dry season (Guinart Sureda 1997, Aguape Abacay 1997). In the wildlife management plans we helped develop, many riparian areas consequently were designated as off-limits to hunters. BOLFOR supported the management efforts of the hunters in many ways in addition to providing population data, such as facilitating workshops related to monitoring programs and publishing educational materials that were distributed in local schools.

Our research on wildlife management was much more appealing to the communities of Lomerío than our more extensive and very participatory work on forest management, mostly for cultural reasons. Although the financial viability of forest management on a commercial scale was demonstrated, there was only weak local commitment to forestry, at least as it was envisioned by BOLFOR (Markoupoulous 1998, McDaniel 2002). In fact, the community's hard-won FSC certification was allowed to lapse after five years (Markoupoulous 1998). While they were operating with FSC certification, the communities made profits in one year, but reportedly the sawmill director absconded with the money, defeating the objective of equitable sharing among community members. It became increasingly apparent that community forest operations take place within a very different framework than a business, one in which market-oriented development options are embedded in a broader livelihood system (see chapter 11). McDaniel (2002) points out that the Chiquitanos, like many rural producers, prefer subsistence farming to wage labor.

On private lands and timber concessions in the broader region of Chiquitania, resource economists working with BOLFOR found that there are substantial financial impediments to widespread implementation of sustainable forest management or even adoption of methods to sustain timber yields. With a matrix-based model constructed with stand data from permanent sample plots in Lomerío, Boltz (2003) argued that rapid forest liquidation is the financially most attractive land use option and that following all the guidelines of the 1996 Forest Law does not result in sustained timber yields. Other studies show that additional silvicultural interventions are needed to achieve the sustained yield goal, but the most effective combination of incentives and regulation has not yet been developed. In a related study on the economic drivers of deforestation in the region, Merry et al. (2002) found that the additional profits from modest increases in stumpage prices will provide the capital needed to convert forest into cattle pastures. Given the rapid rate of deforestation in this region (Steininger et al. 2001), other mechanisms are clearly needed to promote the maintenance of forest cover.

RESEARCH AT LA CHONTA: PUTTING PIECES TOGETHER

La Chonta is a 100,000-ha timber concession located in Guarayos Province of the Department of Santa Cruz. Agroindustrial Forestal La Chonta, the company that owns the concession, is one of the more advanced forestry companies in Bolivia. It operates a large sawmill at the edge of the concession from which it trucks kiln-dried lumber to its door factory and other processing facilities in Santa Cruz. BOLFOR began working in this concession because of the concessionaire's desire to obtain certification and, after all the trouble and cost of maintaining research in Bajo Paraguá, because of its relative proximity to Santa Cruz (six hours by road). The owner of the La Chonta concession was also representative of large firms that were concerned about sustainability, in contrast to the lack of interest encountered in Lomerío and the active disinterest in Oquiriquia. A further advantage is that the forests of La Chonta are transitional between the dry forests of Lomerío and the humid forests of Bajo Paraguá, which increased the true replication of many of our studies.

BOLFOR's first experience with La Chonta was assisting with the preparation of their management plan. In 1994, during forest management planning, a large wildfire escaped from pasturelands bordering the concession and burned more than one-third of the area. BOLFOR researchers documented that although the fire was of the slow-moving, low-intensity understory variety, only occasionally reaching into the crowns of heavily liana-laden trees, it killed many trees and was followed by massive proliferation of lianas (Pinard et al. 1999b). We also found that, in contrast to the results from the drier forests of Lomerío, postfire regeneration of commercial timber species was sparse (Mostacedo et al. 2001a, Gould et al. 2002). Despite these results, which we made sure were well circulated in the forestry community in Bolivia, little action in regard to fire prevention and control was evident in most concessions or in the surrounding areas. Concessionaires either remained unconvinced about the need for wildfire management, did not have the expertise and other resources to dedicate to wildfire control, or considered the fires to be a social problem that should be addressed with controls on fire use in agriculture. Also, the forests retain a mostly green canopy and may appear unscathed after a fire (see chapter 17). After the fires of 1999, during which 4.5 million ha in the departments of Santa Cruz and Beni burned, including much of the town of Ascension de Guarayos, BOLFOR assisted the Superintendencia Forestal in developing an early warning system for wildfires and sponsored several workshops on firefighting, but most areas still lack effective fire control methods. One obvious lesson from this experience is that even in big concessions, it is a mistake to disregard land use practices and other driving forces in the larger landscape in which they are located (see chapter 17).

The 1994 fire, coupled with evidence of earlier burns (e.g., soil charcoal) motivated us to study the impacts of timber harvesting and silvicultural treatments on forest flammability in La Chonta (G. Blate in preparation). Preliminary results from these studies reveal that, in contrast to the wetter forests of Amazonian Brazil (Holdsworth and Uhl 1997, Nepstad et al. 1998), forest flammability (i.e., ignition potential) in La Chonta is not substantially increased by forestry operations, presumably because the dry season is severe and the canopy of even unlogged forest is fairly open. In contrast, logging increases the intensity of fires that do occur in La Chonta by increasing fuel loads on the ground.

In the 1970s through early 1990s, most of La Chonta's valuable timber was extracted, compelling the concessionaire to harvest and try to market other species. Most of these species were not well known commercially, and the silvicultural needs of nearly all of them were unknown (Mostacedo and Fredericksen 1999). Among these lesser-known species was a fig (*Ficus boliviana*), the harvesting of which engendered environmental concerns, and a number of species with woods prone to develop blue stain fungi (e.g., *Hura crepitans, Schizolobium parahyba,* and *Cariniana ianeirensis*), which stimulated major changes in harvesting practices. Our studies revealed that the impacts of fig harvesting on wildlife populations are unlikely to be severe, given the large residual populations of mature fig trees after logging (Fredericksen et al. 1999b). In regard to the blue stain–susceptible species, we worked closely with the loggers to develop a harvesting system with which they can fell, yard, haul, and saw logs and load the lumber into drying kilns within forty-eight hours, after which fungal infections are likely to destroy the commercial value of the wood. Because each type of timber has different uses and different sawing and drying methods, the loggers need to know the exact location of every harvestable tree, by species, in their working area and thus need detailed and accurate harvest plans. A concern emerging from this need for rapid transformation of standing trees into kiln-dried lumber is that logging crews tend to harvest one species at a time, which means that they reenter different portions of the annual logging coupe several times over a period of up to six months. Unauthorized or inappropriately authorized reentry logging (i.e., relogging before the end of the designated felling cycle) is a major problem in many parts of the tropics but does not have major deleterious impacts in La Chonta as long as stands are completely closed six months after the initial entry. Although some seedlings recruited onto skid trails are destroyed when an area is reentered after a few months, the overall impacts on regeneration are minor, and increased skidding seems to benefit the regeneration of most species (Jackson et al. 2002, Fredericksen and Pariona 2002). As for the additional costs of this unique form of reentry logging, they too are minor

(Boltz and Quevedo 2002). Research on the very practical aspects of timber harvesting solidified relationships between the concessionaire, logging crews, and the research team, and gradually La Chonta became our
principal study site.

Scarcity of regeneration of the principal species being harvested for
timber in La Chonta prompted an ongoing series of studies on phenology (Justiniano and Fredericksen 2000), seed production by trees retained
in logging areas for this purpose (Fredericksen et al. 2001), seed dispersal, germination, and seedling survival (Severiche 2002, Fredericksen and
Pariona 2002). We found that most regeneration of commercial timber
species was occurring in areas with disturbed soil and high light, such as
logging roads and portions of logging gaps where skidders had traveled.
Very few commercially valuable species were recruiting in the forest understory or in the portions of logging gaps undisturbed by skidders. Currently, studies are being carried out to determine whether intentional
soil scarification by skidders in logging gaps will increase recruitment.
Preliminary data show a significant increase in the abundance and
growth of seedlings of valuable shade-intolerant species, although shade-
tolerant species are negatively affected (Jaldin 2001). Costs are not high
because it takes only three to five minutes to scarify a logging gap, and
it can be done at the same time as log extraction.

Although exposure of mineral soil and opening of large felling gaps
seem to stimulate the reproduction of a number of commercially important timber species, lack of planning of felling directions and some other
timber harvesting practices cause more damage to the residual forest
than is desirable (Jackson et al. 2002, Krueger 2004). Furthermore, a
study of trees wounded by skidders revealed an increased incidence of
fungal infections, perhaps rendering trees that suffer even minor damage
useless for future harvesting (McDonald et al. 2000). It was clear that
some of the damage to residual trees and soil could be avoided if logging
ceased during wet weather and if the logging crews were better supervised, but logging performance is seldom evaluated to determine
whether logging crews are correctly applying RIL techniques. To facilitate
performance evaluations, BOLFOR produced a guide to evaluating logging
operations (Contreras et al. 2001). We also held numerous workshops for
chainsaw operators and skidder drivers and published well-illustrated
guides to RIL techniques (e.g., Tanner 1997); despite these efforts, logging
practices could still improve substantially.

Advanced regeneration of commercial tree species is generally scarce
in La Chonta, and where it exists in logging gaps its growth typically is
impeded by competing vegetation. We could reduce competition by

broadcast spraying of a 5–10 percent solution of glyphosate with a back-pack sprayer or by mechanical scarification of gaps with the blade of the skidder at the time of timber yarding, but these site preparation treatments are not advisable because they eliminate both weeds and commercial seedlings. In contrast, treatments directed toward liberating saplings in gaps (advanced regeneration) are potentially useful. To test this more selective approach to seedling and sapling liberation, we released advanced regeneration from weeds in La Chonta using selective application of herbicides or by manual cleaning with machetes to a distance of 1–2 m around each sapling in logging gaps (Fredericksen and Pariona 2002). For reasons that we are still trying to determine, in response to liberation, the sapling diameter growth rate increased, but survival and height growth did not. Manual liberation was at least as effective as herbicide spraying and was less costly. One frustrating part of these liberation treatments was that the advanced regeneration was dominated by only two of the ten to fifteen species for which the forest is being managed. Although costs were not high for this treatment, it entails an additional stand entry. Given that the modest returns from the treatments will not be recovered until the end of the rotation, the cost-effectiveness is dubious. Furthermore, there are legitimate concerns about recommending herbicide spraying in Bolivia unless accompanied by adequate training programs about herbicide use and safety.

As in our other study sites, lianas are a major silvicultural problem for timber stand management in La Chonta. Although slightly less vine infested than the forests of Bajo Paraguá, La Chonta has one of the highest reported liana densities of all tropical forests in the literature (Alvira et al. 2004); 73 percent of trees in La Chonta have at least one liana, and the average infested tree hosts more than nine. On average, lianas cover 35 percent of the area of commercial tree crowns. Fortunately, cutting lianas on current and future crop trees is not expensive, costing only $1–2/ha (Fredericksen 2000). Costs could be lowered more if liana cutting were carried out during the tree census done six months to a year before harvesting, thus eliminating the need for an additional stand entry. A further advantage of prefelling liana cutting, in addition to reducing logging damage and the risks to tree fellers, is that the treatment results in lower liana coverage in felling gaps (Alvira et al. in press). To avoid the more severe biodiversity impacts and the high costs of complete liana cutting, we recommended liberating only trees to be harvested and future crop trees.

In addition to liana cutting, we evaluated the growth benefits of removing large noncommercial trees that overtop future crop trees. To correct imbalances in stand composition resulting from selective harvesting and to provide opportunities for regeneration of commercial tree species, we also poison-girdled large, malformed noncommercial trees regardless of whether they were overtopping commercial stems. Chainsaw girdling followed by herbicide application was preferred to felling of unwanted trees in these stand improvement treatments because girdled trees die gradually (over the period of a year or two) without causing much damage to surrounding trees and without an abrupt environmental shock that might reduce the growth or survival of commercial trees underneath them. In all cases, girdling was successful only when followed by herbicide application to the girdle cuts (Pariona et al. 2003). Herbicides were applied using a squirt bottle, which resulted in far less chemical being used than with broadcast spray applications.

Despite the long list of failures with enrichment or gap planting in the tropics (e.g., Dawkins and Philip 1998), we experimented with this approach where regeneration failures were attributable to lack of seed trees. We conducted our enrichment planting experiments with mahogany seeds and seedlings in logging gaps after different methods of site preparation and subsequent weeding treatments. The costs of site preparation and planting either twenty to forty seeds or fifteen to twenty seedlings in a single gap averaged $8 (K. Ohlson, unpublished data 2002). Growth and survival data are still preliminary, but long-term efficacy must be very good to justify the high costs of these treatments.

In keeping with USAID regulations, all studies that might lead to recommendations of silvicultural treatments were complemented by studies of their biodiversity impacts. At La Chonta, we compared wildlife populations in logged and unlogged blocks of forest (Woltmann 2000, Fredericksen and Fredericksen 2001) and in logging gaps and the surrounding undisturbed forest in logged blocks (Flores et al. 2001, Fredericksen and Fredericksen 2001, 2002b). Studies were also conducted on the impact of logging on fleshy fruit abundance (Fredericksen et al. 1999b, Ruiz in preparation). These studies revealed modest effects of logging on fruit production and only minor impacts on wildlife species abundance or diversity, with some species or guilds benefiting from harvesting and others being negatively affected. Taxa most negatively affected by forest management activities included ants, beetles, and frogs; groups that typically benefited included reptiles, small mammals, and frugivorous and nectarivorous birds. The minor impacts on fauna observed in these studies may be attributed partly to the low logging intensities (less than 10 m^3/ha), the matrix of undisturbed forest in which the logged areas are imbedded, and the effective prohibition of hunting, as specified by the 1996 Forestry Law and FSC certification guidelines.

INDUSTRIA PARKET

Industria Parket (INPA), unlike other heavily used BOLFOR research sites, is privately owned. INPA hires private contractors to selectively log their 30,000-ha forest on a planned cutting cycle of twenty years. Product use is restricted to parquet wood flooring. Our research began at the site in 1997 with the previous owner of the property, Amazonic Sustainable Enterprises. Despite its proximity to the humid forests of La Chonta (120 km), the forests of INPA are much drier and trees there have a longer deciduous period; only 8 percent of the species of trees more than 10 cm dbh are shared between the two sites. This site is located along the western border of the Chiquitano dry forests and is similar in environmental characteristics and species composition to the forests of Lomerío. It was certified by the FSC in 1998; the certification was passed on to the new owners with the sale of the property in 2000.

Our initial research at what was then Amazonic concerned the costs and impacts of RIL compared with conventional logging using a large (100-ha) single replicate of each treatment. Although we observed similar levels of damage per unit road and skid trail length and per logging gap in reduced-impact and conventionally logged areas (Parra 2002), a reduction in total skid trail length resulted in lower costs and overall damage in the reduced-impact area (A. Alarcon, unpublished data 1999). Studies focusing on liberation of advanced regeneration in logging gaps and timber stand improvement that were conducted at La Chonta were replicated at what is now the INPA site, with similar mixed results. For example, prescribed burning and machete cleaning were found to increase the density and growth of commercial regeneration, especially for light-seeded shade-intolerant species such as *Anadenanthera colubrina* (Heuberger et al. 2002). However, recruitment and growth were not significantly higher in the cleaned or burned treatments than in the control treatment for most species. In addition, the costs and risks of using prescribed fire in logging gaps were judged to be prohibitively high.

While the land was owned by Amazonic Sustainable Enterprises, BOLFOR research at the site was temporarily set back by a land dispute between the forest company and adjoining landowners. The dispute, as well as a financial crisis that beset the company, temporarily shut down logging activities and research at the site. A new research partnership was formed between BOLFOR and INPA in 2000, and the site was the second location for installation of blocks of Long-Term Silvicultural Research Project plots (discussed later in this chapter).

GUARAYOS: TOWARD COMANAGEMENT OF COMMUNITY FORESTS

From the inception of the project, extension foresters from BOLFOR were engaged with indigenous groups and other rural communities to manage their forests for commercial timber and nontimber forest products. The Law of Popular Participation of 1994, the Law of Administrative Decentralization of 1995, and the 1996 Forestry Law, together with the related implementation policies, resulted in substantial portions of lowland Bolivia becoming legally titled to these communities (Pacheco and Kaimowitz 1998). With the opportunities provided by the new laws and the ensuing influx of new players into the forestry sector, BOLFOR emphasized helping local groups initiate forest management projects, assisting them in conducting the inventories and writing the management plans needed to commence commercial logging. BOLFOR also assisted local management organizations with training focused on institutional strengthening, basic bookkeeping, and other business skills. These efforts remain to be summarized elsewhere, but it is clear that a great deal of time and effort is needed for people to transform themselves from subsistence farmers into commercial forest managers. Progress toward this goal appears to be somewhat faster where community members had worked in logging concessions or were "pirate" loggers before taking advantage of the opportunities of the 1996 Forestry Law. As we learn more about the distinct responses to logging across Bolivia's forest ecosystems and the varied needs for regeneration of commercial species recommended for management, it is becoming increasingly clear that community groups are being asked to make management decisions in the face of a surprisingly complex and uncertain future. In many cases good management decisions will be based on their detailed indigenous knowledge of local conditions, but it is also likely that they will need to draw on the results of researchers, particularly in understanding phenomena that are not readily apparent because of their scale or complexity.

An extension activity that was initially intended to familiarize community members with RIL techniques allowed us to identify an opportunity for collaboration between Guarayo communities experimenting with forest management, BOLFOR's biophysical research and community forestry programs, and other institutions. In the forests surrounding La Chonta five communities have recently gained approval for their forest management plans. BOLFOR community foresters provided three of these communities with technical assistance to develop their plans and market their timber. In the communities of Cururu and Salvatierra these efforts were augmented by CIFOR's Adaptive Collaborative Management Program, which has introduced participatory methods to help the communities strengthen their management organizations and distribute benefits equitably (Cronkleton in press). Because many of the community members were unfamiliar with RIL and some had never seen any logging operation up close, the BOLFOR–CIFOR team decided to organize a series of visits to the nearby research areas in La Chonta to give the community members a better perspective for making initial decisions about their management plans. Community representatives were impressed by the logging system used in La Chonta and by some of the research under way. They were especially intrigued by the silvicultural treatments being used to promote regeneration, given that their forests were high-graded by logging companies in the 1980s and early 1990s. Based on requests from several community members that similar work be done on their land, we began exploring the opportunity for collaborative research in community forests.

This work is still at a preliminary stage, but promising opportunities have been revealed. When one of the community leaders saw the soil scarification treatments in logging gaps, he asked whether they might plant crops in some gaps instead. His question was motivated by the challenge of providing their logging crews with food given that areas designated for timber management are far from their agricultural fields. This suggestion evoked ideas about forest management that are interesting to both community members and forest scientists. Perhaps in addition to planting food crops in logging gaps near their camps, the forest workers could plant and tend seedlings of valuable commercial timber species. These discussions fit so well with our increased awareness of human impacts on the forests we were trying to manage that the topic became a theme for the next phase of research in the area.

OVERVIEW AND CONTINUATION OF BOLFOR RESEARCH

Our retrospective analysis of natural forest management research sponsored by BOLFOR may convey the impression that the project ran smoothly and as planned, which was not always the case. BOLFOR was a huge ICDP funded by the U.S. government that was very much involved in reforming the forestry sector in Bolivia; not surprisingly, it had it share of detractors. Dissension also became apparent when Conservation International, a member of the founding consortium, withdrew from the project because of fundamental philosophical concerns about forest management as a conservation and development strategy. It also took some time for our foresters, wildlife biologists, and social scientists to develop respect for one another and learn to work together. Furthermore, throughout the project we found it extremely difficult to deliver the results of our applied research to decision makers, even when the work was on topics they had identified as priorities.

A number of important lessons emerged from BOLFOR research (box 5.1), and BOLFOR staff bolstered local institutions, including the Superintendencia Forestal, but the longest-lasting impacts of the project are likely to be in human capacity building. In hindsight, we believe that more should have been invested in postgraduate training, but at about $80,000 per M.S. student and twice that for a Ph.D., even a project the

---

Box 5.1   Major Lessons Emerging from BOLFOR Research on Natural Forests

- Silvicultural treatments that promote regeneration and growth of commercial species can be modest in cost and have few deleterious biodiversity impacts but should be based on thorough ecological information and are likely to be applied only where forest tenure is secure.
- Certification guidelines and government regulations in Bolivia are big steps toward sustainable forest management, but more attention must be paid to promoting silvicultural treatments when the recruitment of the species being harvested depends on interventions in addition to reduced-impact logging. The option of maintaining volume yields while allowing species composition to change should be evaluated from financial and environmental perspectives.
- Forest history should be considered in developing silvicultural guidelines, especially where regeneration of trees being harvested has been linked to agricultural activities or other intensive disturbances.
- Vines, ground bromeliads, and giant herbs can play major roles in determining the rates and patterns of forest regeneration.
- The biodiversity impacts of selective logging are minor, or at least difficult to detect, where logging intensities are low and forest canopies are fairly open before harvesting.
- Forest management decisions and impacts are driven by the broader sociopolitical context, especially livelihood systems and land use practices in the larger landscape.

size of BOLFOR found it difficult to justify very many fellowships for study abroad. Furthermore, with such a small forest research community, the fellowship recipients were sorely missed while they were taking classes abroad; it helped that most of them conducted their thesis research in Bolivia. Providing financial and academic support to local students for their undergraduate thesis project research helped to prepare them for further study and was a cost-effective way of raising the level of technical support available for forest management initiatives.

A substantial proportion of BOLFOR research funds was expended on biodiversity impact studies, as stipulated by USAID and in keeping with the interests of a number of BOLFOR scientists. Our studies of the impacts of logging and other silvicultural treatments on insects, amphibians, reptiles, birds, and mammals generally revealed that impacts were modest, varied by species, and diminished rapidly once an area was left to regenerate. In keeping with the trend evident in the literature, most of the studies compared logged and unlogged forest, or forests logged at different intensities, all fairly low. If biodiversity studies of the sort sponsored by BOLFOR are to continue, we recommend that they focus on silvicultural interventions that are severe enough to secure the sustained yield of the light-demanding commercial tree species that are being so rapidly depleted. We also recommend that the nature of suitable control areas be considered because the forests in which BOLFOR worked have histories of substantial human interventions.

Although forest management in Bolivia must improve further before it will be generally sustainable, improvements over the tenure of BOLFOR (1994–2003) were substantial, particularly the reduction in hunting pressure from logging crews. Before passage of the 1996 Forestry Law in Bolivia, with its explicit links to FSC certification, hunting was a major concern in forestry concessions. Today, with some exceptions, there is fairly strict enforcement of hunting bans at least in certified concessions, and increases in wildlife populations have been observed in these areas. Perhaps of more consequence than hunting bans, now that logging activities each year are restricted to designated areas representing at most one-twentieth of each concession, the impacts of logging crews are greatly reduced. Hunting is still permitted on indigenous lands, but the impact of hunting there is less than that observed in the past in concessions (Rumíz et al. 2001). Wild game hunting is now a problem primarily in northern Bolivia, where it continues to feed Brazil nut and palm heart gatherers (Paredes 2001, Rumíz and Aguilar 2001), as it did the rubber tappers before them, contributing to the scarcity of wildlife in these forests.

Like many other groups of forest scientists around the world, BOLFOR researchers became increasingly aware that many forests considered to be pristine were actually shaped by former human occupants (Denevan 1992, Balee 1994, Fairhead and Leach 1996). We encountered pottery shards and soil charcoal in all study areas, which we mostly disregarded, and started detailed studies on ecological history late in the project in La Chonta in 2001. Preliminary studies indicate that soils attributable to intensive human activity (*terra preta do indio,* black soils, or anthrosols) cover about 15 percent of the concession in La Chonta (Paz Rivera 2003). The distributions of several tree species useful to humans (e.g., edible fruit-producing taxa), including some timber species, appear to be related to the distribution of *terra preta* and the less radically altered soil we call *terra moreno.* Although this evidence of prior human occupancy resembles that reported from other parts of the Amazon, the study sites in La Chonta are far from rivers and other permanent sources of water, which makes them somewhat surprising. Two samples of charcoal that was mixed with pottery at 10 cm and 15 cm below the surface revealed carbon 13 dates of 380 and 420 years before present, respectively, but we are not yet sure how to interpret these data. Perhaps with the active involvement of several Bolivian archaeologists in the project, coupled with our recent discovery of what we believe are dependable annual growth rings on several species that are being logged, we will be able to determine whether regeneration of many of the trees now being harvested was associated with land abandonment a few hundred years ago. Although these studies are still preliminary, it does appear that prior land use practices influenced current stand structure and composition, including the regeneration of timber species with which we now have silvicultural difficulties. Such findings suggest that mimicking the disturbances that created this forest might entail silvicultural practices that increase disturbance. Such a strategy is almost diametrically opposed to current management philosophies of minimizing intrusion into tropical forests in the name of biodiversity protection and RIL. The compromise solution to these opposing strategies might be to create the types and intensity of disturbances necessary for recruiting regeneration while minimizing or eliminating unnecessary disturbances (Wadsworth 2001).

In collaboration with several Guarayo communities, we are planning a series of silvicultural experiments that reflect our growing awareness of the relevance of forest history and that specifically center around the idea of farming felling gaps. The approach will be something of a combination of the *taungya* system developed in Burma in the mid-nineteenth century (Dawkins and Philip 1998), without its negative geopolitical implications (Bryant 1994), and the enrichment planting approaches with which we experimented earlier in the project. It will differ from precolonial, pre–metal axe farming practices because the agricultural cropping periods will be short and the forest fallows long (Denevan 2002). Guarayo agroforesters plan to plant agricultural crops mixed with seedlings of commercially valuable timber species in large felling gaps near their temporary logging camps. After a season or two of farming, during which the tree seedlings will be tended, the gaps will be allowed to develop as enriched forest. With this approach, some of the problems associated with trying to manage fallowed fields for long-rotation crops, such as timber (Gould and Quiviquivi 2000), will be avoided because the felling gaps are in areas dedicated to forestry, not agriculture. We hope that by using this approach, we may satisfy the often-conflicting demands on forest managers to use treatments that are both socially appropriate and silviculturally effective.

To promote continuity of the research started by BOLFOR, to help secure the continued participation of international researchers, and to improve the chances of securing continued funding from a wide variety of sources, we used the final years of project funding to build a strong base for future research. Our approach was to establish sets of large-scale, permanent experimental plots in La Chonta, INPA, and a wet forest site in the northern state of Pando collectively called the Long-Term Silvicultural Research Project (LTSRP; BOLFOR 2000). We plan to set up additional plots using the same basic design in indigenous reserves in Guarayos and elsewhere in the Bolivian Amazon. Each established site is equipped with a simple screened research building with bathrooms, work tables, and storage areas. Most researchers tent camp near the main building, where they have access to solar power, running water, and a weather station. The facilities are located within a few kilometers of all of the research blocks. The plots are large enough (20–27 ha, depending on the site) to allow industrial-scale research on logging and other silvicultural treatments and studies on the biodiversity impacts of these treatments.

The central LTSRP studies are comparisons of four different management and silvicultural treatments in replicated blocks in different forest types. The treatments are based on a wide variety of silvicultural studies, many of which were sponsored by BOLFOR and summarized in a recently published volume on the topic (Mostacedo and Fredericksen 2001). The four basic treatments are no harvesting, typical planned harvesting, planned harvesting with additional silvicultural treatments, and intensive harvesting with additional silviculture. Other, smaller-scale manipulative experiments are superimposed on these basic treatments (e.g., controlled burns, wildlife exclosures, and soil scarification). The treatment plots are arranged in randomized complete blocks, with two to four blocks per site. The experiment will yield information on relative costs and efficiencies of logging operations and selected silvicultural treatments (e.g., marking of future crop trees to avoid damage, vine cutting, soil scarification, tree liberation, and timber stand improvement). The study will also yield long-term data on tree growth, forest dynamics, and the impact of harvesting and other silvicultural treatments on biodiversity.

At the time of this writing (late 2003), forest policies in Bolivia are in a moderate state of flux, particularly in regard to the setting of the annual area-based fees paid by loggers and the distribution of these funds. Another component of the 1996 Forestry Law that is being revisited is the requirement that for each 1000 ha logged, a 1-ha permanent plot for growth and yield monitoring should be established. The motivation for this regulation is obvious, especially given the arbitrary nature of the twenty-year minimum cutting cycle, but its implementation is widely understood to be a fiasco. The few plots that were established were inappropriately located and so poorly installed and measured that the few data emerging are of dubious quality. We hope that the LTSRPS will provide the data needed for setting cutting cycles and for prescribing preharvest and postharvest silvicultural treatments for enhancing regeneration and growth of timber trees. In exchange for this service to the forestry sector, we also hope that some of the funds needed to maintain the plots will be provided to the supporting institution from the forest fees (*patente*) paid to the government by loggers.

As the scheduled termination of BOLFOR and the cessation of USAID funding were drawing close, weaknesses of the project's exit strategy became apparent. The size of the project in a country that was not investing heavily in forestry made it nearly inevitable that BOLFOR would assume some of the characteristics of a permanent institution. Although we endeavored to support local institutions throughout the project, including the Museo de Historia Natural Noel Kempff Mercado and the now-defunct research wing of the Bolivian Forest Industry Association (Promobosque), there was no apparent Bolivian institution that could take over for BOLFOR when the project ended. In particular, there were no Bolivian institutions whose mission included the extension and technical services for natural forest management, including the applied research carried out by BOLFOR. After a long series of consultations with representatives of the NGO community, government, and the forestry sector, the Instituto Boliviano de Investigación Forestal (IBIF) was formed to promote and conduct research in a network of permanent sample plots throughout lowland Bolivia. This network will be based on the LTSRPS but will also include smaller permanent sample plots established by IBIF and collaborating institutions.

The first in what is planned as a biennial series of national forestry congresses that was held in June 2002 in Santa Cruz is among the most compelling indicators that progress toward sustainable natural forest management will continue in Bolivia. This three-day congress, attended by about 200 researchers, industrial representatives, and policymakers, featured more than 100 papers and posters on topics including silviculture, biodiversity impacts of forestry operations, rural sociology, the economics of community-based forest management, and forest policy. Although some of the presentations followed strict disciplinary lines (e.g., silviculture or rural sociology), most were interdisciplinary in their perspectives. There is still a great need for more capacity building in Bolivia, but the culture of the research community—indeed, of the entire forest sector—seems to have improved in Bolivia in the past decade.

REFERENCES

Aguape Abacay, R. 1997. *Frutos del bosque ribereno de Lomerío y su importancia para la fauna silvestre, Santa Cruz, Bolivia.* B.S. thesis. Santa Cruz, Bolivia: Universidad Autónoma Gabriel René Moreno.

Alvira, D., F. E. Putz, and T. S. Fredericksen. 2004. Liana loads and post-logging liana densities after liana cutting in a lowland forest in Bolivia. *Forest Ecology and Management* 190: 73–86.

Antelo Paz, E. K. 1997. *Aplicacion de tratamientos silvicultuales en bosque aprovechado en la zona de Lomerío.* B.S. thesis. Santa Cruz, Bolivia: Universidad Autónoma Gabriel René Moreno.

Asquith, N. M., M. T. Vargas, and J. Smith. 2002. Can forest-protection carbon projects improve rural livelihoods? Analysis of the Noel Kempff Mercado Climate Action Project, Bolivia. *Mitigation and Adaptation Strategies for Global Change* 7: 323–337.

Balee, W. 1994. *Footprints of the forest.* New York: Columbia University Press.

Barker, M. G. and D. Pérez-Salicrup. 2000. Comparative water relations of mature mahogany (*Swietenia macrophylla*) trees with and without lianas in a subhumid, seasonally dry forest in Bolivia. *Tree Physiology* 20: 1167–1174.

BOLFOR. 2000. *LTSRP: The Long-Term Silvicultural Research Project study plan.* Santa Cruz, Bolivia: Proyecto BOLFOR.

Boltz, F. 2003. *Optimal management of Bolivian tropical dry forest.* Ph.D. dissertation. Gainesville: University of Florida.

Boltz, F. and R. Quevedo. 2002. *La conservación al servicio de la economia? Beneficios potenciales de la planificatión de pistas de arrastre para la reducción de daños a árboles de futura cosecha.* Bulletin no. 25. Santa Cruz, Bolivia: Proyecto BOLFOR.

Bryant, R. L. 1994. Shifting the cultivator: The politics of teak regeneration in colonial Burma. *Modern Asian Studies* 28: 225–250.

Camacho Mercado, O. 1996. *Analisis del impacto de un aprovechamiento forestal sobre el bosque seco sub-tropical de Lomerío, Santa Cruz, Bolivia.* B.S. thesis. Santa Cruz, Bolivia: Universidad Autónoma Gabriel René Moreno.

Centurión, T. R. and I. J. Kraljevic, eds. 1996. *Las plantas utiles de Lomerío.* Santa Cruz, Bolivia: Proyecto BOLFOR.

Contreras, F., W. Cordero, and T. S. Frederiksen. 2001. *Evaluación de aprovechamiento forestal.* Santa Cruz, Bolivia: Proyecto BOLFOR.

Contreras-Hermosilla, A. and M. T. Vargas Rios. 2002. *Social, environmental and economic dimensions of forest policy reforms in Bolivia.* Bogor, Indonesia: Center for International Forestry Research; Washington, D.C.: Forest Trends.

Cronkleton, P. In press. Gender, participation and the strengthening of indigenous forestry management. In C. J. P. Colfor, ed., *The equitable forest: Enhancing equity in forest management.* Bogor, Indonesia: Center for International Forestry Research.

Dawkins, H. C. and M. S. Philip. 1998. *Tropical moist forest silviculture and management: A history of success and failure.* Oxford, U.K.: CAB International.

Denevan, W. 1992. The pristine myth: The landscape of the Americas in 1492. *Annals of the Association of American Geographers* 82: 369–385.

Denevan, W. 2002. *Cultivated landscapes of native Amazonia and the Andes.* Oxford, U.K.: Oxford University Press.

Fairhead, J. and M. Leach. 1996. *Misreading the African landscape: Society and ecology in a forest–savanna mosaic.* Cambridge, U.K.: Cambridge University Press.

Flores, B., D. Rumíz, T. S. Fredericksen, and N. J. Fredericksen. 2001. *Uso de claros de aprovechamiento por las aves en un bosque húmedo tropical Boliviano.* Technical document no. 100. Santa Cruz, Bolivia: Proyecto BOLFOR.

Frederiksen, N. J. and T. S. Fredericksen 2001. *Impactos del aprovechamiento forestal selectivo en poblaciones de anfibios de un bosque tropical húmedo de Bolivia.* Technical document no. 105. Santa Cruz, Bolivia: Proyecto BOLFOR.

Frederiksen, N. J. and T. S. Fredericksen. 2002a. *Impacts of selective logging on wildlife indicator species in a Bolivian tropical humid forest.* Technical document. Santa Cruz, Bolivia: Proyecto BOLFOR.

Frederiksen, N. J. and T. S. Fredericksen. 2002b. Terrestrial wildlife response to logging and wildfire in a Bolivian tropical humid forest. *Biodiversity and Conservation* 11: 27–38.

Fredericksen, T. S. 2000. Selective herbicide application to control lianas in tropical forests. *Journal of Tropical Forest Science* 12: 561–570.

Fredericksen, T. S., L. McDonald, K. Wright, and B. Mostacedo. 1999a. Ecology of the ground bromeliad *Pseudananas sagenarius. Boletín de Sociedad Botánica Boliviana* 2: 165–173.

Fredericksen, T. S., B. Mostacedo, J. Justiniano, and J. Ledezma. 2001. Seed-tree retention consideration uneven-aged management in Bolivian tropical forests. *Journal of Tropical Forest Science* 13: 352–363.

Fredericksen, T. S. and W. Pariona. 2002. Effects of skidder disturbance on commercial tree regeneration in logging gaps in a Bolivian tropical humid forest. *Forest Ecology and Management* 171: 223–230.

Fredericksen, T. S. and F. E. Putz. 2003. Silvicultural intensification for tropical forest conservation. *Biodiversity and Conservation* 12: 1245–1453.

Fredericksen, T. S., F. E. Putz, P. Pattie, W. Pariona, and M. Peña-Claros. 2003. Tropical forestry in Bolivia: The next steps from planned logging towards sustainable forest management. *Journal of Forestry* 101: 37–40.

Fredericksen, T. S., D. Rumíz, M. J. Justiniano, and R. Aguape. 1999b. Harvesting free-standing figs for timber in Bolivia: Potential implications for sustainability. *Forest Ecology and Management* 116: 151–161.

Gonzales Paniagua, V. H. 1997. *Caracterizacion de bosques residuales en la reserva forestal de produccion Bajo Paraqua*. B.S. thesis. Santa Cruz, Bolivia: Universidad Autónoma Gabriel René Moreno.

Gould, K., T. S. Fredericksen, F. Morales, D. Kennard, F. E. Putz, B. Mostacedo, and M. Toledo. 2002. Post-fire tree regeneration in two Bolivian tropical forests: Implications for fire management. *Forest Ecology and Management* 165: 225–234.

Gould, K. A. and E. Quiviquivi. 2000. *Regeneracion arborea posterior a la agricultura de chaqueo y quema en el oriente Boliviano: Implicaciones para el manejo forestall*. Technical document no. 93/2000. Santa Cruz, Bolivia: Proyecto BOLFOR.

Guinart Sureda, D. 1997. *Los mamiferos del bosque semideciduo neotropical de Lomerío (Bolivia). Interaccion indigena*. Ph.D. dissertation. Barcelona: Universitat de Barcelona.

Gullison, R. E., J. J. Hardner, and A. Shauer. 1997. The percentage utilization of felled mahogany trees in the Chimanes Forest, Beni, Bolivia. *Journal of Tropical Forest Science* 10: 94–100.

Gullison, R. E., S. N. Panfil, J. J. Strolse, and S. P. Hubbell. 1996. Ecology and management of mahogany (*Swietenia macrophylla* King) in the Chimanes Forest, Beni, Bolivia. *Botanical Journal of the Linnaean Society* 122: 9–34.

Guzman Gutierrez, R. A. 1997. *Caracterizacion y clasificacion de especies forestal en gremios ecologicos en el bosque sub-humedo estacional de la region de Lomerío, Santa Cruz, Bolivia*. Postgraduate thesis. Turrialba, Costa Rica: Centro Agronomico Tropical de Investigacion y Ensenanza.

Heuberger, K. A., T. S. Fredericksen, M. Toledo, W. Urquieta, and F. Ramirez. 2002. Mechanical cleaning and prescribed burning for recruiting commercial tree regeneration in a Bolivian dry forest. *New Forests* 24: 183–194.

Holdsworth, A. R., and C. Uhl. 1997. Fire in Amazonian selectively logged rain forest and the potential for fire reduction. *Ecological Applications* 7: 713–725.

Jackson, S. M., T. S. Fredericksen, and J. R. Malcolm. 2002. Area of disturbance and damage to residual stand following selection logging in a Bolivian tropical humid forest. *Forest Ecology and Management* 166: 271–284.

Jaldin, E. 2001. *Impactos preliminares de escarificación de suelo con skidders in claros de aprovechamiento*. Undergraduate thesis. Cochabamba, Bolivia: Escuela Forestal.

Johns, A. D. 1985. Selective logging and wildlife conservation in tropical rainforest: Problems and recommendations. *Biological Conservation* 31: 355–375.

Justiniano, M. J. and T. S. Fredericksen. 2000. Phenology of tree species in Bolivian dry forests. *Biotropica* 32: 276–281.

Kaimowitz, D., C. Vallejos, P. Pacheco, and R. Lopez. 1998. Municipal governments and forest management in lowland Bolivia. *Journal of Environment and Development* 7: 45–59.

Kennard, D. K. 2002. Secondary forest succession in a tropical dry forest: patterns of development across a 50-year chronosequence in lowland Bolivia. *Journal of Tropical Ecology* 18: 53–66.

Kennard, D. K., T. S. Fredericksen, and B. Mostacedo. 2001. Potencial de las quemas controladas para el manejo de especies maderables de bosques secos: Estudio de caso de Lomerío. In B. Mostacedo and T. S. Fredericksen, eds., *Regeneración y silvicultura de bosques tropicales en Bolivia*, 203–204. Santa Cruz, Bolivia: Proyecto BOLFOR.

Killeen, T. J., A. Jardim, F. Mamani, and N. Rojas. 1998. Diversity, composition and structure of a tropical semideciduous forest in the Chiquitania region of Santa Cruz, Bolivia. *Journal of Tropical Ecology* 14: 803–827.

Krueger, W. 2004. Costs and benefits of future crop tree flagging and improved skid trail planning relative to conventional planned diameter-limit logging in Bolivian tropical forest. *Forest Ecology and Management* 188: 381–393.

Markoupoulous, M. 1998. The impacts of certification on community forest enterprises: A case study of the Lomerío Forest Management Project, Bolivia. IIED Forest and Land Use Series, no. 13. Oxford, U.K.: International Institute for Environment and Development.

McDaniel, J. 2002. Confronting the structure of international development: Political agency and the Chiquitanos of Bolivia. *Human Ecology* 30: 369–396.

McDonald, E., M. A. Pinard, and S. Woodward. 2000. *Invasión micótica de lesiones artificiales en* Ficus glabrata. Technical document no. 94. Santa Cruz, Bolivia: Proyecto BOLFOR.

Merry, E. A. 2001. *Effects of vine cutting on understory birds in a Bolivian lowland forest: Implications for management.* M.S. thesis. Gainesville: University of Florida.

Merry, F. D., P. E. Hildebrand, P. Pattie, and D. R. Carter. 2002. An analysis of land conversion from sustainable forestry to pasture: A case study in the Bolivian lowlands. *Land Use Policy* 19: 207–215.

Mostacedo, B. and T. S. Fredericksen. 1999. Status of forest tree regeneration in Bolivia: Assessment and recommendations. *Forest Ecology and Management* 124: 263–273.

Mostacedo, B. and T. S. Fredericksen, eds. 2001. *Regeneracion y silvicultura de bosques tropicales en Bolivia.* Santa Cruz, Bolivia: Proyecto BOLFOR.

Mostacedo, B., T. S. Fredericksen, K. Gould, and M. Toledo. 2001a. Responses of structure and composition to wildfire in dry and sub-humid Bolivian tropical forests. *Journal of Tropical Forest Science* 13: 488–502.

Mostacedo, B., J. Justiniano, M. Toledo, and T. Fredericksen. 2001b. *Guia dendrologica de especies forestales de Bolivia.* Santa Cruz, Bolivia: Proyecto BOLFOR.

Navarro, S. G. 1995. *Clasificacion de la vegetacion de la region de Lomerío en el Departamento de Santa Cruz, Bolivia.* Report no. 10. Santa Cruz, Bolivia: Proyecto BOLFOR.

Nepstad, D. C., A. Moreira, A. Veríssimo, P. Lefebvre, P. Schlesinger, C. Potter, C. Nobre, C. Setzer, T. Krug, A. Barros, A. Alencar, and J. R. Pereira. 1998. Forest fire prediction and prevention in the Brazilian Amazon. *Conservation Biology* 12: 951–953.

Nittler, J. B. and D. W. Nash. 1999. The certification model for forestry in Bolivia. *Journal of Forestry* 97: 32–36.

Pacheco, P. B. and D. Kaimowitz, eds. 1998. *Municipios y gestion forestal en el tropico boliviano.* La Paz, Bolivia: Center for International Forestry Research, Centro de Estudios para el Desarrollo Laboral y Agrario, Taller de Ininciativas en Estudios Rurales y Reforma Agraria, and Proyecto de Manejo Forestal Sostenible.

Paredes, L. 2001. *Evaluación de uso de la fauna silvestre durante la zafra castañera en el bosque Amazónico.* Pando, Bolivia: Proyecto PANFOR.

Pariona, W., T. S. Fredericksen, and J. C. Licona. 2003. Comparison of three girdling treatments for timber stand improvement in Bolivian tropical forests. *Journal of Tropical Forest Science* 15: 583–592.

Parra, J. L. 2002. *Diferencias de impactos entre aprovechamiento forestal planificado y no planificado en un bosque seco tropical.* Undergraduate thesis. Santa Cruz, Bolivia: Universidad Autónoma Gabriel René Moreno.

Paz Rivera, C. L. 2003. *Forest-use history and the soils and vegetation of a lowland forest in Bolivia.* M.S. thesis. Gainesville: University of Florida.

Peña-Claros, M. 1996. *Ecological and socioeconomic impacts of palm heart extraction on populations of* Euterpe precatoria *in Bolivia.* M.S. thesis. Gainesville: University of Florida.

Pérez-Salicrup, D. R. 2001. Effect of liana cutting on tree regeneration in a liana forest in Amazonian Bolivia. *Ecology* 82: 389–396.

Pérez-Salicrup, D. R. and M. G. Barker. 2000. Effect of liana cutting on water potential and growth of adult *Senna multijuga* (Caesalpinoideae) trees in a Bolivian tropical forest. *Oecologia* 124: 469–475.

Pérez-Salicrup, D. R., A. Claros, R. Guzman, J. C. Licona, F. Ledezma, M. A. Pinard, and F. E. Putz. 2001a. Cost and efficiency of cutting lianas in a lowland liana forest of Bolivia. *Biotropica* 33: 34–47.

Pérez-Salicrup, D. R., V. L. Sork, and F. E. Putz. 2001b. Lianas and trees in a liana forest of Amazonian Bolivia. *Biotropica* 33: 34–47.

Pinard, M. A. and J. Huffman. 1997. Fire resistance and bark properties of trees in a seasonally dry forest in eastern Bolivia. *Journal of Tropical Ecology* 13: 727–740.

Pinard, M. A. and F. E. Putz. 1996. Retaining forest biomass by reducing logging damage. *Biotropica* 28: 278–295.

Pinard, M. A., F. E. Putz, and J. C. Licona. 1999a. Tree mortality and vine proliferation following a wildfire in a subhumid tropical forest in eastern Bolivia. *Forest Ecology and Management* 113: 201–213.

Pinard, M. A., F. E. Putz, D. Rumíz, R. Guzmán, and A. Jardim. 1999b. Ecological characterization of tree species for guiding forest management decisions in seasonally dry forests in Lomerío, Bolivia. *Forest Ecology and Management* 113: 201–213.

Pinard, M. A., F. E. Putz, and J. Tay. 2000. Lessons learned from the implementation of reduced-impact logging in hilly terrain in Sabah, Malaysia. *International Forestry Review* 2: 33–39.

Pinard, M. A., F. E. Putz, J. Tay, and T. E. Sullivan. 1995. Creating timber harvest guidelines for a reduced-impact logging project in Malaysia. *Journal of Forestry* 93: 41–45.

Pinard, M. A., R. Veizaga, and S. A. Stanley. 1997. Mejora de la regeneracion de especies arboreas en los claros de corta de un bosque estacionalmente seco en

Bolivia. *Las memorias del Simposio Internacional sobre Posibilidades para el Manejo Forestal Sostenible en America Tropical.* Santa Cruz, Bolivia: IUFRO/BOLFOR.

Pollack, H., M. Mattos, and C. Uhl. 1995. A profile of palm heart extraction in the Amazon estuary. *Human Ecology* 23: 357–385.

Putz, F. E., G. M. Blate, K. H. Redford, R. Fimbel, and J. G. Robinson. 2001a. Biodiversity conversation in the context of tropical forest management. *Conservation Biology* 15: 7–20.

Putz, F. E., L. K. Sirot, and M. A. Pinard. 2001b. Tropical forest management and wildlife: Silvicultural effects on forest structure, fruit production, and locomotion of non-volant arboreal animals. In R. Fimbel, A. Grajal, and J. Robinson, eds., *The cutting edge: Conserving wildlife in managed tropical forests,* 11–34. New York: Columbia University Press.

Rumíz, D. I. and F. Aguilar. 2001. Rain forest logging and wildlife use in Bolivia: Management and conservation in transition. In R. Fimbel, A. Grajal, and J. Robinson, eds., *The cutting edge: Conserving wildlife in logged tropical forests,* 649–664. New York: Columbia University Press.

Rumíz, D. I., D. Guinart, S. R. Luciano, and J. C. Herrera. 2001. Logging and hunting in community forests and corporate concessions: Two contrasting case studies. In R. Fimbel, A. Grajal, and J. Robinson, eds., *The cutting edge: Conserving wildlife in logged tropical forests,* 333–358. New York: Columbia University Press.

Sanchez Acebo, L. 1997. *Regeneracion de bejucos despues del corte, en un bosque tropical estacional del Bajo Paraguá.* B.S. thesis. Santa Cruz, Bolivia: Universidad Autónoma Gabriel René Moreno.

Santillan Dávalos, H. 1996. *Effectos del aprovechamiento en dos sitios de estudio Oquiriquia Bajo Paraguá.* Technical thesis. Santa Cruz, Bolivia: Universidad Mayor de San Simon Escuela Tecnica Superior Forestal.

Schoonenberg, T., M. A. Pinard, and S. Woodward. 2003. Responses to simulated fire wounding in tree species characteristic of seasonally dry tropical forest of Bolivia. *Canadian Journal of Forest Research* 33: 1–10.

Severiche, W. 2002. *Regeneración de especies comerciales en caminos abandonados en la concesión forestal La Chonta, Santa Cruz, Bolivia.* Undergraduate thesis. Santa Cruz, Bolivia: Universidad Autónoma Gabriel René Moreno.

Steininger, M. K., C. J. Tucker, P. Ersts, T. J. Killeen, Z. Villegas, and S. B. Hecht. 2001. Clearance and fragmentation of tropical deciduous forest in the tierras bajas, Santa Cruz, Bolivia. *Conservation Biology* 15: 856–866.

Tanner, H. 1997. *Tecnica de corta dirigida: Manual ilustrado.* Santa Cruz, Bolivia: Proyecto BOLFOR.

Wadsworth, F. H. 2001. Not just reduced, but productive logging impacts. *International Forestry Review* 3: 51–53.

Woltmann, S. 2000. *Comunidades de aves del bosque en áreas alteradas y no alteradas de la concesión forestal La Chonta, Santa Cruz, Bolivia.* Technical document no. 92. Santa Cruz, Bolivia: Proyecto BOLFOR.

Chapter 6

THE BUSINESS OF CERTIFICATION

Joshua C. Dickinson, John M. Forgach, and Thomas E. Wilson

Maintenance of viable tropical forest ecosystems outside parks and equivalent reserves can benefit substantially from voluntary third-party forest management certification, especially as coordinated by the Forest Stewardship Council (FSC). Certification can also enhance the well-being of people living in and around forests. Addressed here is the apparent bottleneck between well-managed forests and discerning consumers, which is the business of certified forestry in tropical, developing country settings. *Business* in this context refers to many considerations, including business management and entrepreneurship at the company or community level, attractiveness to venture capital and outside investors, government policies, and marketing and consumer preferences.

When consumers buy produce, canned tuna, or a blouse from Guatemala, the label "organic," "dolphin friendly," or "Fair Trade Federation" assures them that they have done their bit for the environment or that a Mayan was paid fairly for her handiwork. When they buy wood products, the FSC logo assures consumers that the best available methods were used to maintain the ecological integrity of the forest from which the tree was harvested and perhaps that a rural community enjoyed economic benefits from logging. We explicitly assume here that FSC certification is one of the best available tools for ensuring that forests in the tropics are managed in an environmentally responsible, socially beneficial, and economically viable manner. Furthermore, we assume that in regard to conservation, certified forests complement but do not replace protected forests, as specified in the FSC policy on high–conservation value forests (HCVFS; see http://www.fscoax.org).

The chainsaw is a blunt instrument for conserving tropical forests. Nevertheless, until alternative or complementary products and services such as carbon credits and ecotourism can bring more income to forest users, logging often remains the only economically attractive alternative to converting the forest to pasture and cropland. Nontimber forest products (NTFPS) alone generally ensure little more than sustainable poverty (Browder 1992, Southgate 1998). Unfortunately, NTFPS tend to either be high in value but low in abundance, making the resource vulnerable to overexploitation (e.g., incensewood), or low in value but high in abundance (e.g., fuelwood), making the resource challenging to use for poverty alleviation. In contrast, timber is both abundant and moderately valuable (Salafsky et al. 1998).

It is well recognized that for certification to work as a market incentive for good forest management, consumer demand for certified forest products must increase (Dickinson 1999). Less appreciated as an impediment to the success of certification are the organizational and entrepreneurial deficiencies common to both the private sector and rural communities that manage forests in developing countries. These deficiencies become particularly apparent in the international market for certified products.

CERTIFICATION IN A GLOBALIZED ECONOMY

The globalization process is upon us, with all its wonders and warts. On the positive side, *The Lexus and the Olive Tree,* a primer on globalization, lists dozens of examples of how countries that want to participate in the world market are forced to adopt internationally accepted standards governing transparency, accounting methods, and quality control (Friedman 2000). International certification of good forest management takes advantage of economic globalization to achieve environmental and social goals. A retailer in the United Kingdom can escape the ire of environmentalists concerned about tropical deforestation by stocking furniture made in China from wood harvested from a certified forest in the Amazon basin. To take advantage of this marketing opportunity, some loggers in the tropics are actually obeying the forest laws, adopting unheard-of forestry practices to conserve biodiversity, and breaking with a 400-year tradition of exploiting local communities by engaging in good faith negotiations to solve territorial disputes. Brazil, a global player in the certified market, has gone so far as to form a certified product buyers' group with the goal of having all wood used domestically certified by 2005 ("Managing the Rainforest" 2000), although this is reminiscent of the International Tropical Timber Organization's (ITTO) futile call for all production forests in the tropics to come under sustainable management by 2000.

Forest management certification is a tool for assuring interested parties that a specific forest is being well managed (Viana et al. 1996). Ecological, social, and economic sustainability, central tenets of certification, are complex concepts, best thought of as goals to be pursued and redefined in the process (Putz 1994). Elements of sustainable forest management on which FSC certification is based include the following:

- Maintenance of ecological functions and biological diversity of forest ecosystems
- Assurance that people who inhabit or work in the forest share in the benefits of forest management
- Financial returns from forest management and value-added activities that are profitable and competitive with conversion to alternative uses

Certification of the FSC variety is voluntary and is based on market incentives created by consumers and a wide array of retailers, industries, and architects who have agreed to stock, manufacture, and specify the use of wood from well-managed forests. For many along the certified product market chain, the appeal of doing the right thing transcends market incentives. For example, a number of community and industrial forest management operations have become certified mostly because of their desire to be recognized for practicing good forestry in addition to wanting to secure access to green markets.

Establishing the FSC as a global organization to address what constitutes good forest management in boreal, temperate, and tropical regions from ecological, economic, and social perspectives was a complex challenge. The FSC encountered strong resistance from many in the forest sector who preferred the status quo. Organizational support, education, and pressure by nongovernmental organizations (NGOs) played a critical role in launching the certification movement. Financial support for launching this new organization came from philanthropic foundations and international development assistance agencies. For many supporters, creation of the FSC was a response to widespread frustration with command-and-control regulation of forest use by governments (Kiker and Putz 1997).

Creation of the FSC certification system in 1993 triggered the launching of several competing certification systems with varied methods and standards. These include the Sustainable Forestry Initiative (SFI) of the American Forest and Paper Association, the Pan European Forest Certification scheme, and the Canadian Standards Association's Sustainable Forest Management Program. The short-lived Forest Management Awards program of the Washington, D.C.–based Tropical Forest Foundation (TFF) and ITTO's ill-fated Year 2000 Initiative also drew attention from the FSC in its early years. These alternatives to the FSC detracted from efforts to make certification an effective market incentive to improve forest management practices, mostly because they caused confusion among consumers (Ozinga 2001, Atyi and Simula 2002). Less widely appreciated were the damaging effects of a number of well-intentioned international and national groups that set out to independently develop their own principles and criteria for sustainable forest management rather than work with the FSC (e.g., the Center for International Forestry Research, Lembaga Ekologi Indonesia, and the Malaysian Criteria and Indicators Working Group). Although we fully recognize the contributions made by these groups, many logging industries delayed implementation of any of the obviously needed changes in their operations in the name of waiting for the research to be completed. Although competing certification schemes could be viewed as beneficial under ideal circumstances, the rapid depletion and degradation of tropical forests globally makes such competition counterproductive. As one prominent representative of the logging industry (and member of the TFF board) said, "You keep talking, we'll keep logging" (B. Chan, pers. comm. 2001).

Although several competing certification schemes are ongoing, others have joined forces with FSC or disappeared. The FSC currently has eleven independent, accredited certifiers that perform initial assessments and periodic audits of field performance based on established principles and criteria (http://www.fscoax.org). As of December 2003 there were 566 certified forest operations in fifty-eight countries with a worldwide total of more than 40 million ha. The FSC also provides chain-of-custody certification to allow the tracking of certified products from the forest through processing stages to the end consumer. In addition to recognizing good forest managers, FSC certification provides consumers with highly credible assurance that products they buy come from forest operations managed in environmentally and socially responsible manners.

FSC certification is a delicate balancing act between environmental, social, and economic interests. The dominant actors have been representatives from the environmental community that see certification as a tool for conserving forest ecosystems outside protected areas. They are supported, particularly in the context of developing countries, by social welfare activists who see certified management primarily as a means to strengthen community-based forestry and reinforce tenure claims but also as a way to ensure worker and forest dwellers' rights.

The area of certified forest in the tropics in late 2002 was 3.5 million ha, only 12 percent of the world total certified. Why do tropical countries lag behind countries with temperate and boreal forests in terms of the area of forest certified? The answers are complex and often intertwined, but many are related to the fact that temperate and boreal forests are found mostly in northern hemisphere developed countries. Factors that promote certification in developed countries in the North and limit its expansion in the South are listed in box 6.1.

A principal hurdle for good forestry is that commercial timber interests in the tropics must find certified management more attractive than conventional logging. If timber companies fail to make money in certified forestry, or even if they fail to make as much money as they would otherwise, the whole elaborate construct is likely to fall apart.

Financial institutions and development assistance organizations that conditioned their loans and other support on the recipient forest operations becoming certified have contributed substantially to recent improvements in tropical forest management. For example, the Overseas Private Investment Fund of the United States cites FSC guidelines in the

---

Box 6.1   Factors Promoting Certification in Developed Countries in the North and Limiting Its Expansion in the South

Factors that favor certification in the North:
- Certification originated in the North, and the most widely used certifiers are based in the United States and United Kingdom.
- Forest management in developed countries is practiced more often under the direction of trained foresters who can readily adapt their practices to meet certification standards.
- Temperate and boreal coniferous and hardwood ecosystems are well understood (although what constitutes good management often remains controversial).
- The opportunity costs of monitoring and managing forests are low because most areas that are forested are not suitable for other land uses.
- Laws governing environmental impacts, land tenure, workers' rights, and transparency of financial transactions are widely enforced.
- Environmental organizations are strong because of the financial and philosophical backing of a large segment of the educated public.
- Capital for forestry is available at competitive rates.

(continued)

Box 6.1 (continued)

Factors that discourage certification in the South:

- Certification is introduced from the outside by international non-governmental organizations (NGOS) or assistance projects via local NGOS, companies, and communities with other priorities (e.g., weak environmental and social action NGOS have little leverage in the forest sector).
- Tropical forest ecosystems are highly diverse and poorly understood both silviculturally and ecologically, and there are few foresters in tropical countries who can manage them.
- Tropical forests generally are not managed at all, making the change to certified management difficult and expensive.
- Many forest areas are destined for conversion (planned or spontaneous), making sustainable forest management impossible. The opportunity costs of maintaining and managing forests in some areas are high because the sites can sustain other, more intensive and more profitable land uses (e.g., oil palm or pulpwood plantations).
- Indigenous people, environmentalists, loggers, colonists, and ranchers have divergent perspectives on the values of forests.
- Law enforcement is lax and corruption common, making the practice of certifiable forestry difficult and expensive relative to competing illegal logging operations.
- Business management, marketing, and technical skills are limited in the forest sector and even worse in rural communities.
- Tropical countries have difficulty attracting investors and joint venture partners with needed capital, skills, and market connections, and loans often are not available to the forest sector.

"Standards" section of its *Environmental Handbook* (http://www.opic.gov). Similarly, the U.S. Agency for International Development (USAID) Mission in Bolivia conditioned funding of a forestry project on the operations being FSC certified. In Brazil, the venture capital firm A2R conditions its financing on operations becoming certified. Precious Woods, a Swiss holding company with forest operations in Brazil, voluntarily chose FSC certification as a means of validating the quality of forest management and gaining access to the market for certified forest products.

By late 2002, most of the world's area of certified tropical forest was in Bolivia and Brazil. Therefore it seems relevant to ask what we can learn from their experiences with certification that is relevant to other tropical countries. Bolivia and Brazil share a common border in the Amazon basin, with many of the same commercial tree species. Both have forest protection advocates, indigenous groups, and commercial agriculture and ranching interests, as well as growing peasant agricultural populations and logging operations of various scales, all competing for a shrinking forest resource. Differences are also striking. For example, Brazil is a large and advanced developing country, whereas Bolivia is one of the poorest countries in the hemisphere, which results in substantial differences in the scale and sophistication of the private and public institutions that affect forest resources. Brazil has a well-developed road and riverine transportation system, providing access to both a large domestic market and export markets for forest products. Bolivia has a small domestic timber market and high export transportation costs because of its mediterranean location. In Bolivia, most forest is held by the government, with timber rights obtained through long-term concessions for which the private sector pays US$1/ha per year. Indigenous and peasant communities obtain timber harvesting rights for lower fees. In Brazil, in contrast, forested land may be purchased for $25–60/ha. An external initiative by a development agency prompted Bolivia's adoption of certification, whereas progressive industrialists brought certification to Brazil. In Bolivia, 1 million ha of natural forest was under certified management as of 2002. Certification of 1 million ha in Brazil began with eucalypt plantations and was later expanded to forests in the Amazon basin.

BOLIVIA: CERTIFICATION VIA DEVELOPMENT ASSISTANCE

Much of the initiative to participate in certified forestry in Bolivia came from the Bolivian Sustainable Forestry Project (BOLFOR), funded by USAID (Nittler and Nash 1999, see also chapter 5). In 1993, the project designers chose to use the certification scheme established by the newly created FSC to ensure that tropical forest management followed ecological and social standards with wide international acceptance. With BOLFOR sponsorship, the director of SmartWood, an FSC-accredited certifier, conducted a series of workshops for representatives from forest industries, NGOS, and government agencies in 1994 to acquaint stakeholders with the concept of certification. Successive Bolivian governments have worked with BOLFOR to establish and implement a new forest law and related legislation that is compatible with sustainable forestry and the long-term access to forest resources by the private sector, peasant communities, and indigenous groups (Contreras-Hermosilla and Vargas Rios 2002). The 1996 Bolivian Forest Law was designed to foster sustainable management of the nation's forests (MDSMA 1996). Forest operations complying with the law need few modifications of their practices to become FSC certified. Furthermore, the Bolivian Forest Service (Superintendencia Forestal) recognizes the annual audits performed by FSC-accredited certifiers as meeting forest law–mandated inspections. To promote forest certification and to develop FSC guidelines for Bolivia, the Bolivian Council for Voluntary Forest Certification (CFV) was established in 1995 as the FSC-recognized national office (Cordero 2002). After initial resistance, FSC-certified forest management received the official endorsement of the forest industry's trade organization, the Cámara Forestal. In recognition of their contribution to bringing 1 million ha of forest under certified management, the Cámara and its members received the World Wide Fund for Nature (WWF) Gift to the Earth award in 2002.

The Bolivian experience with certification is an indication of what can be accomplished with adequate, decade-long financing, applied research on issues related to sustainable forestry, and an integrated approach to policy frameworks, social issues, and technical aspects of forest management (Nittler and Nash 1999). As of late 2002, some 20 percent of the forests in timber concessions were FSC certified, the largest area in the tropics. That forest concessionaires would adopt globally recognized standards for environmentally and socially sound forest management is not the result of a green epiphany but rather a response to a perceived opportunity: certified markets. Starting in 1998, several companies were exporting to certified markets in Europe and North America. Unfortunately, their exports represent a small percentage of the potential production from Bolivia. Efforts are under way to double the certified forest area, largely through work with community and indigenous forest holders.

Despite notable success in expanding the area of certified forests in Bolivia, the future of the business side of this effort remains uncertain. Companies were ill prepared to compete under conditions imposed by the forest law and certified management, with the result that export volumes have fallen dramatically. The basic problem is that a certified tree in the forest does not readily translate into money in the bank. Business management and entrepreneurship skills are woefully lacking. Distance from forests to processing centers and markets coupled with a poor transportation infrastructure compound this problem because they impose a high shipping cost threshold. High-value woods, principally mahogany, could be exported profitably despite high transport costs, but such woods were very scarce in Bolivia by the mid-1990s. Furthermore, timber high-grading is not permitted under the new forest law and not certifiable under FSC standards. Nevertheless, when Thompson Mahogany of

Philadelphia pulled its purchasing agents out of Bolivia after thirty-five years, they blamed the 1996 Forest Law, FSC certification, and BOLFOR but not the near exhaustion of the resource.

Forestry is a neglected sector in Bolivia, as in most other tropical countries. Governments generally view forests as a settlement frontier awaiting conversion to farmland and pasture. Agrarian reform laws often define deforestation as an improvement an aspiring landowner must make to secure a land title (Laarman 1999). Logging typically is a salvage operation carried out by a rudimentary operator with chainsaws, a skidder, and a few trucks operating without apparent concern for forest regeneration, local communities, or biodiversity. Forest-to-market roads are not a government priority. In contrast, east of Santa Cruz, farm-to-market roads, machine-planted and -harvested soybeans, sunflowers, and wheat fields extend through the windrowed remnants of what was until recently the most extensive and biologically rich tropical dry forest in the hemisphere, financed largely by the World Bank Lowlands Project (http://www.wrm.org.uy.actors/WB/Ipreport2.html). Ironically, Bolivia's premier exporter of certified forest products complained that although he could get a loan on highly favorable terms to plant soybeans, he could not obtain a penny for forestry operations (C. Roda, pers. comm. 2001).

Multilateral development banks such as the World Bank provide countries with sector loans for agriculture, mining, energy, and transportation but generally not for tropical forestry (http://www4.worldbank.org/projects/). The rationale for not creating sector loan packages in forestry may relate to the vehement protests of environmental groups against past World Bank insensitivity to tropical deforestation issues (http://www.rainforestweb.org). Certified forest management has been shown to contribute to development while maintaining the integrity of forest ecosystems and has the support of a wide array of environmental and social advocacy organizations and progressive elements of the business community (Howard and Stead 2001). Unfortunately, unbending advocates of forest protection have steadfastly opposed technical and financial support of the forest sector in the tropics (e.g., Rice et al. 1997).

It is easy to identify the changes in the forest sector that are needed if it is to be profitable as well as sustainable; implementation is another matter. Common changes include more efficient extraction and milling, high-quality value-added processing, effective use of lesser-known species, and full use of residual shorts and scrap, changes unthinkable for the mahogany logger. These changes cost money or at least reduce profits. Lack of access to capital at a competitive cost has repercussions on two levels. First, the capability of a certified forest industry to modernize its processing capability is severely limited. Second, lack of working capital plagues the exporter of finished products, who must wait until timber has been milled, dried, processed, shipped overseas, and accepted by the customer before being paid. This situation contrasts sharply with an earlier era in Bolivia when dealers competing for a dwindling supply of mahogany and other high-value woods paid for the product at the sawmill or even paid for the logs in advance of harvesting.

Access to capital is only one of the challenges facing enterprises seeking to modernize their operations. Value-added processing of lesser-known species results in a product that derives its value from characteristics other than the name of a species. Design, utility, color, finishing characteristics, and price may be variables imparting value to the product. The U.S. market has tended to be more willing to accept products made from lesser-known species based on documented technical characteristics than the European market, which still prefers known species. Ability to provide on-time delivery of agreed-upon volumes of the quality specified may be crucial to repeat sales. Effective advertising and sales presentation, market presence, adaptation to change, and rapport with customers are all factors contributing to success. If the enterprise meets all the appropriate requirements and is certified, it will have a competitive edge in the market (Anonymous 2001). If certification becomes the standard, then it simply becomes a precondition for competing.

If the factors just discussed are impeding the success of established forest enterprises, the limitations on community-based forest product marketing efforts are likely to be even more severe. Illiteracy and innumeracy are common in most communities of subsistence farmers in Bolivia and throughout the tropics (Reimers 2002). It seems naive to expect these communities to rise to the challenges of corporate forestry without substantial human capacity building over an extended period of time. Linking forest-rich communities with established forest industries can benefit both (Mayers and Vermeulen 2002) but often does not. Despite the numerous impediments, the future of large areas of tropical forest and millions of tropical people depends on the success of these partnerships.

Implementation of the 1996 Forest Law in Bolivia was akin to a meteor impact on the forest sector insofar as it resulted in the demise of all but the most viable companies. A subsequent unrelated economic downturn eliminated a number of other firms already weakened by the increasing scarcity of mahogany. The law requires that all concessions pay an annual fee of approximately US$1/ha per year as an alternative to the notoriously corruption-prone practice of collecting a fee on the volume of timber removed. This area-based fee resulted in a reduction in the area of forest under concessions from more than 20 million ha to nearly 5 million ha as companies either reduced their concession size or abandoned forestry altogether. Concessions are required to develop management plans based on a twenty-year cutting cycle, which precludes highgrading of dispersed valuable species and necessitates the use of lesser-known species. There are ongoing discussions regarding the efficacy of the concession pricing and the length of the cutting cycle. Securing the environmental and socioeconomic benefits of certified tropical forest management entails overcoming the basic entrepreneurial weaknesses that plague the companies and communities that harvest, mill, process, and sell certified products. Although a few companies may achieve a successful breakthrough on their own, most need some combination of external assistance and engagement of venture capitalists or international partner companies. Community-based forest management operations suffer from even more fundamental problems.

The indigenous community of Lomerío (population ca. 5000), with 53,000 ha of forest, was the first operation certified in Bolivia (early 1996). The Lomerío experience illustrates a number of the constraints that will challenge the advocates of broader community participation in the benefits of certified forestry (see chapter 5). Some of these constraints include long-term dependence on external financial and technical assistance, the weakness of socially oriented NGOs as business consultants, ill-adapted social structure for efficient business management and agile response to market signals, and the difficulty in finding an honest broker to serve as an intermediary between an evolving community enterprise and an unforgiving international marketplace (Markopoulous 1998). That this is not a problem unique to Bolivia is amply illustrated by an assessment of community-based forest operations in Asia (Salafsky et al. 1998).

To complement the BOLFOR initiative by providing technical assistance on the business side of certified forest operations in Bolivia, the Amazonian Center for Sustainable Forest Enterprise (CADEFOR) was established in 1998 with initial support from the Forest Management Trust, through grants provided by the MacArthur Foundation and USAID. CADEFOR assists private sector companies, community-based microenterprises, and indigenous forest enterprises in the process of becoming certified and then helps them to benefit from certification. Indigenous groups and other rural communities engaged in forest management are largely dependent on a successfully exporting private sector as a market for their lumber. Exporters, as well as others along the market chain, face multiple internal constraints in attracting investors, including the following:

- *Lack of business management skills:* Companies are ill equipped to compete in a global market because of limited management skills, technological problems, low efficiency, and lack of strategic planning.
- *Opaque finances:* Closely held family businesses generally keep multiple sets of unaudited books.
- *Poor marketing skills:* Without market familiarity and links, companies are not responsive to changing customer preferences, pricing strategies, and competition.
- *Lesser-known species:* Woods that are not necessarily inferior but unfamiliar to the market must gain market acceptance.
- *Costly financing:* Bank interest rates are higher than in developed countries, and credit lines available to other sectors such as agriculture and energy are not available to forest enterprises.

Given the magnitude of the need for business management and entrepreneurial capacity building, CADEFOR has suffered from chronic underfunding since its inception. Priorities of USAID and the Bolivian government under BOLFOR were at first focused on bringing large areas of forest under certified management, with a modest component addressing business development and marketing. Emphasis has shifted to community forestry. Unfortunately, without a dynamic, successful private sector, communities have no market for the products from their certified forests. Although it has achieved modest successes in export promotion, CADEFOR has lacked the critical mass of internationally and domestically respected expertise and supporting resources needed to make Bolivian forest industry a significant exporter of products from its certified forests. For example, at the November 2002 wood product export exhibition in La Paz (Expo Madera), few of the twenty-five Bolivian exporters encountered were even aware of CADEFOR's existence.

Bolivia has achieved remarkable results in the forest sector. First came the creation of a policy framework conducive to good forest management, followed by a program that has brought large areas of natural forest under certification and made almost all forest enterprises aware for the first time that management is an option. Efforts began later and have moved more slowly in to improve the business management and entrepreneurship skills needed to compete in global markets. A lesson learned was that investment in the business side of certification should parallel assistance to companies and communities in certified forest management.

BRAZIL: CERTIFICATION VIA NGO AND VENTURE CAPITALIST INITIATIVES

Mais grande do mundo—"the biggest in the world"—applies to many things Brazilian including the Amazon River, the Amazon forest, and soon the area of certified tropical forest. On a more somber note, Brazil has also had a high rate of deforestation and a very high (80 percent) rate of illegal logging (Elliott 2002). Brazil has also demonstrated the capacity to launch some of the world's most forest-destructive development schemes, with Avança Brasil (Forward Brazil) being the latest (Goodland and Irwin 1975, Laurance et al. 2001). Can forest certification help in a "save the Amazon" strategy? History gives the optimist pause, but if any country has the energy, intellect, entrepreneurship, and capacity to accomplish such a near miracle, it is Brazil.

Certification has taken a different trajectory in Brazil than in Bolivia. Brazil was active in the creation of FSC, forming part of a nine-country consultive group in 1992 (May 2002). Brazilian representatives of the FSC then carried out an extensive national consultation embracing a wide range of stakeholders including environmental and social NGOs, universities, the forest sector (including the timber, paper, and charcoal industries), and the steel industry, which is a large producer and consumer of eucalypt wood (Viana et al. 1996). The Brazilian program of the WWF played a decisive role in establishing a FSC presence in Brazil with the formation of a National Working Group in 1995, which subsequently achieved National Initiative status in 2001. In 1999, a buyers' group of more than sixty members including private sector companies, state and city administrators, architects, and furniture manufacturers was formed under the leadership of Friends of the Earth. Other members of Brazil's strong NGO community supporting certification included the Institute for Man and Environment of the Amazon, Greenpeace Brazil, and the Pro-Nature Foundation. The Institute for Forest and Agriculture Management and Certification, the SmartWood Network certifier in Brazil, Scientific Certification Systems, Société Générale de Surveillance Qualifor, and Skal International performed FSC certification assessments in Brazil. Of the tropical countries in the 1992 consultive group that helped form FSC, only Brazil has gone on to certify large areas of forest.

Brazil began FSC certification outside the Amazon region with large plantations owned by fiberboard and pulp and paper companies such as

Eucatex, Duratex, and Klabin. These companies had the business structure, technical expertise, and capital necessary to incorporate certification into their operations with little outside assistance. This allowed certified forestry operations to become major players in Brazil and abroad before entering the more controversial realm of natural tropical forest certification.

Although forest industries in Brazil and Bolivia suffer from the same lack of long-term funding for forestry, a different set of capital constraints obtain in the former. In Brazil, pressure of the discount factor (e.g., 20 percent per annum in Brazil) is a tremendous disincentive to the long-term investments needed for sustainable, certified forest enterprises. Part of this problem derives from the very heavy presence of the Brazilian government as a borrower at very high interest rates, which saturates the market. This factor, coupled with an unfriendly tax and fiscal environment, has virtually killed the Brazilian stock market, which is a quarter of the size it was twenty years ago, and has stifled long-term investment prospects. There is no way companies can financially justify a twenty-five–year investment in forestry at an average real return of about 12 percent per annum if they are competing with 13–15 percent per annum (U.S. dollar- indexed) interest rates on twenty-year Brazilian government sovereign debt. Partially in response to this problem, A2R established a Biodiversity Enterprise Fund that has come to play a key role in overcoming this capital crunch by supporting sustainable forestry in Brazilian Amazonia (http://www.fundoterracapital.com). How does A2R assure investors of a satisfactory return on their investments in tropical forest management? Four important considerations are as follows:

- FSC certification assures investors that the forest enterprises will be well managed according to internationally credible standards and scientific information, resource tenure is secure, the operations benefit local communities, and the products will have a growing market among environmentally and socially responsible consumers.
- Brazilian forest land can be privately owned and is greatly undervalued. At an average land cost of about US$50/ha, a marketable standing volume of 30 m^3, a value of sawn wood of US$250/$m^3$ (35 percent conversion efficiency from log to sawn wood), and an annual harvest of 4 percent of the property, for a vertically integrated forest product company the land investment can be recouped in less than a year.

- A2R client companies are initially undervalued because of past dependence on the domestic market, past unsustainable resource use practices, inefficient management, and lack of quality control. A2R provides its client companies with a package of services including facilitation of access to multilateral and bilateral funding, assistance with production technologies, market information and introductions, hands-on operational support, specialized consultancy services, and product certification guidance. To provide project-specific management training, A2R created the Brazilian Institute for Education in Sustainable Business (http://www.ibens.org).
- Values of the forest that are maintained under certified management and could eventually yield an aggregate value comparable to that of timber include carbon sequestration, bioprospecting, wildlife habitat maintenance, ecotourism, and watershed protection.

Another example of the pivotal role of certification in Brazil is Mil Madeireira Itacoatiara, a project of the Swiss holding company Precious Woods. Shareholders in this company seek to make investments that are ecologically sound, socially just, and economically feasible. The project's main objective is to demonstrate the economic feasibility of sustainable forest management closely integrated with value-added processing. The 80,000-ha project was initiated in 1994 and received its FSC forest management and chain-of-custody certification from SmartWood in 1997. One self-generated incentive for good management came when research conducted by the company revealed that use of reduced-impact logging technologies reduced both logging costs and collateral damage to advance regeneration. Of the more than 100 tree species identified in the project area, 65 were found to have actual or potential market value. The company is also well aware of the importance of maximizing exports from Brazil given that timber on the domestic market sells for an average of $30/m^3$ whereas exports are valued at $350–650/m^3$. In their mill, they increased the yield of exportable timber from the typical 35–40 percent to as much as 55 percent. They are also making effective use of residuals to make value-added, semifinished, and finished furniture components, which has prompted development of specialized processing methods and improved marketing skills.

Mil Madeireira Itacoatiara has gone through a long and costly learning process en route to profitability, but the investors have shown their willingness to take a long-term perspective and make substantial up-front capital investments. Other green investor-backed projects can profit from lessons learned by the Swiss:

- *Introduction of lesser-known species:* In an area with limited volumes of well-known species (e.g., mahogany and cedar) it is necessary to develop markets for many species that were previously little known. First steps needed are to identify the species and to assemble the necessary technical data for the species' use.
- *Forest–industry–market relations:* Once management practices are refined, lesser-known species characteristics analyzed, and a full inventory completed, then analysis of market demands is needed to guide manufacturing.
- *Harvestable volumes:* Data from permanent plots are needed on the recruitment and growth of commercial species to determine what is a truly sustainable volume to be harvested and to set rotation cycle lengths.
- *Forest management costs:* A management model specific to each stand is needed to calculate the cost of management plan implementation.

CERTIFICATION AND PROTECTION: COMPLEMENTARY STRATEGIES

The U.S. government spends more money, rhetoric, and political capital trying to stop the growing of coca than it does on addressing the socioeconomic factors driving the insatiable demand for drugs at home. In an analogous situation, scarce talent, energy, and money are expended by an array of NGOs, governments, and international agencies to stop the legal and illegal pillaging of tropical forests by loggers (McKenney 2002), while little is being done to change the behavior of consumers whose demand for floors, doors, and windows drives the global market for tropical wood. From the business perspective, it is critical to recognize that although consumption of high-value species has historically been concentrated in the export market, domestic consumption also must be addressed. For example, Brazil is both the largest producer and the largest consumer of tropical timber (http://www.fao.org/forestry/).

A recent publication of the Union of Concerned Scientists (Gullison et al. 2001) proposes fifteen strategies for stopping industrial logging in HCVFS, which, according to the authors, include much of the world's remaining forests. The strategies range from legal challenges to boycotts and protests, most of which work against the interests of governments, forest industries, and workers in the forest sector. Working against people's interests is costly, be they coca growers or timber companies. In an appendix listing examples of how each strategy has worked in practice, certification is relegated to the end of the list, with a lukewarm endorsement, and no examples of its efficacy are provided. The authors also state that there is insufficient consumer demand for certified wood to displace all production from HCVFS, but, curiously, they also state that the "supply of FSC-certified wood is grossly insufficient to meet demand" (Gullison et al. 2001:79). It seems obvious that the claim about public demand for certified products will be true only after awareness has been created by campaigns and advertising. The first effective efforts at promoting certification were initiated by environmental advocacy groups that pressured several large chains of home improvement stores to pledge to stock FSC-certified wood. Comparatively little has been done to urge consumers to demand certified products. It is unfortunate that influential environmental groups such as the Union of Concerned Scientists are unwilling to effectively support certification as a tool for conserving tropical forests.

The arguments that forest protection is the only effective mode of tropical forest conservation because sustainable forest management is financially uncompetitive with conventional logging (Rice et al. 1997, Pearce et al. 2003) rest on the assumption that governments are unable or unwilling to enforce regulations that ensure the sustainability of forest operations. The willingness of the Bolivian government to create and implement a progressive forest law leaves room for hope. The Bolivian forest sector has fared poorly in the international market not because of competition from conventional logging but because of business practices that are not competitive given new market conditions.

The social and economic well-being of people living in and around forests is an important humanitarian and social justice issue in itself (Brechin et al. 2002, Wilshusen et al. 2002). Forest protection programs that ignore the human dimension do so at the expense of their conservation goals. In contrast, FSC certification is one of the most powerful tools available to ensure that the economic and social interests of communities and indigenous people are protected and enhanced. How forest industries deal with land tenure issues, indigenous rights, worker rights, and local employment opportunities are explicitly addressed in FSC Principles (see Principles 2, 3, 4, and 5 at http://www.fscoax.org). Many forest communities and indigenous groups chose to certify their lands as much to enhance their tenure security as to exploit potential market opportunities. Being certified also gives them annual feedback on the sustainability of their operations.

With rare exceptions, rural communities are constrained to selling to domestic processors because they harvest small volumes, are undercapitalized and consequently lack large and dependable harvesting equipment, lack business acumen, and have few market connections (Scherr et al. 2002). When a successful certified industrial export economy exists, communities have unprecedented opportunities to benefit if NGOs and assistance programs help them to develop their capacity. Vertically integrated industrial operations generally have a processing capacity that exceeds the annual allowable cut on their forests. Therefore, they must buy from local certified communities, with the fairness of the transaction being required under FSC Principle 5. Where communities and indigenous groups gain legal control over a significant proportion of the forest estate, as has occurred in much of the tropics (White and Martin 2002), they gain marketing clout in negotiations with larger and more sophisticated chain-of-custody certified processors of forest products.

As the sustainability of forestry operations in regions of low conservation value is increased, a great deal of biodiversity can be maintained. Unfortunately, forest management and forest protection often are framed as alternative rather than complementary conservation strategies. The FSC recognizes the complementarity of management and protection in Principle 9, which addresses the protection of HCVFs. This perspective is clearly articulated by WWF in their *Global Vision for Forests 2050* (Elliott 2002), in which the goal for tropical forests of 40 percent protected, 40 percent extensive production, and 20 percent intensive production forests by 2050 was set. Whether it is the Global Vision of WWF or any other vision on which conservationists agree, it must be presented to all stakeholders as a coherent whole.

FSC certification is the most credible tool currently available to assure stakeholders that forests under extensive and intensive production are well managed. For potential of the FSC to be realized, a widespread educational effort is needed to convince consumers that they can contribute to maintaining ecologically viable forests and to the well-being of those who live and work in the forests by buying certified forest products. Several large home improvement outlet stores have pledged to buy certified products, but they need clear signals from consumers that their commitment will pay off. Potential multipliers along the certified product value chain are many and include architects, builders, and government-funded construction specifiers that ascribe to green building codes. Similarly, venture capitalists, bankers, and development agencies concerned with their images and the long-term viability of their investments can do a great deal to promote good forestry through certification. Forest management certification assures producers, processors, retailers, and consumers that environmental concerns are addressed and that there will be a sustained availability of products at fair prices while reducing the threat of boycotts, bans, and legal suits.

Globalization of the world economy and communication can work in favor of broad acceptance of the common principles of good forest management, as represented by the FSC certification process. Internet-linked consumers and advocacy groups, mobilized by a common set of environmental and social values, have unprecedented power to influence whether good forest management in the tropics remains the exception or becomes the rule.

REFERENCES

Anonymous. 2001. *Environmental marketing claims*. Atlanta, Ga.: The Home Depot.

Atyi, R. E. and M. Simula. 2002. *Forest certification: Pending challenges for tropical timber*. Background Paper, ITTO International Workshop on Comparability and Equivalence of Forest Certification Schemes, Kuala Lumpur, April 3–4, 2002.

Brechin, S. R., P. R. Wilshusen, C. L. Fortwangler, and P. C. West. 2002. Beyond the square wheel: Toward a more comprehensive understanding of biodiversity conservation as a social and political process. *Society and Natural Resources* 15: 41–65.

Browder, J. 1992. The limits of extraction. *BioScience* 42: 174–182.

Contreras-Hermosilla, A. and M. T. Vargas Rios. 2002. *Social, environmental, and economic dimensions of forest policy reforms in Bolivia*. Bogor, Indonesia: Center for International Forestry Research; Washington, D.C.: Forest Trends.

Cordero, W. 2002. *La certificación forestal voluntaria en Bolivia*. La Paz: Boletín Instituto Boliviano de Comercio Exterior.

Dickinson, J. C. 1999. Forest certification as a tool for conservation. *The Geographical Review* 89: 431–439.

Elliott, C. 2002. *A vision for forests in the 21st century*. Presentation to the Forest Leadership Forum, sponsored by the Certified Forest Products Council and World Wildlife Fund. Atlanta, Georgia, April 25–27, 2002.

Friedman, T. 2000. *The Lexus and the olive tree*. New York: Anchor Books.

Goodland, R. J. A. and H. S. Irwin. 1975. *Amazon jungle: Green hell or red desert?* Amsterdam: Elsevier.

Gullison, R. E., M. Melnyk, and C. Wong. 2001. *Logging off: Mechanisms to stop or prevent industrial logging in forests of high conservation value*. Cambridge, Mass.: Union of Concerned Scientists Publications.

Howard, S. and J. Stead. 2001. *The forest industry in the 21st century*. Washington, D.C.: World Wildlife Federation.

Kiker, C. F. and F. E. Putz. 1997. Ecological certification of forest products. Economic challenges. *Ecological Economics* 20: 37–51.

Laarman, J. G. 1999. *Government policies affecting forests. Forest resource policy in Latin America*. Washington, D.C.: Inter-American Development Bank.

Laurance, W. F., M. A. Cochrane, S. Bergen, P. M. Fearnside, P. Delmônica, C. Barber, S. D'Angelo, and T. Fernandes. 2001. The future of the Brazilian Amazon. *Science* 291: 438–439.

"Managing the rainforest." *The Economist*. May 12, 2000, pp. 83–85.

Markopoulous, M. 1998. *The impacts of certification on community forest enterprises: A case study of the Lomerío forest management project, Bolivia*. London: IIED Forest and Land Use Series no. 13.

May, P. H. n.d. *Forest certification in Brazil: Trade and environmental enhancement*. Paper prepared at the request of the Consumer Choice Council.

Mayers, J. and S. Vermeulen. 2002. *Company–community partnerships: From raw deals to mutual gains*. London: International Institute for Environment and Development.

McKenney, B. 2002. Questioning sustainable concession forestry in Cambodia. *Cambodia Development Review* 6.

MDSMA (Ministry of Sustainable Development and Environment). 1996. The Bolivian Forest Law. Law no. 1700 of July 12, 1996.

Nittler, J. B. and D. W. Nash. 1999. The certification model for forestry in Bolivia. *Journal of Forestry* 97: 32–36.

Ozinga, S. 2001. *Behind the logo: An environmental and social assessment of forest certification schemes*. Online: http://www.fern.org.

Pearce, D. F., F. E. Putz, and J. K. Vanclay. 2003. Sustainable forestry: Panacea or pipedream? *Forest Ecology and Management* 172: 229–247.

Putz, F. E. 1994. Towards a sustainable forest: How can forests be managed in a way that satisfies criteria of sustainability? *ITTO Tropical Forest Update* 4: 7–9.

Reimers, F. 2002. *The politics of educational inequality: The struggle for educational opportunity in Latin America*. Working Papers on Latin America no. 02/03-2. Boston: The David Rockefeller Center for Latin American Studies.

Rice, R. E., R. E. Gullison, and W. Reid. 1997. Can sustainable management save tropical forests? *Scientific American* April: 44–49.

Salafsky, N., B. Cordes, M. Leighton, M. Henderson, W. Watt, and R. Cherry. 1998. *Chainsaws as a tool for conservation? A comparison of community-based timber production enterprises in Papua New Guinea and Indonesia*. Rural Development Forestry Network Paper no. 22b. London: Overseas Development Institute.

Scherr, S. J., A. White, and D. Kaimowitz. 2002. *Making markets work for forest communities*. Washington, D.C.: Forest Trends.

Southgate, D. 1998. *Tropical forest conservation: An economic assessment of the alternatives in Latin America*. New York: Oxford University Press.

Viana, V. M., J. Ervin, R. Z. Donovan, C. Elliot, and H. L. Gholz, eds. 1996. *Certification of forest products: Issues and perspectives*. Washington, D.C.: Island Press.

White, A. and A. Martin. 2002. *Who owns the world's forests? Forest tenure and public forests in transition*. Washington, D.C.: Forest Trends.

Wilshusen, P. R., S. R. Brechin, C. L. Fortwangler, and P. C. West. 2002. Reinventing a square wheel: Critique of a resurgent "protection paradigm" in international biodiversity conservation. *Society and Natural Resources* 15: 17–40.

PART II

Working Forests and Community Development in Latin America

Chapter 7

COMMUNITIES, FORESTS, MARKETS, AND CONSERVATION

Marianne Schmink

In keeping with the polemic approach of Putz (chapter 2), this chapter might be titled "Are You a Conservationist or a Human Rights Advocate?" Are we forced to choose between preservation of forests and respect for the rights and needs of people who live in or near them? Believing this to be a false dichotomy, many initiatives over the past few decades have tried to address conservation and development in an integrative framework, one that would benefit local peoples and the natural systems on which they depend. Despite the promise of this approach, there have been many failures. Partly in reaction to this mixed record, there are indeed signs of a new polarization. The development establishment is abandoning sustainability in favor of a return to poverty alleviation and productivity goals, and the conservation community is retreating from attempts to integrate local people into conservation strategies (Sanderson 2002, Wilshusen et al. 2002).

Yet strategies that separate conservation from development also have been shown to be bankrupt. The preservationist paradigm that focuses only on protected areas in the absence of humans is doomed unless the needs and behavior of people with interests in resources in and around these areas are addressed. Approaches to community development that do not address the sustainability of resource use, especially in relation to market dynamics, likewise can succeed only in the short term. The failures in projects and strategies stem not from the integrative perspective itself but rather from flaws in design and implementation and from the magnitude of commercial pressures for resources.

Under what conditions can community forest management be an effective strategy for conservation through sustainable management? In this chapter, I argue that these conditions include not only healthy forests, market access, and business skills but also an appreciation for the complexity of social systems in which community forest enterprises are embedded. This includes not only local culture, institutions, and livelihood systems but also the broader socioeconomic and political forces that determine the viability of forest management initiatives.

COMMUNITIES AND FORESTS

The enabling conditions for sustainable forest management are substantially different for communities than for commercial timber operations. This reality seems to be ignored in much of the current enthusiasm for linking communities with markets for timber and other forest commodities. Community forest management is embedded inextricably in a social community, in a specific historical and ecological setting; it is not simply a forest enterprise. For example, Wollenberg (1998) sees forest product conservation and development as situated in a set of three-way relationships between the market, the forest, and the villagers' economy. This embeddedness also determines the insertion of the community forestry enterprise into the broader policy environment and markets and the ecological and socioeconomic impacts of forest management. Among the many community-level factors that affect forest enterprises are multiple uses, multiple tenure forms, institutional arrangements, cultural and ethnic divisions, gender relations, demographic patterns, and unequal resource distribution within communities.

Communities live in specific ecological settings that are the result of historical patterns that preceded their own practices. On one hand, growing evidence suggests that many tropical forests have been significantly shaped by human use (see chapters 1 and 2). The current habitats of rural communities have been altered through practices of ancestral groups or other predecessors whose actions may have favored certain species and eliminated others. In some instances, these practices have left behind patches of fertile soil or groves of useful trees as a gift for later generations. In other instances, communities have found their territories impoverished of timber resources through high-grading logging operations. It is the history of resource use and its impact on current ecological systems that set the management parameters for current use.

Because community forest enterprises are embedded in specific social communities, they have a completely different character from private sector businesses. For these communities, forest management typically is only one of a variety of elements in their complex livelihood systems. These systems include multiple uses of forest resources for different products, used by distinct groups within the community. Forest resources provide both income and a safety net (Hladik et al. 1993, Wollenberg and Ingles 1998), as well as noneconomic values. Investing time and resources in one activity, such as timber management, affects all other elements of the livelihood system, having a ripple effect throughout the social system that will certainly affect the long-term success of forest management efforts (Richards 1997a, Becker and León 2000).

These complex livelihood systems often are tied to distinct indigenous cultural and institutional systems (Richards 1997a, Becker and León 2000, Fisher 2000). Community resource use is governed by complex institutions and recognized formal and informal rules that are an essential part of the community's social capital (Gibson et al. 2000, Colfer and Byron 2001). These local institutions, including common property regimes, vary greatly between communities and change with demographic and market pressures as producers adapt to new conditions and as cultures evolve (Berkes 1989, Ostrom 1990, Ascher 1995, Richards 1997a, Agrawal 2001, Agrawal and Gibson 2001). Multiple tenure forms also distinguish different social groups and land uses both between and within communities (Wollenberg 1998; see also chapter 9). Different rules and structures may govern individual, collective, and common property because it is used for different purposes. The complexity of tenure situations provides crucial constraints and opportunities for conservation and sustainable development initiatives (Banana and Gombya-Ssembajjwe 2000, Gibson and Becker 2000).

Thus, ecological and sociocultural histories dictate a great diversity among communities in terms of social origins, forms of organization, cultural systems, and relationships to forest resources. But most proponents of community forest management have not yet recognized the importance of understanding the complexity of each community and the need to tailor forest management plans to the overall social system in which they are embedded (but see Richards 1997, Fisher 2000, Agrawal 2001, and chapter 13, this volume,). The diversity of community sociocultural systems, like the diversity of forests, necessitates approaches adapted to each particular situation. Taking a cookie-cutter approach to community forest plans is akin to applying a predesigned harvest plan to a forest in which no inventory has been carried out. An inventory of the social system would analyze (among other things) how people make a living, what institutions and social relations determine access to resources for different purposes, who controls decision making and captures benefits from forest use, the values placed on forests, and how these conditions are changing (Lecup et al. 1998). This information is needed to provide the basis for designing, testing, and adapting a forest management plan appropriate to the social system in which it is embedded. A variety of methods must be developed to support iterative information gathering at different scales, with the direct participation of communities, to support adaptive management under conditions of high uncertainty and complexity (Fisher and Dechaineux 1998, Gibson et al. 2000, Colfer and Byron 2001).

Besides the diversity of community systems, resources and benefits also are distributed unequally between community members, both participants and nonparticipants in development projects (McDougall 2001). Yet many forest management proposals assume that communities, like firms, have a unitary utility function and a single representative decision maker. New initiatives and market links are likely to exacerbate internal inequities within communities, increasing socioeconomic differentiation by favoring those directly involved in the enterprise over others. For example, the highly successful system of açaí management on the island of Combú masks significant internal differentiation between landowners, land controllers, and landless extractivists (Nugent 1993; see also Anderson and Ioris 1992). This is yet another reason why forest management project leaders must understand community systems, including people who do and do not directly participate in forestry enterprises. The effects of unequal distribution have ramifications for the sustainability of enterprises and for long-term socioeconomic and environmental impact.

In addition to these complex internal socioeconomic dimensions, communities also are embedded in a broader socioeconomic and policy context, one that often is not very favorable to forest communities. These policies tend to favor large-scale corporate interests over smallholders and generally provide few incentives for socially grounded, place-based systems of resource management and tenure such as those typical of rural communities (see chapters 8 and 21). Institutional and policy failures, including unresolved land tenure issues and privatization, have been the main problem for common property management regimes for forest management in Latin America (Richards 1997a, 1997b).

This policy bias is not simply a technical matter: Policies that benefit large enterprises and elite business interests reflect the relative social power in societies and the perception (not always borne out in reality) that large-scale enterprises are more equipped to carry out sustained management and can be monitored more easily. The debate over national forest policies in Brazil raises many of the relevant issues. From a policy standpoint, it seems rational to promote forest management in government-controlled national forests through large-scale concessions (see chapter 3). However, the alternative model that supports community-based timber management, an ambitious challenge given the complexities described earlier, has never really been attempted despite its far greater potential for spreading social benefits and the opportunity to foster forest management across a range of landscapes already used by rural producers (see chapters 13 and 22).

The social inequities that underlie policy decisions pose significant challenges to efforts to level the playing field for small producers, as advocated by Scherr et al. in chapter 8. Real-world policy "is the net result of a tangled heap of formal and practical decisions by those with varying powers to act on them" (Mayers and Bass 1999:ii; see also Silva 1994). Empowerment of local communities to negotiate their own interests is needed to change policy outcomes in their favor.

COMMUNITIES AND MARKETS

Given the negative environmental and social impacts of commercial forest management and the untapped potential for community-based management, linking communities with markets for forest products seems to be a promising alternative. White and Martin (2002) estimate that 60 million indigenous people live in the rainforests of Latin America, West Africa, and Southeast Asia, and an additional 400 to 500 million people depend directly on forest resources for their livelihood. Many of the remaining forested areas in Latin America are in the hands of communities; for example, peasant *ejidos* and indigenous groups control 70 percent of Mexico's forests (Richards 1997a). There is strong potential for successful community forests in the tropics: Tens of millions of people could benefit in different ways from forest management (see chapter 8). Among these groups of producers are both smallholders who manage individual forest plots and communities that manage common property resources.

Yet the inherent asymmetries involved in linking rural communities to markets call for caution. There are many ways in which increased market involvement may have a negative impact on communities. Why should this be so? The problem goes beyond the lack of community expertise in business management. Often overlooked in the enthusiasm for community forest management initiatives is the reality that markets also are embedded in social systems, and in those social systems small producers operate at a distinct disadvantage. The same unequal power relations that underlie policies that favor large corporate interests over smallholders also systematically distort market relations in favor of vested interests (Richards 1997a). Equity and social justice are not outcomes to be expected from market mechanisms. Even well-established and independent producers in an expanding, favorable market situation often remain at the margins of the market because of factors such as inequities in land tenure and market access (see chapter 19). Moreover, increased market dependency may undercut community food security by diverting energies from subsistence activities to market-oriented forest management activities that are subject to changes in international prices and commodity demands, factors out of the communities' control.

Because communities operate at a disadvantage in the market, community forest management necessitates special precautions to protect these smallholders from negative effects. This realization typically leads to calls for community-level training in business skills and other measures to improve community market position by strengthening organizations and partnerships (see chapter 8). However, technical training addresses only one part of the problem (the lack of trained business personnel within communities) and may inadvertently undermine traditional leaders by empowering younger and more educated men (Fisher 2000). Moreover, the time frame of the market and of well-intentioned funders usually underestimates the amount of time a community needs to become successful in the market. Experience has shown that, even with training, most community forest management enterprises remain dependent on outside organizations, especially with respect to market connections. If this is true for the Mexican *ejidos,* with their secure land tenure, established social organizations, and long-term support from the Plan Piloto Florestal, it seems unrealistic to expect more from the majority of communities that lack these advantages.

Similar dilemmas confront proposals for partnerships between communities and private companies. Mayers and Vermeulen (2002) found that such partnerships could provide many positive benefits to communities, including economic returns and diversification, land tenure security, and infrastructure. However, they also found such partnerships to suffer from high transaction costs, frequent misunderstandings between partners, and negative environmental and social effects, including low wages, unequal land distribution, and exclusion of disadvantaged community members. So far, even the best partnerships have not raised poor people out of poverty (Mayers and Vermeulen 2002). Still, the proliferation of such experiments is providing new models of more equitable arrangements that may hold promise for future adaptation.

The embedded nature of forest enterprises means that market initiatives must be carefully integrated into community cultural and livelihood systems. Expectations of business success may collide with other community priorities, undermining the social capital in communities that is the basis for sustainability in the face of changing conditions. Market demands also may increase pressures on forest resources beyond sustainable harvest levels. Given these considerations, under what conditions should communities take on corporate features in order to undertake forest management, as Putz suggests in chapter 2? Perhaps a better question is, What models can be developed for communities that allow them to balance their multiple interests and values with the demands of market-oriented forest management?

Community forestry is not for everyone. Many communities or small producers lack market access, good forest resources, and other prerequisites to compete successfully, and forest dependence may trap them in poverty (Wunder 2001). The best question may be, Under what conditions can communities engage with the market on their own terms?

Despite the challenges, many communities have responded positively to market opportunities and have actively fought to conserve forests (Richards 1997a). Appropriate institutions and policies are needed to encourage local control through capacity-building approaches that recognize and respect specific ecological and social contexts in which community forest management is embedded, guarantee rights to land and resources, and empower local people to negotiate their interests (Mayers and Bass 1999, Mayers and Vermeulen 2002). This is a tall order, given the entrenched power of commercial and political interests in the forest markets. However, innovative and effective ways to combine capitalistic and traditional forms of organization may emerge from such approaches (Fisher 2000). Decentralized, democratic forms of policymaking, with special support for community groups, are important steps toward development of more flexible, adaptive management systems that draw on learning from different stakeholders (Mayers and Bass 1999, Wollenberg and Ingles 1998). For the moment, this is our best hope in developing the human and social capacity for communities to negotiate their natural resource market connections.

COMMUNITIES AND CONSERVATION

Most of the remaining tropical forests in Latin America are inhabited by people, many of whom have a long-term commitment to place and to future generations. Some elements of their community systems favor conservation, but others do not, especially during times of change (Colfer and Byron 2001). What are the most effective incentives for these communities to conserve their forests? Despite the current enthusiasm for market incentives to promote conservation, there is evidence that, for communities, a broader approach is necessary.

Because of the higher profitability of conventional logging, sustainable forestry will not work very well without additional incentives (Pearce et al. 2003). Given the vulnerability of communities in commodity markets and the essential nonmarket benefits that the traditional forest management provides to the broader society, mechanisms that can channel environmental service payments or social and legal support to small producers in exchange for forest management and protection are particularly appropriate (Richards 1997a, 1997b). One way to address the inherent disadvantages of local people is to provide subsidies, something that large producers have been adept at negotiating throughout history (see chapter 21). De Jong (chapter 13) demonstrates from a study in Mexico that carbon mitigation systems can be developed at low cost in natural forests and secondary vegetation managed by small producers as long as these proposals are compatible with community land use goals. In Brazil, four communities demonstrated clear understanding of connections between their resource use activities, the environmental services they provided, and the potential for receiving transfer payments to compensate for these services (Instituto Vitae Civilis 2002). Proactive, comprehensive efforts will be needed to enable communities to compete effectively in the evolving global carbon market (Smith and Scherr 2002).

Traditional community resource use practices and policies typically offer a number of advantages compared with commercial regimes (Berkes and Folke 2002). Local people have an intimate knowledge of the ecosystem and are capable of more intensive, species-specific management, including enrichment and restoration to retain a diverse forest. The presence of communities in forests often has provided protection from outside invaders. Given the expanses of forest land managed by communities and smallholders, these are positive arguments in favor of subsidies to support their forest management systems.

Although less visible to outsiders, nonmarket environmental, cultural, and spiritual values may provide the strongest incentives for communities to conserve (Richards 1997a). Transforming forest goods into market commodities may not always be the best conservation or development strategy. Indigenous communities with limited market exposure are especially vulnerable to market involvement that may undermine traditional exchange systems, remove traditional checks on wealth accumulation, and erode group cooperation (Colchester 1989, Chase Smith 1995, Richards 1997a, 1997b). Market-driven conservation initiatives often erroneously assume that indigenous people and other traditional populations, once introduced to the market, orient their resource use to market signals, rarely questioning what the cultural costs of such a shift might be. Yet unlike business firms whose main objective is to turn a profit, communities often value, above all, the guarantee of rights to resources that can support them and their descendants, as well as the cultural ties to a place that they call home.

ACKNOWLEDGMENTS

The author thanks Bob Buschbacher, Karen Kainer, Francis E. Putz, and Daniel Zarin for their insightful thoughts and suggestions, especially on communities and conservation.

REFERENCES

Agrawal, A. 2001. Common property institutions and sustainable governance of resources. *World Development* 29(10): 1649–1672.

Agrawal, A. and C. C. Gibson, eds. 2001. *Communities and the environment: Ethnicity, gender and the state in community-based conservation.* London: Rutgers University Press.

Anderson, A. and E. Ioris. 1992. Valuing the rain forest: economic strategies by small-scale forest extractivists in the Amazon estuary. *Human Ecology* 20: 337–369.

Ascher, W. 1995. *Communities and sustainable forestry in developing countries.* San Francisco: ICS Press.

Banana, A. Y. and W. Gombya-Ssembajjwe. 2000. Successful forest management: The importance of security of tenure and rule enforcement in Ugandan forests. In C. C. Gibson, M. A. McKean, and E. Ostrom, eds., *People and forests: Communities, institutions, and governance*, 87–98. Cambridge, Mass.: MIT Press.

Becker, C. D. and R. León. 2000. Indigenous forest management in the Bolivian Amazon: Lessons from the Yuracaré people. In C. C. Gibson, M. A. McKean, and E. Ostrom, eds., *People and forests: Communities, institutions, and governance*, 163–191. Cambridge, Mass.: MIT Press.

Berkes, F., ed. 1989. *Common property resources: Ecology and community-based sustainable development.* London: Belhaven Press.

Berkes, F. and C. Folke. 2002. Back to the future: Ecosystem dynamics and local knowledge. In S. H. Gunderson and C. S. Holling, eds., *Panarchy: Understanding transformations in human and natural systems*, 121–146. Washington, D.C.: Island Press.

Chase Smith, R. 1995. *The gift that wounds: Charity, the gift economy and social solidarity in indigenous Amazonia.* Paper presented at the Symposium on Community Forest Management and Sustainability in the Americas, University of Wisconsin, Madison, February 3–4, 1995.

Colfer, C. J. P. and Y. Byron, eds. 2001. *People managing forests: The links between human well-being and sustainability.* Washington, D.C.: Resources for the Future.

Colchester, M. 1989. Indian development in the Amazon: Risks and strategies. *The Ecologist* 19: 249–254.

Fisher, R. J. and R. Dechaineux. 1998. A methodology for assessing and evaluation the social impacts of non-timber forest product projects. In E. Wollenberg and A. Ingles, eds., *Incomes from the forest: Methods for the development and conservation of forest products for local communities,* 189–199. Bogor, Indonesia: CIFOR.

Fisher, W. H. 2000. *Rain forest exchanges: Industry and community on an Amazonian frontier.* Washington, D.C.: Smithsonian Institution.

Gibson, C. C. and C. D. Becker. 2000. A lack of institutional demand: Why a strong local community in western Ecuador fails to protect its forests. In C. C. Gibson, M. A. McKean, and E. Ostrom, eds., *People and forests: Communities, institutions, and governance,* 135–161. Cambridge, Mass.: MIT Press.

Gibson, C. C. M. A. McKean, and E. Ostrom, eds. 2000. *People and forests: Communities, institutions, and governance.* Cambridge, Mass.: MIT Press.

Hladik, C. M., A. Hladik, O. F. Linares, H. Pagezy, A. Semple, and M. Hadley, eds. 1993. *Tropical forests, people and food: Biological interactions and applications to development.* Paris: UNESCO and the Parthenon Publishing Group.

Instituto Vitae Civilis. 2002. *Protecting social and ecological capital through compensation for environmental services (CES).* São Paulo, Brazil: Editora Fundação Peirópolis.

Lecup, I., K. Nicholson, H. Purwandono, and S. Karki. 1998. Methods for assessing the feasibility of sustainable non-timber forest product-based enterprises. In E. Wollenberg and A. Ingles, eds., *Incomes from the forest: Methods for the development and conservation of forest products for local communities,* 85–106. Bangor, Indonesia: CIFOR.

Mayers, J. and S. Bass. 1999. *Policy that works for forests and people.* London: International Institute for Environment and Development.

Mayers, J. and S. Vermeulen. 2002. *Company–community forestry partnerships: From raw deals to mutual gains?* London: International Institute for Environment and Development.

McDougall, C. L. 2001. Gender diversity in assessing sustainable forest management and human well being. In C. J. P. Colfer and Y. Byron, eds., *People managing forests: The links between human well-being and sustainability,* 50–71. Washington, D.C.: Resources for the Future.

Nugent, S. 1993. *Amazonian Caboclo society: An essay on invisibility and peasant economy.* Oxford, U.K.: Berg.

Ostrom, E. 1990. *Governing the commons: The evolution of institutions for collective action.* Cambridge, U.K.: Cambridge University Press.

Pearce, D., F. E. Putz, and J. K. Vanclay. 2003. Sustainable forestry in the tropics: Panacea or folly? *Forest Ecology and Management* 172: 229–247.

Richards, M. 1997a. Common property resource institutions and forest management in Latin America. *Development and Change* 28: 95–117.

Richards, M. 1997b. Tragedy of the commons for community-based forest management in Latin America? *Natural Resource Perspectives* 22: 1–8.

Sanderson, S. 2002. The future of conservation. *Foreign Affairs* 81: 162–173.

Silva, E. 1994. Thinking politically about sustainable development in the tropical forests of Latin America. *Development and Change* 25: 697–721.

Smith, J. and S. J. Scherr. 2002. *Forest carbon and local livelihoods: Assessment of opportunities and policy recommendations.* Bogor, Indonesia: CIFOR.

White, A. and A. Martin. 2002. *Who owns the world's forests? Forest tenure and public forests in transition.* Washington, D.C.: Forest Trends/Center for International Environmental Law.

Wilshusen, P. R., S. R. Brechin, C. L. Fortwangler, and P. C. West. 2002. Reinventing a square wheel: Critique of a resurgent "protectionist paradigm" in international biodiversity conservation. *Society and Natural Resources* 15: 17–40.

Wollenberg, E. 1998. Methods for assessing the conservation and development of forest products. In E. Wollenberg, and A. Ingles, eds., *Incomes from the forest: Methods for the development and conservation of forest products for local communities,* 1–16. Bogor. Indonesia: CIFOR.

Wollenberg, E. and A. Ingles, eds. 1998. *Incomes from the forest: Methods for the development and conservation of forest products for local communities.* Bogor, Indonesia: CIFOR.

Wunder, S. 2001. Poverty alleviation and tropical forests: What scope for synergies? *World Development* 29: 1817–1833.

Chapter 8

MAKING MARKETS WORK FOR FOREST COMMUNITIES[1]

Sara J. Scherr, Andy White, and David Kaimowitz

Forests and trees play a critical role in the livelihoods of the world's poor. Some one-fourth of this group depends fully or in part on forest resources to meet subsistence needs for staple and supplemental foods, construction materials, fuel, medicines, cash, and local ecosystem services, as well as farm inputs such as animal feed and nutrients for crops. But many of these same rural people are also forest producers, from indigenous communities with vast tracts of natural tropical forests to individual farmers who plant trees along their farm boundaries (box 8.1). Low-income farmers may earn 10 to 25 percent of their household income from nontimber forest products (NTFPS) such as mushrooms, fruits, or medicines (Wunder 2001). Small-scale processing of forest products such as furniture, tools, and baskets also is a large source of rural nonfarm employment (Arnold 1994).

For many poor rural people in forested and marginal agricultural lands, commercial markets for forest products and ecosystem services offer one of the few available and sustainable options to overcome their poverty.

As we enter the twenty-first century, the debate about forestry is intensifying, particularly with regard to the three seemingly contradictory goals of conserving forests, meeting fast-growing market demand, and promoting sustainable development to reduce rural poverty. Development assistance efforts in recent years have focused on forests as safety nets for low-income forest dwellers. These efforts emphasize access to forest resources for the poor to meet their subsistence needs. But much less has been done to help local people exploit their forest assets in a

Box 8.1   Major Types of Low-Income Forest Producers

- Indigenous and other community groups who manage collectively owned forest resources
- Local individuals or groups who co-manage or harvest products from public forests
- Smallholder farmers who manage remnant natural forests or plant trees in or around their crop fields and pastures
- Individuals or groups who engage in small-scale forest product processing
- Employees of forest production or processing enterprises

sustainable manner to take advantage of the opportunities and cope with the pressures of growing demand for forest products.

Some development organizations have become disenchanted with forestry, arguing that it has contributed little to poverty reduction. There is also concern that greater commercial activity by low-income forest populations would threaten conservation.

However, it is unlikely that large-scale conservation can be achieved *without* engaging local people in marketing their forest products and services. Furthermore, fundamental changes under way in forest supply, demand, and governance offer new opportunities for low-income producers (box 8.2). With well-designed assistance for community-based enterprises, supportive policies, and the active engagement of the private sector, tens of millions of poor households can benefit from forest markets.

Promoting commercial forest market development while also reducing rural poverty will require new vision and targeted action. This chapter identifies the most promising market opportunities for local producers in developing countries and illustrates possible business models with real-life examples. Strategies for realizing that potential also are presented.

RECONCILING CONSERVATION WITH COMMERCIAL DEVELOPMENT

Resistance to opening markets for low-income forest producers has stemmed in part from forest conservation concerns. This stance ignores the fact that most remaining "wilderness" areas contain indigenous residents with legitimate claims to the land. The fact that communities are as good and often better managers of their local forests than governments also is disregarded. There is much evidence that local people can and do

Box 8.2   Global Forest Transitions Creating Opportunities for Small-Scale Producers

- *Increased control of forests:* Nearly one-fourth of the forest estate in the most forested developing countries is now owned (14 percent) or de facto controlled (8 percent) by indigenous and rural communities as a result of recent government recognition of local claims and devolution. Local ownership offers opportunities to capitalize on forest assets.
- *Growing product demand:* Although demand for forest products in developed countries is growing slowly, demand in developing countries is growing rapidly, and this demand will have to be met mainly by domestic production. New processing technologies are creating demand for small-diameter, lower-quality wood, which communities can and do produce.
- *Increasing scarcity raises the value of natural forests:* The supply of tropical hardwoods from natural forests has declined greatly because of deforestation, overharvesting, establishment of protected areas, and civil disturbance. Therefore stands of natural tropical hardwoods are becoming more valuable, and local people hold a substantial and increasing share of these stands.
- *Forest intensification:* Demand has prompted intensified forest management. Forest scarcity, increased prices of timber relative to those for grain, expansion of farming into marginal lands, tree domestication, and outgrower arrangements have stimulated extensive tree growing and commercialization on small farms.
- *Globalizing markets:* Although globalization often favors highly efficient, lower-cost producers, it is also opening opportunities to non-traditional suppliers as new niche markets arise and buyers become more proactive in seeking and securing reliable sources of scarce forest commodities.
- *Environmental service demand:* Environmental concerns are creating new markets for certified forest products and ecosystem services. Socially and environmentally aware investors are exploring opportunities to invest in sustainable forest management, including local farm and community producers.
- *More democratic governance:* Investor and consumer demands for socially responsible forestry are beginning to drive improved social protections for forest communities. Democratization is fostering reforms in forest governance that give greater voice to local people. International norms increasingly support indigenous land rights.

protect forests and ecosystem services of local value (Shepherd 1992, Pof-ferberger and McGean 1996, Gibson et al. 2000, Colfer and Byron 2001).

Some influential policymakers have argued that forest conservation can best be achieved by concentrating commercial forest activity in very high-productivity areas and subsidizing plantations (Victor and Ausubel 2000). This argument is fundamentally flawed for countries with large, poor rural populations and large domestic forest markets. This approach does not re-duce domestic demand for wood. It reduces the economic incentive to in-vest in more sustainable production in natural forests, driving producers into unsustainable, illegal, low-return systems. Furthermore, it denies communities the use of their assets for their own economic benefit.

Still other policymakers propose that conservation can best be achieved by imposing public ownership on lands already locally owned. Rather than continue to ignore and deny indigenous and other commu-nities rights to use their forests, conservationists and the forest industry should partner with indigenous peoples to support conservation and sus-tainable production. This shift would greatly extend the area of natural forest effectively under long-term conservation. In forest-scarce areas, broad-based regulatory, tenure, and market reforms can provide incen-tives to reforest degraded ecosystems.

POTENTIAL COMPETITIVE ADVANTAGES HELD BY POOR PRODUCERS

For many producers, reforms in policies and business support will allow their forests to increasingly contribute to their own economic develop-ment. Low-income forest producers have potential competitive advan-tages for important segments of commercial forest markets:

- Nearly a fourth of the forest estate in the most forested develop-ing countries is owned (14 percent) or de facto controlled (8 per-cent) by indigenous and rural communities as governments rec-ognize local land claims or devolve control to local populations. In forest-scarce regions, agroforestry has expanded greatly on small farms; in Bangladesh, for example, farms account for most timber production.
- Forest dwellers located near populated centers with growing do-mestic demand, particularly inland cities far from commercial ports, have lower transport costs, are more familiar with local preferences, have the flexibility to supply small quantities as needed by local traders, and can provide fresher supplies of NTFPs.
- Some producers can supply products at lower prices than large-scale commercial suppliers. Many have lower opportunity costs

for land and labor, and many value the collateral benefits of community employment or ecosystem services. In agroforestry systems, the costs of tree production may be lower because of joint production with crops and livestock. Trees may even have a positive effect on the income of associated crops, as in the case of windbreaks.

- Some forest communities can be competitive because they have resident owner-managers, whereas corporations must account for the cost of hired management and labor.
- Often, communities are eager to adopt sustainable management systems to avoid boom-and-bust cycles.
- Because they are present and because they are highly motivated to protect their long-term community interests, local people may better monitor and protect forest resources from risks such as urban encroachment, theft, and fire.
- Forest dwellers have an advantage in branding for specialty markets, enabling them to target consumers or investors sensitive to reputation or involved in socially responsible market niches.

COMMERCIAL OPPORTUNITIES FOR LOW-INCOME PRODUCERS

Global forest transitions are creating new opportunities for small-scale producers in particular markets. This section highlights several important examples. Greater detail is provided in table 8.1), including estimates of the number of producers with potential to participate in each market by 2025 and the potential for this participation to increase household incomes.

- *Commodity wood (construction grade, poles, fuelwood):* Rapidly growing domestic demand for commodity wood—for urban settlements, industry, fuel, and infrastructure—offers the largest potential market. Community forest owners and farmers in forest-scarce locations near rapidly growing inland population centers can be competitive suppliers, as can some user groups co-managing public forests.
- *High-quality timber (appearance grade):* Community forest owners of natural forests with high-quality, accessible timber, strong community organization, and good marketing and management skills can profitably sell tropical hardwoods. In forest-scarce areas with high income growth and good market access, small-scale farmers can profitably sell high-value timber from agroforestry.

Table 8.1 Main Market Opportunities and Possible Business Models for Low-Income Forest Producers: A Preliminary Assessment

A. Commodity Wood (construction grade, poles, woodfuel)

Low-Income Group	Where Main Opportunities Will Be Found	Scale of Market Opportunity for Poor	Business Models	Potential to Raise Incomes	Examples
Community forest owners	Countries where public forest area for commercial use is limited and producers face low transport costs to major inland markets; humid, subhumid areas, closed-canopy forest, some woodlands	**	Stumpage, logs, poles, fuel sold locally by community to national or international traders or loggers.	*	*Ejidos* in northern Mexico's Chihuahua and Durango.
			Wood-using companies contract or agree to harvest wood from community forests.	**	Export of construction wood from Papua New Guinea.
Public forest users	Countries with large public forests and weak public management capacity or devolution to local governments; diverse forest types	**	Local people produce wood in public forests, under co-management agreements, to sell to local traders or public agency.	**	Most public forest co-management programs in India and Nepal.
Small-scale farmers	Forest-scarce inland regions with rapid income or population growth; humid and subhumid areas	***	Farm forestry products are sold to local traders.	**	Eucalyptus farming in India (Dewees and Saxena 1995).
			Farm forestry or outgrower schemes directly link producers with large-scale sawmills, commodity wholesalers, or final users.	***	Match Company farm forestry scheme with 30,000 farmers on 40,000 ha in Uttar Pradesh, India; Kolombangara Forest Products, Ltd., informal sawlog grower scheme with 100 growers (Desmond and Race 2000).
			Farm forestry operates with cooperative wood marketing organization.	***	Widespread in India, Philippines, Bangladesh, Nepal.

Table 8.1   (continued)

B. High-Quality Timber (appearance grade)

Low-Income Group	Where Main Opportunities Will Be Found	Scale of Market Opportunity for Poor	Business Models	Potential to Raise Incomes	Examples
Community forest owners	Areas with more secure tenure rights over forests with high-quality timber, accessible at market prices, and strong community organization, with marketing and management skills, mainly for export markets; mostly closed-canopy forest in humid and subhumid areas	**	Communities sell stumpage or logged wood locally to traders (national or international).	*	Community forests in Oaxaca, Mexico (PROCYMAF 2000).
			Communities actively market to international buyers.	**	Ecoforestry operations in Papua New Guinea (Flier and Sekhran 1998).
			Forest communities manage timber in partnership with private company.	***	Iisaak Forest Resources, Ltd. (Baird and Coady 2000).
			Forest communities lease concessions to industry or government.	**	Community forests in Bolivia (Pacheco 2001); government loggers pay royalties to Pakistan community forests (Ahmed and Mahmood 1998).
Public forest users	Public forests co-managed for high-value timber, promoted by local government or end users; mainly closed-canopy forest in humid and subhumid areas	*	Producer organizations manage public forest concessions.	**	National Council for Protected Areas in Guatemala, multiple-use zone of the Mayan Biosphere Reserve (Ortiz 2000).
Small-scale farmers	Mainly forest-scarce regions with growing incomes and demand for high-value products; good market access; areas with secure tenure; mainly in humid and subhumid areas	**	Small farms or communities participate in outgrower or crop share schemes with private companies to establish plantations of improved high-value timber.	**	Prima Woods project for teak production in Ghana (Mayers and Vermeulen 2002).
			Farmers grow timber at low densities in agroforestry systems and remnant forest to sell cooperatively.	*(*)	Philippines Agroforestry Cooperatives (ICRAF 2001).

Table 8.1 (continued)

C. Industrial Pulpwood (for chemically treated wood products)

Low-Income Group	Where Main Opportunities Will Be Found	Scale of Market Opportunity for Poor	Business Models	Potential to Raise Incomes	Examples
Community forest owners	Countries with most large forest areas under secure community ownership and with large pulp and paper or engineered wood industry; communities located near mills; humid and subhumid areas	*	Joint ventures and leases operate with shared equity between industries and communities for pulpwood production.	**	Mondi pulp and paper company in South Africa's Eastern Cape provides technical assistance and start-up capital to communities organized in common property associations (Mayers and Vermeulen 2002).
			Community forest land is leased to private companies for pulpwood production.	**	Tasman Forest Industries in New Zealand leases land from 27 Maori groups on 11,000 ha; landholders retain hunting and grazing rights (Mayers and Vermeulen 2002).
Small-scale farmers	Densely settled, forest-scarce countries with large pulp and paper or engineered wood industry and limited foreign exchange; farmers located near pulp mills; humid and subhumid areas	**	Outgrower arrangements: Industry helps farmers establish and manage pulpwood plantations in guaranteed supply contracts.	***	Aracruz Cellulose timber partner program in Brazil (Desmond and Race 2000, Saigal and Kashyap 2000).
			Farm forestry: Farmers establish plantations with technical support from industry; sell output without purchase contracts.	**	ITC Bhadrachalam Paperboards, Ltd., integrated pulp and paper mill in Andhra Pradesh State, India (Lal 2000, Saigal and Kashyap 2000).
			Farmers lease land to private companies for pulpwood production.	**	Jant Limited wood chipping operation in Madang, Papua New Guinea (Mayers and Vermeulen 2002).

Table 8.1 (continued)

D. Certified Wood

Low-Income Group	Where Main Opportunities Will Be Found	Scale of Market Opportunity for Poor	Business Models	Potential to Raise Incomes	Examples
Community forest owners	Forest communities with high capacity for natural forest management and marketing, that can achieve low certification costs	*	Forest communities selling stumpage or logs have established contracts or agreements with certified wood users or market intermediaries.	**	Certification of 53,000 ha in the indigenous community of Lomerío, Bolivia (Contreras-Hermosilla and Vargas 2001).
Public forest users	Forest user groups with high capacity for natural forest management, mainly where forests have high biodiversity or carbon value and supportive public forest institutions	*	Long-term community concessions in public forests or co-management agreements involve established contracts or agreements with certified wood users or market intermediaries.	**	National Council for Protected Areas in Guatemala, multiple-use zone of the Mayan Biosphere Reserve (Ortiz 2000).
Small-scale farmers	Farmer groups, mainly in humid and subhumid regions, with high capacity for natural forest management and marketing, that can achieve low certification costs	*	Farm producer groups have established contracts or agreements with certified wood users or market intermediaries.	**	Klabin pulp and paper company of Brazil helps outgrowers obtain certification and supply local furniture company demand (Dubois and Grieg-Gran, pers. comm. 1999).

Table 8.1 (continued)

E. Nontimber Forest Products (NTFPS)

Low-Income Group	Where Main Opportunities Will Be Found	Scale of Market Opportunity for Poor	Business Models	Potential to Raise Incomes	Examples
Community forest owners	NTFPS (from all types of forest) with high national or international demand that do not have domesticated substitutes are available; strong community organization, including a sustainable management or conservation plan for wild resources	***	Forest communities collect or grow, process, and sell NTFPS to local processors or traders.	*	Most NTFP producers.
			Forest communities collect and sell NTFPS to processing and marketing collective or parastatal.	*	Brazil nut producer organizations supported by the Rainforest Alliance (Clay 1996).
			Forest communities contract to collect, process, and sell NTFPS to private industrial processor or retailer.	**	Indigenous producers in Marajo Pará, Brazil, who collect heart of palm for local processing plant (P. Moles, pers. comm. 2000).
	Community with biodiverse forests and capacity to negotiate deals with private firms	*	Forest community makes bioprospecting agreement with private company.	*	Bioprospecting agreements with communities in Latin American rainforests (Reid 1993).
Public forest users	Producer groups can obtain exclusive or guaranteed access to raw materials; NTFPS have high value; mainly national demand	**	Groups collect, process, and sell NTFPS to local processors or traders.	*	Bamboo producers and artisan cooperatives in Andhra Pradesh, India (Kumar et al. 2000).
			Groups collect NTFPS and sell to parastatal or collective.	**	Tribal Development Cooperative Corporation of Orissa, Ltd., in India (Neumann and Hirsch 2000).
			Groups contract to supply processor or retailer.	**	Rattan producers belonging to the Manipur Crafts Society of India (Belcher 1998).
Small-scale farmers	NTFPS have large, deep national or international markets with growth; no major economies of scale in production	***	Small farmers grow, process, and sell NTFPS to local processors or traders.	**	Most small farm NTFP producers.
			Small-scale farmers grow and sell NTFPS to processing and marketing collectives.	**	Many nationally and internationally traded domesticated spices, dyes, seeds, oilseeds, leaf for fodder, ornamentals.
			Small-scale farmers grow and sell NTFPS through outgrower schemes or contracts with private industry.	**	Same as above.

Table 8.1 (continued)

F. Forest Product Processing

Low-Income Group	Where Main Opportunities Will Be Found	Scale of Market Opportunity for Poor	Business Models	Potential to Raise Incomes	Examples
All groups	Simple preprocessing to increase income and access markets by reducing waste, increasing quality, or reducing transport costs.	**	Community or group enterprise	**	Drying forest fruits to improve product quality, reduce pest loss, or allow storage; chemically treat rattan to prevent fungal damage and staining (Hyman 1996).
	Simple tools, furniture, other basic commodities for poor consumers in growing rural or urban areas	**	Community or group enterprise.	**	Small-scale processing firms in Africa (Arnold et al. 1994).
	Sawmilling, in markets where large-scale, high-efficiency mills do not compete (humid and subhumid forest regions)	*	Cooperative community, farmer, or group operates sawmill enterprise with identified buyers.	**	Small-scale logging in the Amazon (Padoch and Pinedo-Vasquez 1996).
	Finished processing, where commercial links can be forged with businesses serving higher-income consumers; groups with capacity for standardized, high-quality production	*	Forest community or farmers operate cooperative for sale direct to wholesalers or retailers.	***	Community producers in Oaxaca, Mexico, selling finished wood products to the Puertas Finas Company.

Table 8.1 (continued)

G. Payments for Environmental Services

Low-Income Group	Where Main Opportunities Will Be Found	Scale of Market Opportunity for Poor	Business Models	Potential to Raise Incomes	Examples
Community forest owners	Forest-rich regions with resources of very high environmental value (for biodiversity, tourism)	*	Business partnerships for nature tourism are established between forest communities and private companies or public agencies.	**	Agreement between the community of Zancudo and Transturi, a major ecotourism operator in Ecuador (Wunder 2000).
	Regions where forest ecosystem services are needed to reduce economically important types of degradation (especially watershed protection)	**	Governments, farmer groups, and conservation agencies make direct payments to communities.	*	New York City water; Perrier-Viettel (Johnson et al. 2001); Costa Rica farm payments (Chomitz et al. 1999).
Public forest users	Forest-scarce regions with potential for rapid forest growth, or forest-rich regions threatened by rapid deforestation (carbon)	*	Direct or indirect payments are made to forest communities to sequester carbon within a framework of emission trading.	*	Noel Kempff Project, Bolivia (Smith and Scherr 2003).
Small-scale farmers	Forest-scarce regions where agency capacity to manage public forests for ecosystem services is weak or expensive	*	Public forest dwellers or users are compensated for managing or protecting public forest for ecosystem services.	*	Financial payments to forest community households for forest protection in Vietnam (FAO 2001).
	Forest-scarce regions for environmental services and sites of high value to buyers (e.g., biodiversity corridors)	*	Private deals are made to provide highly valued ecosystem services.	*	Payments to upstream forest landowners by Irrigator Associations in Cauca River, Colombia (Johnson et al. 2001).
	Areas where forest ecosystem services are needed to reduce economically important types of degradation (e.g., forest buffers to reduce nutrient pollution)	**	Municipalities, farmer groups, or conservation agencies make direct payments to farmers.	*	Payments to control salinity in New South Wales, Australia (Brand 2000).
	Regions with low forest cover and existing institutions to reduce transaction costs	**	Direct or indirect payments are made to farmers to sequester carbon within a framework of emission trading.	*	Scolel-Te, Mexico, forest carbon project (de Jong et al. 2000).

Scale of potential market participation by poor producers in developing countries by the year 2025:
***high (tens of millions), **moderate (millions), *small (fewer than a million).

Potential for market participation to raise producer household income: ***major income increase,
**moderate income increase, *mainly as supplemental income or safety net.

- *Industrial pulpwood (chemically treated wood products):* In densely settled, forest-scarce countries with large markets for pulp, farmers or communities near mills can produce pulp, especially on lower-quality lands. To protect food security and the environment, plantings should be in mosaics with natural forest and cropland.

- *Certified wood:* Some community forest owners and some farmers can benefit from certified wood markets if they have direct links to export for wholesale or retail buyers, if they have partners willing to underwrite certification costs, and if they are already operating at levels close to certification standards (see chapters 5 and 6).

- *Nontimber forest products:* Economic potential for the greatest number of low-income producers lies in growing or collecting products for which demand increases as consumers' incomes increase. Especially promising are those with qualities that make them difficult to grow in large-scale intensive plantations, such as certain kinds of mushrooms. Accountable intermediary trading organizations are needed. Export potential is limited by the high costs of conducting transactions, meeting quality standards, achieving volumes, and retaining competitiveness. Enterprises based on collection of wild species in community or public forests need conservation plans.

- *Forest product processing:* Many local producers will benefit from preprocessing to reduce waste, increase quality, or reduce transport costs and from production of furniture and commodities for poor consumers in growing markets. Small-scale sawmilling will be viable in markets where industrial high-efficiency mills do not compete. High-value finished products, such as decorative flooring or furniture, may be viable where commercial links can be forged with higher-income consumers and producers can standardize product quality (see chapter 14).

- *Payments for ecosystem services:* Some forest dwellers in areas with high ecosystem values, such as watershed protection or biodiversity habitat, can sell those services in private or public deals. Many more may begin receiving public payments for ecosystem services that prevent or reverse environmental degradation, such as flood control and dam sedimentation prevention. Once agreements are in place for carbon offset trading, millions of local producers also will benefit if operational guidelines are set with local producers in mind and if mechanisms are developed to reduce monitoring and transaction costs (Mundy and ARM 2000; see chapter 12).

MARKETS ARE NOT FOR EVERYONE

In many cases, small-scale producers cannot compete with low-cost industrial producers or products from land-clearing and illegal extraction. For some rural communities and farmers with low-quality forest resources and poorly developed market infrastructure, commercial markets will not play an increased role in livelihoods. Even where forest market conditions are favorable to small-scale forest holdings, many of the very poor will benefit mainly as hired laborers for small forest enterprises or from the employment multiplier effects of local forest development. For these people, forestry development should focus primarily on subsistence and environmental values.

A FRAMEWORK FOR ACTION

Although these opportunities are exciting for many low-income producers, under current conditions they face serious constraints to successful forest market participation (Wunder 2001; Neumann and Hirsch 2002). To realize potential market benefits, targeted action is needed on two fronts: developing small-scale forest enterprises and removing the barriers constructed by certain policies.

Developing Forest Enterprises

Improve Market Position
To raise incomes significantly, producers need to analyze the value chain in their markets and establish a competitive position. This may mean improving production and marketing technology, product quality, or supply reliability. Local sales of low-value wood products and NTFPs with stagnant demand can play an important role in the livelihoods of forest dwellers. But long-term income growth will depend on a successful response to growing demand for domestic forest commodities. This entails building supply networks that link producers to markets and increased production efficiency. Small-scale producers' potential for successfully supplying commodity markets is illustrated by the pulpwood outgrower schemes in South Africa (box 8.3).

To access high-value specialty markets and ecosystem services, producers must be highly responsive to consumer preferences and have

Box 8.3 South African Farmers Produce Industrial Pulpwood

In the 1980s, farmers in KwaZulu-Natal, South Africa, entered into outgrower schemes with the international pulp and paper companies Sappi and Mondi. The two firms now contract with more than 10,000 growers on nearly 18,000 ha. The average plot sizes are 1.5 ha for the Mondi project and 2.7 ha for the Sappi project. Farmers, more than half of whom are women, grow trees on their own land under purchasing agreements with the companies. The companies provide material goods such as seedlings, tools and fertilizer; low- or no-interest loans, and assistance with establishing and maintaining small eucalyptus woodlots. In return, the companies expect to harvest from each plantation after a growing cycle of six years on the coast and seven years inland. There is little competition with food crops for land or labor.

The schemes were started as corporate social responsibility exercises, but the partnership is good business for the companies. Because the land is held under communal tenure, it would otherwise be unavailable for purchase or lease agreements. Although the costs of administering the schemes per ton of fiber appear to be higher than those incurred from commercial plantations, the additional land rental fees associated with commercial land probably offset such costs. Furthermore, the outgrower system generates the fiber supply needed to maximize the economies of scale in the companies' pulp mills.

Because the farmers obtain cash income at harvest, trees are seen as a form of savings. Even highly vulnerable households are able to join the outgrower schemes if they have sufficient land. Outgrower schemes contribute 12 to 45 percent of the income needed for a household to remain above the abject poverty line.

Source: Mayers and Vermeulen (2002).

good marketing strategies. Low-income producers need to manage risks through a portfolio of products in different income and risk categories, maintaining the capacity to switch products as demand changes. Those revenue streams may derive from harvesting different products from a multipurpose tree, harvesting at different ages, or harvesting from a diverse mix of species. Market development should occur over time as producer capacity develops.

Strengthen Producer Organizations

Often, strong local producer organizations are needed. Commercial development can require producers to make capital investments, undertake processing activities, organize marketing deals, and establish product quality or conservation controls. Groups can contract with intermediaries to ensure supplies to a buyer. In regions with underdeveloped market institutions, groups of producers can work together to overcome value chain gaps, for example, by setting up reliable transport services, recruiting regional traders, establishing log sorting yards, or agreeing to quality standards. The payoff for strengthening producer organizations has been demonstrated by the business and environmental outcomes of Proyecto de Conservación y Manejo Sostenable de Recursos Forestales (PROCYMAF) in Mexico (box 8.4).

Box 8.4   Organizing Forest Communities in Mexico

In the early 1980s, indigenous communities in the poor, mountainous southern states of Mexico, angered by watching their forests degraded by outside loggers, formed a regional organization and succeeded in stopping the government from renewing timber concessions. Many of these communities went on to establish their own community forest enterprises. In 1997, the Proyecto de Conservación y Manejo Sostenable y Recursos Forestales (PROCYMAF), co-financed by the government and the World Bank, began to operate in the pine–oak forests of the state of Oaxaca.

The project works on a demand basis, helping 256 communities to become more organized and build capacity. Communities that are not actively engaged in commercial forestry first develop land use plans and evaluate their land governance systems. Communities that are already engaged in forestry activities use project funds to develop new management plans, establish new community protected areas, or explore new business or marketing options. Training courses regularly provide information about silviculture, management, and marketing of wood and nonwood forest products. The project has a separate component that involves private sector consulting services for communities.

Since the project's start, the area under forest management has expanded from 500,000 to 650,000 ha, and total wood production has increased from 400,000 to 660,000 m^3 annually. These communities sell

(continued)

Box 8.4 (continued)

their timber to a local door manufacturer at a premium of 15 percent. This new volume generates at least an additional $10 million in value annually. About 1300 new permanent jobs in forest management and processing have resulted, and an additional 175 jobs have been generated in nontimber forest product activities including mushroom production and fresh water bottling. As a result, the state of Oaxaca is taking in an additional $1 million a year in tax revenue, and communities' social expenditures, apart from salaries and wages, have increased by at least $1 million a year.

Forests are also better managed. Some 13,500 ha of permanent old-growth reserves have been established. Some 90,000 ha have already been certified by the Forest Stewardship Council.

Sources: DeWalt et al. (2000), PROCYMAF (2000).

Promote Strategic Business Partnerships

Strategic business partnerships can benefit both private industry and local producers. At least fifty-seven countries have at least one community–company forestry partnership (Mayers and Vermeulen, 2002). Through these arrangements, industrial firms can access wood fiber and nonwood products at a competitive cost, along with forest asset protection, local ecosystem expertise, and social branding opportunities. Business partners can provide local producers with high-quality planting materials, technical assistance, quality control, investment resources for expansion, and marketing and business expertise. An effective partnership requires a long-term perspective for business development, flexible contract terms, special attention to reducing business risks (such as spreading sources of supply among different producer groups), and mechanisms to reduce transaction costs. Industrial partners, accustomed to specialization, need to respect the diverse livelihood strategies of their lower-income partners. The potential for successful business partnerships between indigenous communities and industrial companies is illustrated by Iisaak Forest Resources in Canada (box 8.5). Third parties, such as conservation organizations, nongovernmental organizations, and public forest agencies, have successfully brokered partnerships between large firms and small-scale producers.

Box 8.5   First Nations of British Columbia Partner with Multinational Firm

Iissak Forest Resources is a company owned by the indigenous, or First Nations, populations of Canada's Clayoquot Sound and Weyerhaeuser Corporation's British Columbia Coastal Group. Iisaak is working toward an economically viable way of conserving and managing valuable coastal old-growth forests that are not formally protected.

Iisaak, which now has tenure rights to 87,000 ha of land, originated from an intense social conflict over industrial harvest in Clayoquot Sound's old-growth forests. Widespread civil disobedience brought both logging and expansion of protected areas to a halt in 1993. In 1994–1995, a scientific panel evaluated the rainforest ecosystem and identified uses consistent with conservation. In 1998, initiatives to develop a new joint venture began. The partnership took two years to develop as trust was established between the previously conflicting partners. Individuals deemed trustworthy by both sides took an innovative step by agreeing to share a single strategic planning office. The negotiations involved not only First Nations and Weyerhaeuser but also local governments, the federal government, environmentalists, and unions. A Memorandum of Understanding, eventually signed in 1999 with five major environmental nongovernmental organizations, resolved the historic conflict while also respecting First Nations' traditional ownership of their territories, enhancing local sustainable economic development opportunities, and providing stability for local communities. In 2000, the United Nations Educational, Scientific and Cultural Organization Biosphere Program named the region a World Heritage Site. First Nations, who have majority ownership of Iisaak, consider this a step toward full government recognition of their territorial claims.

Iisaak has plans for three business segments. The commercial timber segment is producing high-quality cedar sawlogs for specialty products. Second, new business will be based on nontimber forest products, recreation, and ecotourism. The third component will develop and market conservation values such as carbon storage and biodiversity habitat.

Source: Baird. and Coady (2000).

Promote Essential Business Services

Local business success also depends on access to essential business services, tailored to meet the special needs of lower-income producers. These include management services; organizational support; technical assistance for production, conservation, and processing; market information; insurance; marketing assistance; and financing. In the early stages of local forest market development, such services rarely exist in most rural communities. They must be provided by nonprofit public or civic agencies, such as PROCYMAF in Mexico, or a private entity such as a venture capital fund in Brazil (box 8.6). As local capacity and scale of production expand, the private sector can find profitable opportunities. Research support is needed to help forest enterprises increase productivity and reduce costs. Leaders of forest producer organizations need training in community facilitation, technical forest management, and marketing.

Target Education and Research to Community Forestry

Forming a commercially viable community forestry sector will entail developing, disseminating, and adapting to new production, processing, and management systems. Education and training programs must foster this new expertise, integrating sustainable forest management, business, and marketing skills with community facilitation. Research should focus on technical, economic, institutional, and policy problems relevant to forest communities and small-scale farmers.

Removing Policy Barriers

Secure Forest Access and Ownership Rights of Local People

Currently, uncertainties about forest tenure and restricted forest access are the most binding constraints to development and expansion of local forest businesses. Half to two-thirds of all forests are state controlled, including large deforested areas, degraded forests, and farmlands on steep slopes (White and Martin 2002). Clear tenure rights authorize local people to protect forests against outside encroachment and to enter into business contracts. Transferring or returning forest assets to the ownership or long-term use of local people is a politically and financially feasible first step for poverty reduction. Many countries have begun to formally devolve ownership or long-term usufruct rights to local households or communities. Still, a high level of state control often remains, and the state either retains the highest-quality forests or claims a disproportionate share of income from those lands. In Indonesia and the Philippines, some local groups have successfully negotiated new rights

Box 8.6   Venture Capital Firm Builds Sustainable Industry with Amazon Communities

Small and medium-sized Latin American companies are earning competitive profits while increasing biodiversity with the help of A2R's Terra Capital. The venture capital fund reflects a partnership between Axial RR of Brazil and GMO-RR of Boston. Investment areas include organic agriculture, sustainable forestry, nontimber forest products, ecotourism, and bioprospecting. Several Terra Capital investments involve community-based forestry in the Brazilian Amazon, including a processing plant for palm heart, a babaçu palm processing company, and a large, certified sustainable softwood production and processing enterprise. A2R is committed to improving local livelihoods and conserving forest resources as part of its core business strategy. An interdisciplinary team of financial and technical specialists from A2R visits the enterprises frequently to provide business support.

For example, A2R acquired a financial interest in a palm heart processing plant on a remote island in Marajo, in the state of Pará, which was suffering from unreliable raw material supply and poor administrative and financial management. A2R helped to resolve local land conflicts and to secure local rights for growing palm fruits, thereby ensuring a regular and secure source for the processing plant. Within three years, the enterprise achieved sales of us$4 million, supporting 100 factory employees and increasing incomes and assets for 5000 producing families in one of the poorest parts of the Amazon. A2R also helped local people produce the palm fruits more sustainably. They have begun to seek Forest Stewardship Council certification, which would establish the first certification for heart of palm in Brazil.

Source: P. Moles, A2R (pers. comm., 2000).

by demonstrating sustainable forest management (Scherr et al. 2001). More secure forest access and ownership rights for local people must be pursued aggressively, including the establishment of property rights for ecosystem services.

Remove Regulatory Barriers
Reducing the excessive regulatory burden on local forest producers is essential if they are to use their own forests or public forests for economic

development. Market activity in most developing countries is choked by excessive state regulation. In some regions of India, for example, ten separate permits are required for community forest producers to complete a timber sale (Saxena, pers. comm., 2000). In other countries, indigenous communities have long-term rights to extensive tracts of natural forest, but they are denied the right to commercially exploit them. Complex, poorly understood, and contradictory regulations from various agencies make compliance difficult, encouraging selective enforcement. This drives millions of people to operate illegally. In many cases regulations can be replaced by strong technical assistance programs that promote and monitor best practices or by certification programs (see chapter 6). The requirements of forest management plans and certification must be radically simplified for small-scale producers to comply.

Level the Playing Field in Forest Markets

Forest market policies that discriminate against small-scale producers also must be reformed. Lower-income forest producers benefit most from a level playing field consisting of markets with many buyers and sellers, few limitations on market entry or operation, flexible quality and volume requirements, and no subsidies or regulations that favor large-scale actors. Yet most governments subsidize or provide privileged access to large-scale producers and processors. They have a plethora of rules that distort markets and burden small-scale producers, maintain product standards biased against producers (such as overdimensioning of lumber), establish official monopoly buyers, and set excessive taxes and forest agency service charges. In most countries, the reforms necessary to benefit the poor would benefit the business sector and the forests as well.

In Bolivia, for example, far-reaching forest policy reforms have not only included formal recognition of indigenous groups' forest rights; they also have exempted small-scale forest producers from some requirements. Their concession fees have been lowered, the process for accessing municipal forests has been simplified, and assistance with marketing and forest certification has been provided (Contreras-Hermosilla and Vargas 2001).

Involve Local Producers in Policy Negotiations

Local producers' active involvement in forest policy negotiations will result in more practical, realistic, and lower-cost laws, market regulations, and development plans. In some countries, democratization has enabled greater participation. It has forced greater transparency in forestry markets. Forest rights and regulatory reforms have been achieved through political alliances involving local producer networks, private industry, government agencies, and environmental groups that stand to benefit from forest market development.

Protect the Poorest

Mechanisms must be developed to protect the interests of the poorest forest users and producers without sacrificing others' potential income gains from commercialization of public forests. It is most important to retain forests' safety net function, particularly ensuring access to subsistence products or harvest rights at certain times of the year. This involves sharing the benefits of communal forest enterprises, granting plantation gleaning rights to the landless poor, and giving the landless a voice in forest management.

Roles for Key Actors

Efforts to reduce poverty through commercial forestry should be realistic but ambitious. Risks will be lowest for low-income producers with strong competitive positioning. This includes areas where communities have competitive advantages, secure tenure rights, and established organizations; where major policy barriers are limited; where businesspeople want to partner with community forest enterprises; and where industry is open to sustainable and socially responsible forestry.

Private businesses including forestry industry, community organizations, and private financial and business service providers will necessarily play central roles. Business attention should be attracted first to the more promising sustainable forestry management opportunities. Businesses that can identify the competitive advantages of forming partnerships and working with local producers will strengthen their long-term supply and cost position. Innovative financing strategies can be pursued with socially and environmentally responsible investors. Business leaders can play an active role in governments' policy reform.

National, state, and local governments can help to strengthen local forest tenure rights and producer associations, reform market laws to level the playing field for low-income producers, simplify regulations and taxation, make industry–producer partnerships more attractive, encourage business support services, provide or facilitate strategic financing for market development, and involve local producers in policy formulation. At the same time, governments must safeguard and strengthen the safety net role of forests.

Development and conservation organizations can play a catalytic role in raising awareness of business opportunities, promoting policy changes, facilitating viable business partnerships, and establishing business support services targeted to low-income producers and community foresters. These groups can assist in developing guidelines for forest management plans, certification processes, transparency, and other global industry norms that enable full participation by local producers. Low-cost information services, through the Internet and other media, can provide broad access to available data, market information, and resources.

Research organizations can work with community forest owners and farmers to develop and field-test production and processing systems that are more efficient, profitable, and accessible. Researchers can analyze the financial and organizational viability of different business models for local enterprises and producer–industry partnerships.

The next generation of community forest investments should concentrate in areas where market, organizational, and policy conditions make it possible to have a major impact on rural poverty while showing the economic viability of sustainable forestry management as a business model. Successes can serve as examples for policymakers, businesspeople, and conservationists. These examples illustrate the possibilities while creating a skilled, experienced, and well-networked community of practice to mentor a new generation of business leaders.

NOTE

1. This chapter is based on a longer report by the same authors, published by Forest Trends and CIFOR (Scherr et al. 2003).

REFERENCES

Ahmed, J. and F. Mahmood. 1998. *Changing perspectives on forest policy.* Policy That Works for Forests and People Series no. 1. Islamabad and London: IUCN-Pakistan and International Institute for Environment and Development.

Arnold, J. E. M. 1994. *Nonfarm employment in small-scale forest-based enterprises: Policy and environmental issues.* EPAT/MUCIA Working Paper no. 11. Madison: University of Wisconsin.

Arnold, J. E. M., C. Liedholm, D. Mead, and I. M. Townson. 1994. *Structure and growth of small enterprises using forest products in southern and eastern Africa.* OFI Occasional Paper no. 47. Oxford, U.K.: Oxford Forestry Institute.

Baird, L. and L. Coady. 2000. A new economic model for conservation-based forestry in temperate old growth forests. Presentation at the conference "Developing Markets for Environmental Services of Forests," Forest Trends, British Columbia Ministry of Forests, University of British Columbia Faculty of Forestry, Vancouver, Canada, October 4, 2000.

Belcher, B. 1998. A production-to-consumption systems approach: Lessons from the bamboo and rattan sectors in Asia. In E. Wollenberg and A. Ingles, eds., *Incomes from the forest: Methods for the development and conservation of forest products for local communities*. Bogor, Indonesia: Centre for International Forestry Research and IUCN–The World Conservation Union.

Brand, D. 2000. *Emerging markets for forest services and implications for rural development, forestry industry and government*. Paper presented to conference on "Developing Commercial Markets for Environmental Services of Forests," Vancouver, Canada, October 4–6, 2000.

Chomitz, K., E. Brenes, and L. Constantino. 1999. Financing environmental services: The Costa Rican experience and its implications. *The Science of the Total Environment* 240: 157–169.

Clay, J. W. 1996. *Generating income and conserving resources: 20 lessons from the field*. Washington, D.C.: World Wildlife Fund.

Colfer, C. J. P. and Y. Byron, eds. 2001. *People managing forests: The links between human well-being and sustainability*. Washington, D.C.: Resources for the Future and Center for International Forestry Research.

Contreras-Hermosilla, A. and M. T. Vargas. 2001. *Social, environmental and economic impacts of forest policy reforms in Bolivia*. Washington, D.C.: Forest Trends and Centre for International Forestry Research.

de Jong, B. H. J., R. Tipper, and G. Montoya-Gomez. 2000. An economic analysis of potential for carbon sequestration by forests: Evidence from southern Mexico. *Ecological Economics* 33: 313–327.

Desmond, H. and D. Race. 2000. *Global survey and analytical framework for forestry outgrower arrangements*. Rome: Food and Agriculture Organization of the United Nations.

DeWalt, B., F. Olivera, and J. Betancourt Correa. 2000. *Mid-term evaluation of the Mexico community forestry projects*. Washington, D.C.: World Bank.

Dewees, P. A. and N. C. Saxena. 1995. Wood product markets as incentives for farmer tree growing. In J. E. M. Arnold and P. A. Dewees, eds., *Tree management in farmer strategies: Responses to agricultural intensification*. Oxford, U.K.: Oxford University Press.

FAO. 2001. *Vietnam country profile*. Paper prepared for the FAO Forum on "The Role of Forestry in Poverty Alleviation," Tuscany, Italy. Rome: Food and Agricultural Organization.

Flier, C. and N. Sekhran. 1998. *Papua New Guinea: Loggers, donors and resource owners*. Policy That Works for Forests and People Series no. 2. London: International Institute for Environment and Development.

Gibson, C. C., M. A. McKean, and E. Ostrom, eds. 2000. *People and forests: Communities, institutions and governance*. Cambridge, Mass.: MIT Press.

Hyman, E. 1996. Technology and the organization of production, processing and marketing of non-timber forest products. In M. Ruiz Perez and J. E. M. Arnold, eds., *Current issues in non-timber forest products research*. Proceedings of the workshop "Research on NTFP," Hot Springs, Zimbabwe, August 28–September 2, 1995. Bogor, Indonesia: Center for International Forestry Research.

ICRAF. 2001. *Agroforestry cooperatives in the Philippines*. Bogor, Indonesia: International Centre for Research in Agroforestry.

Johnson, N., A. White, and D. Perrot-Maître. 2001. *Developing markets for water services from forests: Issues and lessons for innovators*. Washington, D.C.: Forest Trends, World Resources Institute and the Katoomba Group.

Kumar, N., N. Saxena, Y. Alagh, and K. Mitra. 2000. *India: Alleviating poverty through forest development.* Evaluation Country Case Study Series. Washington, D.C.: The World Bank.

Lal, P. 2000. *Private sector forestry research: A success story from India.* Andhra Pradesh, India: ITC Bhadrachalam Paperboards Limited.

Mayers, J. and S. Vermeulen. 2002. *Company–community forestry partnerships: From raw deals to mutual benefits?* London: International Institute for Environment and Development.

Mundy, E. and ARM. 2000. *Risk mitigation in forestry: Linkages with Kyoto and sustainable forestry management.* Washington, D.C.: Forest Trends.

Neumann, R. P. and E. Hirsch. 2002. *Commercialisation of non-timber forest producers: Review and analysis of research.* Bogor, Indonesia: Center for International Forestry Research.

Neumann , R. P. and R. Hirsch. 2000. *Commercialisation of non-timber forest products: Review and analysis of research.* Bogor, Indonesia: Centre for International Forestry Research and Food and Agriculture Organization.

Ortiz, S. 2000. Community forestry for profit and conservation: A successful community management experience in timber production and marketing in Guatemala. *Tropical Forest Update* 10(1). Online: http://www.itto.or.jp/newsletter/v10n1/4.html.

Pacheco, P. 2001. *Bolivia: Country profile.* Background paper for Inter-Agency Forum on "The Role of Forestry in Poverty Alleviation." Tuscany, Italy, September 2001. Rome: FAO.

Padoch, C. and M. Pinedo-Vasquez. 1996. Smallholder forest management: Looking beyond non-timber forest products. In M. Ruiz Perez and J. E. M. Arnold, eds., *Current issues in non-timber forest products research.* Bogor, Indonesia: Center for International Forestry Research.

Pofferberger, M. and B. McGean. 1996. *Village voices, forest choices: Joint forest management in India.* Oxford, U.K.: Oxford University Press.

PROCYMAF. 2000. *Proyecto de conservacion y manejo sustentable de recursos forestales en Mexico. Informe y avance 1998–2000. Mision de evaluacion de medio termino.* Mexico: SEMARNAP.

Reid, W. V. 1993. *Biodiversity prospecting.* Washington, D.C.: World Resources Institute.

Saigal, S. and D. Kashyap. 2000. *Review of company-farmer partnerships for the supply of raw material to the wood-based industry.* Substudy for the Instruments for Sustainable Private Sector Forestry Project. London: International Institute for Environment and Development/Ecotech Services.

Scherr, S. J., M. E. Amornsanguasin, D. Chiong-Javier, S. Garrity, Sunito, and Saharuddin. 2001. *Local organizations in natural resource management in the uplands of Southeast Asia: Policy context and institutional landscape.* Paper presented to the SANREM conference on "Sustaining Upland Development in Southeast Asia: Issues, Tools and Institutions for Local Natural Resource Management," Makati, Metro Manila, Philippines, May 28–30, 2001.

Scherr, S. J., A. White, and D. Kaimowitz. 2003. *Making forest markets work for low-income producers.* Washington, D.C.: Forest Trends and CIFOR.

Shepherd, G. 1992. *Managing Africa's tropical dry forests: A review of indigenous methods.* London: Overseas Development Institute.

Smith, J. and S. J. Scherr. 2003. Capturing the value of forest carbon for local livelihoods. *World Development* 31: 2143–2160.

Victor, D. G. and J. H. Ausubel. 2000. Restoring the forests. *Foreign Affairs,* November–December, pp. 127–145.

White, T. A. and A. Martin. 2002. *Who owns the world's forests?* Washington, D.C.: Forest Trends.

Wunder, S. 2000. Ecotourism and economic incentives: An empirical approach. *Ecological Economics* 32: 465–479.

Wunder, S. 2001. Poverty alleviation and tropical forests: What scope for synergies? *World Development* 29: 11.

Chapter 9

INSIDE THE POLYGON

EMERGING COMMUNITY TENURE SYSTEMS AND FOREST RESOURCE EXTRACTION

Tom Ankersen and Grenville Barnes

> Tenure is not the "silver bullet." But because it is the factor most often neglected in addressing forestry issues, it requires immediate and careful attention in the development of forestry policy and programs.
>
> —Bruce and Fortmann 1992:496

Formal tenure systems have generally focused on defining the outside boundary of community tenure systems, resulting in a homogeneous polygon that is treated as communal property by the formal legal system. In fact, if one looks inside this polygon, most of these "communal" tenure systems are a complex web of individual and shared rights that deal with the use and allocation of community resources. In this chapter we describe and compare three community tenure systems and delve into the tenure system operating inside the polygon.

Many valuable forested areas in developing countries fall under a community tenure system. The traditional approach toward formalizing these areas is to grant a communal land title or concession transferring exclusive use rights to the forest dwellers. The title or concession defines the perimeter of the area (outside polygon) and registers the rights to the titled territory in the name of the group. In this way the formal tenure system divides up these territories into a set of polygons in space. The formal document may specify broad limits on deforestation and require some form of land use plan, but in many cases it does not really address the de facto land tenure and resource management structure inside the polygon. The result is a de jure "tenurial shell" (*sensu* Alcorn and Toledo 1998), which should facilitate interactions outside the polygon but in many instances actually constrains such interactions.

Bromley and Cernea (1989:15) have defined common property regimes (CPRS) as

> corporate group property. The property-owning groups vary in nature, size, and internal structure across a broad spectrum, but they are social units with definite membership and boundaries, with certain common interests, with at least some interaction among members, with some cultural norms, and often their own endogenous authority system.

Much of the mainstream literature on CPR focuses on the critical enabling conditions for sustaining common property systems (e.g., Ostrum 1990, Agrawal 2001). While sharing the ultimate goal of sustainability, we approach CPR or community tenure systems from a somewhat different perspective. By focusing on the land and resource tenure system, we seek to understand the current situation with respect to the allocation, use, transfer, and control of forest and other resources inside the polygon. In analyzing this de facto tenure system, we also compare it with the external de jure system to identify inconsistencies and possible areas of conflict.

Given the dynamic nature of both tenure and resource systems, we are also concerned with identifying and managing the information needs to support sustainable extractive practices between parties inside and outside the polygon. We contend that as community tenure systems come under increasing pressure, internal as well as external, it will be necessary for these communities to improve their local land administration capabilities and maintain more detailed tenure information if they are to be sustainable across generations. Information that focuses only on forest resources, not on who holds the use and extractive rights and the exact nature of those rights, is insufficient for the effective management of working forests.

OVERVIEW OF CASE STUDIES

To pursue our investigation we selected three case studies in which communities in tropical regions of Latin America are managing forest resources under some form of community tenure regime. These regimes include the community concessions of the Maya Biosphere Reserve in Peten, Guatemala, the extractive reserves of Brazilian Amazonia, and the forest *ejidos* of Quintana Roo, Mexico.

The communities managing forest resources in these community tenure regimes share certain characteristics. Each involves closely knit multiethnic communities, the majority of whose members (or their descendants) migrated to frontier forests in response to emerging markets for nontimber forest products (NTFPS) and in search of opportunities for land and livelihood. In each case, the opportunity presented was principally to extract latex-based NTFPS by ranging within a standing forest and collecting resin from living trees, a process known as tree tapping. In each case, the latex products have suffered steep market declines because of the development of synthetic substitutes for chewing gum and rubber. Each case study can also be traced to some extent to social movements that coalesced around issues related to social justice and land reform and, subsequently, sustainable development. Each community now has a delineated external polygon registered by the national land registry within which some form of community forest management occurs. In addition, each community must demonstrate some form of community governance authority that is subject to state approval.

These community tenure regimes also diverge at a fairly fundamental level. In the case of the community concessions and extractive reserves of Guatemala and Brazil, the form of land tenure is limited and contingent. The land underlying the polygon remains in the public domain (*dominio publico*). The usufruct rights granted to the community are limited to a specific duration (twenty-five and thirty years, respectively, or approximately one generation), with a right of renewal that is contingent on performance and a fee schedule. In the case of Mexico, on the other hand, the community is granted full ownership (*dominio pleno*) over the land. In addition, certain individual rights can be established within the polygon under circumstances specified by national law. The extent to which the communities are engaged in timber harvesting differs in each case. The tenurial shell provided by each of these systems also varies substantially in terms of its security, its marketability, and the rules that govern property transactions both inside and outside the delimited polygon. The different tenure attributes of the case studies are compared in table 9.1.

CASE STUDIES

Case 1: Community Concessions of Guatemala

The Maya Forest is the contiguous forest that covers parts of southern Mexico, Belize, and the northern Guatemala department known as El Peten (Nations et al. 1998). Once densely settled with the pre-Colombian Maya civilization, the forest closed in over ancient Maya ruins, and the

Table 9.1 Comparison of Community Tenure Systems in Guatemala, Brazil, and Mexico

Tenure Attributes	Community Concession	Extractive Reserve	Forest *Ejido*
Membership eligibility	Resident within community	Resident within community	*Ejidatarios* residing in *ejido* (capped?)
Internal organizations	Officially recognized community governance entity	Resident associations	Assembly, *comisariado, consejo de vigilancia*
Land tenure	Land owned by government	Land owned by federal or state government	Land owned privately by *ejido*
Common property	Exclusive use rights to forest resources for 25 years (renewable)	Joint use rights	Forest and other land held in undivided shares
Individualized tenure	Subgroup use rights	"Authorization to use" contracts signed with each *colocação*	Agricultural parcels and house lots
Transfers allowed			
Inheritance	N/A	Use rights may be transferred	Allowed to a single descendant
Sales (internal)	Prohibited	Improvements can be sold with government and resident association permission	Agricultural parcels and house lots
Sales (external)	Prohibited	Improvements can be sold with government and resident association permission	Agricultural parcels and house lots
Forest use restrictions	Subsistence use of timber allowed, commercial uses pursuant to management plan	Maximum of 10% deforestation allowed per family unit; domestic use of timber allowed	May not be subdivided; reserve set aside
Protected forest reserve	Yes	No	Yes

Guatemalan Peten was a nearly forgotten frontier until late in the twentieth century. Like legal Amazonia in Brazil, the Peten has in the past been accorded special status, including a period of quasiautonomy under military control. Land administration north of the seventeenth parallel was governed by the autonomous Institute for the Promotion and Economic Development of Peten (FYDEP) (Beavers 1995, Kaimowitz 1995). Land that was not granted to large private interests was retained by the state.

For most of Guatemala's history the Peten has been viewed as a frontier suitable for only the hardiest natural resource extractivists: *chicleros* who roamed the state forest extracting natural latex (chicle) for chewing gum, loggers high-grading mahogany and cedar for the tropical timber trade, and looters sacking the region's rich archaeological wealth (Schwartz 1990). In this milieu, *chiclero* communities coalesced in the forest around informal territories based on their unique extraction needs (Dugleby 1998). In the southern Peten, on the other hand, land was cleared by large cattle ranching interests and invaded by landless highland peasants.

In the late 1980s international and conservation groups grew alarmed over the rapid rate of deforestation in the department and a road construction proposal certain to spur colonization (Ponciano 1998). Competing groups vied for their vision of the Guatemalan frontier to become state policy. A 1989 *National Geographic* article describing the "Ruta Maya" captivated the international community and introduced tourism as a policy alternative for development in the region (Garrett 1989). International nongovernmental organizations (NGOs) extolled the potential of NTFPS, the most important of which included chicle; xate, an ornamental palm used in flower arrangements; and allspice, a fragrant seed used in cooking. In addition, the entire Peten basin was underlain by oil concessions, and drilling was under way in the Xan field of Laguna del Tigre, Central America's largest wetland (Bowles et al. 1999). Forestry remained commercially important, and subsistence agriculture and hunting also contributed to the local economy.

In 1990, backed by international donors, especially the U.S. Agency for International Development (USAID), the Guatemalan government created the Maya Biosphere Reserve (MBR), encompassing most of the remaining forested land in the northern Peten. The reserve was divided into three zoning units based on the protected areas paradigm promoted by the United Nations Educational, Scientific and Cultural Organization (UNESCO) (Dyer and Holland 1991). These biosphere reserves include core areas of strict protection, a multiple-use zone where ecologically consistent resource extraction is permitted, and a buffer or transition zone where human development is expected to be more intense. The legal framework for reserve administration is hierarchical and based largely on the Western protected areas management model. A framework law and subsidiary regulations govern the management of the reserve as a whole and authorize a reserve-wide regulatory master plan (Decreto 5-90 [Reserva de la Biosfera]). The master plan calls for unit-by-unit long-term management plans and annual operational plans for individual management units (CONAP 1996b). In practice, the buffer zone is largely deforested and colonized. The remaining forested areas are found in the core and multiple-use zones. It is in the multiple-use zone where Guatemala's experiment with forest management based on community resource tenure has been launched and where the MBR departs from most Western forest management models.

During the MBR's formative period, a logging ban was instituted while government and nongovernment institutions wrestled with how to administer forestry in the region. Continued illegal logging increased the pressure on the Guatemalan government and the NGOS to formalize tenurial arrangements in the multiple-use zone. International NGOS promoted community forestry and NTFP extraction based on principles of natural forest management and modeled after the extractive reserve paradigm (Gretzinger 1998). These interests ultimately prevailed.

The Guatemalan National Protected Areas Council (CONAP), charged with implementing the reserve's management plan, established a regulatory process through which the communities in the multiple-use zone could petition to receive twenty-five-year exclusive forest use concessions (CONAP 1994). The concession process requires a boundary demarcation and a management plan, both of which are incorporated into a binding agreement signed by CONAP and the legal representative of the community. The legal representative of the community must be officially sanctioned by the municipality and the governor of the Peten. The concession boundary must be registered with the National Institute of Agrarian Transformation (INTA), the national land titling agency.

Land ownership in the concession areas is expressly reserved by the state, but the communities gain exclusive use of surficial forest resources subject to the management plan and the reserve's legal framework (figure 9.1). Subsurface exploitation rights are retained by the state subject to a provision authorizing payment for natural resource damages caused by exploitation. Agriculture is permitted only in already cleared areas. The public is given the right to pass and to use existing roads. Community members are permitted to exercise their "traditional and customary laws," which must be negotiated between the community and the municipality and incorporated into the management plan. Communities must pay a concession fee to the government of Guatemala, which has the effect of requiring that some income be derived from the forest (CONAP 1996a).

The legal framework for the MBR recognizes that humans settled the Peten before the reserve's establishment. Human settlement is addressed in different ways depending on zoning category. No new properties may be individually or collectively titled in the MBR. Preexisting private property in the multiple-use zone (e.g., property for which a legal title has

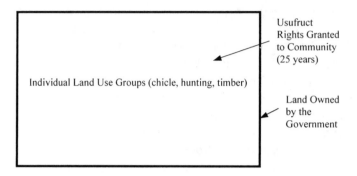

Figure 9.1   Tenure structure of Guatemalan concessions.

been conferred) must be registered with CONAP, and a management plan for the property must be approved. The property owner must maintain the boundaries and report land invasions to CONAP. Sale of the property must be reported to CONAP, and a management plan from the subsequent land owner must be accepted by CONAP.

Untitled settlements in the multiple-use zone are also addressed. This category includes historic *chiclero* communities, such as Uaxactun and Carmelita, within the community concessions. In this case the community must present CONAP with a list of male inhabitants with their national identification numbers and the name of the spouses and names and ages of the children. No additional people are permitted to settle in the community, and the sale, rental, or subdivision of property is prohibited. Each family is entitled to use a maximum of 45 ha for agroforestry purposes only. Cattle ranching is expressly prohibited. Subsistence hunting is permitted as provided for in the concession management plan (CONAP 1996a).

By the end of the 1990s almost all the multiple-use zone of the MBR had been partitioned into forest use concessions under the control of communities in the forest. Uaxactun (83,000 ha) and Carmelita (53,000 ha), both centers of chicle production, are the largest community concessions. However, these concessions are smaller than the chicle extraction territories suggested by Dugelby (1998) for these communities.

By most accounts deforestation slowed as communities exercised their right to exclude non–community members from the concession areas. Anecdotal evidence even suggests that one community evicted a family for violations of the management plan, and it is reported that efforts by non–community members to settle in some concessions have been repulsed by communities jealously guarding their exclusive use rights.

Case 2: Extractive Reserves of Brazil

The extractive reserve tenure model, as the name implies, is an attempt to establish a tenure system that explicitly balances economic development goals with environmental conservation goals. This tenure model was first proposed in Brazil in 1985 by the National Council of Rubber Tappers as a strategy for gaining greater tenure security for this group of extractivists. In response to repeated challenges to their land by colonization schemes and the expansion of cattle ranching across the western Amazon, their leader, Chico Mendes, championed the idea of extractive reserves as a viable alternative to the conventional rectangular subdivision and privatization of land rights (Mendes 1989).

Extractive reserves are built around former rubber estates established in response to the rubber boom in the late 1800s. (The Chico Mendes Extractive Reserve, for example, incorporates nineteen former rubber estates.) Rubber barons created expansive rubber estates (*seringais*) in the western Amazon and imported workers, mainly from northeast Brazil, to carry out the labor-intensive job of extracting latex from the rubber trees. With the decline in the rubber market and increased competition from Malaysia, the rubber barons lost interest in their estates and left the workers to their own devices. Many *seringueiros* stayed on the land, and in addition to continuing to extract latex, they began to harvest Brazil nuts and other forest products. Although there has been outmigration, the *seringueiros* encountered in today's extractive reserves are largely the descendants of these earlier pioneers (Schmink and Wood 1992, Melone 1993).

Initially, extractive settlements were created through the agrarian reform agency Instituto Nacional de Colonizaçaó e Reforma Agrária (INCRA), in accordance with an administrative directive passed in 1987 (Portaria no. 627 of 7/30/87). This marked a significant departure from the conventional settlement model in that the community as a whole was given use rights, and the concept of sustainable development, including goals of both economic development and environmental protection, was incorporated into the government strategy for agrarian reform (ELI 1995). Building on this experience, the Brazilian government passed a decree in 1990 to establish and create extractive reserves (Decree no. 98,897/90). This law gave the Brazilian Government Institute for the Environment and Renewable Resources (IBAMA) the responsibility for supervising and operating these reserves and specified the organizational structure and approach for managing the reserve. In 1996 a further administrative decree (Portaria no. 268 of 10/23/96) was passed providing

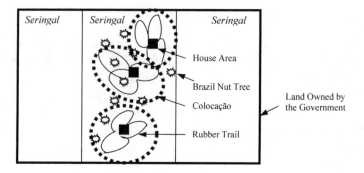

Figure 9.2   Tenure structure of Brazilian extractive reserves.

for agroextractive reserves, which replaced the extractive settlement tenure model and are also administered by INCRA.

The fundamental tenure characteristics shared by both models of the extractive reserve are as follows (figure 9.2):

- The federal (through INCRA or IBAMA) or state government sets aside and owns the land of the reserve.
- The community acquires a concession for joint usufruct rights over the extractive reserve (usually for thirty years).
- Use rights are transferable by inheritance.
- A Utilization Plan, laying out how the community will manage their resources in a sustainable manner, must be prepared as part of the concession (ELI 1995).

IBAMA has established guidelines (Portaria no. 51 of 5/11/94) for creating and legalizing an extractive reserve that includes substantial details on the Utilization Plan, including the prohibition of commercial hunting and the recognition of common areas such as rivers, lakes, pathways, beaches, banks, and jointly managed areas in the reserve; also, timber may be extracted for commercial purposes, but the extent of this extraction will be specified in the Utilization Plan and a management plan prepared and approved by the residents' association or union or IBAMA (Art. 8.3.2, Portaria no. 51). The Utilization Plan of most reserves prohibits residents from deforesting more than 10 percent of their family holding.

Extractive reserves are composed of a complex distribution of individual and community rights that are most often dictated by the spatial distribution pattern of the resource, as opposed to a homogeneous geometric pattern typically imposed in other tenure regimes. Each family on the former rubber estates occupies an area known as a *colocação,* which contains the rubber trails or *estradas de seringa*. An average family usually works three trails, each of which could contain as many as 150 rubber trees. The resource rights in this case therefore are defined initially by the location of the rubber trees and then by the trails that link them. The *seringueros* allow others to pass freely through their *colocação*, but the areas encompassed by the trails are regarded as mostly exclusive. In addition, each family has a cleared area where they live, cultivate a few subsistence crops, and raise small animals (Murrieta and Rueda 1995). Brazil nuts are the second most important extractive product, and the trees are generally regarded as the property of a particular *colocação*. The same is true for individual trees with value, such as cedar and mahogany. The *seringueros* also exercise hunting rights over particular areas of the forest.

These resource-driven (as distinct from land-driven) rights result in a complex spatial pattern on the ground: linear in the case of rubber trails, polygonal in the case of hunting, and a series of points for the cases of Brazil nut and other trees. This is a far cry from the simplicity of conventional land parcels, which are typically bounded by a simple geometric figure and encapsulate a homogenous tenure system. In western Brazil each rubber trail is estimated to contain 100 ha, but in reality the boundaries of the *colocaçoes* are not known. This means that it is impossible to determine whether individual *seringueros* have exceeded the 10 percent deforestation limit. Current estimates are based on general measurements for the whole *seringal* divided by the number of *colocaçoes*, and this indicates that in some instances they are fast approaching the legal limit (Gomes 2001).

In a study of land use dynamics in four *seringais* with the highest deforestation rates in the Chico Mendez Extractive Reserve, Gomes (2001:113) concludes that "key household characteristics have influenced land use strategies, suggesting that attention needs to be placed on the household level factors affecting different land use activities." Moreover, there is a proposal to introduce timber extraction in the reserve even though this is forbidden by the Utilization Plan. The younger generation in the reserve tend to be less interested in rubber tapping, and some recognize that cattle provide a more liquid asset that allows them to obtain cash during emergencies. Maintaining the forest while improving the economic situation of the *seringueros* remains the central challenge within the extractive reserves.

Case 3: *Ejidos* of Mexico

The southern Mexican state of Quintana Roo also lies in the Maya Forest bioregion. The forest culture of this state has as much in common with the peoples of the contiguous region in Guatemala and Belize as it does with Mexican states to the north. Like that of Guatemala, southern Mexico's frontier history was dominated by the extraction of forest products, including tropical timber and chicle. Large concessions were given to foreign firms who paid the Mexican government for the privilege of extracting timber from the Yucatán peninsula. Communities in the region received work but little more in exchange for the extractive activities (Snook 1998).

However, southern Mexico differs dramatically from its southern neighbors in terms of the way in which agrarian reforms were carried out. The 1917 Mexican revolution paved the way for the consolidation of the *ejido* system as the primary means of land distribution to the rural poor throughout Mexico. Under the *ejido* system, title to land is vested in communities to be managed as inalienable common property. According to most estimates, at least 50 percent of all arable lands in Mexico were distributed in this manner, and as much as 70 percent of the Mexican forest estate is *ejidal* (World Bank 2001). Among the largest *ejidos* in Mexico are those conferred to several communities in the Maya Forest. One reason for this is that the basis for the creation of *ejidos,* such as Noh Bec (24,215 ha) and Las Caobas (70,000 ha) in the state of Quintana Roo, stemmed from the reliance of these communities on the extraction of chicle from the Maya Forest. The area for these *ejidos* was determined by multiplying an average hectarage estimated for a *chiclero* to sustain his family by tapping chicle trees (approximately 450 ha) by the number of *chicleros* in a community. Even so, in the southern Mexican states these distributions often were ignored, at least in terms of conferring rights to the resources in the *ejidos*. Most *ejidos* were never formally demarcated, and logging continued. Around 1947 the foreign concessions were suspended, and a single Mexican firm took over logging in Quintana Roo. The *ejidal* communities noticed little difference, receiving a small stumpage fee set by the Mexican government (Snook 1998).

In 1983 the Mexican firm's Quintana Roo concession expired, and Mexico's experiment with community forestry, Plan Piloto Forestal, was launched (Galleti 1998). Under this plan, participating *ejidal* communities assumed full responsibility for forest management and could determine allowable cuts and set prices. One of the first steps participating communities took was to declare an area of the *ejido* off-limits to agriculture and other incompatible activities: the forest reserve. A management plan divided the forest reserves into twenty-five blocks based on a twenty-five-year cutting cycle. Chicle and other NTFPS could still be extracted from the forest reserve. Economies of scale dramatically changed *ejidal* production capacity because of the decentralization that the conversion to management implied, making it more difficult to compete in open markets. In the early 1990s the *ejidos* of Las Caobas and Noh Bec were certified by the Forest Stewardship Council, a private entity that guarantees consumers that timber harvested from the forests it certifies complies with a set of standards designed to ensure the social and environmental sustainability of the forest (http://www.fscoax.org/principal.htm; see chapter 6).

In 1992, a watershed year in *ejidal* history, Mexico approved a sweeping reform to Article 27 of its Constitution, which provides the legal basis for *ejidal* ownership (De Aguinaga 1993). In the interest of modernizing the Mexican agricultural economy and preparing Mexico for its entrance into the North American Free Trade Agreement (NAFTA), the Article 27 reforms provided a means for *ejidos* to enter into property transactions with outside investors and, in some circumstances, to privatize land within the *ejido*. However, permanent forest lands may not be alienated. Fundamental policy decisions concerning the *ejidal* land base are first made by the *ejidal* assembly, comprising all *ejido* members.

A new agrarian law was passed to implement the Article 27 reforms and a government program set up to demarcate and regularize *ejidal* land titles. The law creates a special office, the Procuduria Agricultura, to protect the rights of *ejidatarios* and other small land holders. *Ejidal* titles, defining the external polygon and the different regimes inside the polygon, must be registered in the social property registry, known as the National Agrarian Registry. This registry records the names of *ejidatarios* and documents the distribution of the land base within the *ejido*.

The law recognizes three primary bodies for the internal administration of the ejido (Art. 21, Ley Agraria). The Assembly, comprising all the *ejidatarios,* is the ultimate authority in the *ejido*. The *ejidal* Comisariado is the executive arm of the *ejido*, responsible for implementing agreements made by the Assembly and general administration of the *ejido*. Among other functions, the Comisariado is required to maintain a registry book noting the names and "basic identification data" of the *ejidatarios* (Art. 22). The Consejo de Vigilancia acts as a watchdog council for Comisariado governance.

Three different categories of land are recognized in the polygon (Art. 44: figure 9.3):

- Land for residential purposes (*asentamiento humano*)
- Land for common use (*uso común*)
- Land that is subdivided into parcels (*parceladas*)

A different form of land tenure applies to each of these categories. The land area designated for residential purposes cannot be sold or mortgaged

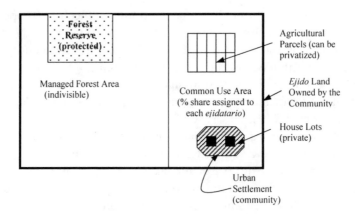

Figure 9.3   Tenure structure in Mexican forest *ejidos*.

and is not subject to prescription. House lots (*solares*) on this land are assigned without cost to *ejidatarios,* and any remaining lots may be rented out or alienated in favor of people who want to become residents of the *ejido* (Art. 68). House lots can be sold to others within and outside the community.

The individual interest in common use areas is provided through an agrarian use right (*derecho de uso común* or *derecho agrario*) that consists of an indivisible share, represented as a percentage that is based on the number of hectares in common use divided by the number of *ejidatarios.* The *ejido* may transfer part of the area under *uso común* to social or business subgroups within the *ejido,* such as *chicleros* (Art. 75). The common use area may include public space and buildings as well as permanent forest estate. Land under forest or tropical jungle cannot be divided into parcels (Art. 59). In many ways this property regime resembles the Western model of a condominium, in which one owns a unit privately and holds an indivisible share in the common areas.

Parcelas remain communally owned, but individual use rights apply, usually based on historic cultivation by individual *ejidatarios.* *Parcela* use rights may be transferred within the *ejido,* but no *ejidatario* may own more than 5 percent of the total *ejido* land area. *Parcelas* may also be mortgaged or rented to third parties within or outside the *ejido,* without the need for assembly approval (Art. 79). Upon agreement of the *ejidal* assembly, *ejidatarios* may convert their *parcela* use rights to full ownership (*dominio pleno;* Art. 81). In these cases the title is issued by the National Agrarian Registry but registered in the general Property Registry. It does not appear that the transfer of a *parcela* diminishes the percentage share accorded to the *ejidatario*. Furthermore, if an *ejidatario* sells to an outsider, he or she does not lose other *ejidatario* rights unless he or she has no further legal interest in the community (Art. 83).

Although the law appears to anticipate entry of new landed *ejidatarios* into the *ejido*, our interviews revealed that community members believe that the number of *ejidatarios* was fixed on the date of registry and cannot be increased. Part of this belief may be based in the legal requirement that inheritance rights transfer to only one successor, who could be the spouse or common-law partner, a child, a relative, or someone who was economically dependent on the deceased *ejidatario* (Art. 18).

In the new *ejidal* community tenure regime, property rights are being unbundled and redistributed both internally and externally. In the case of the Noh Bec *ejido*, the total area available through the *derecho de uso común* is 110 ha, most of which is forested. *Ejidatarios* are contemplating internal regulations that would cap the size of any individual agricultural *parcela* at 35 ha. Few *ejidatarios* currently cultivate this maximum. This would enable the *ejido*, through its forestry cooperative, to buy back the uncultivated land rights within the 35-ha maximum and retire it to the permanent forest estate.

EVOLVING TENURE SCENARIOS

The increasing complexity of community tenure regimes suggests a need for better-managed tenure information. The community tenure regimes we observed belie the traditional conceptions of common property as indivisible, inalienable, and incapable of being encumbered. We noted increasingly sophisticated formal and informal land and resource transactions occurring in communally owned or managed property, and at the same time we noted that external influences are driving a greater demand for information certainty. In our research we identified a number of instances in which a system providing such certainty may be warranted and speculate on how such scenarios may arise in the future.

Scenario 1: Conservation Easements in Guatemala

> An international conservation organization wants to purchase timber harvest rights from a communally managed concession and retire these rights to prevent them from being exercised.

Recently an international conservation organization presented the community forest concessions in Guatemala with an intriguing possibility. The organization is considering offering to buy and retire all or a portion of a community's right to harvest commercially valuable trees. Called a conservation incentive, the proposed acquisition of an exclusive use right begins to resemble the contemporary conservation easement, or *servidumbre ecologico*, as it is called in Latin America. In both common law and civil law jurisdictions these kinds of easements are generally regarded as perpetual, running with the land. Nonetheless, there are examples of limited-duration easements that run for a person's lifetime or for some specified period (Gustanski and Squires 2000). In the Guatemala scenario, the conservation incentive concession holder would be the legal representative of the community that signed the community concession agreement. Because the concession is given by the government for the twenty-five-year duration, the government may also have to consent to the agreement and may even be a necessary third party to the agreement, especially if the conservation organization wanted to retire the right in perpetuity.

One approach to this scenario would be to have the conservation incentive agreement mirror the twenty-five-year cutting cycle established for the concession in its management plan. Thus payments would be paid out for each forest block as it comes on line for harvesting. Restrictions could also be placed on how the money would be used as it is paid out, to guarantee that it would contribute to the community's sustainable development.

To ensure that timber harvest rights subject to the agreement will not be exercised, it may be necessary to georeference and record individual trees or blocks of trees. This would be particularly true if this form of easement became perpetual. Already, trees subject to harvest each year in the community concessions are georeferenced and marked for cutting. However, in the long term, where the intent is to maintain the tree for its biodiversity value, both the marking of the tree or tree block and the recording of the tree use rights transferred would necessitate a more robust information system, especially in an intergenerational context.

Scenario 2: Transfer of Deforestation Rights in Brazil

> *Colocação* A seeks to expand cattle production by trading for *colocação* B's 10 percent deforestation rights.

Transfers of development rights (TDRS) were first introduced as a means of averting development that would negatively impact or destroy the aesthetic value of historic buildings in the United States.[1] In simple terms it involves taking the development right out of the bundle of rights attached to a parcel of land (or historic building) and transferring that right to another parcel of land in another location. The primary motivation behind TDRS is to preserve a certain area (known as the sending zone) by exercising the development rights in an area designated for development (known as the receiving zone). In addition to preserving historic buildings, TDRs have been used extensively to preserve farmland and threatened natural resources (http://www.plannersweb.com/tdr.html).

Although this mechanism for protecting community resources has been used for more than thirty years in the United States, it challenges the mainstream view of property as a unified bundle of rights that is permanently affixed to a specific piece of land. In TDRs the landholders in the protected or sending zone split off their development right from the full bundle of rights and recoup the value of this right by selling it as "development credits" that can be exercised in the receiving zone. Deed restrictions, or conservation easements, are placed on the properties in the protected zone, ensuring that they are used only for activities that would not alter the predominant land use. Developers who purchase development credits are permitted to implement higher-density development projects in the receiving zone than their counterparts who choose not to purchase these credits. This provides the incentive for an active market in development credits.

Turning to the situation in Brazil, we envisage a scenario in which a family in *colocação* A wants to expand its pasture land to accommodate more cattle. Let us assume that they have already reached their 10 percent deforestation limit and so are restricted by the Utilization Plan from clearing more forest. Immediately adjacent to *colocação* A lies *colocação* B, which has pristine forest on all but 2 percent of their land. Family A approaches family B with an offer to purchase their remaining deforestation rights (8 percent) and transfer them to *colocação* A. In exchange, family B commits to no further deforestation on their *colocação*. The result of this arrangement is that the total area deforested is no more than that allowed by the Utilization Plan over the whole reserve or *seringal*.[2]

The advantage of the TDR arrangement is that it provides greater flexibility for accommodating differences in natural resource stocks, differences in economic activities, and differences in capabilities (labor and capital) between different *seringueiros* while retaining the same overall limit on deforestation. The difficulty, as was mentioned earlier, is defining the *colocação* boundaries, monitoring activities in this area, and enforcing the new limits conveyed by the TDR. A scenario like this is particularly challenging in the frontier context of the Brazilian Amazon.[3]

Scenario 3: Tenure Conversions in the *Ejidal* Polygon in Mexico

> The *ejido* Nuevo Progreso wants to acquire the rights to individual agricultural parcels and redesignate them as permanent forest estate.

Ejidal leaders have expressed a desire to increase the area of community forest land by acquiring all or portions of usufruct tracts allocated to individual *ejidatarios* for conversion to agricultural parcels. This is particularly desirable where the soil is no longer suitable for agriculture or where *ejidatarios* are allocated their indivisible share of agricultural land but need only a portion of this to conduct their enterprise. Because the agricultural parcels are subject to a different set of tenure rules than the forest area (see table 9.1), this will involve a tenure conversion between these two categories. Essentially, the *ejido* assembly would use profits from the existing forestry enterprise to buy back the undeveloped agricultural usufruct and return it to the permanent forest estate, thereby expanding the forest area available for commercial forestry. This scenario creates an internal market in property use rights, suggesting the need for a more sophisticated community land information system.

THE COMMUNITY CADASTRE: IMPROVING INFORMATION SYSTEMS IN THE POLYGON

> The social norms of traditional forest cultures often support conservation practices. Increasing their tenure security and granting rights to manage trees generally enhances their capacity to maintain those practices.
> —Forster and Stanfield 1993:vi

Management plans typically identify the resources in the community and then estimate sustainable harvest rates. Recognizing that sustainable harvesting is a function of both the resource and the people who have rights to the resources, we feel it is important to focus on this human resource relationship, which is encapsulated in the tenure system. In this section we make the case for developing a community-based tenure information system or cadastre.

The modern concept of a cadastre for maintaining land tenure information has been around since the *Domesday Book* was developed in the eleventh century in England (Barnes 1990). In Latin America it is often interpreted as an information system for property taxation purposes, reflecting the early generation of cadastres designed for this purpose in Europe. But since those early times, the cadastre, or more specifically the legal cadastre, has come to mean a land information system that defines the legal dimensions and geolocation of the primary tenure unit: the parcel. It can be distinguished from a geographic information system (GIS), commonly used in land and resource management, through the following attributes:

- It is updated transactionally, not periodically, thereby remaining current.
- It is linked to the property registry, which describes the formally recognized tenure rights.
- It contains a complete record of all parcels in a jurisdiction.
- The emphasis is on legal tenure information as opposed to natural resource information.
- The basic spatial unit is the cadastral parcel.

A cadastre has also been recognized as a device for organizing, administering, and controlling people by centralized state structures (Scott 1998). We accept that historically the cadastre has been used for social engineering, but in this chapter we view the cadastre as a community tool for understanding who holds what rights where. Furthermore, we do not see it as necessarily a "neoliberal tool" for facilitating private, individual tenure but rather as a means of improving land and resource administration in the increasingly sophisticated transactional environment that is occurring in a number of community tenure systems. Finally, we believe it is an appropriate tool only in community tenure systems in which property-based transactions are going on inside the polygon and rights to resources are being divided internally. We argue that compiling geographic information on resources for purposes of land and resource management is only half the picture. As these systems become more transactionally complex, often driven by the need for more perfect information both internally and externally, some form of community cadastre may be needed to provide the sort of tenure security that many accept as a sine qua non for intergenerational resource protection (Otsuka and Place 2001).

The question addressed in this section is, Is it time to begin thinking about a community cadastre that would support and facilitate sustainable extraction? Cadastral initiatives in Latin America and elsewhere have promoted the decentralization of cadastral institutions, but this has typically reached only the county or municipal level. Furthermore, the focus has generally been on land under private, individual tenure, not under community tenure. Cadastral experience in Latin America has shown that it is difficult to update the cadastral information, and as informal transactions resume the formal cadastre will increasingly become outdated. This is particularly true in communities where there are small landholdings, often spread across several distinct parcels, and where land transactions are limited primarily to community members. In many of these cases the cost of formalizing a transaction may exceed the value of the land. We argue that in such cases the only viable option is to develop a community cadastre that is administered by the local community.

The three scenarios presented in the previous section of this chapter illustrate the need for more detailed tenure information. The concept of a conservation concession (Guatemala) necessitates information that supports the transfer of usufruct rights in individual trees or at least small blocks of forest. This information is both spatial and legal in nature. The transfer of deforestation rights scenario (Brazil) takes a specific right from one bundle of rights and transfers it to another bundle of rights in a different location. Keeping track of transactions of the individual sticks in the bundle, as opposed to the whole bundle, also necessitates more specific cadastral information. In addition, this information must be linked to land cover information if deforestation is to be properly monitored. In the third scenario (Mexico), the conversion of land under individual tenure to indivisible tenure necessitates cadastral information on specific parcels within the parcelized agricultural area of the *ejido*.

As the bundle of rights in any individual property is split apart and placed under different tenure regimes involving multiple parties, both inside and outside the polygon, the need for detailed cadastral information will increase. We believe the only realistic approach is to develop local capacity to manage this information within a community cadastre. This would not necessarily entail high-tech computerized information systems, but capacity would need to be developed to manage spatial and textual information using an appropriate level of technology.

CONCLUSION

We have examined three distinct tenure responses to the challenge of facilitating both conservation and development (see table 9.1). The cases of the extractive reserves in Brazil and the *ejidos* in Mexico demonstrate that the inside of a communally owned or managed polygon is not a homogeneous common property but a complex mix of individual and group rights that is becoming increasingly disaggregated. In the *ejidos*, transactions are allowed both internally and externally, involving third parties outside the polygon. These tenure arrangements play a crucial role in describing the socioecological relationships in the community. They describe the institutions, rules, rights, and obligations with respect to the use of forest and other land-based resources. However, land and resource tenure is dynamic, and we have presented three scenarios that incorporate innovative tenure approaches toward emerging demands of conservation and development. These scenarios have already played out in developed countries such as the United States and are being seriously contemplated in the tropical tenure systems described in this chapter.

Finally, we conclude that a community-based information system or cadastre would be a useful tool for conservation and development, particularly where resource rights are being actively disaggregated internally from a pure communal property situation and transacted both externally and internally. Information on resources alone is only half of the socioecological equation; what is lacking is valuable cadastral information that ties individuals or groups to the resources and promotes the sustainable use of these resources now and in the next generation.

NOTES

1. See *Penn Central Transp. Co v. New York City*, 438 U.S. 104, 98 S.Ct. 2646, 57 L.Ed.2d 631, where the New York City Landmarks Preservation Law of 1965 was challenged as being unconstitutional by Penn Central Transportation Co. The court held that the law was constitutional and did not constitute a taking of property.

2. The Utilization Plan (Art. 16) of the Chico Mendes Agro-Extractive Reserve in Cachoeira specifies 10 percent of the area of the *colocação,* which cannot exceed 30 ha.

3. This scenario was presented by Brazilian researchers during a workshop sponsored by the United States Agency for International Development in the context of large private Amazonian land holdings, where the deforestation limit is 20 percent for individual holdings.

REFERENCES

Agrawal, A. 2001. Common property institutions and sustainable governance of resources. *World Development* 29: 1649–1672.

Alcorn, J. and V. Toledo. 1998. Resilient resource management in Mexico's forest ecosystems: The contribution of property rights. In F. Berkes and C. Folke, eds., *Linking social and ecological systems,* 216–249. Cambridge, U.K.: Cambridge University Press.

Barnes, G. 1990. The evolution of the cadastre concept: From *Domesday Book* to LIS/GIS network. *Surveying and Land Information Systems Journal* 50: 5–9.

Beavers, J. 1995. *Tenure and forest exploitation in the Peten and Franja Transversal del Norte regions of Guatemala.* Washington, D.C.: World Bank, Guatemala and Natural Resource and Management Study.

Bowles, I., A. Rosenfeld, C. Kormos, C. Reining, J. Nations, and T. Ankersen. 1999. The environmental impacts of international finance corporation lending and proposals for reform: A case study of conservation and oil development in the Guatemalan Peten. *Environmental Law* 29: 103–132.

Bromley, D. and M. Cernea. 1989. *The management of common property resources: Some conceptual and operational fallacies.* World Bank Discussion Paper no. 57. Washington, D.C.: World Bank.

Bruce, J. and L. Fortmann. 1992. Property and forestry. In P. Nemetz, ed., *Emerging issues in forest policy,* 471–496. Vancouver, B.C.: UBC Press.

CONAP. 1994. *Normas de adjudicación de concesiones.* Guatemala City, Guatemala.

CONAP. 1996a. *Asentamientos humanos en las diferentes zonas de la Reserva de la Biosfera Maya: Derechos y obligaciones.* Guatemala City, Guatemala.

CONAP. 1996b. *Plan maestro de la Reserva de la Biosfera Maya.* Guatemala City, Guatemala.

De Aguinaga, A. 1993. The new agrarian law: Mexico's way out. *St. Mary's Law Journal* 24: 883–901.

Dugelby, B. 1998. Governmental and customary arrangements guiding chicle latex extraction in Peten, Guatemala. In R. Primack, D. Bray, H. Galletti, and I. Ponciano, eds., *Timber, tourists and temples: Conservation and development in the Maya Forest of Belize, Guatemala and Mexico,* 155–178. Washington, D.C.: Island Press.

Dyer, M. I. and M. M. Holland. 1991. The biosphere reserve concept: Needs for a network design. *BioScience* 41: 319.

ELI. 1995. *Brazil's extractive reserves: Fundamental aspects of their implementation.* Washington, D.C.: Environmental Law Institute Research Report.

Forster, N and D. Stanfield. 1993. *Tenure regimes and forest management: Case studies in Latin America.* Land Tenure Center Report. Madison: University of Wisconsin.

Galleti, H. 1998. The Maya Forest of Quintana Roo: Thirteen years of conservation and community development. In R. Primack, D. Bray, H. Galletti, and I. Ponciano, eds., *The Maya Forest of Belize, Guatemala and Mexico,* 33–46. Washington, D.C.: Island Press.

Garrett, W., ed. 1989. La Ruta Maya. *National Geographic* 176(4): 424–479.

Gomes, C. V. 2001. *Dynamics of land use in an Amazonian extractive reserve: The case of the Chico Mendes Extractive Reserve in Acre, Brazil.* M.S. thesis, Latin American Studies, University of Florida, Gainesville.

Gretzinger, S. 1998. Community forest concessions: An economic alternative for the Maya Biosphere Reserve in the Peten, Guatemala. In R. Primack, D. Bray, H. Galletti, and I. Ponciano, eds., *Timber, tourists and temples: Conservation and development in the Maya Forest of Belize, Guatemala and Mexico,* 111–124. Washington, D.C.: Island Press.

Gustanski, J. and R. Squires, eds. 2000. *Protecting the land: Conservation easements past, present, and future.* Washington, D.C.: Island Press.

Kaimowitz, D. 1995. *Land tenure, land markets and natural resource management by large landowners in the Peten and Northern Transversal of Guatemala.* Paper presented at the 1995 meeting of the Latin American Studies Association, Washington, D.C., September 28–30, 1995.

Melone, M. 1993. The struggle of the *seringueiros:* Environmental action in the Amazon. In J. Friedmann and H. Rangan, eds., *In defense of livelihood: Comparative studies on environmental action,* 106–126. West Hartford, Conn.: Kumarian Press.

Mendes, C. 1989. *Fight for the forest: Chico Mendes in his own words.* London: Latin America Bureau (Research and Action) Ltd.

Murrieta, J. L. and R. P. Rueda. 1995. *Reservas extractivistas*. Gland, Switzerland: IUCN.

Nations, J., R. Primack, and D. Bray, 1998. Introduction: The Maya Forest. In R. Primack, D. Bray, H. Galletti, and I. Ponciano, eds., *Timber, tourists and temples: Conservation and development in the Maya Forest of Belize, Guatemala and Mexico*, xiii–xx. Washington, D.C.: Island Press.

Ostrum, E. 1990. *Governing the commons: The evolution of institutions for collective action*. Cambridge, U.K.: Cambridge University Press.

Otsuka, K. and F. Place. 2001. *Land tenure and natural resource management: A comparative study of agrarian communities in Asia and Africa*. Baltimore: Johns Hopkins University Press.

Ponciano, I. 1998. Forest policy and protected areas in the Peten, Guatemala. In R. Primack, D. Bray, H. Galletti, and I. Ponciano, eds., *Timber, tourists and temples: Conservation and development in the Maya Forest of Belize, Guatemala and Mexico*, 99–110. Washington, D.C.: Island Press.

Schmink, M. and C. Wood. 1992. *Contested frontiers in Amazonia*. New York: Columbia University Press.

Schwartz, N. 1990. *Forest society: A social history of Peten, Guatemala*. Philadelphia: University of Pennsylvania Press.

Scott, J. C. 1998. *Seeing like a state*. New Haven, Conn.: Yale University Press.

Snook, L. 1998. Sustaining harvests of mahogany (*Swietenia macrophylla*) from Mexico's Yucatan forests: Past, present and future. In R. Primack, D. Bray, H. Galletti, and I. Ponciano, eds., *Timber, tourists and temples: Conservation and development in the Maya Forest of Belize, Guatemala and Mexico*, 61–80. Washington, D.C.: Island Press.

World Bank. 2001. *Mexico land policy: A decade after the ejido reform*. World Bank Report no. 22187-ME. Washington, D.C.: World Bank.

Chapter 10

AIMING FOR SUSTAINABLE COMMUNITY FOREST MANAGEMENT

THE EXPERIENCES OF TWO COMMUNITIES IN MEXICO AND HONDURAS

Catherine Tucker

In a context of global deforestation, and despite widespread good intentions to protect forests, sustainable forest management has proved elusive. Not only do forests comprise highly complex and inadequately understood ecosystems, but they are also subject to competing demands and conflicts between stakeholders in the international, national, and local arenas. With few exceptions, the people who live in or near forests have been excluded from policymaking relevant to the resources on which they depend. This situation has contributed to increasing social inequities, deforestation, and failures of national policies (Ascher 1995; cf. Klooster 1996, Agrawal 2000). Many local populations have struggled to assert their rights to forests. Although successful grassroots efforts to assert rights and manage forests remain the exception to the rule, such cases provide insights to the potential of community organization to challenge unfavorable policies, promote local development, and govern natural resources. This study focuses on the experiences of two communities, one in Mexico and the other in Honduras, that have tried to conserve their forests and derive economic benefit from them.

In the early 1980s, Mexico and Honduras experienced rising local resistance to national forest policies. The *municipio* (similar to a county) of Capulalpam de Méndez (hereafter Capulalpam) in Oaxaca participated in this trend by joining a regional protest to end timber concessions. In Honduras, the *municipio* of La Campa demonstrated its resistance by beginning efforts to terminate contracts for its timber that had been granted to sawmills by the Honduran Forestry Development Corporation (CO-

HDEFOR). Both of these cases involved local movements to gain control over forest resources in the face of state intervention, problematic forest policies, and globalization. These communities' protests culminated in apparent success: The Mexican concessions ended, and COHDEFOR left La Campa. With time, Honduras and Mexico responded to internal and international pressures to devolve certain rights over natural resource management to the local level. This study points to the complexities and the promise of collective action, particularly as collective action relates to community forestry, and the tensions that exist as communities attempt to balance development with conservation in an increasingly global economy. The discussion focuses on two questions: What factors contributed to successful collective action, and how have these communities fared in their efforts to manage their forests wisely?

DATA COLLECTION

This chapter draws on eighteen months of research conducted in Honduras between 1993 and 2000 and three months of field work conducted in Mexico between 1996 and 2001. Methods used to collect data included household surveys, censuses, archival research, and informal and formal interviews with community members, local authorities, and regional officials. At both sites, ethnographic work was supplemented by participatory rural appraisals and forest mensuration carried out by an interdisciplinary, multinational team of investigators (Tucker 1999a, Tucker et al. 1999).

FOREST RESOURCES AND POLICIES IN MEXICO AND HONDURAS

The sustainable management of forest resources represents a critical challenge for Mexico and Honduras, which have extensive forest resources and problems with deforestation. Between 1964 and 1980, Honduras lost nearly a quarter of its forest cover; today barely 65 percent of the land remains in forest (Utting 1993:10, Pineda Portillo 1997:279–280). Mexico's forest area fell by almost 30 percent between 1970 and 1990 (Merino Pérez 1997:141). The challenge of community forestry is particularly notable in Mexico because *ejidos* and indigenous communities own nearly 80 percent of Mexico's forests (Cabarle et al. 1997, Snook 1997:19). Both nations face economic challenges, but their situations differ. Mexico is the largest and wealthiest nation of the Mesoamerican region; Honduras is among the poorest. Mexico produces oil and has more natural resources than Honduras, which struggles to overcome poverty, extreme indebtedness, and a history in which banana companies and outside powers have often exercised inordinate influence to obtain land rights, beneficial infrastructure, and national policies favorable to their business and political interests (Lapper and Painter 1985, cf. Enloe 1989:133–135, Euraque 1996).

Forest policies in Mexico and Honduras contributed to circumstances that provoked community protests in the 1980s. From 1940 to 1980, Mexico attempted to control deforestation with logging bans in overexploited regions while granting concessions in less exploited regions to foster the development of forest industries (Klooster 2000:288). Honduras permitted forest concessions until 1974, when it nationalized trees and the timber export trade with the passage of Decree 103. The law aimed to capture foreign exchange generated by timber trade and gain income for national development (Ascher 2000:14–15). Decree 103 created COHDEFOR and charged it with competing mandates: It was to develop forest industries but also protect forests and watersheds (Utting 1993:136–138). COHDEFOR had the power to grant timber contracts regardless of the land's ownership. In both nations, policies discouraged private and community forest owners from making management decisions. Stumpage fees were set at a fraction of the market value (Bray 1991:16, Tucker 1996:282). Mexico's concessions intended to encourage businesses to manage forests wisely, but the laws were loosely enforced. Concessionaires had few incentives to conserve the resource. In Honduras, businesses received contracts for specified timber quantities. COHDEFOR foresters marked the areas where logging could occur and which trees would be left as seed trees, but enforcement proved ephemeral (Tucker 1999a; cf. AFE-COHDEFOR 1996:204). Mexico and Honduras experienced similar processes; profits accrued largely to the concessionaires and sawmills while communities whose forests were logged faced forest degradation with minimal compensation (Utting 1993:145, Klooster 1996:150, Tucker 1996:281–285, Ganz and Burckle 2002:34, 37).

THE EMERGENCE OF COMMUNITY FORESTRY

Community and social forestry gained attention in the 1970s and 1980s as a way to achieve sustainable management of forest resources and provide benefits to populations living in and near forests (Government of India 1973, cited in Cernea 1992; Gadgil and Vartok 1976, FAO 1978, Arnold 1992). The theoretical foundations for community-based approaches held that local control and benefits were essential prerequisites for successful conservation. When local users gain legal rights to forest ownership and management, it is reasoned that they have greater livelihood security and improved incentives for wise management through the legal exploitation and marketing of forest products. In addition, the resource and the people may benefit from the integration of indigenous knowledge into local management practices. Conservationists expect that biodiversity and natural resources become more relevant to local populations when they have a stake in economic benefits and preservation (Cabarle et al. 1997, Schelhas et al. 2001). Studies of common property institutions offer support for social forestry by showing that groups can self-organize to manage resources effectively when fundamental conditions are met, such as recognized rights to the resource (Berkes et al. 1989, Ostrom 1990, McKean and Ostrom 1995). Moreover, community forestry has the potential to reduce government expenditures by devolving some of the responsibilities for forest protection and management to local communities (Runge 1986; cf. Mayo and Craig 1995).

Mexico and Honduras designed policies in the 1970s to permit community participation in forestry, but in reality they allowed little local autonomy over forest management (Utting 1993:139). In Mexico, the national Forestry Subministry (Subsecretaria Forestal) promoted community silviculture policies (ca. 1975) to spur production in less accessible regions where large companies could not operate. These policies marked a shift toward socially oriented forestry, but they did not apply to communities with concessions (Carabias Lillo et al. 2000:15, Merino Pérez et al. 2000:132–133). In Honduras, the Social Forestry System that began in 1974 intended to provide rural populations with direct and indirect benefits from forest protection and production, to ensure their participation in development. The Social Forestry System encouraged communities to form groups for resin tapping; it also supported the formation of manual sawmill cooperatives, but few became operational (Stanley 1991, SECPLAN/DESFIL/USAID 1989:148–149, AFE-COHDEFOR 1996:176–177, 187, 203–204). Honduran forestry technicians maintained a high degree of control and intervention. Although some resin-tapping cooperatives proved profitable and enduring, many cooperatives foundered with organizational problems and volatile market prices. Support for the Social Forestry System waned through the 1980s as results proved disappointing (AFE-COHDEFOR 1996).

OVERVIEW AND DESCRIPTION OF THE COMMUNITIES

The study communities share several similarities that facilitate comparison. The populations are descended from indigenous peoples; although most inhabitants no longer speak native languages, their heritage endures through rituals and beliefs. Both communities obtained communal land

Table 10.1   Forest Characteristics of Capulalpam and La Campa

	Capulalpam, Mexico (N = 64 plots)[a]	La Campa, Honduras (N = 79 plots)[a]
Dominant tree species	Quercus spp.[b]	Pinus oocarpa
Dominant species basal area	13.11 m²/ha	11.09 m²/ha
Codominant species	Pinus spp.[c]	Quercus spp.[d]
Codominant species basal area (trees[e])	13.00 m²/ha	1.67 m²/ha
Total basal area (trees[e])	31.61 m²/ha	12.95 m²/ha

[a]Plots were randomly selected for a subset of the forest area. In Capulalpam, a total of 20,096 m² was sampled in 1906 ha of forest, composed of the management areas defined as silvicultural forest, domestic use forest, and wildlife refuge. In La Campa, a total of 24,612 m² was sampled in 629 ha of forest, composed of four private forests, three communal forest areas (designated woodlots and forest pasture), and the resin-tapping cooperatives' forest, all of which had been affected by logging or resin tapping before 1987.

[b]Q. laurina and Quercus spp. that could not be identified at a species level.

[c]P. leyofil, P. oaxacana, P. oocarpa, P. rudis, P. patula, P. pseudostrobus, and P. teocote.

[d]Q. sapotaefolia, Q. peduncularis var. sublanosa, and several unidentified oaks.

[e]Trees are defined as having a diameter at breast height of at least 10 cm.

titles during the colonial period. The communities are located in mountainous areas with steep slopes, generally thin soils, and inadequate infrastructure. Pine and oak trees dominate the natural vegetation (table 10.1), and forests provide important environmental services such as watershed protection. The forests have a long history of human intervention under low population densities, at least since the population declines associated with the Spanish conquest (Newson 1986; Díaz-Polanco and Burguete 1996). The people use many forest products, particularly firewood, timber, and forest pasture. The cultivation of maize and beans is central to their culture and their diet; slash-and-burn agriculture once was the most important factor in forest transformation. Both regions experience periodic forest fires caused by natural events and human activities. Community members fight forest fires cooperatively, and human-caused forest fires have declined since the communities regained forest management rights. Moreover, slash-and-burn methods, often associated with forest fires, have become rare as farmers adopted intensive agricultural methods and soil conservation measures (Tucker et al. 1999, Southworth and Tucker 2001).

Capulalpam de Méndez, Mexico

Capulalpam de Méndez (hereafter Capulalpam) is located approximately 60 km northeast of Oaxaca City, in the Sierra Juarez (part of the Sierra

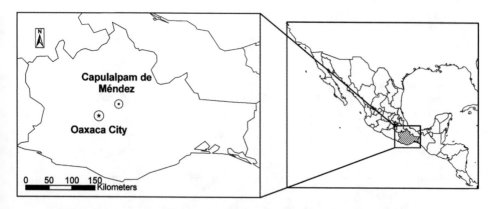

Figure 10.1   Location of Capulalpam de Méndez in the State of Oaxaca with reference to Mexico.

Norte) of Oaxaca (figure 10.1). This Zapotec community, composed of a single settlement, had a population of 1424 at the time of field work in 1999. The *municipio* covers an area of 3665 ha; more than 88 percent is forested (table 10.2). Historically, many men worked in a nearby silver mine. Today nearly half of the households have a member employed in a salaried position in business, education, or government, a number of them in the neighboring *municipio* of Ixtlán or Oaxaca City (Salazar Ventura et al. 1999).

The community has strong institutions for self-government. The Asamblea de Comuneros (Community Members' Assembly, hereafter Asamblea) oversees communal lands, including forests. The Asamblea meets regularly and involves all men born in the community (*comuneros*), widows of *comuneros* (*comuneras*), and a few immigrants who have passed a trial period to become *comuneros*. The Asamblea makes decisions regarding management of communal land, forest use, and protection of municipal borders. *Comuneros* must serve the community in capacities related to the traditional cargo system, through which they fulfill increasingly important ritual responsibilities and official capacities as they gain experience. All of the community's adult male residents, regardless of whether they are *comuneros*, are expected to provide periodic labor contributions, or *tequios*, for community projects, infrastructural maintenance, and border protection (Tucker et al. 1999).

Before the 1960s, Capulalpam's forests did not experience heavy logging. The community permitted selective logging of the pine forests to supply beams for the silver mine. Most of the forest was not logged because it was inaccessible. In 1955, the Mexican government

Table 10.2   Summary Data for Capulalpam and La Campa

	Capulalpam, Mexico[a]	La Campa, Honduras
Total area	4,144 ha	12,805 ha
Total forest area	3,665 ha[b]	8,643 ha[c]
Percentage of area in forest	88.4%	67.5%
Area in agriculture, settlements, and other nonforest	479 ha	4,162 ha[d]
Area planted in coffee	0[e]	255.5 ha[f]
Average annual precipitation	1,800 mm	1,300 mm[g]
Elevation range	2,005–3,080 m	1,130–1,800 m
Mean slope	26°	19°

[a]Tucker et al. (1999).

[b]Forest area as defined by Capulalpam's 1993 management plan and verified by field observations. It includes open canopy forest, dense canopy forest, regenerating areas, and some patches without significant tree cover. The latter include rocky outcroppings and small clearings within the forest, so the total forest cover is slightly overestimated. This total also includes a forested area of 1241 ha that Capulalpam claims but that is under litigation because of competing claims by two neighboring municipalities.

[c]Based on analysis of a Landsat Thematic Mapper satellite image from March 17, 1996. Southworth and Tucker (2001) describe the methods used for image registration, calibration, and classification. Forest includes areas with more than 25% canopy cover based on forest measurements. With few exceptions this excludes shade-grown coffee fields, which in La Campa tend to have less than 25% canopy cover because of recent establishment.

[d]Agriculture includes agricultural fields (including coffee), house gardens, pastures, and young fallows. Settlements include village areas, house lots, and sports fields.

[e]Coffee does not grow in Capulalpam because of its high elevation and low temperatures.

[f]J. Zelaya, president, La Campa AHPROCAFE (pers. comm., August 18, 1998).

[g]Tucker (1996).

granted most of the Sierra Juarez as a concession to Fabricas de Papel Tuxtepec (FAPATUX), a paper mill in northern Oaxaca. Under the concession, communities could sell timber only to the concessionaire, and they could not run their own forest enterprises (Klooster 1996:148, Bray 1997:24–25, Anta Fonseca et al. 2000:18). By the 1960s the paper mill was extracting timber from Capulalpam. FAPATUX paid Capulalpam a fixed fee for timber rights but gave men employment as lumberjacks (Tucker et al. 1999; cf. Ganz and Burckle 2002:35). Capulalpam's elders recall that they soon became dissatisfied with the concession's low wages. Regionally, strikes in demand of better wages occurred from 1967 to 1971 (Carabias Lillo et al. 2000:18–19). Frustration with FAPATUX and its environmental impacts grew through the 1970s.

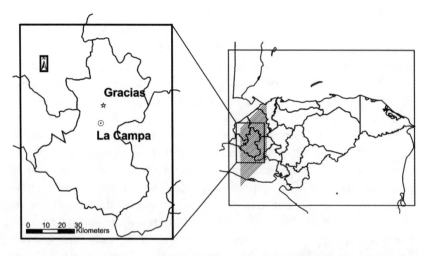

Figure 10.2   Location of La Campa in the Department of Lempira with reference to Honduras.

La Campa, Honduras

La Campa is located in the Department of Lempira, barely 16 km from Gracias, the departmental capital (figure 10.2). Approximately 5000 people live in the *municipio,* which encompasses nine villages and nearly 12,805 ha. More than 60 percent of the area is pine–oak forest (Southworth and Tucker 2001). The majority of the population, descendants of the Lenca people, depend on subsistence production of maize and beans, with occasional migration to Honduras's major cities for temporary jobs in factories, construction, and domestic service.

A council composed of locally elected officials and representatives from each of the villages governs the *municipio.* The council is the principal decision-making entity for the management of municipal land. Although council members are male, any male or female resident can attend council meetings and submit complaints or requests. The council resolves disputes, grants individual usufruct to land, plans projects, and establishes regulations. Residents must contribute labor to municipal projects and serve as representatives when nominated. Although most of the land is held under communal village and municipal titles (a small number of residents have obtained private title), individuals have de facto private rights to agricultural fields, house lots, and pastures (Tucker 1999b:207).

La Campa experienced minimal logging until the 1970s. In 1973 a regional sawmill owner negotiated with the council to harvest 5000 m³ of timber. Within months, the contract was nullified by the passage of Decree 103. Thereafter, the sawmill obtained a permit through COHDEFOR for a lower timber price than that negotiated with La Campa. The sawmill and its successors did not employ local labor, so La Campa's men did not learn logging methods. The *municipio* had to petition COHDEFOR to receive payment for the timber, and sawmill vehicles damaged roads and bridges (Tucker 1996:273–303).

Logging and its ramifications caused resentment, but COHDEFOR's Social Forestry Program initially counteracted it. The program employed residents for work in forests (clearing underbrush, thinning saplings) and provided payment with staple foods. Three resin-tapping cooperatives formed in La Campa, but resin prices proved volatile. Price shocks in the late 1970s and mid-1980s led to resignations of resin tappers from cooperatives. Moreover, the market was controlled by only a few resin-processing companies, and they kept prices low. Throughout Honduras, the Social Forestry Program faltered as market prices, problems with CO-HDEFOR, and local organizational difficulties constrained most cooperatives' success (Stanley 1991, Utting 1993:139, AFE-COHDEFOR 1996).

COHDEFOR imposed harsh fines on Lacamperos who harvested even a few trees without authorization. Although Lacamperos could obtain permits to cut trees for carpentry, tempering artisanal pottery, or house construction, they found the bureaucratic process and travel to the regional office to be costly and time-consuming. By contrast, COHDEFOR officials did not apply sanctions to sawmills, despite flagrant environmental violations and excessive harvesting documented by COHDEFOR technicians. Residents found it profoundly unjust that sawmills overexploited their forests with impunity. The early 1980s brought increasing enmity between COHDEFOR and Lacamperos, but internal tensions in La Campa initially impeded efforts to organize against logging (Tucker 1996:299–311).

ORGANIZED RESISTANCE AND SUCCESSFUL COLLECTIVE ACTION

Capulalpam, Mexico

The preconditions for grassroots organization and resistance were laid in the labor and financial arrangements enforced by the concessionaire and the national government. Capulalpam's frustrations with FAPATUX had regional resonance, and in the late 1970s it joined with twelve other communities to form the Organization for the Defense of Natural Resources and Social Development of the Sierra Juárez (Organización en Defensa de los Recursos Naturales y el Desarrollo Social de la Sierra Juárez [OR-

DRENASIJ]). The organization included Zapotec and Chinantec communities. Despite different cultures and languages, they shared a common goal: ORDRENASIJ aimed to end the concession and obtain community rights to manage forests (Bray 1991, Ascher 1995:145, Carabias Lillo et al. 2000:18–19). When the FAPATUX concession came up for renewal in 1981, the government moved to renew it in perpetuity. ORDRENASIJ responded with passionate protest. Communities lobbied state and federal government representatives, formed alliances with sympathetic students and professionals, and publicized their position through the mass media. They refused to work for the concession, blocked roads, and threatened to damage logging equipment if FAPATUX operated in their forests (Bray 1991, Carabias Lillo et al. 2000:14–15, Wilshusen et al. 2002).

As resistance rose, the national government evaluated the concessions' performance. Profits were poor, and high-grading methods had proven unsustainable. Intact forests lay increasingly distant from roads, so additional transportation and road-building costs would be incurred to extract timber. Community resistance further interfered with production and threatened to raise costs. The problems could not be resolved by enforcing the concessions' renewal. Moreover, many forestry technicians and development agencies supported greater community involvement in forest management. Social forestry provided an alternative to concessions and the potential to support local development. With the combination of community resistance, unprofitable concessions, and a viable alternative, the Mexican government decided in 1982 not to renew forest concessions (Bray 1991, Utting 1993:145).

La Campa, Honduras

In 1986, La Campa's relationship with COHDEFOR collapsed in the wake of two forest fires, one caused by a COHDEFOR "controlled burn" and another by careless loggers. More than 300 Lacamperos met to form the Society for the Defense of Village Rights (Patronato Pro-defensa de los Derechos del Pueblo [PPDP]). Similar to ORDRENASIJ, but on a smaller scale, PPDP gained support through meetings with the region's chief military officer, the governor, and a congressman. PPDP also sought legal counsel and met with a journalist from a national newspaper (Tucker 1996:318–323).

COHDEFOR responded to PPDP's activism by proposing the creation of a COHDEFOR office and an Integrated Management Area in La Campa, which would permit community involvement in forest management under COHDEFOR supervision (AFE-COHDEFOR 1996:176). Lacamperos interpreted the proposal as a COHDEFOR stratagem to increase its domination.

Subsequently, COHDEFOR issued a new timber contract and compelled La Campa's mayor to sign it. PPDP responded by taking their mayor hostage and blocking an access road. A national newspaper published a story on La Campa's efforts to end logging in the *municipio*. PPDP called on the governor, the parish priest, and Lempira's military leadership to intervene; in the following week the parties met in La Campa. COHDEFOR agreed to end its activity in La Campa, but it retained the right to return if La Campa allowed commercial forest production. La Campa banned logging and restricted harvesting to local needs (Tucker 1996:322–325).

WHAT FACTORS CONTRIBUTED TO SUCCESSFUL COLLECTIVE ACTION?

The successful grassroots organization that gained forest rights for Capulalpam and La Campa in the 1980s resulted from the interaction of local, regional, and national circumstances. At the local level, they had experience with local governance and self-organization; this prepared them to act jointly against more powerful interest groups and subsequently create institutions to manage common property forests. In the Sierra Norte, ORDRENASIJ drew on a shared history of strategic resistance and skillful accommodations to the Mexican state to build a regional movement that crossed ethnic and linguistic lines (cf. Anta Fonseca et al. 2000, Carabias Lillo et al. 2000). Secure land titles probably contributed to the communities' confidence that they would benefit from their efforts if they could regain rights to manage forests for their own purposes.

At the regional level, timber businesses faced growing costs for road construction, log extraction, and transportation. The emergence of strong community resistance coincided with administrative and management shortcomings in Mexican concessions and COHDEFOR that undermined their viability. At the national level, environmental institutions and forest laws had failed to meet public and political expectations, creating conditions that were conducive to change (Peckenham and Street 1985:239–244, Bray 1991, Jansen 1998:7–8). Organized protests and media coverage won public support, and the movements found political allies. International donor agencies also influenced the process as national economic woes led to structural adjustment programs. In these complex circumstances, the national governments chose not to respond with oppressive tactics, the potential costs of which presumably were judged to exceed the potential benefits. Thus, multiple pressures contributed to the official decision to recognize community rights to forest management (Bray 1991) and revise policies. The new laws that were implemented brought new opportunities and challenges for Capulalpam and La Campa.

HOW HAVE THESE COMMUNITIES FARED IN THEIR EFFORTS TO MANAGE THEIR FORESTS WISELY?

Capulalpam, Mexico

The end of the concessions gave Capulalpam the right to manage its own forests. In 1986, a new forest law was approved; it increased national support for community forestry. But that same year, Mexico's incorporation into the General Agreement on Tariffs and Trade (GATT) negated many elements of the new law. GATT lifted controls on market prices, reduced tariffs and import substitution policies, and cut national funding for public projects. Subsequently, the Mexican government privatized financial institutions, which led to more restrictive lending procedures and reduced credit availability for small-scale producers (Biles and Pigozzi 2000:4–6, Carabias Lillo et al. 2000:94–95). These conditions posed a challenge for the development of community forestry enterprises.

Communities in the Sierra Norte faced internal and external obstacles to managing their forests. *Comuneros* had gained practical experience in forest harvesting in the concession years, but communities lacked people with the experience necessary to run a forest enterprise (Bray 1991, Ascher 1995:146–147). Moreover, communities had to meet legally set, national standards for forest management plans and pay for expensive technical services. In 1989, Capulalpam joined with four other communities to form the Zapotec and Chinantec Union (UZACHI) to develop sustainable forestry enterprises, share the costs of technical forestry services, and train their own people in forestry. UZACHI sought technical and organizational training from a regional nongovernmental organization (NGO), Estudios Rurales y Asesoría (ERA). The NGO worked with the UZACHI communities, providing advice and practical training (Bray 1991, Ascher 1995:146–147). To meet national regulations, Capulalpam worked with ERA to develop a forest management plan.

The Asamblea purchased a sawmill and created the position of sawmill manager, to which a member is elected every two to four years. The system maintains control under the Asamblea, but the cost of training is high, and managers' inexperience has led to shortcomings in sawmill operations. *Comuneros* have begun to consider hiring a permanent manager, but they are concerned that this change would necessitate hiring an outsider, devolve too much power, and constrain Asamblea control. Despite management challenges, the sawmill has proven profitable, and the Asamblea reinvests the profits in community projects. The Asamblea approves harvest levels far below those recommended by UZACHI foresters, yet lumber sales have provided income to build a new health center and a high school, pave the town's main roads, and pay for community fiestas.

The community sought to strengthen its technical knowledge and debated how to integrate scientific approaches with local traditions and priorities. A major strategy was to provide technical training for young people. An UZACHI technician explains the approach: "We can say that the people already have much of the understanding needed for natural resource management, but at a certain moment, through the assistance of outside people, we combine traditional elements with technical elements of management" (Carabias Lillo et al. 2000:30).

The passage of the North American Free Trade Agreement (NAFTA) in 1994 subjected Mexico's forestry enterprises to increased international pressures. Lower-cost lumber from the United States flooded the Mexican market, and community forestry enterprises faced difficulties as they were forced to compete with U.S. prices (Bray 1997:6, Richards 1997). In an effort to strengthen enterprises threatened by the impacts of NAFTA, Mexico's National Development Plan (1995–2000) has encouraged financial and technical support for Oaxaca's forest sector. Mexico gained support from the World Bank and the Japanese Development Agency to encourage and strengthen community forestry. The funding led to a series of programs: Programa de Desarrollo Forestal, Programa Nacional de Reforestación, and Programa para Conservación y Manejo Forestal (PRO-CYMAF) (Anta Fonseca et al. 2000). Capulalpam actively pursued the potential assistance.

In 1997, Capulalpam and the other UZACHI communities obtained certification from SmartWood and the Forest Stewardship Council (FSC) for sustainable forestry. A U.S. forester, a Mexican ecologist, and a Mexican rural sociologist conducted the certification evaluation over nine months. UZACHI and Capulalpam shared the costs of the team's ground transportation, food, and lodging; UZACHI paid the team's honorariums, and SmartWood covered the teams' airfare (F. Chapela, pers. comm. 2002). The community hoped that certification would result in higher lumber prices (Anta Fonseca et al. 2000). Unfortunately the market demand for certified lumber has remained low, but Capulalpam maintains its commitment to sustainable forestry and renewed its FSC certification in 2001. The second evaluation proceeded under similar arrangements, but the World Wildlife Fund and PROCYMAF covered part of the costs.

Moreover, the evaluation was expanded to include chain-of-custody certification (F. Chapela, pers. comm. 2002).

Seeking to diversify its forestry business, Capulalpam is exploring ways to harvest and market nontimber forest products. Individuals collect local matzutake mushrooms for export to Japan and grow shiitake mushrooms on oak logs thinned from the forest to sell in regional markets (D. Dodds, pers. comm. 2002; Anta Fonseca et al. 2000:114–115). Capulalpam has more forest cover today than when FAPATUX departed, and several of the experimental silvicultural treatments have resulted in rapid regeneration. Despite clear successes, the community faces questions of whether it should hire a permanent sawmill manager to improve efficiency and how to market its products more effectively (Tucker et al. 1999).

La Campa, Honduras

The years of COHDEFOR domination over La Campa's forests led to a pent-up demand for agricultural land and created a new demand for private forests. After COHDEFOR's departure, farmers laid claim to logged areas that were flat and suitable for agriculture. Logged areas on steep slopes, unsuitable for farming, began to regenerate. Farmers with sufficient labor and financial resources fenced land for private woodlots with council approval. This broke with custom; historically, usufruct was recognized only if a farmer cleared the land within six months of council permission to claim the parcel. After COHDEFOR's intervention, people saw advantages in privately held forests (Tucker 1999a).

In the late 1980s, agronomists representing Honduras's coffee institute (Instituto Hondureño del Café) visited La Campa and its few coffee plantations. The agronomists declared La Campa's highlands suitable for growing export-quality coffee and provided information on national programs that supported coffee production. The municipal council welcomed the news that La Campa qualified for a national subsidy under Decree 175-87 that funded roads in coffee-producing *municipios* (cf. AFE-COHDEFOR 1996). Farmers who requested land for coffee received council support, although most of the land was in communal forests. Lacamperos' commitment to protecting highland forests waned with the incentives to grow coffee. By the mid-1990s, most of La Campa's highland forests (with the exception of areas designated for community woodlots and watershed protection) had been subdivided into usufruct plots, mainly by farmers who hoped to plant coffee. Even so, only 255.5 ha (less than 2 percent) of La Campa were planted in coffee by 1998 (J.

Zelaya, pers. comm. 1998). Planting proceeds slowly; coffee takes three years of expensive labor and chemical inputs before the first harvest, and local conditions necessitate that it be grown in shade. Many farmers cannot afford to cultivate coffee, and those who do have small plantations. La Campa's largest grower owns 14 ha in coffee; most have less than 1.5 ha (J. Zelaya, pers. comm. 1998).

By 1990 the Honduran government faced increasing pressure from international donor agencies to allow private enterprise to manage forests. COHDEFOR's budget was cut by 15 percent (Utting 1993:44), reflecting its failure to fulfill its contradictory responsibilities of promoting forest industries while also protecting forests. Meanwhile, Honduras faced continuing trade deficits, and structural adjustment programs required fundamental changes to favor export markets and private enterprise. The Agricultural Modernization and Development Law of 1992 addressed these issues. The law reverted the ownership of trees and productive decisions to the land's legal owners, and COHDEFOR's responsibilities were confined to forest conservation and evaluation of management plans under the National Forest Administration (AFE) (AFE-COHDEFOR 1996). Reforms to municipal laws also gave *municipios* legal rights and responsibilities to manage and conserve their natural resources. These policies gave La Campa a legal foundation for the rights they had claimed.

With the legal reforms, former resin tappers saw an opportunity to pressure the council for a resin-tapping permit. They proposed a resin-tapping reserve in lowland forests away from the coffee-producing region and agricultural fields. The council agreed in exchange for a harvesting fee. The resin tappers formed a new cooperative and entered into a contract with a privately owned resin-processing company based in Comayagua. The cooperative began operation in 1995, deeply in debt to AFE-COHDEFOR for the cost of the management plan and to the resin-processing company for the materials needed to tap and store the resin.

As coffee production gradually expanded and resin tapping resumed, La Campa's total area in pine–oak forest increased slightly between 1987 and 1996. Forests grew back in previously logged areas at lower elevations unsuitable for coffee. But the principal factor in forest regrowth appeared to be the abandonment of marginal agricultural plots, associated with agricultural intensification and adoption of chemical inputs (Southworth and Tucker 2001). The *municipio* also implemented rules over local harvesting of pine trees and enforced its logging ban. In 1995, La Campa received second place in a national competition to recognize successful cases of forest conservation (F. Amadeo Santos, pers. comm. 1997).

CONCLUSION

Both communities have achieved clear successes but also encountered challenges in forest management. They have built on a conviction that they could manage their forests more wisely than any outside entity. Capulalpam chose to harvest timber, pursue diversification into non-timber forest products, and use the profits for municipal development. Integral factors in its success include strong institutional arrangements, cooperation with neighboring communities to share the costs of technical services, and wise selection of advisors. Community institutions have gained experience with forest management and continue to expand their horizons. La Campa chose to ban logging and commercial sales of forest products because these activities would have necessitated COHDEFOR's continuing intervention. Distrust and anger at COHDEFOR stiffened the population's resolve. Policy changes in the 1990s opened the door for La Campa to pursue local forestry more autonomously, particularly resin tapping.

The community's human and natural resources influenced their choices. Capulalpam's men had worked as lumberjacks; they knew that logging could be profitable, and they believed it could be done sustainably. Despite the degradation that FAPATUX caused, the *municipio* still had commercially valuable timber within reach of feeder roads. By contrast, Lacamperos had not worked with the sawmills, so they did not perceive it as a feasible occupation. Most of La Campa's lowland forests had been stripped of commercially valuable timber by 1987, as low basal areas attest (table 10.1). Given their experience with sawmills, people doubt that logging can be accomplished without environmental degradation, so they continue to oppose it.

The ability of Capulalpam and La Campa to manage their community forests, despite different approaches, conform to theoretical expectations that secure tenure, strong local institutions, and organizational experience are fundamental components of successful common property institutions (Ostrom 1990; Stanley 1991). Moreover, theory argues that in order to organize collectively and manage resources jointly, people must share the understanding that the benefits will exceed the costs (Ostrom 1992; cf. Klooster 1996). The current cases provide support, as well as qualifications, for this tenet. Generally speaking, Capulalpam has been more effective in establishing a systematic approach to forest management, and it has obtained community as well as economic benefits from forest management while fostering an expansion in total forest area. Despite the trend in natural forest regrowth (particularly in the drier, lowland forests that are not suitable for coffee production), La Campa has faced more severe challenges to forest conservation than Capulalpam. Most of these threats relate to the economic pressures the population experiences. Other than subsistence uses, Lacamperos perceive few benefits from the forest, and most households have inadequate incomes or resources to meet basic needs. They recognize that the costs of increased forest protection—including organizational costs—would be high. Although the resin tappers' cooperative benefits from a forest product, it has operated with high debts since its inception, and resin prices remain volatile. Incentives for coffee production have led to forest clearing in the uplands. If these forests had been providing income or other highly valued benefits, perhaps the people would have been more committed to conserving highland forests.

Nevertheless, both communities value their forests for more than just economic benefits. Interviews with adults in both places reveal that many see forests as having social and aesthetic worth; they also recognize environmental services (e.g., watershed protection) along with the subsistence and market value of forest products. These perceptions appear to be related to their experiences of logging by external entities. Forest degradation and denial of their autonomy accentuated the recognition that forests are integral for their livelihoods and for their children's futures. As a result, Capulalpam's *comuneros* refuse to harvest as much timber as their own foresters recommend because many doubt that logging can be conducted without incurring environmental risks. For similar reasons, La Campa residents remain committed to the logging ban. Lacamperos have also resisted COHDEFOR pressure to thin the forests regenerating in formerly logged areas, even though thinning would remove less fit trees, improve tree growth, and bring money to municipal coffers through sales of poles. Coincidentally, a precipitous drop in coffee prices in the late 1990s evidently slowed the conversion of highland forests to coffee plantations.

These communities represent success stories for collective action and, with qualifications, for community forestry management. Their experiences of forest degradation by outside agents served as a catalyst not only for resistance but also for subsequent development of institutions for forest management. Their determination to govern their forests, resist temptations to permit extensive logging, and protect forests for the future was forged as they saw their forests ravaged by outside entities. But their collective action would have faced greater opposition had the broader contexts and public opinion not favored conciliatory responses by the national governments.

The future of community forest management remains unclear, for many threats to common property exist, and in some regions the failures outweigh the successes (Richards 1997, Campbell et al. 2001). Community forestry often is criticized for being less profitable and efficient than private forest industries, but this evaluation fails to recognize the value of sustainability (Ascher 2000:14). Market failures and systemic inequities exacerbate the challenges faced by communities to organize and benefit from their forests. Local decisions and actions may do little to change international processes but can mediate them and can prompt creative approaches. Collective action at the local level is a vital means for innovative responses to market integration and globalization (cf. Robinson 1998). Moreover, in Latin America common property survives among many indigenous groups and rural populations and provides a more promising context than other forms of tenure for achieving sustainable forest management and more equitable distribution of benefits from natural resources (Richards 1997). As Capulalpam and La Campa illustrate, the promise of community forestry endures. The alternative of denying local rights to resource management has a history of failure for resource conservation and local development. As one Oaxaca authority states, "Today you cannot talk of development, you cannot talk of conservation, if the opinions of the communities are not taken into account" (Carabias Lillo et al. 2000:110).

ACKNOWLEDGMENTS

A National Science Foundation Dissertation Improvement Program Grant (SBR-9307681) funded the 1993–1994 research in Honduras. Grants from the Social and Behavioral Science Institute of the University of Arizona and the Comins Fund of the Department of Anthropology at the University of Arizona provided support for Honduras research in 1995. Research in Mexico and Honduras in 1996, 1997, 1998, 1999, and 2000 was supported by the National Science Foundation (SBR-9521918) through the Center for the Study of Institutions, Population, and Environmental Change at Indiana University. Honduran field work benefited from the invaluable research assistance of Jessica Fonseca, Stephen McLaughlin, Martha Moreno, J. C. Randolph, José Rosa Sánchez, Jane Southworth, Paul Turner, José Atanacio Valentín, and Craig Wayson. In Mexico, the research team combined the talents of Krister Andersson, Jon Belmont, Theresa Burcsu, David Dodds, and Salvador Espinosa. The teams are deeply grateful to the people of Capulalpam and La Campa. Special thanks goes to Benjamin Luna, Ricardo Ramírez, Francisco Chapela, and the staffs of the Comisariado de Bienes Comunales, the Alcaldía Municipal, and UZACHI in Capulalpam. In Honduras, I am indebted to municipal council members (1992–2000), the Honduran Association of Coffee Producers in La Campa and Gracias, the COHDEFOR office in Gracias, and many more people than can be named.

REFERENCES

AFE-COHDEFOR, 1996. *Analisis del sub-sector forestal de Honduras.* Tegucigalpa, Honduras: Cooperación Hondureña-Alemana, Programa Social Forestal.

Agrawal, A. 2000. Small is beautiful, but is larger better? In C. Gibson, M. McKean, and E. Ostrom, eds., *People and forests: Communities, institutions and governance,* 57–86. Cambridge, Mass.: MIT Press.

Anta Fonseca, S., A. Plancarte Barrera, and J. M. Barrera Terán. 2000. *Conservación y manejo comunitario de los recursos forestales en Oaxaca.* Oaxaca, Mexico: Secretaría de Medio Ambiente, Recursos Naturales y Pesca, Delegación Oaxaca.

Arnold, J. E. M. 1992. *Community forestry: Ten years in review.* Rome: Food and Agriculture Organization of the United Nations.

Ascher, W. 1995. *Communities and sustainable forestry in developing countries.* San Francisco, Calif.: Institute for Contemporary Studies.

Ascher, W. 2000. Understanding why governments in developing countries waste natural resources. *Environment* 42: 8–18.

Berkes, F., D. Feeny, B. J. McCay, and J. M. Acheson. 1989. The benefits of the commons. *Nature* 340: 91–93.

Biles, J. and B. W. Pigozzi. 2000. The interaction of economic reforms, socioeconomic structure and agriculture in Mexico. *Growth and Change* 31: 3–22.

Bray, D. B. 1991. The struggle for the forest: conservation and development in the Sierra Juarez. *Grassroots Development* 15: 12–25.

Bray, D. B. 1997. La reconstrucción permanente de la naturaleza: Organizaciones campesinas y desarrollo popular sustentable. In L. Paré, D. B. Bray, J. Burstein, and S. Martínez Vásquez, eds., *Semillas para el cambio en el campo: Medio ambiente, mercados y organización campesina,* 3–18. Mexico City: Universidad Autónoma de México, Instituto de Investigaciones Sociales, La Sociedad de Solidaridad Social "Sansekan Tinemi," Servicios de Apoyo Local al Desarrollo de Base en México, A.C.

Cabarle, B., F. Chapela, and S. Madrid. 1997. Introducción: El manejo forestal comunitario y la certificación. In L. Merino, ed., *El manejo comunitario en México y sus perspectivas de sustentabilidad,* 17–33. Cuernavaca, Mexico: Centro Regional de Investigaciones Multidisciplinarias, UNAM.

Campbell, B., A. Mandondo, N. Nemarundwe, B. Sithole, W. de Jong, M. Luckert, and F. Matose. 2001. Challenges to proponents of common property resource systems: Despairing voices from the social forests of Zimbabwe. *World Development* 29: 589–600.

Carabias Lillo, J., J. Delvalle Cervantes, and G. Segura Warnholtz. 2000. *Voces del monte: Experiencias comunitarias para el manejo sustentable de los bosques en*

Oaxaca. Mexico City: Proyecto de Conservación y Manejo Sustentable de Recursos Forestales en México, Secretaría de Medio Ambiente, Recursos Naturales y Pesca.

Cernea, M. 1992. A sociological framework: Policy, environment and the social actors in tree planting. In N. P. Sharma, ed., *Managing the world's forests: Looking for balance between conservation and development,* 301–335. Dubuque, Iowa: Kendall/Hunt.

Díaz-Polanco, H. and A. Burguete. 1996. Sociedad colonial y rebellion indígena en el Obispado de Oaxaca (1660). In H. Díaz-Polanco, ed., *El fuego de la inobedencia: Autonomía y rebellion India en el obispado de Oaxaca,* 17–52. Oaxaca, Mexico: Centro de Investigaciones y Estudios Superiores en Antropología Social.

Enloe, C. 1989. *Bananas, beaches and bases: Making feminist sense of international politics.* Berkeley: University of California Press.

Euraque, D. A. 1996. *Reinterpreting the banana republic: Region and state in Honduras, 1870–1972.* Chapel Hill: University of North Carolina Press.

FAO. 1978. *Forestry for local community development.* Rome: Forestry Department, Food and Agriculture Organization of the United Nations.

Gadgil, M. and V. P. Vartok. 1976. The sacred groves of the Western Ghats in India. *Economic Botany* 30: 152–160.

Ganz, D. J. and J. H. Burckle. 2002. Forest vegetation in the Sierra Juarez, Oaxaca, Mexico: History of exploitation and current management. *Journal of Sustainable Forestry* 15: 29–49.

Government of India. 1973. *Interim report of the National Commission on Agriculture and Social Forestry.* New Delhi: Government of India.

Jansen, K. 1998. *Political ecology, mountain agriculture, and knowledge in Honduras.* Amsterdam: Thela.

Klooster, D. 1996. Como no conservar el bosque: La marginalización del campesino en la historial forestal mexicana. *Cuadernos Agrarios* (Mexico City) 14: 144–156.

Klooster, D. 2000. Community forestry and tree theft in Mexico: Resistance or complicity in conservation? *Development and Change* 31: 281–305.

Lapper, R. and J. Painter. 1985. *Honduras: State for sale.* London: Latin American Bureau (Research and Action) Limited.

Mayo, M. and G. Craig. 1995. Community participation and empowerment: The human face of structural adjustment or tools for democratic transformation? In C. Mayo and M. Mayo, eds., *Community empowerment: A reader in participation and development,* 1–11. London: Zed.

McKean, M. A. and E. Ostrom. 1995. Common property regimes in the forest: Just a relic from the past? *Unasylva* 46: 3–15.

Merino Pérez, L. 1997. Organización social de la producción forestal comunitaria. In L. Paré, D. B. Bray, J. Burstein, and S. Martínez Vásquez, eds., *Semillas para el cambio en el campo: Medio ambiente, mercados y organización campesina,* 141–154. Mexico City: Universidad Autónoma de México, Instituto de Investigaciones Sociales, La Sociedad de Solidaridad Social "Sansekan Tinemi," Servicios de Apoyo Local al Desarrollo de Base en México, A.C.

Merino Pérez, L., P. Gerez Fernández, and S. Madrid Zubirán. 2000. Políticas, instituciones comunitarias y uso de los recursos comunes en México. In M.

Bañuelos, coord., *Sociedad, derecho y medio ambiente: Premier informe del programa de investigación sobre aplicación y cumplimiento de la legislación ambiental en México,* 57–143. Mexico City: CONACYT/SEP, Universidad Autónoma Metropolitana, Secretaría de Medio Ambiente, Recursos Naturales y Pesca/Procuraduría Federal de Protección al Ambiente.

Newson, L. 1986. *The cost of conquest: Indian decline in Honduras under Spanish rule.* Boulder, Colo.: Westview.

Ostrom, E. 1990. *Governing the commons: The evolution of institutions for collective action.* Cambridge, U.K.: Cambridge University Press.

Ostrom, E. 1992. The rudiments of a theory of the origins, survival and performance of common-property institutions. In D. W. Bromley, ed., *Making the commons work: Theory, practice and policy,* 293–318. San Francisco, Calif.: ICS Press.

Ostrom, E. 1998. *Self-governance and forest resources.* Paper presented at the conference on Local Institutions for Forest Management, Center for International Forestry Research, Bogor, Indonesia, November 19–21, 1998.

Peckenham, N. and A. Street. 1985. *Honduras: Portrait of a captive nation.* New York: Praeger.

Pineda Portillo, N. 1997 (3d ed.). *Geografía de Honduras.* Tegucigalpa, Honduras: Editorial Guaymuras.

Richards, M. 1997. Common property resource institutions and forest management in Latin America. *Development and Change* 28: 95–117.

Robinson, W. I. 1998. (Mal)development in Central America: Globalization and social change. *Development and Change* 29: 467–497.

Runge, C. F. 1986. Common property and collective action in economic development. *World Development* 14: 623–624.

Salazar Ventura, J., F. S. Olmedo Bernal, and R. E. Perez Garcia. 1999. *Diagnóstico de salud 1999, centro de salud de un núcleo básico: Capulalpam de Méndez.* Oaxaca, Mexico: Secretaria de Salud.

Schelhas, J., L. E. Buck, and C. C. Geisler. 2001. Introduction: The challenge of adaptive collaborative management. In L. E. Buck, C. C. Geisler, J. Schelhas, and E. Wollenberg, eds., *Biological diversity: Balancing interests through adaptive collaborative management,* 245–260. Boca Raton, Fla.: CRC Press.

SECPLAN/DESFIL/USAID. 1989. *Perfil ambiental de Honduras 1989.* Tegucigalpa, Honduras: SECPLAN/DESFIL/USAID.

Snook, L. K. 1997. Uso, manejo y conservación forestal en México. In L. Paré, D. B. Bray, J. Burstein, and S. Martínez Vásquez, eds., *Semillas para el cambio en el campo: Medio ambiente, mercados y organización campesina,* 19–35. Mexico City: Universidad Autónoma de México, Instituto de Investigaciones Sociales, La Sociedad de Solidaridad Social "Sansekan Tinemi," Servicios de Apoyo Local al Desarrollo de Base en México, A.C.

Southworth, J. and C. M. Tucker. 2001. The influence of accessibility, local institutions, and socioeconomic factors on forest cover change in the mountains of western Honduras. *Mountain Research and Development* 21: 276–283.

Stanley, D. 1991. Communal forest management: The Honduran resin tappers. *Development and Change* 22: 757–779.

Tucker, C. 1996. *The political ecology of a Lenca Indian community in Honduras: Communal forests, state policy, and processes of transformation.* Unpublished doctoral thesis, University of Arizona, Tucson.

Tucker, C. 1999a. Manejo forestal y políticas nacionales en La Campa, Honduras. *Mesoamérica* 37: 111–144.

Tucker, C. 1999b. Private vs. communal forests: forest conditions and tenure in a Honduran community. *Human Ecology* 27: 201–230.

Tucker, C., S. Espinoza, and K. Andersson. 1999. *Resumen preliminar del trabajo de campo de* CIPEC *en Capulalpam, Oaxaca, Mexico*. Working Paper. Bloomington, Ind.: CIPEC.

Utting, P. 1993. *Trees, people and power: Social dimensions of deforestation and forest protection in Central America*. London: Earthscan.

Wilshusen, P. R., L. Raleigh, and V. A. Russell. 2002. By, for and of the people: The development of two community-managed protected areas in Oaxaca, Mexico. *Journal of Sustainable Forestry* 15: 113–126.

Chapter 11

COMMUNITY FORESTRY FOR SMALL-SCALE FURNITURE PRODUCTION IN THE BRAZILIAN AMAZON

David G. McGrath, Charles M. Peters,
and Antônio José Mota Bentes

A large proportion of Amazonia is occupied by smallholders who obtain their livelihood through shifting cultivation and the extraction of forest resources. With the rise of the extractivist movement in Brazil in the late 1980s, interest was generated in the potential of these groups for the sustainable management of Amazonian forests (Schwartzman 1989, Allegretti 1995). This movement has been highly successful in pressuring the Brazilian government to pass and implement policies in support of its agenda, and to date twenty-five extractive reserves of various types have been created, covering 3.8 million ha and including 154,000 people (including both extractive reserves and *assentamentos extrativistas* [IBAMA, Centro Nacional de Populações Tradicionais, Belém, pers. comm. 2002]).

Unfortunately, these political gains have not been matched by comparable success in consolidating the economic base of extractive reserves or establishing forest management as a viable economic strategy for smallholders. Despite much effort and expense, extractive reserves are still a long way from being economically viable. At the same time, the community forestry approach has come under criticism from economists, who argue that forest extraction does not provide a viable economic base for developing traditional communities (Homma 1989, 1993, Browder 1992, Rice et al. 1997), and from biologists, who argue that traditional extractive activities are degrading forest resources and depleting game species that perform vital ecological roles in forest ecosystems (Redford 1992, Salafsky et al. 1993, Peres 1994, Terborgh 1999, Putz et al. 2001). Given that the total area in Amazonian reserves where human presence and use are permitted is 30 percent larger than all the parks and biological reserves combined (ISA 1999) and six times larger if indigenous reserves are included, successful resolution of these economic and ecological problems is critical to the well-being of an enormous area of Amazonian forest, not to mention the hundreds of thousands of people whose future is inextricably tied to these reserves.

Although criticisms of traditional forest extraction are in some cases valid, this certainly does not imply that forest extraction has no potential for successfully reconciling development and conservation objectives (Schwartzman et al. 2001). The main problem is an overly naive view of the organizational capacity of smallholder groups and the promotion of inappropriate strategies for developing extractive economies (Smith 1995). In a few places in the Amazon and elsewhere in the neotropics, an alternative strategy for developing community-based forestry is emerging that could be called boutique capitalism, in contrast to the commodity capitalism approach that characterizes conventional logging and extraction of nontimber forest products such as rubber. This approach combines small-scale production of high-quality finished products for green consumer markets with emphasis on developing the local organizational capacity needed to administer these enterprises.

In this chapter we describe a project in the Tapajós–Arapiuns Extractive Reserve in western Pará, Brazil, in which smallholder community groups are managing forest resources to produce wood for small-scale furniture workshops. This project, called the Caboclo Workshops of the Tapajós (Oficinas Caboclas do Tapajós), was designed to facilitate development of group organizational capacity and to promote the production of simple, high-quality hand-made furniture for local and regional markets. Forest conservation was also a key consideration in the design of the project, and all activities of the furniture enterprise ultimately depend on the sustainable management of community forests.

TAPAJÓS–ARAPIUNS EXTRACTIVE RESERVE

The Caboclo Workshops of the Tapajós project is a collaborative effort involving the Amazon Institute for Environmental Research, the Woods Hole Research Center, and the communities of Nova Vista, Nuquini, and Surucuá in the Tapajós–Arapiuns Extractive Reserve (figure 11.1). The project is one outcome of a process that began in the early 1980s when communities of the west bank of the Tapajós River organized to oppose commercial logging in what they considered to be their territory. After several years of conflict and mounting political pressure, the Instituto

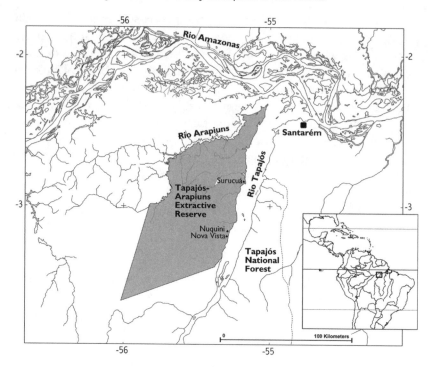

Figure 11.1   The Tapajós–Arapiuns Extractive Reserve, Brazil, and location of the three communities involved in the Caboclo Workshops of the Tapajós project.

Nacional de Colonização e Reforma Agrária (INCRA), the government agency responsible for titling federal lands, granted the communities a 13-km-wide, 64-km-long forest reserve on the western shore of the Tapajós River. The area encompassed the seventeen communities that were most actively involved in the struggle. The communities divided the reserve into two main zones paralleling the river. The first 3 km inland from the river was designated for settlement and agricultural activities, and the remaining 10 km was set aside as a forest reserve.

Ten years later, in the mid-1990s, the Tapajós communities joined with communities of the south bank of the Arapiuns River, a tributary of the Tapajós, to lobby for creation of an extractive reserve encompassing the lands between the two rivers (see figure 11.1). In 1998 the 647,611-ha Tapajós-Arapiuns Extractive Reserve was created over the fierce opposition of logging companies, local business interests, and the municipal government.

Since 1984, communities of the original forest reserve created by INCRA, now incorporated into the extractive reserve, have had varying success in restricting agricultural activities to the first 3 km, as originally agreed upon. Especially in the larger communities closer to Santarém, pressure for agricultural land and from commercial loggers has been intense. Many communities in need of new land for farming or income from timber sales have ceded to pressure and permitted farmers or commercial loggers to exploit areas in their forest reserve. However, several communities, including Nova Vista and Nuquini, have been largely successful in protecting their forest resources. The existence of these reserves provided the initial motivation for this project.

COMMUNITY STRUCTURE

Communities along the Tapajós River range in size from 35 to 120 families, with Nova Vista, Nuquini, and Surucuá having 35, 46, and 86 families, respectively. The local population is typically *caboclo*, of mixed European, African, and Indian descent. Communities tend to have a linear settlement pattern, with houses arranged on either side of one or more roads parallel to the river. Most have well-defined cores with a Catholic church, a community center, and a primary school. As part of the original settlement with INCRA and the logging companies, community territories were defined averaging 4 km frontage along the river and extending inland 13 km. Within this territory, families own current and fallowed agricultural fields, which they obtain from the village council. However, as is typical of communities with fairly abundant forest resources, tenure arrangements are still quite fluid, and there is much lending of land between families. Most fields are located within an hour's trip by bicycle, roughly 5 km from the community center.

Reserve communities have a long tradition of grassroots activism. Most have an elected leadership based on a presidential system that may include a community council. Two other important organizations are the Rural Workers' Union of Santarém (Sindicato dos Trabalhadores Rurais de Santarém) and the Catholic church, both of which have played critical roles in training community leaders and developing local organizational capacity. Most communities also have their own community associations and may participate in one of the two intercommunity associations that provide access to government credit programs for farming and some extractive activities. Communities are serviced several times a week by two or three ferryboats, which provide access to markets and government services in Santarém. Transport costs for passengers and goods tend to be fairly high by local standards, and for more distant communities they constitute a significant barrier to stronger participation in the regional market.

LOCAL ECONOMY

The major economic activity of the Tapajós communities is farming, and the main crop is manioc, which is processed into *farinha* (meal). Shifting cultivation is the predominant agricultural system. Fields average 1 ha, and the normal sequence involves two plantings of manioc and then fallowing of fields for five or more years. Families produce three to five 50-kg sacks of *farinha* per month, most of which is sold in the community or in Santarém. Farmers cultivate a variety of other crops, the most important being corn, squash, and beans, but none of these contributes significantly to household incomes. Most families also cultivate fruit trees around their homes, but few produce a surplus for market. Animal husbandry is limited and largely subsistence oriented. Almost all families have a few chickens and ducks, and some raise pigs. Large animals, such as cattle and horses, are raised by only a few families. Fishing is the main source of animal protein for most households, followed by hunting. People also exploit a variety of forest products, of which the most important economically is rubber, collected from trees planted in the community and from wild stands in the forest. A processing plant in Santarém and a government price support program for natural rubber are the main reasons for continued interest in this commodity.

INSTITUTIONAL CONTEXT

With the creation of the Tapajós–Arapiuns Extractive Reserve, communities were integrated into a new institutional framework within the Brazilian Institute of the Environment and Renewable Resources (IBAMA), the agency responsible for the federal reserve system. Within IBAMA, extractive reserves are the responsibility of the National Center for Traditional Populations. The official governing body of the reserve is the Director Council, composed of representatives of reserve communities, various government agencies, and local nongovernmental organizations working in the reserve. However, the reserve-wide organization, Tapajoara, whose leadership is elected by reserve residents, is responsible for governing the reserve, with the Director Council simply ratifying its decisions.

CABOCLO WORKSHOPS OF THE TAPAJÓS PROJECT

The Caboclo Workshops of the Tapajós project began in 1998 in the communities of Surucuá and Nuquini and was later joined by a third community, Nova Vista. By coincidence, the first contact with the communities was made during a regional meeting held in Nuquini to plan efforts to wrest the area that would later become the extractive reserve from the two logging companies that controlled much of the land inland from the communities. A representative of a logging company also attended the meeting and presented a proposal to purchase timber in the Nuquini forest reserve. The fact that community members were at least willing to listen to the logger's offer was evidence of their concern over the poor condition of community infrastructure and their recognition that the timber resources they had guarded for so long were more than sufficient to address their needs. As one community member put it, "We've preserved this forest for all these years for what?" The Tapajós furniture project was developed to answer this question by finding a way in which communities could tap the resources they had so zealously guarded without depleting the productive potential of their forest.

The project's approach is to develop sustainably managed community forest reserves to supply wood for local furniture workshops. Artisans use locally available hand tools to produce simple pegged furniture designed to bring out the natural beauty of Amazonian hardwoods. At present, furniture is sold locally, with plans to expand into national and possibly international markets as production increases.

The furniture workshop and forest reserve contribute directly and indirectly to community development. The enterprise contributes directly by generating employment for participating artisans and indirectly via investment of part of the workshop's profits in a community development fund for improving community infrastructure, both social and economic. As the enterprise grows in both employment and sales volume, the fund will become an increasingly important source of support for community development initiatives.

Caboclo Workshops was designed to be consistent with local technology and ways of doing things. However, it should be emphasized that the enterprise itself, including the workshops, furniture, forest management system, and organization needed to manage the overall business, is entirely new to the community members involved. There is no local or regional precedent for Caboclo Workshops that could serve as a model and source of experienced advisers.

The initial vision for the project was largely that of the two project coordinators, an American geographer and a locally born Brazilian sociologist, who have been working in the region since the early 1990s. They proposed the project to the communities and, once communities had confirmed their interest, sought external funding for the initiative. However, neither project coordinators nor community members had prior experience in community forestry, so development of the project has been a learning experience for all those involved. Through this process, local artisans are acquiring the skills and experience they need to transform the project into a self-sufficient business.

Project staff consists of three full-time and two part-time members, including specialists in community organizational development, community management of natural resources, agricultural extension, and woodworking. Funding for the project has been provided by the U.S. Agency for International Development, Ford Foundation, and Funbio, a Brazilian funding program supported by the Global Environmental Facility. The annual budget for the last three years has averaged us$70,000. Work during this period has focused on four main areas: organizational development, furniture production, forest management, and marketing.

Organizational Development

Caboclo Workshops operates at three interdependent organizational levels: the community workshops, the Caboclo Workshop association, and the communities in which each workshop is located. The main focus of project activity thus far has been on organizing the community workshops. Workshops began with fifteen to twenty members each. Over the course of the first year, membership declined, stabilizing at six to twelve, depending on the community. Most are men, and ages range from twenty to fifty. Only one group has significant participation by women. Groups are responsible for all phases of local forest management and furniture-producing activities, and thus far most capacity building and organizing activities have taken place at this level. Each group has an elected coordinator and vice-coordinator responsible for organizing workshop activities and representing the workshop in regional meetings and other activities.

Although workshops are independent organizations within each community, the two are closely linked through the design of the project in which workshops are intended to serve as a vehicle for community development. A fundamental link between workshop and community is that the furniture enterprise exploits community forest resources. Communities have granted workshops the right to exclusive use of timber resources in a designated management area. In return, each workshop contributes part of its profits to a development fund managed by community leadership.

Influence of the project on the community extends further than negotiating use rights. Furniture projects grew out of broader discussions of the value of community forest resources and development options. Communities take pride in being the home of workshops and in having established formal forest management areas. In fact, several people who are not members of the workshops but support the idea participated in the forest inventories. The success of the workshops has also helped move discussion of forest resources out of the abstract realm and has encouraged communities to be more concerned with conservation. For example, there is a notably stricter adherence to the rules regulating the location of agricultural activities in collaborating villages, and several community fire prevention programs have been developed to protect forests.

The Caboclo Workshop Association is the least developed organizational level thus far. The association will have a two-tier structure consisting of community workshops and the regional association. The actual division of labor between these two levels will be worked out as the organization develops, but the plan is for workshops in each community to operate as largely autonomous management and production units within the association, with local members responsible for managing their own workshops and forest resources. The Regional Workshop Association will be responsible for furniture marketing, overall logistical support, financial management, and institutional relations.

At this point, most of the logistical and organizing activities are still undertaken by project staff, but with increasing participation of workshop members. With the workshop level increasingly consolidated, emphasis is turning toward development of the regional organization. Efforts are now focused on developing and implementing a business plan to guide the process of structuring the workshop association to take responsibility for marketing furniture in major national markets such as Rio de Janeiro and São Paulo, and all that implies in terms of business operations. Although a coordinating group composed of representatives of the community workshops will oversee operations, it is likely that an outside administrator will be hired to manage day-to-day activities associated with marketing, financial administration, and logistical support. As group members with administrative talent emerge and acquire business management skills, they will assume greater responsibility, perhaps replacing the outside manager.

Production

Development of community workshops began with a series of two-week training sessions in which artisans acquired woodworking skills, experimented with different furniture designs and types of wood, and developed

Figure 11.2 Furniture workshop in the village of Nuquini, Tapajós–Arapiuns Extractive Reserve, Brazil.

the basic production system followed today. Artisans locate fallen trees in the forest and agricultural fields, cut them into boards and other pieces with chainsaws, and carry them back to the workshop on bicycles. Pieces are worked with hand tools, including hand saws, brace and bit, hand adze, chisels, and plane (figure 11.2). Furniture is simple in construction, and pieces are pegged and glued together. Designs seek to take advantage of the shape, grain, knots, and holes of each piece. Pieces are finished with paste wax and branded with the Caboclo Workshop logo.

Thus far, workshop output consists primarily of stools, coffee tables, and cutting boards of varying design, although a number of other types of furniture and kitchen implements are produced in smaller quantities. Groups are constantly experimenting with new designs and, once accepted, standardize measurements for each. The number of wood species used has not yet stabilized and varies from workshop to workshop, depending on local availability. Thus far, groups have worked with roughly twenty species each, for an overall total of thirty-four species for the three communities.

Productive activities are organized in terms of individual effort rather than productivity. The authorship of individual pieces is not recorded, and in many cases pieces are the product of several members' efforts. However, the group keeps a record of the amount of time each member works, and individual shares of workshop sales are calculated on the basis of time worked in the previous period. Workshops also keep track of the amount of time consumed in making each piece to provide a basis for estimating costs and productivity.

Although workshops are now functioning on a regular basis, they are a part-time activity so as not to interfere with other important economic activities such as farming. The groups started out working one week per month and plan to increase their time commitment to two weeks. This period covers all activities associated with the workshops, including locating and removing wood from the forest. Groups produce an average of ten to twelve pieces per month of all types. The total volume of wood used is surprisingly small, even when wastage is included. Average monthly consumption is around 0.2 m^3 per workshop, or 2.5 m^3 annually. The small volume of wood and number of pieces reflects both the fact that only five to ten days per month are dedicated to all workshop activities, including obtaining wood in the forest, and to low labor productivity resulting from the use of simple hand tools. We expect the volume of wood consumed to increase significantly as workshops systematize furniture production, possibly introduce some electric tools, and increase the amount of time in operation.

Forest Management

In contrast to the approach usually taken in timber management projects, groups began by producing furniture and only a year later began research for developing forest management plans. During this year groups worked with wood from fallen and dead trees found in the vicinity. This approach was largely fortuitous, the result of ad hoc responses to immediate choices, but in retrospect it turned out to have been an effective way of developing the project. The decision to start this way was made because we had the project staff to train people in producing furniture and to organize the workshops, but we did not have a forester to coordinate forest management activities. To avoid tinkering with a forest that we knew very little about, we decided to use waste wood scavenged from active and abandoned swiddens.

By concentrating on furniture production, groups tackled something they could easily understand and incorporate into their lives. Producing and selling furniture, artisans acquired a detailed understanding of what they would be managing the forest for—the kind of wood and the quantities they would need to sustain furniture production. Starting with dead wood also makes sense in retrospect. There is quite a lot of it in the vicinity of communities, and from a furniture-making perspective it is of excellent quality. The wood is still hard, and as a result of aging, there is much less danger of parts shrinking and splitting than there would be with conventionally dried wood. We will incorporate this natural aging into our management plan.

The management strategy involves selective felling of the annual increment of desirable furniture woods in the forest and conscientious monitoring of regeneration levels after harvest as a basis for silvicultural treatment. Management planning is based on quantitative, diagnostic information, and these data are collected in a participatory fashion by the villagers themselves. Although the exact timing and sequence of operations were modified slightly between villages, the forestry activities initiated in Nova Vista, Nuquini, and Surucuá include delineation of management area, species selection, quantitative forest inventory, growth and yield studies, definition of allowable cut, and monitoring.

Delineation of Management Area

A specific tract of forest to be used for producing furniture woods was designated by each community. Nova Vista and Nuquini each set aside areas of 200 ha, whereas Surucuá, which is closer to Santarém and has smaller, patchier tracts of undisturbed forest, set aside a 100-ha management area. The management areas for Nuquini, Nova Vista, and Surucuá are located 4, 6, and 10 km, respectively, from the village. All three tracts are (mostly) accessible by bicycle, which is how the wood, bucked into small bolts for easy transport, will be removed from the forest.

Species Selection

Initial meetings were held in each community to discuss the concept of sustainability, forest management, and the importance of collecting baseline information on the density and abundance of desirable wood species. After this discussion, a list of preferred wood species was compiled. Most communities also included several nontimber forest resources (e.g., edible fruits, medicinal plants, and oilseeds) on the list, in anticipation of the day when management activities would also extend to these important resources.

There was a surprising degree of overlap in the species lists produced by each village. There are apparently forty to fifty species of desirable furniture woods in the forests of the Tapajós–Arapiuns Extractive Reserve, and at least thirty of these species occur in the management areas of each community. The furniture woods compiled from the village surveys are listed in table 11.1.

Forest Inventory

The forest inventory design for use in the Caboclo Workshops of the Tapajós project was based on several considerations. The method had to be sufficiently transparent to be understood and faithfully replicated by local field crews. The sample intensity had to be large enough to provide a statistically reliable assessment of species abundances and size distributions yet small enough that the field work could be completed in a time frame agreeable to a group of people who had other things to do. Finally, the placement of sample units had to facilitate forest typing and mapping of species volumes and provide a permanent means of access for periodic entry into the area.

For these reasons, a systematic strip sample based on 10-m-wide, parallel transects was used to sample the wood resources in each management area. The distance between transects was fixed at 100 m, yielding an overall sample intensity of 10 percent. Each transect was 1 km long and composed of fifty 10- by 20-m segments, or plots; the results for each plot were tallied separately. Slope corrections, although rarely needed, were applied as necessary.

In each plot, the crew carefully searched a 5-m belt on either side of the line, and every tree on the species list at least 5 cm in diameter at breast height (dbh) was tallied and measured with a diameter tape. For plots that contained at least two tally trees, one tree was selected and its height measured using a clinometer. Although even small branches can be used for making furniture, height to the first branch was used to provide a conservative estimate of wood volume. Each crew was composed of a compass person, two *materos* ("ones who know the woods") to look for, identify, and measure trees, one person to tally the data, and one or two people to pull the transect rope and brush the line. Three to five crews performed the inventory work. Depending on the

Table 11.1 List of Furniture Woods Compiled from the Villages of Surucuá, Nova Vista, and Nuquini

Common Name	Scientific Name	Family	Community		
			Nova Vista	Nuquini	Surucuá
Angelim bordado	*Hymenolobium* sp.	Leguminosae		■	
Angelim pedra	*Dinizia excelsa* Ducke	Leguminosae	■	■	■
Angelim vermelho	*Hymenolobium petraeum* Ducke	Leguminosae	■	■	■
Cajurana	*Pouteria elegans* (A.DC.) Baehni	Sapotaceae			■
Carapanaúba	*Aspidosperma nitidum* Benth. ex Muell. Arg.	Apocynaceae	■		■
Cuiarana	*Terminalia dichotoma* G. Meyer	Combretaceae	■		
Cumarú branco	*Dipteryx odorata* (Aubl.) Willd.	Leguminosae	■	■	■
Cupiúba	*Goupia glabra* Aubl.	Celastraceae			■
Envira preta	*Guatteria poeppigiana* Mart.	Annonaceae	■		■
Fava amargosa	*Vatairea paraensis* Ducke	Leguminosae	■	■	■
Fava preta	*Vatairea* sp.	Leguminosae		■	
Ipê amarelo	*Tabebuia serratifolia* Nichols	Bignoniaceae	■	■	■
Ipê roxo	*Tabebuia impetiginosa* (Mart. ex DC.) Standl.	Bignoniaceae	■	■	■
Itaúba preta	*Mezilaurus itauba* (Meisn.) Taub. ex Mez	Lauraceae	■	■	■
Jacarandá	*Dalbergia spruceana* Benth.	Leguminosae	■		
Jarana	*Lecythis lurida* (Miers) S. A. Mori	Lecythidaceae	■	■	■
Jatobá	*Hymenaea courbaril* L.	Leguminosae	■		■
Jutaí	*Hymenaea parvifolia* Huber	Leguminosae			■
Louro preto	*Ocotea baturitensis* Vattimo	Lauraceae	■	■	
Macacaúba	*Platymiscium duckei* Huber	Leguminosae			■
Marupá	*Simarouba amara* var. *typica* Cronquist	Simaroubaceae		■	
Muiracatiara	*Astronium lecointei* Ducke	Anacardiaceae	■		■
Muirapixuna	*Chamaecrista scleroxylon* (Ducke) Irwin & Barneby	Leguminosae	■	■	■
Muiratauá	*Apuleia leiocarpa* Macbr.	Leguminosae	■	■	
Pororoca	*Dialium guianense* (Aubl.) Sandw.	Leguminosae	■	■	■
Sucupira amarela	*Diplotropis purpurea* (L.C. Rich.) Amsh.	Leguminosae	■	■	■
Sucupira preta	*Bowdichia nitidia* Spruce ex Benth.	Leguminosae	■	■	
Sucuúba	*Himatanthus sucuuba* (Spruce) Woodson	Apocynaceae	■	■	
Tatajuba	*Maclura tinctoria* (L) D. Don ex Steud.	Moraceae			■
Tauarí	*Couratari guianensis* Aubl.	Lecythidaceae			■

All taxonomic determinations should be viewed as tentative.

number of species encountered and the condition of the forest, the crews were able to complete 1.0 to 1.5 km of line a day.

Growth Studies

To document diameter growth rates in the management area, growth studies of selected species were initiated in each management area concurrent with the inventory work using stainless steel, vernier-type dendrometer bands (Liming 1957). These bands are custom made for the sample tree and provide a very sensitive measure of diameter growth. Their construction is also very simple, and villagers quickly learned the process. To date, more than 250 trees have been banded in the reserve, and data on the first year of growth have been collected from about 60 trees at Nova Vista and Nuquini. In addition to their utility for management planning, these data ultimately will provide an interesting comparison with those collected across the river in the Tapajós National Forest (Silva et al. 1985, 1995, DeCarvalho 1992).

There were several reasons for conducting community-level growth studies rather than simply using the growth data from the Tapajós National Forest. First, different species were measured by the villagers, and the land use history of their sites is also very different from that of the national forest. Preliminary results suggest that annual growth rates in the extractive reserve are higher than those in the national forest, probably as a result of the canopy opening caused by a fire that swept through the area several years ago. Second, helping the villagers learn to manage their forests is one of the main objectives of the project. Although it would have been much simpler to use the growth rates from the national forest, the villagers would have no idea where these numbers came from or what was involved in collecting them. By conducting their own growth studies, they learned how to make dendrometer bands and read a vernier caliper, and they have a very clear understanding of the relationship between canopy cover and tree growth.

Defining an Allowable Cut

Using the data from the forest inventories and composite growth data from the Tapajós National Forest and the community management areas, a stand table projection (*sensu* Davis and Johnson 1987) was performed to estimate the annual growth in volume of the furniture wood resource in each management area. The general results from these analyses are presented in table 11.2, which shows the density, volume, and annual volume growth of all merchantable trees of at least 40 cm dbh at Nova Vista, Nuquini, and Surucuá. Because of its short-term importance

Table 11.2 Basic Inventory and Growth Projection Results from the Caboclo Workshop of the Tapajós Project, Tapajós–Arapiuns Extractive Reserve, Brazil

Community	Management Area (ha)	Merchantable Trees/ha	Standing Volume/ha (m³)	Dead Wood/ha (m³)	Mean Annual Increment (m³/ha/yr)
Nuquini	200	13.25	34.42	1.21	0.60
Nova Vista	200	17.90	51.18	4.80	0.92
Surucuá	100	25.7	114.26	3.79	1.64

Volume calculations based on diameter, commercial height, and a taper factor of 0.8 for merchantable species ≥40 cm dbh.

to the furniture initiative, the total volume of dead wood available is also presented.

The forests at Surucuá have the largest number of merchantable trees per hectare, contain the most volume per hectare, and have the highest mean annual increment. Although the Surucuá management area is only half the size of those at Nuquini and Nova Vista, the former site contains a higher total volume of furniture wood. Nova Vista exhibits the highest volume of dead wood per hectare, followed by Surucuá and then Nuquini. The large volumes of dead wood recorded probably also are a result of recent forest fires.

To put these numbers in perspective, it is useful to translate them into quantities of furniture that can be manufactured. Given a knowledge of the specific gravity of certain woods and the weights of different types of furniture, rough estimates of the wood needed for different products can be calculated. Based on these calculations, 1 m³ of wood contains about 1000 cutting boards, 190 stools, or 50 coffee tables. Stated another way, the 200-ha management area at Nova Vista produces 184,000 cutting boards, 34,960 stools, and 9200 coffee tables each year. This bodes well for the sustainability of the management effort because these quantities exceed by a large margin what the workshops can consume. Suffice it to say that there is a lot of room for the Caboclo Workshops market to grow.

Monitoring

Cutting only the growth from a forest is just one parameter in the sustainability equation. If the harvest species are not regenerating, even a conscientious, controlled level of tree felling can gradually lead to over-exploitation. To avoid this, the management plans for all three communities include procedures for monitoring the growth response of residual trees (which could actually increase the allowable cut), the overall floristic composition of the forest, and the impact of logging on the regeneration and establishment of important tree species. These observations will be collected from a network of permanent continuous forest inventory plots established in each management area.

Marketing

In contrast to the wholesale marketing strategy typical of many community forestry initiatives, the strategy being developed here concentrates on retail sales to the urban consumer. As in other aspects of the project, we have taken an incremental approach in marketing furniture, beginning with the local Santarém market and later expanding to larger urban markets elsewhere in Brazil. Thus far, the major share of sales has occurred during local trade and craft fairs in Santarém, although people are increasingly coming to the project office to buy furniture. This arrangement has given artisans the opportunity to sell what they have produced, generating some income but without becoming involved in commitments that the workshops are not yet ready to assume. The experience of representing the workshops at fairs and talking to customers has also been of great importance in building artisans' confidence in the value of their work and the potential of the project. We have used this time to concentrate on developing standard designs for a product line and systematizing production techniques and measurements.[1] Groups are now setting monthly production targets for their main designs.

The groups are increasingly ready to consider marketing their output outside Santarém. If the project is to grow in volume of output and sales, it will be necessary to develop markets in the major urban centers of the south, where consumers are willing to pay more. This will necessitate substantial improvement in the organizational capacity of the workshops because it involves not just much larger volumes and tighter production schedules but also mechanisms for quality control, customer relations, shipping logistics, and financial administration. The main logistical problem is transport. The furniture is sturdy and exceptionally heavy because of the dense woods used, and it is quite bulky. Direct highway connection to the south is precarious, and alternative routes involve shipment by riverboat to Belém and then overland by truck to markets elsewhere in Brazil. As a result, transport logistics are a significant factor in a national marketing strategy.

To a large extent the decision to begin developing a national-scale marketing strategy was precipitated by articles in three national magazines highlighting the Oficinas products. In response to this publicity, requests for information on products soared, as have orders from all over Brazil. Unfortunately, this free publicity came before the workshops were adequately structured, and they must move quickly to take advantage of the opportunity before interest fades. Toward this end, a consulting firm that provides business assistance to community-based initiatives has been contracted to work with the project to develop and implement a business plan for the workshops.

The project plans to obtain some kind of internationally recognized certification for the workshops that recognizes the fact that furniture is made from wood obtained from forests that are sustainably managed by community groups. However, we do not see the market for certified products as necessarily absorbing much of the workshop's production.

EVALUATION

Earlier we identified several concerns in assessing the potential of community forest management initiatives such as this one: resource constraints, financial returns, organizational capacity, and overall applicability. Although many important components of the project are not yet fully operational, the experience does provide sufficient information for a preliminary evaluation.

Resource Availability

One of the major concerns in tropical forest management is whether resource productivity is sufficient to ensure economic viability at sustainable harvest levels. The 120 m^3 of wood available from each 40-ha plot in Nuquini, for example, is almost sixty times the current level of consumption. If we narrow the number of species down to the number being exploited at present, the volume of wood available is half that of the total inventory but still almost fifteen times current consumption levels. Furthermore, the ecological integrity of the managed forests is unlikely to be affected by the volume of wood that will be removed under the proposed management plan. In fact, the proposed cut of 0.6 m^3/ha for Nuquini is well below the maximum cut permitted without a management plan under Brazilian law.

Financial Returns

A second criticism of community forestry has focused on the low economic returns to labor of extractive activities. Although it is not yet possible to undertake a complete financial analysis of the workshops because several major components of the enterprise such as forest management and business administration are not yet functioning, we do have enough information on labor inputs, production volumes, and sales to obtain a rough idea of the economic viability of workshops in their present state of development. In general, artisans devote five to ten days per month to workshop activities, including removal of wood from the forest and furniture production, for a total monthly labor input of thirty person-days per workshop. The value of monthly production at current prices is estimated at 300 reais. Because of project subsidies in the form of tools, some supplies, and staff support for sales and financial management, it is not yet possible to accurately estimate average monthly costs. Partial information available indicates that they average roughly 10 percent, or 30 reais, so the net monthly return to labor is 270 reais. This corresponds to 43 reais per person per month for the six workshop members, about two-thirds the average cash income per family from *farinha* production. This return corresponds to slightly less than the legal minimum wage. Although there is undoubtedly room to increase the efficiency of the workshops, workers will have to increase the productivity of labor through use of some electric tools and obtain higher prices for furniture than is possible in the Santarém market if they are to significantly increase incomes.[2]

There is also room to expand the scale of the enterprise. Based on earlier estimates of the available volume of wood and the income figures presented earlier, the gross value of furniture that could be produced at current prices ranges from 90,000 to 180,000 reais per workshop per year, depending on the number of species used. Even doubling current levels of wood consumption, the existing management area could provide employment for up to forty-five half-time workers, or at least one member of each family in the average-sized reserve community. In this case, gross monthly income would be between 84 and 168 reais for half-time workers.

Organizational Capacity

The third issue is local organizational capacity to operate a successful business. In this regard, although the project is still developing and far from ready to function independently, there is reason to believe that the group will be able to achieve this objective, although a professional manager may be needed for some time. The experience thus far confirms that reported from community forestry initiatives in Mexico (Klooster 2000). Organizational capacity is not something to be taken for granted, nor is it some intangible quality. Rather, through a systematic educational process geared to the level of the participants, it is possible to develop the organizational capacity needed to effectively manage community-based enterprises. We designed this project to take this problem into account in five ways: selection of communities with an initially high level of organizational capacity, simple organizational demands, an incremental approach to project development, a major investment in developing group awareness and organizational skills, and a transfer of responsibility for running the operation from project staff to workshop members that is in pace with development of local capacity.

Potential Applicability of This Approach

Finally, although it is too early for a definitive answer, we believe that the approach to forest management taken here has widespread applicability as a forest management strategy for smallholder communities elsewhere in the Brazilian Amazon. First, the small volume of wood used and the high added value of furniture production mean that resource availability is unlikely to be the limiting factor in most situations. In fact, this approach is especially attractive for those whose forests have been degraded by logging, forest fires, or clearing for agriculture because these are all situations in which there is likely to be an abundant supply of dead wood. Second, because of the simple, low-cost technology used, capital and skill thresholds are low. In this regard, the main issues are woodworking skill and aesthetic sense, both of which can be instilled through training programs. Products are also suitable for a fairly wide range of markets, regional, national, and international, so that demand is not likely to be a limiting factor initially. Although economic returns are fairly low in the early stages, there is the potential for major increases in income as workshops develop, invest in more productive equipment, and tap into larger urban markets. Finally, for all these reasons, this approach has the potential to make an important contribution to community development, providing not only jobs but also funds for improving community infrastructure and services.

CONCLUSION

Despite the criticisms leveled by many conservationists, community-based forest management can be an effective strategy for reconciling the conservation and development of tropical forest resources. Although many difficult challenges must be addressed, in most cases they can be resolved; in fact, the number of successful community-based management experiences throughout the tropics is increasing. The main problem in many cases has been the choice of inappropriate economic strategies that do not take into account the organizational capacities of smallholder communities. Rather than rejecting the model because of earlier mistakes, what is needed now is a renewed effort that draws on lessons from past successes and failures to develop management strategies that take advantage of the enormous potential of community forestry for the conservation of tropical forests. Managed forests are an essential complement to parks and reserves, and the much larger total area now occupied by traditional peoples and colonists is critical to a region-wide conservation strategy for the tropics. Any realistic conservation strategy for tropical forests must be based on recognition of the critical role to be played by forest management.

NOTES

1. At the time of writing, furniture prices are as follows: stools, 40–60 reais; animal stools, 50–100 reais; chairs, 60–85 reais; coffee tables, 100–150 reais; breadboards, 10 reais. One real is worth us$0.33 at prevailing exchange rates.

2. The productivity of furniture production alone is fairly high by local standards, about twice the average daily wage. The problem is that about half their time is devoted to support activities, bringing down the average return per day.

REFERENCES

Allegretti, M. 1995. Reservas extrativistas: Parâmetros para uma política de desenvolvimento sustentável na Amazônia. In R. Arndt, ed., *O destino da floresta,* 17–47. Rio de Janeiro, Brazil: Dumará.

Browder, J. 1992. The limits of extractivism. *BioScience* 42: 174–182.

Davis, K. P. and N. Johnson. 1987 (3d ed.). *Forest management.* New York: McGraw-Hill.

DeCarvalho, J. O. P. 1992. *Structure and dynamics of a logged over Brazilian Amazonian rain forest.* Ph.D. dissertation, University of Oxford, Oxford, U.K.

Homma, A. 1989. Reservas extrativistas: Uma opção de desenvolvimento viável para a Amazônia? *Pará Desenvolvimento* 25: 38–48.

Homma, A. O. 1993. *Extrativismo vegetal na Amazônia: Limites e oportunidades.* Brasília, Brazil: EMBRAPA.

ISA. 1999. *Amazonia Brasileira: 2000.* São Paulo, Brazil: Instituto Socio-Ambiental.

Klooster, D. 2000. Institutional choice, community, and struggle: A case study of forest co-management in Mexico. *World Development* 28: 1–20.

Liming, F. C. 1957. Homemade dendrometers. *Journal of Forestry* 55: 575–577.

Peres, C. 1994. Indigenous reserves and nature conservation in Amazonian forests. *Conservation Biology* 8: 586–589.

Putz, F., G. Blate, K. Redford, R. Fimbel, and J. Robinson. 2001. Tropical forest management and conservation of biodiversity: An overview. *Conservation Biology* 15: 7–20.

Redford, K. 1992. The empty forest. *BioScience* 42: 412–422.

Rice, R., R. Gullison, and J. Reid. 1997. Can sustainable management save tropical forests? *Scientific American* 276: 34–39.

Salafsky, N., B. Dugeby, and J. Terborgh. 1993. Can extractive reserves save the rainforest? An ecological and socioeconomic comparison of nontimber forest product extraction systems in Petén, Guatemala, and West Kalimantan, Indonesia. *Conservation Biology* 7: 39–53.

Schwartzman, S. 1989. Extractive reserves: the rubber tappers' strategy for sustainable use of the Amazon rainforest. In J. Browder, ed., *Fragile lands of Latin America: Strategies for sustainable development,* 150–165. Boulder, Colo.: Westview.

Schwartzman, S., A. Moreira, and D. Nepstad. 2001. Rethinking tropical forest conservation. *Conservation Biology* 14: 1351–1357.

Silva, J. N. M., J. O. P. de Carvalho, J. do C. A. Lopes, B. F. de Almeida, D. H. M. Costa, L. C. de Oliveira, J. K. Vanclay, and J. P. Skovsgaard. 1995. Growth and yield of a tropical rain forest in the Brazilian Amazon 13 years after logging. *Forest Ecology and Management* 71: 267–274.

Silva, J. N. M., J. do C. A. Lopes, and J. O. P. Carvalho. 1985. Inventário florestal de uma area experimental na Floresta Nacional do Tapajós. *Boletim de Pesquisa Florestal* 10/11: 38–110.

Smith, R. 1995. *The gift that wounds: Charity, the gift economy and social solidarity in indigenous Amazonia.* Paper presented in the Conference "Forest Ecosystems in the Americas: Community Management and Sustainability," University of Wisconsin, Madison, February 1995.

Terborgh, J. 1999. *Requiem for nature.* Washington, D.C.: Island Press.

1996

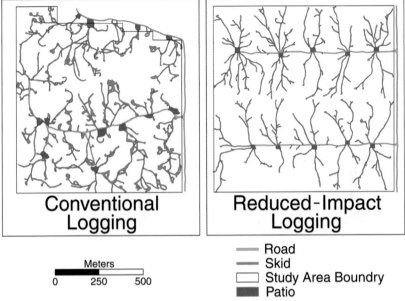

Conventional Logging

Reduced-Impact Logging

Meters

0   250   500

Road
Skid
Study Area Boundry
Patio

Plate 1 Areas of ground damage in two forest areas of about 100 ha each. Ground damage indicates areas where soil has been compacted by mechanical disturbance. It includes log storage decks, skid trails, and roads. A total of 8.9% of the conventional logging block suffered ground damage, compared with 4.8% of the reduced-impact logging block in this example. *Source:* Reprinted from Pereira et al. (2002), with permission.

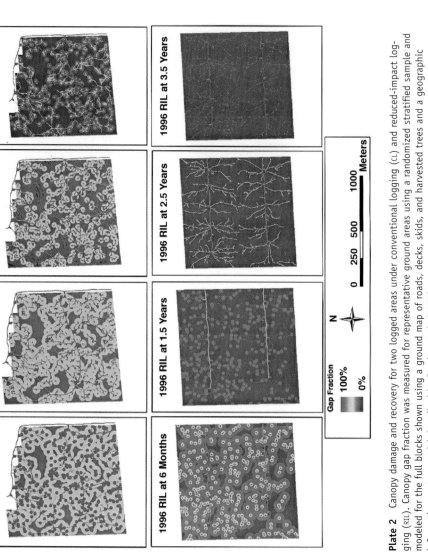

Plate 2 Canopy damage and recovery for two logged areas under conventional logging (CL) and reduced-impact logging (RIL). Canopy gap fraction was measured for representative ground areas using a randomized stratified sample and modeled for the full blocks shown using a ground map of roads, decks, skids, and harvested trees and a geographic information system model described by Pereira et al. (2002).

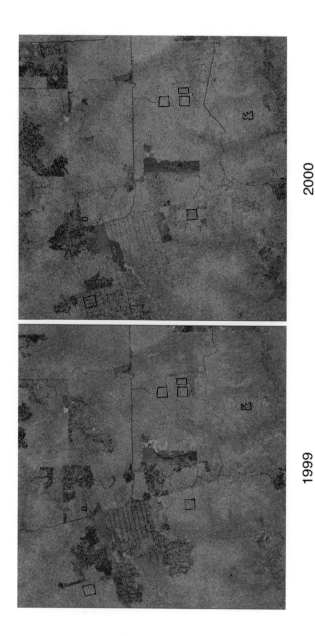

1999

2000

Plate 3 Color composite images of the automated Monte Carlo unmixing output for 1999 and 2000 in the vicinity of the Fazenda Cauaxí. Red indicates bare soil, green indicates forest canopy with shading, and blue indicates exposed nonphotosynthetic vegetation (slash in logged areas). Logging research areas used for bottom-up analyses are delineated in black. *Source:* Reprinted from *Remote Sensing of Environment*, Vol. 87, G. P. Asner, M. M. C. Bustamante, and A. R. Townsend, "Scale dependence of biophysical structure in deforested lands bordering the Tapajós National Forest, Central Amazon," Pages 507–520, Copyright 2003, with permission from Elsevier.

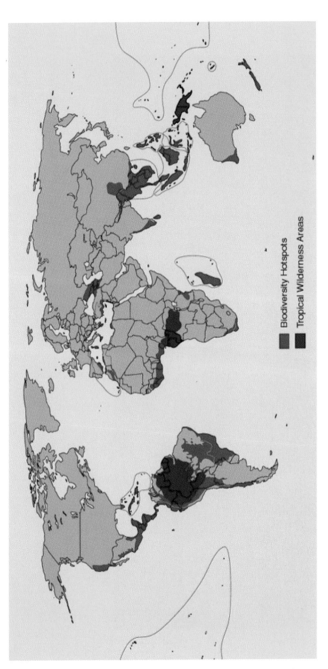

Plate 4 Original extent of the global biodiversity hotspots and major tropical wilderness areas. Of the hotspots in the American tropics, the following percentages remain under native vegetation: tropical Andes, 25%; Chocó–Darién–western Ecuador, 24%; Brazilian Cerrado, 20%; Mesoamerica, 20%; Caribbean, 11%; and Atlantic Forest, 7.5%.

Biodiversity Hotspots

Tropical Wilderness Areas

Plate 5 Hard edge around the Adolpho Ducke Forest Reserve, Manaus, Brazil. Photograph taken in 2000.

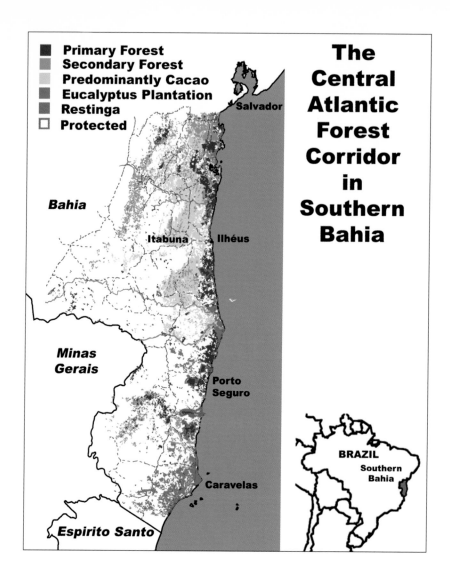

Plate 6 Southern Bahia portion of the central Atlantic Forest corridor, indicating major land uses, remaining forests, and protected areas.

Plate 7 Hypothetical land uses in a portion of a conservation corridor in the Brazilian Atlantic Forest. Orange areas are national parks or private reserves, purple areas are designated for reforestation, and yellow is agroforestry and shade cocoa.

Plate 8 Landsat 7 image mosaic showing anthropogenic pressure around the Kayapo Indigenous Area in the southeastern Brazilian Amazon. The group of territories that make up the Kayapo area cumulatively cover approximately 12 million ha and are demarcated in yellow. Mature forest is shown in green and nonforest in pink. Pink areas around the reserve are largely anthropogenic clearing, and pink areas in the reserve are largely natural savannas.

Chapter 12

COMMUNITY FORESTRY AS A STRATEGY FOR SUSTAINABLE MANAGEMENT

PERSPECTIVES FROM QUINTANA ROO, MEXICO

David Barton Bray

The most sustained case against the ecological and economic feasibility of sustainable management of tropical forests has been developed by researchers associated with Conservation International (CI) (Reid and Rice 1997, Rice et al. 1997, Bowles et al. 1998, Hardner and Rice 1999, Rice et al. 2001a, 2001b). These authors argue that efforts to promote sustainable forest management (SFM) have been largely futile because it will always be more profitable to harvest as many commercial-sized trees in the shortest possible time and invest the profits in other sectors.

The CI group has further argued that policies that promote SFM are doomed to failure because they typically

- Promote the use of lesser-known species (LKSS). But neither prices nor growth rates are any more favorable for LKSS than they are for more commercial species.
- Promote more efficient logging. But industrially efficient logging could also be highly unsustainable.
- Promote tenure security (equated to longer concession durations or private property) but do not improve the financial disincentives for SFM and may even encourage rapid liquidation of the resource.
- Ban log exports, promote value-added processing and more government taxes (rent capture), practices unlikely to contribute to SFM.
- Promote timber certification, which will never add enough marketing value to compensate for the much higher costs of SFM.

Close examination of this literature reveals that this generalization has been made almost entirely on the basis of SFM under one kind of land tenure and contractual condition. The potential for SFM under alternative forms of land tenure and institutional arrangements is barely considered. This chapter provides a contrasting example based on initial evidence from the experience in tropical forest management by communities in Quintana Roo, Mexico. Community forest management under secure tenure arrangements, with community forest enterprises (CFES) managing logging, presents a completely different set of conditions for SFM than logging by private enterprises on public lands under concessions. On a conceptual level, CFES are only one aspect of a multifaceted relationship between a community and its forests; as a result, traditional discount rate calculations fail to capture decision-making processes on forest use in communities and CFES.

Mexico contains the fifth-largest forest area in Latin America, and most of its forest lands are in the hands of local communities, with hundreds of communities managing their own CFES (Ward and Bihun 2001, Bray et al. 2003). Although Mexico may be unique in the amount of national forest lands in community hands, increasing global trends toward decentralization and devolution of forest management and the emergence of neo–common property forms suggest that Mexico may be the face of the future rather than a unique case (Arnold 1998, White and Martin 2002).

The phenomenon of communities managing common property forest for commercial timber production raises questions not asked in the CI literature. Do communities managing tropical forests under secure tenure arrangements respect management plans and overharvest? Do they make the same financial calculations as private sector loggers on public lands? Are intergenerational values factored into implicit financial calculations? Given that community forests are almost by definition multiple-use forests, what values other than timber are generated, and how do all uses contribute to sustainable rural livelihoods? In the following sections I explore some of these questions using data from Quintana Roo and a conceptual framework that describes some of the economic and ecological dimensions of forest management by communities in the state.

COMMUNITY FORESTRY MANAGEMENT IN QUINTANA ROO

The tropical forests of Quintana Roo are classified as medium height and semideciduous. Annual precipitation is around 1300 mm, and 75 percent of the rain falls between May and October. There are an estimated 102 tree species, with an average hectare having up to 30 species:

> The forests of Quintana Roo provide a challenge to those who wish to define some benchmark of "native" biodiversity against which to measure anthropogenic change. The forest community one sees today is the product of more than three thousand years of often substantial human use and intervention, and of infrequent but severe natural catastrophic events in the form of hurricanes and fires. (Kiernan and Freese 1997:97)

The history, problems, and achievements of the Plan Piloto Forestal (PPF), the government program that promoted community forestry in Quintana Roo, have been extensively reviewed elsewhere (Bray et al. 1993, Kiernan and Freese 1997, Flachsenberg and Galletti 1998, Galletti 1998, Vargas-Prieto 1998, Armijo Canto 1999, Taylor and Zabin 2000, Bray 2001). Despite this literature, the PPF is often misunderstood. The prospects for environmentally sound forestry in Quintana Roo have been questioned, but on a mistaken assumption about the logging cycle (Southgate 1998). Community forestry in the state has been equated with industries having agreements with communities to use their forests (Hardner and Rice 1999), when in fact it is a case of communities with their own CFE logging their own forests, a crucial distinction.

The PPF takes place in the context of Mexico's *ejido* system. In common property terms, *ejidos* are both a common pool resource and a common property regime (Ostrom 1990). *Ejidos* are owners of their forests. They are not concessionaires, although their property may be regarded as a form of shared private property, which is not the same as a private enterprise (McKean 2000). Historically, they had to struggle against a government policy of concessions in order to be able to manage their own forest resources, but *ejido* rights over forests were solidified by modifications to the Mexican constitution in 1992 (Wilshusen 2002). The PPF, which emerged with the termination of concessions, was based on the establishment of forest logging estates on *ejido* common property forest, called permanent forest areas (PFAS), thought to be the first time in tropical America that communities declared an end to land use change on portions of their lands; the organization of CFES using the *ejido* governance system as the organizational model; participatory inventories and the institution of permanent sampling plots (Lawrence and Sánchez-Román 1996); and the constitution of second-level organizations serving as assistance providers and political lobbying groups. There are five such organizations that came out of the PPF process. Thus from the beginning the *ejidos* assumed organizational forms and forest management practices quite different from those described for private enterprises operating under concessions.

The management plans of the PPF communities are based on those inherited from the parastatal Maderas Industrializadas de Quintana Roo (MIQROO), the first management plan in tropical America (Snook 1993). This plan is based on a polycyclical system with a twenty-five-year cutting cycle and three turns for a total of seventy-five years, and a minimum diameter limit of 55 cm diameter at breast height. There were also early efforts to develop markets for LKSs but with little success. The PPF process has received significant subsidies over the years, both from federal and state governments and from international donors, although these have been highly variable by period and organization, with most resources being concentrated in only two of the organizations: the Sociedad de Productores Ejidales Forestales de Quintana Roo and the Organización de Ejidos Productores Forestales de la Zona Maya.

TRENDS IN TIMBER EXTRACTION

Figure 12.1 shows the volume of logged mahogany and cedar in Quintana Roo from 1938 to 2001. Three historical periods are reflected in this figure: 1938–1956, when logging was controlled by private concessionaires; 1956–1983, when MIQROO controlled logging in the south and private concessionaires continued in central Quintana Roo; and 1984–2001, the PPF period.

The figure shows little difference in the extracted volume in the concessionaire and the parastatal or private concessionaire period; the MIQROO management plan did not slow down harvesting. The peaks in the mid-1950s resulted from salvage logging after Hurricane Janet in 1954. As the figure makes clear, community management under the PPF process resulted in a dramatic reduction and stabilization of the mahogany and cedar harvest, in three stages. In the first stage, from 1984 to 1988, extracted volumes were 22 percent lower in the five-year period than in the last five-year period (1979–1983) under MIQROO. After this initial logging period, it was realized that there had been measurement problems in the first round of participatory inventories, and more careful participatory inventories were carried out, resulting in further reductions in extracted volumes. Between 1993 and 2001, the average mahogany logging volume was 9904 m^3, a 78 percent reduction from the last five years under the parastatal. This had serious economic impacts at

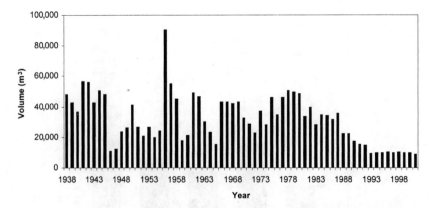

Figure 12.1   Total harvested volume of mahogany (*Swietenia macrophylla*) and cedar (*Cedrela odorata*) in Quintana Roo, Mexico (1938–2001). *Sources:* Dachary and Arnaiz B. (1983), Coldwell (1987), INEGI (1990), Argüelles Suárez (1999), SEMARNAP (2001).

the community level, as communities such as Noh Bec and Laguna Kaná reduced their logging volume by 29 percent and 37 percent just in the first reduction period, despite the fact that logging was a key source of community income, a decision a private logger working on public lands would be unlikely to make.

It has been argued that "most logging companies in the tropics engage in the rapid harvest of a limited number of valuable tree species because it is profitable" (Rice et al. 2001b:171) and that in Bolivia extracted volumes greatly exceeded those in the management plan (Hardner and Rice 1999). This is not reflected in the pattern of logging by Quintana Roo communities. It appears that the sixty-one communities with logging permits in Quintana Roo generally follow the law, respect inventories, and have taken steps toward a more sustainable harvest by reducing their logging volume steadily over time (Bray 2001). LKSS have also been harvested for decades, but current data are highly fragmentary. The LKS harvest rose dramatically in the first years of the PPF process under a state-mandated SFM program but dropped again quickly when it became apparent that markets were insufficient. Although market demand for LKSS has been growing in recent years, the amount of LKSS logged is always far below the authorized volume. For example, for 1999 and 2000, Quintana Roo communities logged 89 percent and 99.5 percent of their authorized volume of mahogany but only 14 percent and 18 percent of their authorized volume of LKSS. This casts doubt on one of the arguments of the CI researchers, that SFM will be more destructive to

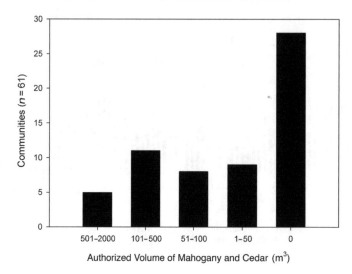

Figure 12.2 Quintana Roo forest communities by authorized extraction volume (m³) of mahogany (*Swietenia macrophylla*) and cedar (*Cedrela odorata*), 2000. *Source:* SEMARNAP (1999), with permission.

the forest because of the high volume of LKS extraction. Although it was proposed as a component of SFM in Quintana Roo, current markets severely limit this option, making it a questionable assumption with which to challenge community SFM.

The particular challenges of community SFM in Quintana Roo are compounded by the great variability in forest resources by the communities in the state. Figure 12.2 graphs communities by authorized amount of logging volume of mahogany and cedar, which closely tracks actual harvest. The figure indicates that only five communities with CFES in Quintana Roo have 501–2000 m³ of annual authorized volume of mahogany and cedar. We may classify these in the state context as large-volume CFES, where the natural resource is sufficient to provide a significant amount of employment, capital reinvestments in the enterprise, and significant profit-sharing flows. Nineteen communities, those with 101–500 m³ and 51–100 m³, are classified as low-volume CFES, where community logging is only a minor component of overall income opportunities (Armijo Canto 1997), and the income flows do not encourage reinvestment in the forest enterprise. The nine communities with less than 50 m³ and the twenty-eight that have logging permits only for LKSS and no authorized volume of mahogany and cedar may be classified as very-low-volume CFES, where the income is extremely minor, with implications for the sustainability of forest management. Sustainable logging may occur at all levels of extraction, but the implications for institutional support and public policies may vary significantly between CFES.

A CONCEPTUAL FRAMEWORK FOR EXPLORING SUSTAINABLE COMMUNITY FOREST MANAGEMENT

In a research project currently under way, a team of an anthropologist, ecologists, and economists has been formed to study the sustainability of community forest management in Quintana Roo, taking several communities as case studies and analyzing existing data on forest production and management. This research project is using the conceptual framework presented here. We believe this framework can be usefully applied to most of the sixty-one communities currently logging in Quintana Roo. Although these communities vary significantly in terms of size, location, ethnic composition, and forest resources, the common structure of the *ejido* system and CFES that are the result of similar government programs has created similarities in the patterns of forest management.

Figure 12.3 shows a conceptual framework that will be used to explore the characteristics and sustainability of community tropical forest management in Quintana Roo, with implications for how it may differ from private exploitation.

A first important feature is the social capital (Dasgupta and Serageldin 2000) constructed by grassroots and government efforts in second-level organizations, represented by the Organización de Ejidos Productores Forestales de la Zona Maya oval on the far right of the framework. Nearly all of the sixty-one logging communities in Quintana Roo belong to one of five different second-level (intercommunity) organizations. Community participation in these second-level organizations has been an important source of social and financial capital for the communities, including subsidies from government and foundation sources, technical support in forestry, and support in price negotiations with buyers.

The framework represents the fact that the community and the individuals within it draw multiple values from the *ejido* territory. Unlike private enterprises, they have far more interests than timber. The *ejido* territory includes both a common property forest area (PFA) and agricultural areas, some of which may also be forested or in secondary succession, creating a managed landscape mosaic. The community and the individuals also draw on the forest and the entire landscape mosaic, but with a complex set of individual and communal appropriations of the *ejido* territory. In common property theory, the natural resources in the entire

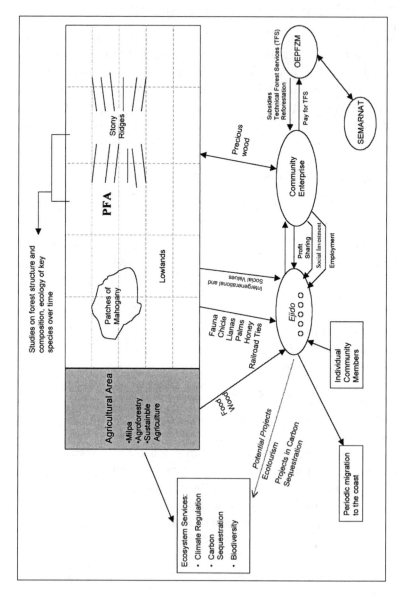

Figure 12.3 Conceptual framework of community tropical forest management in Quintana Roo, Mexico. OEPFZM, Organización de Ejidos Productores Forestales de la Zona Maya; PFA, permanent forest area. The name of the Mexican environmental agency, Secretary of the Environment, Natural Resources, Water, and Fisheries (SEMARNAP), was changed to Secretary of the Environment and Natural Resources (SEMARNAT) in 2000.

ejido territory may be thought of as a stock, with flows that are appropriated either communally (logwood by the enterprise) or individually (other timber products and nontimber forest products [NTFPs]), subject to rules of access (McKean 2000).

Thus the communities have a CFE, which is charged with logging. The community enterprise pays for technical forest services (*servicios técnicos forestales*) from one of the five second-level organizations. In many cases this payment does not entirely cover the costs of those services, with services for reforestation and forest enrichment and representational support subsidized by external support from government and private foundations.

As shown to the left of the CFE box, the CFE pays profit-sharing dividends in cash to community members, generates income through direct employment, and may invest in social infrastructure, pensions, and investments in the enterprise. In addition to common property logging, individual community members also draw multiple timber, nontimber, and agricultural products from the PFA and individual agricultural plots. From the PFA, many communities extracted ten LKSs that were used for railroad ties, although this market disappeared from 1997 to 2001, only to experience a new demand in 2002. More recently a new individually appropriated timber product emerged, the small-diameter timber known as *palizada*, used in tourism construction. Chicle was historically the most important NTFP, but it also terminated because of loss of markets in 1998, although chicle tapping also restarted in 2002. Beekeeping is another important economic activity that draws on the forest mosaic. In many communities there is a growing commercial extraction of palms (*Sabal mexicano*) used in the tourist zone. All community members have access to the forest to provide themselves with subsistence products such as bushmeat, firewood, and timber and palm for housing. Harvest sustainability of many these products has not been established. Notions of wildlife protection are still rudimentary, and local people occasionally kill jaguars who prey on sheep and goats introduced by recent government programs. In some communities, lianas and medicinal plants are also gathered for subsistence and commercial purposes.

The value of the multiple commercial and subsistence uses of the forest accrue almost entirely to the local communities, with economic benefits that vary greatly based on authorized volume. In a high-volume community such as Noh Bec, with 1545 m^3 in authorized volume of mahogany and cedar in 1999, the CFE generates up to 130 full-time or nearly full-time jobs and a profit-sharing dividend of US$1895 per year. Profits are used to invest in community infrastructure, medical services, and old-age pensions. At the other extreme, the community of X-Yatil, with only 24 m^3 authorized volume of mahogany, generates almost no employment and around US$80 of annual profit-sharing dividends from logging (Robinson and Gongóra 2000). Calculations derived from a study of a wider range of forest-based income in two communities in 1996 show that income (including both cash and subsistence values) from commercial timber, chicle, wildlife, and firewood in two communities with low and high authorized volumes of timber ranged from US$405 per community member to US$870 per community member. This compares with an average annual minimum salary of $884 per year if someone were fully employed at the 1997 prevailing minimum wage. This does not include any wage labor, which is also common (Negreros-Castillo et al. 2000). At all levels of forest-based income, all profits in various forms go to local community members with agrarian rights. Notwithstanding persistent problems with local-level corruption in some of the CFES, this is a major step forward in equity and democratic management of natural resources, with consequences for social and political stability. In recent years, communities have also taken important steps toward reorganizing the CFES to prevent corruption (Wilshusen 2002).

In addition to these cash and subsistence incomes from forest use, many of the sixty-one logging communities have been participating in agroforestry and sustainable agriculture programs subsidized by the federal and state government but often channeled by the organizations. Because of government subsidies, up to three-quarters of all members of many communities planted one or more hectares of *taungya* agroforestry. There have also been recent efforts to promote intensive agriculture that could greatly increase yields in smaller areas. *Taungya* agroforestry is intended to leave miniplantations of cedar, mahogany, and LKSS, which also appear to have some degree of volunteer biodiversity and create small forested islands in the agricultural areas (A. Racelis, pers. comm. 2003). Thus these projects tend to create more forested patches on the landscape and to reduce pressure from slash-and-burn agriculture, both steps toward more sustainable land uses. Pressure on forested areas from cattle raising varies from significant in some forest *ejidos* in southern Quintana Roo to insignificant in almost all Mayan *ejidos* in central Quintana Roo.

In addition to all these uses of the *ejido* territory, it appears communities impute an intergenerational value, possibly with other social and cultural values. The forest is seen as a resource to be preserved for their children, with other perceived social and cultural values. The comment of an *ejidatario* from the community of Laguna Kaná is typical:

If we leave our patrimony degraded, we're going to go around begging. We have a firm floor here. It's the patrimony of our fathers. If we don't take care of it for our children, who is going to take care of it?

Current studies will attempt to quantify these expressions of inter-generational values. But this community member implicitly accepts very low discount rates and is untroubled by the low growth rate of tropical timber because the forest is a source of a wide range of values that will extend to future generations. Finally, still unrealized ecosystem service values through ecotourism, biodiversity protection, and carbon seques-tration could be developed in the future.

THE ECOLOGY OF COMMUNITY FOREST MANAGEMENT

As one imperfect but significant measure of sustainability, eleven of the sixty-one logging communities have been certified by the Rainforest Al-liance SmartWood Program and the Mexican Civil Council for Sustain-able Silviculture. However, studies suggest that the current extraction volumes are not sustainable because the seventy-five-year cutting cycle is too short to ensure stocks of commercial-sized mahogany. It has been es-timated that the growth rate of mahogany in these forests is only about half the rate necessary to maintain stocks of commercial-sized timber in the current cycle, and other concerns have been expressed about silvi-cultural and enrichment practices that do not ensure a continued stock of mahogany (Snook 1993, 1997, Negreros-Castillo 2000, Snook and Negreros-Castillo 2002). The current management plan also divides the forest into equal-sized blocks, and it has been observed that mahogany does not have an even distribution in the forest but rather occurs in patches, and communities have sometimes had to go beyond a given annual stand, not following the management plan, to meet the author-ized volume for that year. Current trends in authorized logging volumes vary, partly because of local differences in forest ecology. After a decade of stability in mahogany volumes, statewide authorized volumes de-clined from 10,089 m^3 in 2000 to 8726 m^3 in 2001, but it is not clear whether this trend will persist. Several communities have experienced re-cent declines in their authorized volumes, after years of stability, but one large-volume community has seen its volumes increase. Current propos-als to conduct forest enrichment in logyards, roads, and other large opened areas could maintain or increase harvest levels and reduce im-pact on the natural forest (Flachsenberg and Galletti 1998).

It is not known with any precision to what extent the decades of unsustainable logging, followed by nearly twenty years of more sustainable management by communities, has altered the structure and composition of these natural forests and how close to a sustainable harvest of some timber species current practices may be. Even less is known about harvests of some of the other timber species and NTFPS. But as noted earlier, the natural characteristics of these forests are that they have been highly disturbed for millennia by both natural and anthropogenic causes. In terms of the ecological impact of community logging on wildlife, one observation suggests that the probable reduction of large-diameter mahogany from the forest will affect some bird species (Kiernan and Freese 1997). However, another study found the impact of logging as practiced in Quintana Roo, on both resident and migrant bird populations, to be "benign" (Lynch and Whigham 1995). One of the few studies of the impact of railroad tie logging on the forests found that although it had contributed to a restructuring of the forest near towns and roads, the total gaps opened annually were equivalent to the rate of natural gap formation (Shoch 1999). Community forest management in central Quintana Roo also appears to be one factor that has led to very low rates of land use change over the last twenty-five years. Satellite images show that the landscape in this region is still dominated by a pattern of agriculture within an intact matrix of tropical forest (Bray et al. in press). Chazdon (1998:1296) notes that "a tropical landscape containing a matrix of old-growth forest fragments, second-growth forest, logged forest, and agricultural fields could conceivably protect most of the species present in the regional biota," a characterization that fits this community-managed landscape.

CONCLUSION

The case of community forest management in Quintana Roo suggests that communities and their CFES are an entirely different scenario from private companies logging on public lands under concessions. These communities have an enterprise that logs the forest. They also have a community with multiple economic, social, cultural, and intergenerational relationships with the forest and its associated ecosystems in the *ejido* mosaic. For communities, the forest is not just a financial investment; it is a constellation of economic and cultural values. The CI arguments against SFM are based almost exclusively on a single scenario, private sector logging companies operating under concessions on public lands, and with only two possible outcomes: continued logging by the private company (under two possible scenarios of nonsustainable forestry or SFM forestry) or a protected area. I argue that other outcomes must be recognized and independently evaluated as to their sustainability. Furthermore, the economic benefits from community forest management flow in a far greater proportion to local communities, making significant contributions to social and political stability, economic development, and the democratic management of natural resources.

Hardner and Rice (1999:179) suggest that some of the difficulties "shared by . . . models of community forestry [include] . . . challenges in organizing the communities, ensuring that forest management is more economically attractive than agriculture to local populations, and reversing the negative sentiment about commercial timber producers." In the case of community forestry in Mexico in general, the communities are well organized, the communities have declared the PFAS, and the last stipulation is not relevant because the communities *are* the commercial timber producers, through their own community logging enterprises. CFES in Quintana Roo have not made the decision to harvest as many commercial-sized trees in the shortest time possible. They accept the slow growth of their tropical timber because they know it will be there for their children.

Tenure options are not limited to concessions and individual private property. In common property forms of shared private property, different financial incentives operate, and very low discount rates are accepted (McKean 2000). Although timber certification eventually may be helpful in adding or maintaining value, communities do not need it as an additional economic incentive to maintain their forests. The effort to promote community forestry in Quintana Roo has had multiple subsidies over the years. But concessions on public lands, and consequent problems in revenue collections, imply very large public subsidies to this institutional arrangement (see chapter 21). Thus it is a matter of public policy choice as to whether governments want to use public resources to encourage overharvesting by private industries on public land or to encourage communities to embark on a more sustainable path under common property or co-management arrangements. Protected areas will also need substantial public investments to be viable, with perhaps more uncertain benefits for local communities. For many years, it could be argued that Mexico was a unique historical case and thus not a model. But the recent emergence of community forest management for timber elsewhere in the world (Becker and León 2000, Salafsky et al. 2001a, 2001b, Cronkleton 2002) suggests that Mexico is no longer a unique case but may represent the future of community forest management. Therefore it suggests that CFES may be a viable strategy for conserving forest cover and biodiversity and generating income for local communities.

ACKNOWLEDGMENTS

Thanks to Rosa Cossío-Solano, José Juan Calderón, and Alex Racelis for editorial and research assistance. Special thanks to the William and Flora Hewlett Foundation and the Ford Foundation for their support of the research reported here. Team members include Dr. Juan Manuel Torres-Rojo (Centro de Investigación y Docencia Económica), Dr. Alejandro Velázquez and Elvira Durán (Universidad Nacional Autónoma de México), Dr. Patricia Negreros-Castillo (Iowa State University and FAO), Dr. Alejandro Guevara-Sanguines (Universidad Iberoamericana), and Dr. Henricus F. M. Vester (Colegio de la Frontera Sur).

REFERENCES

Argüelles Suárez, L. A. 1999. *Diagnóstico de las poblaciónes de caoba en Mexico.* Chetumal, Mexico.

Armijo Canto, N. 1997. *Distribución de los beneficios socioeconómicos del bosque.* Chetumal, Mexico: Universidad de Quintana Roo, Departamento para el Desarrollo Internacional (Gobierno Británico).

Armijo Canto, N. 1999. Las sociedades civiles de productos forestales en Quintana Roo. In D. Cazes, ed., *Creacion de alternativas en Mexico,* 85–101. Mexico City: UNAM/Centro de Investigaciones Interdisciplinarias en Ciencias y Humanidades.

Arnold, J. E. M. 1998. *Managing forests as common property.* FAO Forestry Paper no. 136. Rome: Food and Agricultural Organization.

Becker, C. D. and R. León. 2000. Indigenous forest management in the Bolivian Amazon: Lessons from the Yuracaré people. In C. C. Gibson, M. A. McKean, and E. Ostrom, eds., *People and forests: Communities, institutions, and governance,* 163–192. Cambridge, Mass.: MIT Press.

Bowles, I. A., R. E. Rice, R. A. Mittermeier, and G. A. B. da Fonseca. 1998. Logging and tropical forest conservation. *Science* 280: 1899–1900.

Bray, D. B. 2001. The Mayans of central Quintana Roo. In S. C. Stonich, ed., *Endangered peoples of Latin America, Struggles to survive and thrive,* 3–17. Westport, Conn.: Greenwood.

Bray, D. B., M. Carreón, L. Merino, and V. Santos. 1993. On the road to sustainable forestry. *Cultural Survival Quarterly* 17: 38–41.

Bray, D. B., E. Ellis, N. Armijo, and L. Somarriba. In press. The drivers of sustainable landscapes: A case study of the Mayan zone in Quintana Roo, Mexico. *Land Use Policy.*

Bray, D. B., L. Merino-Perez, P. Negreros-Castillo, G. Segura-Warnholz, J. M. Torres-Rojo, and H. F. M. Vester. 2003. Mexico's community-managed forests: A global model for sustainable landscapes. *Conservation Biology* 17: 672–677.

Chazdon, R. L. 1998. Tropical forests: log 'em or leave 'em? *Science* 281: 1295–1296.

Coldwell, P. J. 1987. *Informe de labores del gobierno.* Chetumal, Mexico: Gobierno del Estado de Quintana Roo.

Cronkleton, P. 2002. *Collaboration and adaptation in the marketing of timber by indigenous peoples in lowland Bolivia.* Unpublished paper, "Working Forests in the Tropics: Conservation Through Sustainable Management" conference, Gainesville, Fla., February 2002.

Dachary, A. C. and S. M. Arnaiz B. 1983. *Estudios socioeconómicos preliminares de Quintana Roo: Sector agropecuario y forestal (1902–1980).* Puerto Morelos, Mexico: Centro de Investigaciones de Quintana Roo.

Dasgupta, P. and I. Serageldin, eds. 2000. *Social capital: A multifaceted perspective.* Washington, D.C.: The World Bank.

Flachsenberg, H. and H. A. Galletti. 1998. Forest management in Quintana Roo, Mexico. In R. B. Primack, D. Bray, H. A. Galletti, and I. Ponciano, eds., *Timber, tourists, and temples: Conservation and development in the Maya Forest of Belize, Guatemala, and Mexico,* 47–60. Washington, D.C.: Island Press.

Galletti, H. A. 1998. The Maya Forest of Quintana Roo: Thirteen years of conservation and community development. In R. B. Primack, D. Bray, H. A. Galletti, and I. Ponciano, eds., *Timber, tourists, and temples: Conservation and development in the Maya Forest of Belize, Guatemala, and Mexico,* 33–46. Washington, D.C.: Island Press.

Hardner, J. J. and R. Rice. 1999. Rethinking forest concession policies. In K. Keipi, ed., *Forest resource policy in Latin America,* 161–194. Washington, D.C.: Inter-American Development Bank.

INEGI. 1990. *Análisis estadístico de los Estados Unidos Mexicanos.* Aguascalientes, Mexico: Instituto Nacional de Estadística, Geografía e Informática.

Kiernan, M. J. and C. H. Freese. 1997. Mexico's Plan Piloto Forestal: The search for balance between socioeconomic and ecological sustainability. In C. H. Freese, ed., *Harvesting wild species: Implications for biodiversity,* 93–131. Baltimore, Md.: Johns Hopkins University Press.

Lawrence, A. and F. Sánchez-Román. 1996. The role of inventory in the communally managed forests of Quintana Roo, Mexico. In J. Carter, ed., *Recent approaches to participatory forest resource assessment,* 83–110. London: Overseas Development Institute.

Lynch, J. F. and D. F. Whigham. 1995. The role of habitat disturbance in the ecology of overwintering migratory birds in the Yucatan Peninsula. In M. H. Wilson and S. Sader, eds., *Conservation of neotropical migratory birds in Mexico.* Miscellaneous Publication 727. Orono: Maine Agricultural and Forest Experiment Station.

McKean, M. A. 2000. Common property: What is it, what is it good for, and what makes it work? In C. C. Gibson, M. A. McKean, and E. Ostrom, eds., *People and forests: Communities, institutions, and governance.* Cambridge, Mass.: MIT Press.

Negreros-Castillo, P. 2000. *Restoration of mahogany productivity in southeastern Mexico.* Unpublished manuscript.

Negreros-Castillo, P., J. C. González Nuñez, and L. Merino Pérez. 2000. Evaluación de la sustentabilidad del sistema de manejo forestal de la Organización de Ejidos Productores Forestales de la Zona Maya de Quintana Roo. In O.

Masera and S. López-Ridaura, eds., *Sustentabilidad y sistemas campesinos: Cinco experiencias de evaluación en el México rural.* Pátzcuaro, Michoacan, Mexico: GIRA.

Ostrom, E. 1990. *Governing the commons: The evolution of institutions for collective action.* Cambridge, U.K.: Cambridge University Press.

Reid, J. W. and R. E. Rice. 1997. Assessing natural forest management as a tool for tropical forest conservation. *Ambio* 26: 282–286.

Rice, R. E., R. E. Gullison, and J. W. Reid. 1997. Can sustainable management save tropical forests? *Scientific American* 276(4): 44–49.

Rice, R. E., C. A. Sugal, P. C. Frumhoff, E. Losos, and R. Gullison. 2001a. Options for conserving biodiversity in the context of logging in tropical forests. In I. A. Bowles and G. T. Prickett, eds., *Footprints in the jungle: Natural resources industries, infrastructure, and biodiversity conservation.* New York: Oxford University Press.

Rice, R. E., C. A. Sugal, S. M. Ratay, and G. A. Fonseca. 2001b. Sustainable forest management: A review of conventional wisdom. *Advances in Applied Biodiversity Science* 3: 1–29.

Robinson, D. and E. C. Gongóra. 2000. *An analysis of different forms of organization for forest production in three communities in Quintana Roo, Mexico.* Chetumal, Mexico: Universidad de Quintana Roo.

Salafsky, N., H. Cauley, B. Balachander, B. Cordes, J. Parks, C. Margoluis, S. Bhatt, C. Encarnacion, D. Russell, and R. Margoluis. 2001a. A systematic test of an enterprise strategy for community-based biodiversity conservation. *Conservation Biology* 15: 1585–1595.

Salafsky, N., M. Henderson, and M. Leighton. 2001b. Community-based timber production: A viable strategy for promoting wildlife conservation? In R. A. Fimbel, A. Grajal, and J. G. Robinson, eds., *The cutting edge: Conserving wildlife in logged tropical forests.* New York: Columbia University Press.

SEMARNAP. 1999. *Archivos de aprovechamiento.* Chetumal, Mexico: SEMARNAP.

SEMARNAP. 2001. *Volumen aprovechado de caoba y cedro.* Chetumal, Mexico: Secretaría de Medio Ambiente y Recursos Naturales.

Shoch, D. T. 1999. *An ecological and economic evaluation of railroad tie harvest in the ejido X-Pichil, Quintana Roo, Mexico.* Master's project, Duke University, Durham, N.C.

Snook, L. 1993. Stand dynamics of mahogany (*Swietenia macrophylla* King) and associated species after fire and hurricanes in the tropical forests of the Yucatan Peninsula. Ph.D. dissertation, Yale University, New Haven, Conn.

Snook, L. K. 1997. Uso, manejo y conservación forestal en México: Implicaciones de la tenencia comunitaria y los recientes cambios en las políticas. In L. Paré, D. B. Bray, J. Burstein, and S. M. Vásquez, eds., *Semillas para el cambio en el campo: Medio ambiente, mercados y organización campesina,* 19–35. Mexico City: UNAM; IIS; La Sociedad de Solidaridad Social "Sansekan Tinemi" y Saldebas; Servicios de Apoyo Local al Desarrollo de Base en México.

Snook, L. K. and P. Negreros-Castillo. 2002. *Regenerating mahogany (*Swietenia macrophylla *King) on patch clearcuts in Mexico's Maya Forest: The effects of clearing treatment and cleaning on survival and growth.* Presented at the conference "Working Forests in the Tropics," University of Florida, Gainesville, February 25–26, 2002.

Southgate, D. 1998. *Tropical forest conservation: An economic assessment of the alternatives in Latin America.* New York: Oxford University Press.

Taylor, P. L. and C. Zabin. 2000. Neoliberal reform and sustainable forest management in Quintana Roo, Mexico: Rethinking the institutional framework of the Forestry Pilot Plan. *Agriculture and Human Values* 17: 141–156.

Vargas-Prieto, A. M. 1998. *Effective intervention: External and internal elements of institutional structure for forest management in Quintana Roo, Mexico.* Ph.D. dissertation, University of Wisconsin-, Madison.

Ward, J. R. and Y. Bihun. 2001. Stewardship of Mexico's community forests: Expanding market and policy opportunities for conservation and rural development. In I. A. Bowles and G. T. Prickett, eds., *Footprints in the jungle: Natural resource industries, infrastructure, and biodiversity conservation,* 145–167. New York: Oxford University Press.

White, A. and A. Martin. 2002. *Who owns the world's forests?* Washington, D.C.: Forest Trends, Center for International Law.

Wilshusen, P. R. 2002. *Negotiating devolution: Community conflict, structural power, and local forest management in Quintana Roo, Mexico.* Ph.D. dissertation, College of Natural Resources, University of Michigan, Ann Arbor.

Chapter 13

CARBON SEQUESTRATION POTENTIAL THROUGH FORESTRY ACTIVITIES IN TROPICAL MEXICO

Bernardus H. J. de Jong

The Scolel Té project for carbon management and rural livelihoods in southern Mexico (Scolel Té 1998) began in 1996 after a six-month feasibility study that brought together Mexican and British scientists and representatives of indigenous farmers from the state of Chiapas. The objective of the project was to develop a generic system for planning and administering the production and commercialization of carbon sequestration with the participation of small-scale landowners and communities. The majority of the rural population of Chiapas and other southern states are small-scale indigenous farmers, most of whom live in and operate under communal land ownership of various forms.

Over the past six years, Scolel Té has grown steadily from a vague concept to a small but vibrant organization that is based on the development and commercialization of carbon sequestration assets. Annual income from the sale of carbon services is currently around us$120,000 per year; current customers include the International Federation of Automobiles to offset emissions of Formula 1 races and the World Rally and Future Forests (United Kingdom) to offset emissions of their business partners.

Lessons learned from Scolel Té indicate that carbon mitigation can be developed at low costs because the two principal inputs, land and labor, are cheap compared with other inputs. With an understanding of the local social context, it is possible to develop forestry and agroforestry projects with CO_2 mitigation objectives that simultaneously help finance promising sustainable development programs (Swisher and Masters 1992). Evidence points to low implementation and maintenance costs of various forestry and agroforestry C mitigation options (De Jong et al. 1995).

As part of the feasibility study and subsequent development of the project, the Plan Vivo carbon sequestration planning and management system was designed and refined (http://www.planvivo.org). The system is robust and functions with a core administrative and technical staff of only two to four people and periodic support and advice from scientific agencies such as El Colegio de la Frontera Sur (Ecosur) and The Edinburgh Center for Carbon Management. In Chiapas, the system has been developed during a time of rural tension and conflict and has been accepted by a wide range of political and ethnic groups.

The forestry and agroforestry options that interest the farmers participating in the Scolel Té carbon storage project are the introduction of trees in agricultural systems, such as crop–tree combinations, and the restoration of degraded land. On communally held areas of natural forest or secondary vegetation, the main sequestration strategies are the restoration of degraded forests and the conservation and management of the existing vegetation.

The Scolel Té project is unusual because numerous farmers are participating individually or in groups with a high variety of small-scale practices, and they are distributed over a large area that varies in altitude from 0 to 2000 m above sea level and in rainfall from 1200 to 3000 mm per year. Management practices are site-specific, and farmers adapt them to their particular circumstances based on their personal interests, local conditions, and previous experiences.

Because project implementation began only six years ago, it is still early to judge whether the land use practices initiated through the project are sustainable in the long term. However, there is substantial demand from communities and organizations in the region (as well as in neighboring states) to participate in the project.

The potential of this type of project to mitigate substantial amounts of carbon emissions in a farmer-dominated landscape depends on the responses to two questions, which are presented here and addressed in the remainder of this chapter: Can farmer-selected forestry and agroforestry practices, if implemented at a regional scale, contribute substantially and cost-effectively to the mitigation of CO_2 emissions? What are the main sources and levels of variability in estimates of the carbon sequestration potential of those practices?

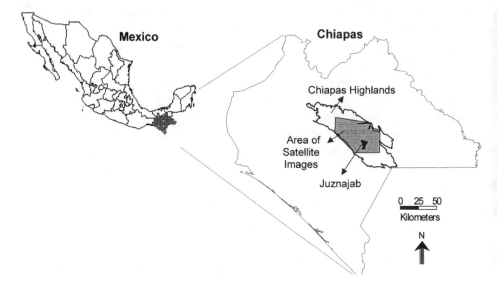

Figure 13.1   Chiapas Highlands study area, the area used for the satellite image interpretation, and the location of Juznajab La Laguna community, Chiapas, Mexico.

ESTIMATING CARBON SEQUESTRATION POTENTIAL AT THE REGIONAL SCALE

Study Area

The Highlands of Chiapas (figure 13.1) encompass all or parts of 30 *municipios* (local government units) and are one of the most densely populated rural areas in Mexico. Tzotzil, Tojolabal, and Tzeltal Maya indigenous groups inhabit these *municipios*. With the rapid improvement of infrastructure from the 1970s onward, including road construction and rural electrification, these populations were increasingly integrated into the economic activities of Chiapas. From 1950 to 1990, the population tripled in size, mainly because of a rapid increase in the number of settlements of between 100 and 2500 inhabitants.

Privatization of communal lands and rapid population growth are among the main driving forces behind ongoing landscape fragmentation (Ochoa-Gaona and González-Espinosa 2000). Whereas only a few decades ago large tracts were still covered with old-growth forest, the landscape is now highly disturbed, with only small areas of disturbed forests in a matrix of cultivated land, tree, and shrub fallows and temporary and permanent grazing lands (Parra-Vázquez et al. 1989). Currently, only a few small patches of old-growth forest remain (Ochoa-Gaona 2001).

Farmers generally combine shifting cultivation and extensive grazing of cattle and sheep with uncontrolled extraction of timber, fuelwood, and other forest products. Farmers with extremely small properties practicing semisubsistence agriculture dominate the rural economy. Each family has a variety of livelihood strategies, which are articulated by means of ecological, technical, and social relationships and production systems, such as the production of corn and beans to sustain the family, temporal or seasonal off-farm paid labor, and trading of surplus products. Any shortage in any of these components obliges the family to search for compensation by trying to increase one of the other components (Fernández et al. 1999). For example, changing coffee plantations into corn and bean fields was one of many farmers' responses to the low coffee price in the early 1990s, whereas the reverse was observed when coffee prices rose again and when additional government subsidies for coffee production became available at the end of the 1990s.

Selection of Forestry and Agroforestry Practices with Carbon Sequestration Potential

Current land use practices were analyzed and potential practice improvements and new alternative practices proposed, discussed, and evaluated based on social, economic, and technical criteria. The selected practices were then evaluated in terms of their carbon offset potential. The costs of implementing each practice were estimated based on the discounted direct costs of improving current land use practices or establishing new practices and the discounted maintenance and opportunity costs.

Evaluating the suitability of forestry and agroforestry for carbon sequestration requires insights into the institutions involved at the implementation level. Our study therefore used participatory methods to identify the major ecological, technical, and socioeconomic constraints related to current practices in the case study area. To begin the project, a multidisciplinary team of scientists and farmers was created. The options were designed and evaluated during workshops in which community representatives and scientific advisers participated (De Jong et al. 1995, 1997, De Jong 2000).

The following parameters were considered in selecting the proposed practices: the area available for forestry or agroforestry, the potential species or species combinations to be planted, the current land use practice in which trees would be incorporated and the planting design, and

Table 13.1 Land Use Options in Selected Land Cover Classes

Land Cover Class	Land Use Options
Closed forest	Integrated community forest management, selective harvesting in compartments, conservation and extraction of nontimber forest products of high-biodiversity cloud forest
Open forest	Forest restoration through natural regeneration or enrichment planting, restriction of grazing activities
Tree and shrub fallow	Forest restoration through natural regeneration or enrichment planting, oak coppicing for fuelwood and charcoal
Milpa agriculture	*Taungya* combined with organic agriculture
Pasture	Agroforestry practices such as fodder banks

the strategy for purchasing seedlings. Table 13.1 highlights land use options that were selected for each current land use and land cover class (De Jong et al. 2000).

Total net carbon accumulation for each alternative management option was estimated for a period of 100 years, based on locally collected data on existing carbon pools and tree growth in relation to site conditions (De Jong 2000), supplemented with published data for those parameters for which no local data were available. In modeling the C fluxes by means of the CO2FIX model (Mohren and Klein Goldewijk 1990, Mohren et al. 1999), we assumed that the carbon dynamics of the rest of the system does not change substantially with the incorporation of the trees and that the site quality remains unaltered during the cycles. The net average increase in C stock was used for this part of the study (De Jong et al. 2000).

Baseline Land Use and Land Cover Change Dynamics

To estimate the carbon sequestration potential of a project, the result of the C flux calculation of the proposed land use practice must be compared with a baseline or nonintervention scenario or current practice. In the case of existing forests, the maintenance or enhancement of the current C stocks through forest conservation or management must be compared with expected future deforestation and forest degradation trends if the project were not implemented. In the case of forest restoration through afforestation or agroforestry measures, the changes in the C stock on a site without the forest restoration activity must be assessed.

To predict future trends in land use and land use change, we assumed that historical trends will continue into the future. To understand the historical trends in land use change and associated carbon fluxes, land cover maps from the 1970s, 1980s, and 1990s were analyzed and compared. These maps were developed and derived from satellite images, aerial photographs, and ground truthing (Tipper et al. 1998, Ochoa-Gaona and González-Espinosa 2000). The land use and land cover (LU/LC) classes that could be distinguished in the images were closed forest, open forest, tree and shrub fallow, pasture, and agriculture (including bare soil and settlements). C densities were assigned to each class, based on field data (De Jong et al. 1999). The surface area occupied by each land use class in 1974, 1984, 1990, and 1996 was multiplied by their respective average C density values.

Whereas most of the aboveground carbon pools, plus some of the root matter and leaf litter, are susceptible to rapid loss caused by land use change, a large proportion of soil carbon remains stable long after land cover changes from forest to open land. The amount of stable humus may vary with soil type, land use history, precipitation, and vegetation, among other factors. Comparing total C pools for each date, we calculated the historical rate of C storage decrease, assuming a stepwise depletion process between periods. C densities in each LU/LC class were assumed to remain constant during the period analyzed. Default baseline scenarios were established as a fixed frame of reference by extrapolation of the yearly rates of C loss into the future.

In a comparison of the LU/LC statistics obtained from the satellite image interpretation of a subarea (308,000 ha, or 49 percent of the whole study area), it appeared that in the late 1970s and early 1980s the total C stocks decreased at a rate of approximately 1.7 percent per year. Between 1984 and 1990 the C stocks increased slightly but diminished rapidly again at about 2.5 percent per year in the 1990s (De Jong et al. 2000). The overall average annual C depletion for the whole period was estimated at 1.4 percent. Given this variation in annual C depletion, a conservative range of baseline emissions through LU/LC change dynamics of 0.5 to 1.5 percent per year was used, from low (0.5 percent) to medium (1 percent) and high (1.5 percent) future baseline C depletion. The medium rate that was used in the baseline estimates matches the average decline observed from 1974 to 1990, whereas the high rate corresponds roughly to the twenty-two-year average C decline (De Jong et al. 2000).

The Costs of Transferring Current Land Use to Forestry and Agroforestry

The interest of farmers to start cultivating trees for timber or other purposes within their current land use strategies varies with economic, social, and cultural factors (Tipper et al. 1998). Some farmers who already have experience with managing trees are likely to enter the project easily, whereas farmers who have seen trees as obstacles for land development are unlikely to become involved in such a project. To estimate the total cost of transferring current land use to the selected practices, only the direct costs related to implementing the project were considered. These costs include implementation, lost opportunities, training in forestry practices, and expected benefits from product sales. To calculate these costs to present value, an income–expenditure profile was constructed for each selected intervention (Tipper et al. 1998, De Jong et al. 2000). Project monitoring is considered a continuous assessment of the functioning of project activities and as such is included in the implementation and management costs (De Jong et al. 1997). The certification of the carbon credits and verification of the projects' performance (Swisher 1992) are excluded from this analysis because their cost will depend on measurement standards and allowable limits of error, which have not yet been agreed upon internationally (MacDicken 1997). External transaction costs are also excluded because they will depend largely on how the Kyoto Protocol is implemented internationally and in Mexico.

Large-scale investment in forestry to sequester carbon will face rising cost functions (Moulton and Richards 1990) when lands with higher productivity or opportunity costs enter the program and when project promotion and forestry training are increasingly needed (Tipper et al. 1998). Therefore four levels (called cost–benefit quartiles) for both opportunity and sociotechnical costs are used in the analysis (De Jong et al. 2000).

The costs of establishing community forestry practices were estimated at US$186/ha for closed forests to US$217.50/ha for open forests and at US$212–285 for the various tree-planting activities. The costs of maintaining the management practices ranged from US$36/year for plantations in agricultural land to US$103/year for plantations in former shrub and tree fallow and from US$63/year to US$101/year for the forest management practices (table 13.2).

The direct opportunity costs of keeping forests were estimated to be lower than those for reforesting agriculture and pastoral land and ranged from US$0/year for the lowest cost–benefit quartile in the open and closed forest class to US$130/year for the highest cost–benefit quartile of the closed forest class (table 13.3). Carbon sequestration by replacing current agricultural practices, fallow, and pasture with agroforestry or plantation forestry costs the most. Replacing agriculture with agroforestry or forestry is only marginally profitable for practices that fall into the first and second cost–benefit quartiles and therefore are the only ones expected to voluntarily enter in a C sequestration forestry program (figure 13.2). The early product revenues from closed forest management

Table 13.2 Costs of Establishing and Maintaining Carbon Sequestration Management Alternatives in Each Current Land Use and Land Cover Class

Land Use and Land Cover Types	Average Cost (us$) of Establishing up to Three Agroforestry Options for Each Current Land Use Class Including Labor (see Tipper et al. 1998 for details)	Operational and Maintenance Costs, Including Project Monitoring (us$/ha/yr)
Closed forest	186–209	63–101
Open forest	217.5	101
Tree and shrub fallow	223–285	75–103
Milpa agriculture	212	36–49
Pasture	282.5	39–65

Source: Adapted from De Jong et al. (2000).

Table 13.3 Annual Opportunity Costs for Each Cost–Benefit Quartile to Convert Current Land Use Practices into Carbon Sequestration Management Alternatives

Production Practice	Opportunity Costs for Each Cost–Benefit Quartile (us$/yr)			
	1st Quartile	2nd Quartile	3rd Quartile	4th Quartile
Closed forest	0–7	7–13	26–65	65–130
Open forest	0	6.5	26	65
Tree and shrub fallow	0	86	150	215
Milpa agriculture	0	140	250	359
Pasture	39	78	107	152

Source: Adapted from De Jong et al. (2000).

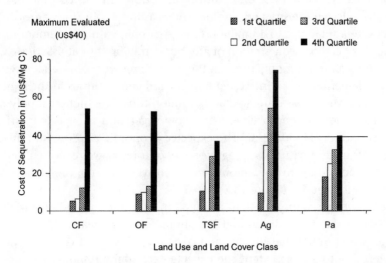

Figure 13.2 Costs of carbon mitigation for the four cost–benefit quartiles of the forestry and agroforestry options that would replace current land use in the following land use and land cover classes: Ag, agriculture; CF, closed forest; OF, open forest; Pa, pasture; TSF, tree and shrub fallow. *Source:* Adapted from De Jong et al. (2000).

offset much of the opportunity and implementation costs, giving a total cost of us$2–13/Mg C, with lower costs associated with closed forest management and higher costs associated with open forests (figure 13.2). Although the latter have low opportunity costs, implementation costs are high (table 13.3).

Modeling the Adoption of Forestry Practices

A spreadsheet model was designed to compile the areas of each LU/LC class, average C storage, and economic inputs and outputs of the alternative management options for each vegetation type.

Cost–benefit flows were discounted to present value to provide an estimate of the net present value (NPV) per hectare of implementing the alternatives for each cost–benefit quartile of each current land use type. A default discount rate of 10 percent was used. In the model it was assumed that if the sequestration purchase price were higher than or equal to the NPV for a particular cost–benefit quartile–management practice–vegetation type combination, then farmers would choose to enter the scheme and implement the new practice.

Under all baseline scenarios, the supply of sequestration was expected to be negligible if incentives were us$5/Mg C or less but would rise sharply when incentives were increased to us$15/Mg C (figure 13.3).

Fankhauser (1997) states that projects that would cost us$5–20/Mg C are cost-effective carbon emission mitigation options. In this cost range, the twelve selected forestry and agroforestry measures in our study area could mitigate a total of 1 to 43 million tons of carbon, with a maximum total supply of carbon sequestration of around 55 million tons at us$40/Mg C.

The maximum supply through the management of communal forests, if implemented by all interested farmers and communities in the region at us$15/Mg C, was estimated at 32 million tons. The highest supply response from the improvement of fallow vegetation is expected with a subsidy of us$15–30/Mg C. The expected economic response to replace agriculture and pasture with agroforestry or forestry was expected to rise slowly according to the amount of incentives paid for the carbon sequestration service (figure 13.3).

A lower discount rate than assumed in this study would give higher present value to medium- and long-term costs, whereas increasing the rate would imply that income and costs over the next five years would determine to a large extent the expected economic response to carbon sequestration incentives. At low discount rates, low levels of sequestration supply were predicted for fallow and development options, where

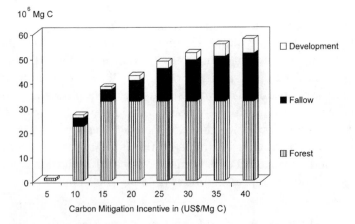

Figure 13.3 Predicted carbon mitigation potential for total, closed, and open forest (*Forest*); tree and shrub fallow (*Fallow*); and agriculture and pasture management (*Development*) options, based on low, medium, and high baseline assumptions. *Source:* From De Jong (2000), reprinted with permission of the author.

future opportunity costs are high. At high discount rates, the maximum supply could be obtained with incentives of around US$20–25/Mg C (De Jong et al. 2000).

The economic model of the potential carbon sequestration supply in relation to the amount of incentives paid for each ton of carbon mitigated is based on the assumption that farmers will react in an economically rational way to price signals. There is evidence that this would hold for southern Mexico. Tipper (1993) and Javier Anaya (pers. comm. 1994) both found that farmers in the northern Highlands of Chiapas switched labor and capital inputs from coffee to maize and bean production in response to a fall in coffee prices in the late 1980s. Experiences to date with the Scolel Té pilot project also indicate that many farmers are eager to enter such a program, even with lower incentive levels than predicted.

VARIABILITY IN THE CARBON MITIGATION POTENTIAL OF FORESTRY ACTIVITIES

A key question still to be resolved is how much variability is inherent in estimates of emission reduction from a given forestry or agroforestry project. A number of methodological questions must be addressed before forestry carbon offset trading can reliably provide verifiable emission reductions (Tipper and De Jong 1998). The emission reduction of any given project must be compared with the carbon fluxes expected from future land use scenarios without that project. To assess the sources and levels of variability that may occur in quantifying the CO_2 mitigation potential of forestry and agroforestry projects, a proposed forest management project for the Juznajab La Laguna community (Juznajab) developed in the context of the Scolel Té pilot project (Scolel Té 1998) was used as an example, comparing in this case two baseline or without-project approaches that have been used in various projects around the world: a regional land use and land use change scenario and a project scenario. Data collected in the field are used to assess the levels of variability that occur in land use and land cover (LU/LC) classification, C stock quantification at a landscape level, and baseline assumptions (De Jong 2000, 2001).

Current Land Use and Proposed Management Activities in Juznajab

The territory of the community Juznajab La Laguna (4004 ha) comprises agricultural land, pasture, secondary shrub and forest vegetation, and well-developed forests. In the past, the community sold the merchantable timber to concessionaires, who in turn cut all harvestable trees. After the harvest, parts of the logged areas were used for slash-and-burn agriculture. When agricultural production dropped, the area was left fallow. During the fallow period, natural regeneration of the predominantly pine and oak species occurred. The secondary forests that are currently present are the result of natural regeneration of lands that were harvested and used for slash-and-burn agriculture in the 1970s. From the late 1980s onward, the community decided not to permit commercial harvesting in the communal forests. Only the collection of fuelwood and construction wood for local consumption and cattle grazing were allowed in the forests. The shrubland originated from degraded pasture and cropland.

The goals and activities of the proposed project have been developed through participatory planning and discussions, coordinated by the community assembly. Therefore the project can be considered compatible with the land use goals of the community. One of the goals is to encourage community-level decision making and to strengthen the planning and technical capacity of the community. The project aims to improve local economies by generating forest-based employment and ensuring the sustained use of natural resources.

The forest management plan that is used as an example for this study is restricted to about 3000 ha of community forests. The remaining 1000 ha of community territory is excluded from the C calculations and includes cropland, settlements, pasture, and shrubland. In the project management option, the community intends to implement improved forest management techniques, which have been successfully applied in other pine-dominated forests of Mexico. The basic principles of the management techniques are to convert the uneven-aged low-productivity forests to more productive, even-aged forest stands through the following silvicultural measures (De Jong 2001):

- Harvesting of well-developed forests in small groups, saving well-formed parent trees to allow natural regeneration of both pine species and various broadleaf species
- Selective thinning of each group in ten-year cycles
- Fire and pest protection measures
- Enrichment planting in areas where natural regeneration does not occur

Table 13.4 lists technologies and carbon emission mitigation impacts included in the project.

The costs of the alternative management system compared with the baseline option include training the community for forest planning and management activities, investment in basic silvicultural and harvesting equipment, forest labor, and temporarily reduced timber and other revenues. Socioeconomic benefits include local involvement in forest management, forestry-based employment, and added value to forest products through investment in community-based forest industries. Ecological benefits include carbon mitigation, watershed protection, and biodiversity conservation.

CARBON DENSITIES

Carbon densities were measured at two levels and scales: major C pools were measured in a set of LU/LC classes at a regional scale, and the tree C

Table 13.4 Technologies and Their Carbon Emission Mitigation Impacts

Technology	Carbon Mitigation Impact
Elimination of land use and land cover changes	Avoided emissions from conversion to other land use
Reduction in harvesting intensity	Avoided emissions from forest degradation
Restoration of degraded lands	Avoided emissions from forest degradation
Extension of the rotation period	Increased C stock in the managed forest and soil
Fire protection	Reduced emissions from burning
Shifting output to long-duration products	C fixed by long-lived forest products

Table 13.5 Land Use and Carbon Density Databases Used in the Analysis for the Highlands and Juznajab, Chiapas, Mexico

Data	Regional Scale: Highlands	Project Scale: Juznajab
Surface area	306,000 ha	3536 ha
Land use	Interpreted Landsat images forestfrom 1974, 1984, 1990, and 1996, using the following classes: closed broad-leaved pine and pine–oak forest, open pine forest, disturbed pine–oak forest, tree and shrub fallow, pasture, and agricultural land (including bare soil and settlements)	Part of the 1996 Landsat TM image, using the following classes: open areas, broad-leaved shrub vegetation, secondary pine and pine–oak forest, well-developed pine, and pine–oak
Carbon densities[a]	39 plots of 0.54 ha each, distributed in the Highlands of Chiapas, separating the following pools: soil organic matter, small roots, herbaceous plants, shrubs, trees, woody debris, stumps, and litter	Trees measured in a total of 102 plots of 0.3 ha each in Juznajab La Laguna

[a]Locally developed allometric equations of biomass in relation to diameter at breast height and height were used to calculate C densities of the tree component for all plots.

densities were measured in a set of LU/LC classes in the community forest (table 13.5). Land use data were also analyzed at these two geographic scales: subregional (part of the Highlands of Chiapas) and community (Juznajab La Laguna). Comparison of the two LU/LC classifications and corresponding tree biomasses in each class (table 13.5) were carried out for a total of 3536 ha, excluding noncomparable classes and areas covered by clouds or shade in the satellite images. The following aggregate LU/LC classes were developed to compare the two classification methods: open areas and shrubland, secondary or degraded forests, and well-developed, closed pine and pine–oak forests.

The land cover estimates of the composite classes varied somewhat between the two classification methods (figure 13.4). The total tree C pool estimate derived from the combination of the two classifications, and biomass measurements (and their errors) varied from 266,500 Mg C (±9.8 percent) using the regional database to 224,000 Mg C (±5.6 percent) with the project database, giving a difference of 42,500 Mg C (±6.4 percent). The overall variation between the two estimates of the tree C pool was 19.3 percent.

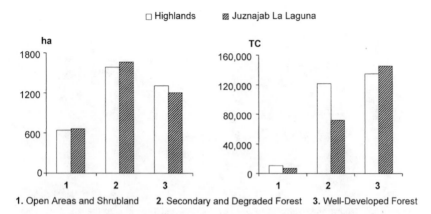

Figure 13.4 Comparison of area (in ha) and tree biomass estimates (in metric tons of carbon [TC]) of Juznajab La Laguna, Chiapas, Mexico, based on data collected in the Highlands and data collected in Juznajab La Laguna. *Source:* Adapted from De Jong (2001).

Historical Evidence of C Storage Depletion

Total C densities were assigned to each LU/LC class and multiplied by the surface area of each class for each evaluation year. We assume that the average C stock in a LU/LC class remains constant over time and that the stock change caused by LU/LC change occurred during the period between each pair of successive years of comparison. The historical rate of annual C storage depletion was calculated for Juznajab La Laguna and the Highlands of Chiapas with the following formula:

$$RR = 1 - [1 - (C_i - C_f)/C_i]^{1/y}, \qquad (13.1)$$

where RR is annual rate of C reduction; C_i is total C in the initial year; C_f is total C in the final year, and y is number of years.

In the Highlands of Chiapas, the area of forest decreased between 1974 and 1996 from 82 to 56 percent of the total area. In Juznajab La Laguna the forest area decreased from 88 to 81 percent (figure 13.5).

The area-weighted sum of variance in total and tree C stock for each LU/LC class was used to estimate the 95 percent confidence interval of the C reduction rates, expressed in percentage of initial C stock. The total C depletion caused by this LU/LC change in the Highlands was estimated to be 18 percent (±3.5 percent), whereas Juznajab La Laguna lost an estimated 11 percent (±4 percent) of the 1974 C pools. The annual decrease in C storage was 0.9 ± 0.1 percent of the 1974 C pools in the Highlands and 0.5 ± 0.1 percent in Juznajab La Laguna (figure 13.5).

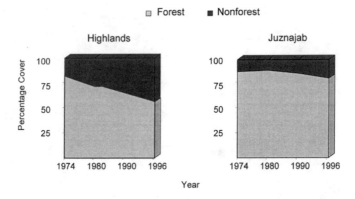

Figure 13.5   Forest and nonforest cover between 1974 and 1996 in percentage of total area in the Highlands and Juznajab La Laguna (based on interpreted 1974, 1984, 1990, and 1996 Landsat images), Chiapas, Mexico.

Baseline Scenario

Baselines should be set at levels that ensure that the emission mitigation activity is additional to what would occur if the project were not implemented. Baseline definitions in the land use sector minimally must deal with delimitation of the project domain and an estimate of LU/LC dynamics and associated greenhouse gas (GHG) fluxes. Information about historical and future land use policies and an estimate of the effect of these policies on LU/LC change dynamics are desirable (Puhl 1998) but not always available. A conservative approach to setting the baseline was applied in this case study:

- Land use change dynamics in Juznajab La Laguna and surroundings will continue until 2010 at a similar rate as over the last twenty-two years, with the depletion rate of carbon stocks continuing as observed during this period. After 2010 this process is expected to slow down until 2020 with improved enforcement of forestry and land use regulations. From 2020 onward it is expected that the C emissions caused by LU/LC change will be counterbalanced by C sequestration of abandoned agricultural land, pasture, or secondary vegetation. A 0.5 ± 0.1 percent annual C reduction rate, as observed in Juznajab, was applied in the baseline management scenario from 2000 to 2010, decreasing linearly to 0 percent in 2020. A sensitivity analysis was applied to the input value of this rate, varying it from 0 percent (without considering future LU/LC change in the baseline) to 0.9 ± 0.1 percent (future LU/LC change will be similar to the historical rate found in the Highlands).

- The community of Juznajab La Laguna will contract a forest concessionaire to harvest all the merchantable timber in 3000 ha of their forests, as they had done in the past. After harvest, the plots will be temporarily converted to slash-and-burn agriculture, leaving only some standing trees. Historically at least 90 percent of the original standing volume was cut in these two activities combined. These values were incorporated in the baseline stand simulations.

Project Scenario

In the project management option, the 3000 ha of forest will be managed by the community if they receive financial assistance in the context of the Scolel Té project.

Members of the community will carry out the forest management activities, for which they will receive training (De Jong 2001). To avoid possible leakage of increasing deforestation outside the community forest, the remaining 1000 ha of nonforest land will be subjected to improved agricultural and silvopastoral techniques. Applying these land use activities to all nonforest land is assumed to produce a sufficient supply of nonforest products to cover future demands of the community.

Carbon Mitigation Potential and Levels of Variation

The overall variation of the C mitigation estimation was calculated with the following formula (IPCC 1996):

$$TU = \sqrt{\Sigma_i(U_i)^2} \qquad (13.2)$$

where TU is the sum of all variation values and U_i is the variance of independent variable i (e.g., C reduction rate, C accumulation, C stock). With the baseline and project scenarios and expected C fluxes of each stand applied, the total C mitigation potential of the improved forest management project was estimated. With the default baseline setting, the C mitigation potential of the community was estimated at 347,000 Mg C ± 10 percent at the end of 100 years. However, with the 0 percent C reduction rate in the baseline scenario, the mitigation potential would decrease to 197,000 Mg C ± 9 percent, whereas the 0.9 ± 0.1 percent C reduction rate, as observed in the Highlands, would result in a mitigation potential of 455,000 Mg C ± 13 percent. The variation in C mitigation estimate varied between

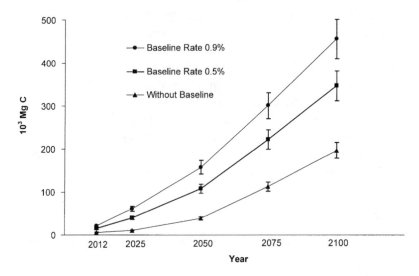

Figure 13.6 Carbon mitigation potential and variability of natural forest management in Juz-najab La Laguna, Chiapas, Mexico. Calculations are based on baseline C reduction rates of 0%, 0.5%, and 0.9%. *Source:* Adapted from De Jong (2001).

5 and 16 percent in each baseline scenario, whereas between the three scenarios the variation fluctuated between 35 and 74 percent (figure 13.6) from the default.

CONCLUSION

Conventional agriculture is only marginally profitable, and modest incentive payments can produce substantial shifts in land use, as was also observed in the United Kingdom (Crabtree 1997). If an appropriate mechanism for distributing mitigation incentives to landowners is implemented, as developed by the Scolel Té project, the amount of carbon emissions that can be mitigated varies between 1 and 38 million tons with incentive levels from us$5 to us$15/Mg C, mainly through natural forest management and fallow improvements. Therefore the management of natural forests and secondary vegetation is the most important element of any large-scale carbon mitigation program in Chiapas and areas with similar conditions in Mexico or elsewhere in Latin America.

The main sources of variability observed in calculating the GHG offset impact of the forestry project were related to calculating C stocks at a landscape level, with variations up to about 10 percent for each classification method and close to 20 percent when comparing variations in tree C stock and LU/LC classifications; historical evidence of LU/LC changes and related GHG fluxes applied in baselines, which gave rise to variations up to about 16 percent; and varying baseline assumptions, which produced differences between 31 and 73 percent in the C mitigation calculations, with variation levels up to 74 percent.

Regional baselines probably will be the most attractive way to calculate the carbon sequestration potential of forest management projects because they will reduce the cost of each project implemented in the region. To reduce variation in the application of baseline depletion rates and to build a series of objectively testable predictions of future changes in terrestrial carbon stocks, a spatial analysis of different predisposing and driving factors of land use change is being carried out. The method that is currently being tested departs from a correlation analysis of causal factors and past land use change. The factors that have the highest correlations with past land use change are used to estimate future carbon emissions, assuming that past trends of change in these parameters (such as population growth) will continue in the future. The model will take into account regional variation in the processes that cause land use change.

Improvements in the factors that cause the variations in the C sequestration calculations described in this chapter, such as appropriate classification of land use and well-defined and acceptable baseline assumptions, cannot eliminate all errors in estimating the C mitigation of a forestry project. However, they point to the main levels of error that may occur in the calculations of GHG offset potential. Thus they could reduce some of the doubts that currently exist about the reliability and verifiability of forestry as a GHG mitigation measure.

REFERENCES

Crabtree, J. R. 1997. Policy instruments for environmental forestry: Carbon retention in farm woodlands. In W. N. Adger, D. Pettenella, and M. Whitby, eds., *Climate-change mitigation and European land-use policies*, 187–197. Wallingford, U.K.: CAB International.

De Jong, B. H. J. 2000. *Forestry for mitigating the greenhouse effect: An ecological and economic assessment of the potential of land use to mitigate CO$_2$ emissions in the Highlands of Chiapas, Mexico*. Ph.D. dissertation, Wageningen University, the Netherlands.

De Jong, B. H. J. 2001. Uncertainties in estimating the potential for carbon mitigation of forest management. *Forest Ecology and Management* 154: 85–104.

De Jong, B. H. J., M. A. Cairns, P. K. Haggerty, N. Ramírez-Marcial, S. Ochoa-Gaona, J. Mendoza-Vega, M. González-Espinosa, and I. March-Mifsut. 1999. Land-use change and carbon flux between the 1970s and 1990s in the Central Highlands of Chiapas, Mexico. *Environmental Management* 23: 373–385.

De Jong, B. H. J., G. Montoya-Gómez, K. Nelson, L. Soto-Pinto, J. Taylor, and R. Tipper. 1995. Community forest management and carbon sequestration: A feasibility study from Chiapas, Mexico. *Interciencia* 20: 409–416.

De Jong, B. H. J., R. Tipper, and G. Montoya-Gómez. 2000. An economic analysis of the potential for carbon sequestration by forests: Evidence from southern Mexico. *Ecological Economics* 33: 313–327.

De Jong, B. H. J., R. Tipper, and J. Taylor. 1997. A framework for monitoring and evaluation of carbon mitigation by farm forestry projects: Example of a demonstration project in Chiapas, Mexico. *Mitigation and Adaptation Strategies for Global Change* 2: 231–246.

Fankhauser, S. 1997. The economic costs of climate change and implications for land-use change. In W. N. Adger, D. Pettenella, and M. Whitby, eds., *Climate-change mitigation and European land-use policies*, 59–70. Wallingford, U.K.: CAB International.

Fernández, J. C., B. De Jong, G. Montoya-Gómez, T. Aleman-Santillan, and M. R. Parra-Vázquez (coords.). 1999. *Programa de desarrollo productivo sustentable en las areas marginadas de Chiapas*. Final Report. San Cristóbal de las Casas, Mexico: Ecosur–Banco Mundial–Sagar.

IPCC. 1996. *Revised 1996 IPCC guidelines for national greenhouse gas inventories reporting instructions*, Vol. 1, Annex 1, *Managing Uncertainties*. Geneva, Switzerland: IPCC.

MacDicken, K. G. 1997. Project specific monitoring and verification: State of the art and challenges. *Mitigation and Adaptation Strategies for Global Change* 2: 191–202.

Mohren, G. M. J., J. F. Garza Caligaris, O. Masera, M. Kanninen, T. Karjalainen, A. Pussinen, and G. J. Nabuurs. 1999. *CO2FIX for Windows: A dynamic model of the CO_2-fixation in forests*, Version 1.2. Research Report no. 99/3. Wageningen, the Netherlands: IBN.

Mohren, G. M. J. and C. G. M. Klein Goldewijk. 1990. *CO2FIX: A dynamic model of the CO_2-fixation in forest stands*. De Dorschkamp, Report no. 624(35). Wageningen, the Netherlands: Research Institute for Forestry and Urban Ecology.

Moulton, R. J. and K. R. Richards. 1990. *Costs of sequestering carbon through tree planting and forest management in the United States*. General Technical Report no. WO-58. Washington, D.C.: USDA Forest Service.

Ochoa-Gaona, S. 2001. Traditional land-use systems and patterns of forest fragmentation in the Highlands of Chiapas, México. *Environmental Management* 27: 571–586.

Ochoa-Gaona, S. and M. González-Espinosa. 2000. Land use patterns and deforestation in the highlands of Chiapas, Mexico. *Applied Geography* 20: 17–42.

Parra-Vázquez, M. R., T. Alemán-Santillán, J. Nahed-Toral, L. M. Mera-Ovando, M. López-Mejía, and A. López-Meza. 1989. *El subdesarrollo agrícola en los altos de Chiapas*. Chapingo, Mexico: Universidad Autónoma de Chapingo.

Puhl, I. 1998. *Status of research on project baselines under the UNFCCC and the Kyoto Protocol*. Information Paper. Paris: OECD and IEA.

Scolel Té. 1998. *Scolel Té: International pilot project for carbon sequestration and community forestry in Chiapas, Mexico*. Online: http://www.ed.ac.uk/~ebfr11.

Swisher, J. N. 1992. Cost and performance of CO_2 storage in forestry projects. *Biomass and Bioenergy* 1: 317–328.

Swisher, J. and G. Masters. 1992. A mechanism to reconcile equity and efficiency in global climate protection: International carbon emission offsets. *Ambio* 21: 154–159.

Tipper, R. 1993. *Technological change in contemporary highland Mayan agriculture.* Ph.D. thesis, University of Stirling, Scotland.

Tipper, R. and B. H. J. De Jong. 1998. Quantification and regulation of carbon offsets from forestry: Comparison of alternative methodologies, with special reference to Chiapas, Mexico. *The Commonwealth Forestry Review* 77: 219–228.

Tipper, R., B. H. J. De Jong, S. Ochoa-Gaona, M. L. Soto-Pinto, M. A. Castillo-Santiago, G. Montoya-Gómez, and I. March-Mifsut. 1998. *Assessment of the cost of large-scale forestry for CO_2 sequestration: Evidence from Chiapas, Mexico.* Report no. PH2/15. London: IEA Greenhouse Gas R & D Programme, U.K.

Chapter 14

AXING THE TREES, GROWING THE FOREST

SMALLHOLDER TIMBER PRODUCTION ON THE AMAZON *VÁRZEA*

Robin R. Sears and Miguel Pinedo-Vasquez

Small villages occupy a significant portion of the banks of the Amazon River on forest land that is periodically flooded. Residents of the *várzea,* as this landscape is called (periodically flooded lands, *sensu* Prance 1979), depend on swidden–fallow agriculture and the extraction of local natural resources for subsistence and income. Although these axe-wielding smallholder farmers necessarily maintain open fields and secondary forests, their role in deforestation is minor compared with that of ranchers, large-scale timber extractors, and industrial development projects that deforest, high-grade, or otherwise degrade the landscape on a large and intensive scale (Hecht and Cockburn 1989, Nepstad et al. 1992). In fact, some farmers in Amazonia maintain substantial tree cover on their landholdings not only for resource production and protection but also to maintain ecosystem structure and function. Many researchers have described these resource management systems—patterns of resource use, or structure and composition—but few have examined their function in terms of economics and ecology (De Jong 2001, Pinedo-Vasquez et al. 2001). The contribution of small-scale farming and forestry to the conservation of biodiversity and preservation of ecosystem functions in otherwise threatened regions remains largely unexplored.

Natural forest management and sustainable forestry are rare in Amazonia. The conventional forest extraction model followed in the Amazon is based on a concession system in which logging operations are carried out with little consideration for long-term timber production (Higuchi 1994, Barros and Uhl 1995). Most concessionaires and policymakers have not considered the environmental, economic, and social damage of conventional logging, where practices often result in high-graded forests with poor regeneration potential (Silva 1989, Lisboa et al. 1991, Fredericksen and Mostacedo 2000), damage to wildlife (Johns 1988, Nepstad et al. 1992), and incidental damage to the residual trees, soil, aquatic bodies, and general habitat (Macedo and Anderson 1993). Resource management authorities often fail to recognize the presence of rural communities in the forests and rarely consult with or ask permission of them when assigning concession contracts to large- and medium-scale extractors. Because both local people and the forest environment suffer damage under conventional forestry practices in Amazonia, resource managers and policymakers need to seek forestry models that combine economic productivity for residents with habitat and species conservation, working for both people and the environment.

Working forests exist in the tropics where rural farmers and indigenous peoples promote a variety of wood and nonwood resources on their landholdings (Padoch and Pinedo-Vasquez 1996, 1999 in Peru and Kalimantan; Anderson 1991 and Pinedo-Vasquez et al. 2001 in Brazil; De Jong 2001 in Peru). The managers of these resources take advantage of natural ecological processes, as in the case of the Ka'apor Indians in eastern Amazonia, who manipulate secondary forest succession (Balée and Gély 1989) to increase the production of desirable species. Farmers in the Amazon *várzea* also practice ecological engineering on their landholdings whereby they create environmental gradients through vegetation management in their agricultural swidden–fallow production systems (Pinedo-Vasquez 1995). Thus farmers are able to promote a variety of timber and fruit tree species with distinct environmental needs (Pinedo-Vasquez et al. 2001).

On a small scale, farmers help to maintain the productivity of the *várzea* by managing threatened resources. The village settlement, lake, crop field, forest, and swamp are all elements of the heterogeneous production landscape of the *várzea*. For example, communities and individuals designate some lakes as production zones for fish to reproduce, manage fruit trees in forests for fishing grounds, and maintain seed trees of important timber species on their landholdings. Many farmers optimize the production in their systems by taking advantage of the heterogeneity of the *várzea* landscape (Denevan 1984).

Shifting markets for nontimber forest products (NTFPS) have prompted changes in forest cover in eastern Brazilian *várzea*. Brondízio and Siqueira (1997) describe the intensification of açaí (*Euterpe oleracea*, Arecaceae) production on the Amazon estuary as farmers transform natural forest into managed palm stands without clearing the land. This practice occurs in a region where agricultural intensification projects nearby have resulted in forest cover loss (Brondízio et al. 1994). Zarin et al. (2001) and Pereira et al. (2002) found that the coverage by palm stands (including açaí) in the region of Macapá doubled over a period of fifteen years, and they attributed the change partially to market changes. Innovative models of timber and NTFP management developed by smallholder farmers such as these should be reexamined because they provide examples of working forests where resource management integrates conservation with income generation.

Here we describe timber management practices and production systems of rural farmers on the Amazon *várzea*. We discuss the characteristics of a market that supports farmers in their production of diverse timber on their landholdings. To understand the connection between the ecological and economic values of timber production in the swidden–fallow system, we analyze the role of one species in the system, *Calycophyllum spruceanum* (Benth) K Schum (Rubiaceae), a tree native to the *várzea* landscape. We focus our discussion on this single timber species to illustrate how timber production systems can be influenced by the flexibility of a species that regenerates in abundance in a dynamic and heterogeneous environment. We discuss *Calycophyllum* in the context of the *várzea* smallholder production systems described elsewhere (Padoch and Pinedo-Vasquez 1999, Pinedo-Vasquez et al. 2001, Pinedo-Vasquez and Rabelo 2002). We also discuss the challenges to timber production by *várzea* farmers and how some have overcome them. Finally, we make recommendations for promoting production in these working forests.

We present data collected from farmers living on *várzea* in three regions of Amazonia: on the Brazilian Amazon estuary near Macapá; in central Amazonia near Tefé, Brazil; and in western Amazonia near Iquitos, Peru. We include these three regions in our analysis because each has a different relationship to the timber market, so we can show how market factors influence the production systems.

PRODUCTION ON THE *VÁRZEA*

In the estuarine *várzea* at the mouth of the Amazon River, under the influence of ocean tides, the river rises and falls several meters twice daily. Inland and up through to the headwaters of the Amazon, the seasonal *várzea* is subject to two to six months of flooding, with river level changes of up to 12 m. This flood pulse dynamic results in erosional and depositional processes that alter the river course and landscape patterns over years, decades, and centuries. The result is a patchy mosaic of landforms associated with a dynamic riparian system such as levees, silt and sand bars, abandoned channels, backswamps, and oxbow lakes. The vegetation types of the *várzea* are as diverse as the landscape elements, with swamps, meadows, early succession forests, old-growth forests, and vegetation associated with swidden–fallow agriculture such as annual crop fields, agroforests, and secondary forests.

Large human populations live on the *várzea* (Denevan 1992, Roosevelt 1999). Natural resources of the *várzea* include timber, fish, and rich alluvial soil suitable for agriculture. Currently, the *várzea* is an important source of protein from fish and agricultural products such as banana, manioc, maize, and rice for populations in large urban centers. Despite the fertile soils of the *várzea* (Furch 1997, Zarin 1999), annual cropping, at least on the seasonal *várzea*, is a risky endeavor because of unpredictable timing and intensity of floods (Chibnik 1994). Alternative economic activities have been developed by *várzea* farmers and include fishing, forestry, and NTFP extraction. In this chapter we explore the forestry systems engineered by smallholder farmers.

Beginning in the 1940s, large-scale timber extraction has been practiced on the *várzea* because of its proximity to fluvial transportation routes (Barros and Uhl 1995). The *várzea* forests host a variety of valuable timber species such as *Cedrela odorata, Ocotea cymbarum, Aniba* spp., *Virola surinamensis, Calycophyllum spruceanum, Ceiba pentandra, Hura crepitans, Calophyllum brasiliense, Minquartia guianensis, Carapa guianensis, Guazuma ulmifolia, Xylopia* spp., and *Aspidosperma excelsum* (table 14.1). The use and market value of each of these species varies with the wood characteristics, extractability, and market trends.

Conventionally, timber is dichotomized into softwood or hardwood, or fast- or slow-growing species. We find it useful, from the point of view of the producer, to use the categories *traditional* and *nontraditional,* terms that are used locally in the Amazon by farmers, loggers, and traders. These categories represent the economic perspective, taking into account the marketability of the species in question (see table 14.1). Stocks of the traditional species, such as *Virola surinamensis* and *Cedrela odorata,* have dramatically declined over the past decade (Lisboa et al. 1991, Anderson et al. 1999, Pinedo-Vasquez et al. 2001), and some species are commercially extinct in some regions. Nontraditional species, such as *Calycophyllum spruceanum,* are gaining importance in the timber industry.

Land Use Patterns

The patterns of land use by *várzea* residents follow the physiographic heterogeneity of the landscape. Although the production systems of smallholder farmers vary between and within regions, they all comprise mosaics of crop fields, agroforests, fallows, house gardens, and forest stands

Table 14.1 Classification of *Várzea* Timber Species

Scientific Name	Common Name		Timber Class		
	Brazil	Peru	Market[a]	Growth[b]	Density[c]
Aniba spp.	Louro	Moena	T	S	H
Aspidosperma excelsum	Carapanaúba	Pumaquiro	T	S	H
Calophyllum brasiliense	Jacareúba	Lagarto caspi	T	S	H
Calycophyllum spruceanum	Pau mulato	Capirona	N	F	H
Carapa guianensis	Andiroba	Andiroba	T	M	H
Cedrela odorata	Cedro	Cedro	T	M	L
Ceiba pentandra	Samauma	Lupuna	T	F	L
Chorisia integrifolia		Huimbá	T	S	L
Copaifera officinalis	Copaíba	Copaíba	T	S	H
Guarea spp.	Jito	Requia	T	S	H
Guazuma ulmifolia	Mutamba	Bolaina	N	F	L
Hura crepitans	Assacu	Catahua	T	F	L
Maquira coriacea	Muiratinga	Capinuri	T	F	L
Minquartia guianensis	Acapú	Huacapú	T	S	H
Ocotea cymbarum	Louro inamui	Moena canela	T	S	H
Pentaclethra macroloba	Pracaxi	Pashaco	N	F	H
Virola surinamensis	Virola, ucuuba	Cumala	T	F	L
Xylopia spp.	Envira vassourinha	Espintana	T	S	L

[a]N, nontraditional timber; T, traditional timber.

[b]F, fast; M, medium; S, slow.

[c]H, high; L, low.

optimizing the environmental complexity of the landscape. Some farmers concurrently manage for the production of annual crops, fruits, and timber, which all mature at different times and in different spaces. This results in a diverse resource base that provides food and income to farm families throughout the year (Padoch and Pinedo-Vasquez 1999). In this system, management activities on any given plot reflect a variety of objectives. These can include annual, semiannual, or perennial crop production; management of wood resources (fuelwood, poles, timber); soil conservation, building, or enrichment; and pest control. For example, weeding a crop field not only reduces competition on the crop plants but also creates appropriate conditions for the establishment of natural regeneration of valuable tree species, and pruning saplings of valuable timber species in an agroforest allows more light to reach interplanted crops.

Timber Management Activities in Smallholder Systems

Floodplain smallholders have a long history of maintaining working forests on their landholdings that yield timber or nontimber resources, provide fishing and hunting grounds, and conserve genetic stocks of otherwise overexploited species. Pinedo-Vasquez et al. (2001) have shown that smallholder farmers in Macapá, Brazil, today produce significant volumes of some of these timbers on their landholdings. For example, properties sampled there contained an estimated 11 m³ of commercial timber (more than 25 cm diameter at breast height [dbh]) per hectare of *Virola surinamensis* and 25 m³ of *Ceiba pentandra,* two traditional timber species. On the Napo River in Peru, of 180 households surveyed, 82 percent of these farmers managed timber on their properties, hosting between seventeen and twenty-three species on each landholding (Pinedo-Vasquez 1995). Their managed forests produce merchantable NTFPs including fuelwood, thatch, medicinals, and fruits, as well as timber products such as sawlogs and poles. By incorporating timber management into an existing swidden–fallow agricultural system, *várzea* farmers enhance the value of labor and inputs while increasing revenue and option value on their landholdings.

Farmers are able to maintain a high diversity of trees by taking advantage of the natural species richness and environmental diversity of the landscape and by engineering a gradient of growing conditions in their fields, fallows, and forests. Pinedo-Vasquez et al. (2001) report that managers facilitate the natural regeneration of a variety of tree species with different ecological needs by creating diverse microhabitats and gradients of light on their landholdings rather than by relying on labor-intensive artificial regeneration. In this way, farmers manage for timber and short-term crops in the same space at the same time.

All components of the swidden–fallow farming systems are important for timber management. By their nature, forests and fallows tend to contain the highest volume of timber on the landholding and provide habitat for seed dispersers, fish, and game. Fields and house gardens are important spaces on the farms, serving as nurseries for natural regeneration and planted or transplanted seedlings and for the genetic improvement of trees. In house gardens, valuable individuals are protected near enough to the house to prevent theft, a common disincentive to timber management.

Mature individuals of overexploited traditional species are protected as seed trees throughout the landholdings: At all our study sites *Cedrela odorata, Virola surinamensis,* and *Ceiba pentandra* were found in higher density on farmer landholdings than in nearby forests. Farmers often transplant seedlings of these valuable species to appropriate spaces. This practice of preserving seed producer trees can be of major conservation importance on a regional scale where high-value species often are commercially extinct in the forest. The seed trees may help repopulate these high-graded forest areas.

Establishment of timber trees and other useful species in the agricultural systems used on the *várzea* occurs by several methods: sparing existing valuable trees during field preparation, sparing seedlings and saplings while weeding during the crop phase, and enrichment planting during the crop or fallow phases. Seedling establishment can occur at any phase of the agricultural cycle, but the crop phase is the most important because the open fields provide favorable germination conditions for heliotropic species. By sparing valuable seedlings during the crop phase, farmers allow selected individuals to become well established in the field before the remainder of the highly competitive fallow vegetation develops at the end of the crop cycle. It is during this phase that farmers select species, determine densities, and decide the management objectives for the field area in the future.

Sapling growth and development of the juveniles are encouraged during the transition from field to fallow by selectively pruning, killing vines, clearing the understory, and thinning the stand to ameliorate growth conditions. Silvicultural manipulation of the fallow vegetation helps promote regeneration and recruitment of diverse species. Large trees in managed forests or fallows usually are eliminated by girdling, which kills the trees slowly and causes little disturbance to surrounding vegetation.

CHARACTERISTICS OF SMALLHOLDER TIMBER MANAGEMENT AND MARKETS

Timber management in smallholder production systems is different from conventional forestry practiced in Amazonia in terms of scale, diversity of species, use of silvicultural treatments, and environmental impacts. Smallholder production is practiced on a much smaller scale than conventional forestry (Pinedo-Vasquez and Rabelo 2002), and income generated is certainly more modest (Pinedo-Vasquez et al. 2001). Whereas timber concessionaires contract thousands of hectares, or logging expeditions extract one or a few species at a time, farmer landholdings range from 5 to 25 ha (rarely as much as 100 ha), and farmers manage up to forty tree species.

There are differences between the three study regions in the ways smallholders participate in the timber market in terms of the number of species and volumes traded and in what form the timber is traded. These differences depend on who is defining the market and what timber is available in the region. In Macapá, for example, smallholders gained control of a sector of the market when they founded family-run sawmills after large-scale logging operations left the region when the industry went bust in the 1960s (Pinedo-Vasquez et al. 2001). These families have developed a locally integrated timber industry by controlling the management, harvest, transportation, sale, and processing of local timbers (Pinedo-Vasquez et al. 2001, Sears et al. in press). They salvaged parts of sawmills abandoned by industrial forestry operators years ago and used their knowledge gained during off-farm labor activities to establish industry infrastructure (for harvest, mills, and transport). This rural infrastructure does not exist in the other study regions. The difference is reflected in the intensity of timber management and smallholder participation in markets.

A key factor in the profitability of maintaining the diverse production systems on the *várzea* is the diversification of the timber market in terms of both species and products traded. As the traditional Amazon timber species become scarce, some buyers become interested in nontraditional species such as *Calycophyllum spruceanum, Guazuma ulmifolia,* and *Pentaclethra macroloba*. The expansion of the market to include nontraditional species dramatically increases the stock of commercial timber and value of standing forest on the farms (Pinedo-Vasquez et al. 2001). For example, in Macapá, farmers manage, market, or use forty-eight tree species, and thirty-six of these are sold in the market (Pinedo-Vasquez et al. 2001) for a variety of wood products. The market in Macapá opened up to these species when the traditional species became scarce in the region.

In Pucallpa, Peru, in 1999, high volumes of the traditional *várzea* timber species were still traded. Seven timber species reportedly were sold to mills in volumes greater than 10,000 m^3, five of which are *várzea* species: *Chorisia integrifolia, Virola surinamensis, Hura crepitans, Cedrela odorata,* and *Copaifera officinalis*. This bulk of this volume probably came from commercial extractors. Nevertheless, forty-eight species were sold to these mills, and twenty species were represented by less than 1000 m^3, ranging from 3 m^3 to 970 m^3 (INRENA 1999). These data from Macapá and Pucallpa suggest that although only a few timber species are of major economic importance, both large- and small-scale extractors can benefit from harvesting diverse species.

A second characteristic that distinguishes smallholder timber production from large-scale extractive operations is that their landholdings comprise mixed-species, multiaged stands where farmers actively manage for a variety of products concurrently. Stands of this character are also multifunctional in that they increase the economic value and ecological value of the landholding. Farmers increase the economic value of their land by producing roundwood for sawmills, fuelwood from poorly formed trees and branches, pole timber for house construction, and a variety of NTFPs such as thatch, fiber, and medicine. Ecological value comes from maintaining a heterogeneous forest environment for plants, fish and other fauna.

Some of the most important nontraditional timbers are fast-growing species. The combination of traditional and nontraditional species and the diversity of commercial and household products yielded from them are important for maintaining farm income. Fast-growing tree species are promoted on short rotations, and farmers rely on them for steady cash income, whereas slow-growing, high-value species are reserved for emergency needs. Eight to ten years after the fallow cycle commences, farmers can produce roundwood of fast-growing species such as *Calycophyllum spruceanum* and *Guazuma ulmifolia*. In four years, pole-sized timber of these species can be produced.

A third difference between smallholder timber production and concession forestry is that farmers, unlike concession loggers, regularly apply silvicultural treatments to their stands or trees. Activities include sparing, pruning, girdling, thinning, weeding, cutting vines, and enrichment planting. The time dedicated to silviculture is difficult to estimate because these activities are carried out concurrently with routine agricultural activities (Putz 2000, De Jong 2001). Farmers also use ecological processes such as natural regeneration and competition to their advantage. Natural regeneration of native species in fields and fallows results in high-diversity stands with little labor input from the farmer. It is common for farmers to enrich their forests and fields with valuable species such as *Cedrela odorata, Swietenia macrophylla,* and *Ocotea cymbarum* as well as some nontraditional species.

The working forests of smallholder farmers adapt to changing environmental and market conditions. By combining short- and long-cycle timber production of both traditional and nontraditional species, smallholders maintain continuous production and forest cover and gain income during difficult years or between harvests. The sale of timber from fallows and forests provides incentives for farmers to leave the land to fallow for longer time periods to allow wood production. In this way these young forests work not only for the farmer but also for the environment by providing soil conservation and increasing forest cover and habitat in a fragmented landscape.

CALYCOPHYLLUM SPRUCEANUM, A COMPONENT OF WORKING FORESTS

One species that occurs in abundance on the *várzea* and is silviculturally favored by farmers is *Calycophyllum spruceanum* (Benth) K Schum (Rubiaceae; known as capirona in Peru and pau mulato in Brazil). This is a nontraditional species that is gaining market importance in both Brazil and Peru. This light-demanding species, hereafter called *Calycophyllum*, is easily identified by its smooth, dark-green to orange-yellow bark that peels in great strips and its high, spreading canopy. The species is but one component of the mixed-species production systems of *várzea* farmers but stands out because it has multiple functions: Its wood is favored for household uses and has commercial value, and it grows at high density, lending itself to rapid establishment of forests in fallows.

The first of the attributes that make *Calycophyllum* suitable for management is that the wood has many uses. The tree provides the most prized fuelwood from *várzea* forests. Pole-sized trees are also highly desired for house construction in both rural and urban settings. In both Peru and Brazil, *Calycophyllum* sawnwood is sold for house framing, doors, window frames, and especially furniture making. In the international market, *Calycophyllum* is exported from Amazonia primarily as parquet. Local people report medicinal and cosmetic uses for the species as well.

A second attribute of *Calycophyllum* in smallholder production systems is that it is a fast-growing species but develops dense wood, a combination of growth characteristics that makes it suitable for management and sale. The wood is very light in color, moderately dense (0.66–0.76 g/cm^3), and resistant to insect attack. The texture of the wood is fine, and its grain varies from straight to interlacing. Trees of *Calycophyllum* can attain 35 m in height and 1.8 m dbh with a regular conical trunk. Young *Calycophyllum* plants grow very quickly under appropriate conditions; saplings in full sun can reach 3 m in height in one year. Diameter growth is also rapid for individuals under high light intensities: Pole-sized trees in one fallow sampled increased by an average of 3 cm in one year (±0.6 cm, $n = 10$), and trees of more than 20 cm dbh averaged 2.1 cm increase in diameter one year (±0.7 cm, $n = 10$) (figure 14.1). *Calycophyllum* is ideal for pole production in as little as three years, and within eight years a managed fallow can yield timber of 20 cm dbh.

A third management attribute is that *Calycophyllum* responds to large clearings and therefore is well adapted to the growing conditions in fields and pastures that receive high light intensities and have exposed mineral soil. The presence of this species in farm systems is an example of how humans can optimize natural processes to increase production of a native plant resource on the *várzea*. The distribution of *Calycophyllum* is patchy in response to the heterogeneity of the complex *várzea* landscape. *Calycophyllum* often dominates stands along the margins of whitewater rivers and the shores of lakes influenced by these rivers because individuals of this native tree species tolerate flood conditions as seeds,

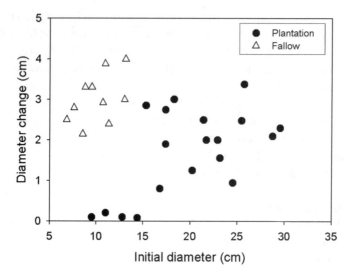

Figure 14.1 Annual diameter growth of *Calycophyllum spruceanum* trees in a 20-year-old mixed-species unmanaged plantation (*n* = 19, mean 1.7 ± 1.1 cm) and a 6-year-old managed fallow (*n* = 10, mean 3.0 ± 0.6 cm) on the floodplain near Iquitos, Peru.

seedlings, saplings, or adults. It also dominates agricultural fallows. The size structures of populations of this species tend toward single-cohort stands. In mature stands, the majority of individuals are large, with few juveniles. Young stands are dominated by pole-sized trees.

Farmers take advantage of the abundant natural regeneration of *Calycophyllum* in their fields and actively manage it, particularly in the last year or two of cultivation before leaving a field to fallow or while establishing a fruit orchard. Silvicultural treatments applied to *Calycophyllum* stands or individuals, as well as to other timber species, include sparing seedlings while weeding crop fields, thinning stands or coppice stems, removing vines, and pruning. Its exfoliacious bark seems to help reduce vine and termite nest infestation.

The density of *Calycophyllum* reflects the site history and management objectives of farmers, and it can be very high (table 14.2). For example, on mineral soil in an unweeded field there were an estimated 1.9 saplings (10 to 30 cm in height) per square meter, or on mineral soil where no other weeds grew at the moment we estimated 385 seedlings (<10 cm in height) per square meter. These two estimates represent the extreme potential of natural regeneration on mineral soil in full sun (ideal establishment conditions) where the field was sampled before the farmer weeded. In contrast, in a field of planted manioc (*Manihot escuelenta*) where the farmer is managing (sparing and protecting selected individuals) *Calycophyllum* re-

Table 14.2 Density and Size of *Calycophyllum spruceanum* Trees and Saplings per Hectare in Agricultural Fields and Fallows and Forests Near Iquitos, Peru

Site (age of stand)	Management Activities	Individuals /ha	Average Diameter at Breast Height (cm) (SD)[a]	Sample Area (ha)
Fallow 1 (9 yr)	Unmanaged	805	9 (4)	0.15
Fallow 2 (4 yr)	Managed for timber, extraction	1200	6 (3)	0.05
Fallow 3 (30 yr)	Managed for timber, extraction	120	30 (10)	0.80
Forest 1	Unmanaged, extraction	334	18 (9)	0.50
Forest 2	Unmanaged, extraction	207	55 (13)	0.50

Regeneration (<1 m ht)		Average Individuals /m^2	Sample Height (cm)[a]	Area (m^2)
Field 1	Clear field, no weeds	386	10	10
Field 2	Field with weeds to 50 cm height	1.9	25	100
Field 3	Manioc with management for *Calycophyllum*	0.16	60	100
Fallow 4 (3 yr)	Unmanaged	0.01	45	100
Fallow 3 (30 yr)	Managed, but not for regeneration	0.002	110	300
Forest 1	Unmanaged, extraction	0	—	1500
Forest 2	Unmanaged, extraction	0	—	1500

[a]Average diameter at breast height and average height are average measures of all stems in each sample.

generation, we estimated 0.16 saplings (average 60 cm in height) per square meter, a density that realistically reflects management goals.

In Macapá, on the Amazon estuary in Brazil, *Calycophyllum* had the highest value of all tree species in six of twelve fallows surveyed, where it made up 53 percent of individuals 2.5 cm dbh or larger (F. Rabelo, unpublished data 2000). In these same landholdings, after *Pentaclethra macroloba*, *Calycophyllum* was the most densely regenerating species in fields, with an average of 3066 seedlings per hectare.

In the Mamirauá Reserve, in central Amazonia, *Calycophyllum* in agricultural fallows ranked eleventh in importance out of eighty-three species in second-growth stands dominated by *Cecropia* spp., *Pourouma* spp., *Theobroma cacao*, and *Inga* spp. Except *T. cacao*, which was an important cash crop in the 1960s, these are all early successional species. In all fields where a *Calycophyllum* seed tree was nearby, saplings were encountered. *Calycophyllum* in young natural forests on the levees ranked second out

Table 14.3 Market Price and Sawmill Production for One Year of Four Timber Species Registered in 1998 with the State Natural Resource Authorities in Pucallpa, Peru

Species	Average Price per Board Foot (us$)	Roundwood Production (m³)	Sawnwood Production (m³)
Calycophyllum spruceanum	0.23	5,605	948
Cedrela odorata	0.78	31,013	16,115
Virola spp.	0.16	20,562	12,690
Swietenia macrophylla	1.17	14,898	8,657

Source: CTAR (1998).

of sixty-five species in stands codominated by *Ficus* spp. and *Cecropia* spp. The species clearly bridges the agricultural landscape and the natural forests on the *várzea*.

Market Profile

The market importance of *Calycophyllum* varies from region to region, and the timber does not fetch a high price. In Pucallpa, the average price of *Calycophyllum* unfinished sawnwood in 1998 was only us$0.23 per board foot (table 14.3). Prices for two high-volume *várzea* species were very different: *Cedrela odorata* was three times that at us$0.78 (16,000 m³), but *Virola* spp. fetched only an average price of us$0.16 over the year (12,700 m³). In comparison, the price of *Swietenia macrophylla,* an upland hardwood, averaged us$1.17 in the same year (8660 m³). In Iquitos and Pucallpa the demand for *Calycophyllum* is very low. The volume of *Calycophyllum* produced annually by registered mills in Pucallpa has fluctuated over recent years and is low, averaging 4300 m³ per year over the past seven years (IN-RENA 1999). Whereas smallholders near Macapá and Tefé, Brazil, sell roundwood for lumber to small-scale mills in the rural areas, farmers in Peru are more likely to sell or trade *Calycophyllum* as fuelwood and poles. This is so partly because transporting logs of *Calycophyllum* is difficult because the fresh logs do not float. The absence of sawmills in the rural areas of Mamirauá, Iquitos, and Pucallpa makes the marketability of *Calycophyllum* far less viable for smallholders in those regions than around Macapá.

CHALLENGES AND SOLUTIONS FOR SMALL-SCALE TIMBER PRODUCTION

Despite the suitability of smallholder production systems for timber management, not all *várzea* smallholders engage in commercial timber production. Market access, fair contracts, limited markets, and forestry policy and politics all present challenges to smallholder farmers who want to engage in the timber industry.

Another general obstacle to smallholder timber production is that most farmers lack access to forestry tools such as chainsaws and mill machinery or saws, which reduces their capacity to harvest and process trees and leaves them dependent on outside extractors and processors. This dependency reduces potential profits from timber management. Failure of agreements between farmers and buyers also causes problems for smallholders. For example, many trees felled on the *várzea* go to waste every year because buyers place orders that they do not honor, or the buyer returns only after the logs have been rendered unmarketable by wood degradation or by prohibitive extraction costs after the floodwaters recede from the forest.

Smallholders in Macapá have largely overcome these problems of mistrust in two ways. First, they control production by taking advantage of mill machinery left behind by fleeing industrial operations to establish family-run rural mills where the timber is first processed. Second, the merchants who buy the timber or lumber in rural areas to sell in the urban centers are from the communities themselves. This allows some degree of trust between seller and buyer. Farmers at the other sites are at the whim of buyers from urban centers or even from other regions of the country lured to the Amazon for quick, exploitive timber trade. In Macapá, rural smallholders control the local dynamics of logging and milling timber.

One disincentive to smallholder timber management is social: Farmers in all three study regions report timber theft as a problem. It is common for commercial extractors to work outside their concession areas, silently stealing the most valuable trees from farmers and communities. Carefully managed *Calycophyllum* poles in farming systems sometimes are stolen by neighbors who do not manage it in their own systems.

Forestry policies present major obstacles to smallholder farmers who want to sell timber from their landholdings. Both Peruvian and Brazilian forestry laws require contracts and authorized forestry management plans for any concession or timber production area.[1] Both countries' new regulations purport to aid rural farmers and communities in developing forestry activities. Despite these government agency efforts, smallholders sometimes cannot afford the required government contract fees or do not have the motivation or expertise to develop the required technical plans.

Another source of frustration to smallholders is that their model of timber production does not mesh with community forestry projects or certification programs that are promoted by nongovernmental organizations and government agencies. Most smallholder farmers manage timber directly on their own landholdings, not on community lands. The community-based model requires individuals to form associations to produce and sell a communal resource, but in the case of timber management by smallholders discussed in this chapter, that resource is not common property. Pushing individuals into a model that is a poor fit results in social and political tension and economic complications. Community forestry programs do function in some villages, as evidenced by other chapters in this volume, but they are not viable everywhere. In Macapá, farmers have run into this problem and are working with the agencies and organizations that promote community-based projects to find a solution. Smallholders in Mamiraú and Peru still struggle with the issue.

CONCLUSION

Both farmers and the environment benefit from the ecological and economic consequences of maintaining a tree component in their production systems. For farmers, the sale of timber supplements an otherwise modest and seasonal income from annual crops and reduces financial stress in years of poor crop production or poor markets. An accessible market that is open to a variety of timber species, both traditional and nontraditional, is added incentive for farmers to maintain diverse tree species and to manage some of them for timber on their landholdings. For the environment, forest cover and tree diversity increase both the ecological and economic value of the farmland, which results in reduced forest conversion and longer fallow periods, and ecosystem structure and function is better conserved.

Large urban timber industry limits rather than helps to promote sustainable forest management for timber production. Industrial companies feed large national and international markets that seek high volumes of only a few species and rely on forest mining (*sensu* Uhl et al. 1997). *Várzea* farmers provide an alternative model of sustainable timber production that contrasts sharply with industrial and plantation forestry models used throughout the region. Recognizing the important role of smallholder farmers in both timber production and forest conservation is critical for changing public and scientific attitudes toward them from destroyers to stewards of Amazon forests.

ACKNOWLEDGMENTS

The authors thank the United Nations University program "People, Land and Environmental Change," the Academy for Educational Development, the Land Institute, and the Association for Women in Science for financial support. Mamirauá Institute in Brazil and the Research Institute of the Peruvian Amazon and the University of San Marcos in Peru provided logistical assistance in the field. The field expertise of Jomber C. Inuma in Mamirauá and Fernando Rabelo in Macapá was invaluable. We are indebted to the many expert farmers of the *várzea* in all three regions, without whose assistance and knowledge these ideas would not come to light. We also thank Daniel Zarin, Francis Putz, and one anonymous reviewer for valuable comments on earlier versions of the manuscript.

NOTE

1. Forestry activities are regulated in Brazil by Law no. 9.649 of May 27, 1999, and a host of provisional measures and normative instructions (most recently Instrução Normativa no. 4, March 4, 2002) and in Peru by the Forestry and Wildlife Law no. 27308 of July 2000 and subsequent instructional regulations.

REFERENCES

Anderson, A. 1991. Forest management strategies by rural inhabitants in the Amazon estuary. In A. Gómez-Pompa, T. C. Whitmore, and M. Hadley, eds., *Rain forest regeneration and management*, 351–360. Paris: Parthenon Publishing Group.

Anderson, A. B., I. M. Mousasticoshvily Jr., and D. S. Macedo. 1999. Logging of *Virola surinamensis* in the Amazon floodplain: Impacts and alternatives. In C. Padoch, M. Ayres, M. Pinedo-Vasquez, and A. Henderson, eds., Várzea: *Diversity, development and conservation of Amazonia's whitewater floodplains,* 119–133. New York: New York Botanical Garden Press.

Balée, W. and A. Gély. 1989. Managed forest succession in Amazônia: The Ka'apor case. *Advances in Economic Botany* 7: 129–158.

Barros, A. C. and C. Uhl. 1995. Logging along the Amazon estuary: Patterns, problems and potential. *Forest Ecology and Management* 77: 87–105.

Brondízio, E. S., E. Moran, P. Mausel, and Y. Wu. 1994. Land use change in the Amazon estuary: Patterns of caboclo settlement and landscape management. *Human Ecology* 22: 249–278.

Brondízio, E. S. and A. D. Siqueira. 1997. From extractivists to forest farmers: Changing concepts of caboclo agroforestry in the Amazon estuary. *Research in Economic Anthropology* 18: 233–279.

Chibnik, M. 1994. *Risky rivers: The economics and politics of floodplain farming in Amazonia.* Tucson: University of Arizona Press.

CTAR. 1998. *Anuario estadistico forestal 1998, region Ucayali.* Pucallpa, Peru: Ministerio de Agricultura.

De Jong, W. 2001. Tree and forest management in the floodplains of the Peruvian Amazon. *Forest Ecology and Management* 150: 125–134.

Denevan, W. 1984. Ecological heterogeneity and horizontal zonation of agriculture in the Amazonian floodplain. In M. Schmink and C. H. Wood, eds.

Frontier expansion in Amazonia, 311–336. Gainesville: University of Florida Press.

Denevan, W. 1992. The pristine myth: The landscape of the Americas in 1492. *Annals of the Association of American Geographers* 82: 369–385.

Fredericksen, T. S. and B. Mostacedo. 2000. Regeneration of timber species following selection logging in a Bolivian tropical dry forest. *Forest Ecology and Management* 131: 47–55.

Furch, K. 1997. Chemistry of *várzea* and *igapó* soils and nutrient inventory of their floodplain forests. In W. J. Junk, ed., *The central Amazon floodplain: Ecology of a pulsing system,* 47–68. New York: Springer.

Hecht, S. and A. Cockburn. 1989. *The fate of the forest: Developers, destroyers, and defenders of the Amazon.* London: Verso.

Higuchi, N. 1994. Utilização e manejo dos recursos madeireiros das florestas tropicais úmidas. *Acta Amazônica* 24: 275–288.

INRENA. 1999. *Estadistica forestal—año 1999: Ambito de la region unidad operativa INRENA–Ucayali.* Pucallpa, Peru: Ministerio de Agricultura, Instituto Nacional de Recursos Naturales.

Johns, A. 1988. Effects of "selective" timber extraction on rain forest structure and composition and some consequences for frugivores and folivores. *Biotropica* 20: 31–37.

Lisboa, P. L. B., E. F. de Terezo, and J. C.-A. da Silva. 1991. Amazônian timber: Considerations on exploration, species extinction and conservation. *Boletim do Museu Paraense Emilio Goeldi, Serie Botânica* 7: 521–542.

Macedo, D. S. and A. B. Anderson. 1993. Early ecological changes associated with logging in an Amazon floodplain. *Biotropica* 25: 151–163.

Nepstad, D. C., I. F. Brown, L. Luz, A. Alechandre, and V. Viana. 1992. Biotic impoverishment of Amazônian forests by rubber tappers, loggers, and cattle ranchers. In D. C. Nepstad and S. Schwartzman, eds., *Advances in economic botany,* 1–14. New York: The New York Botanical Garden.

Padoch, C. and M. Pinedo-Vasquez. 1996. Smallholder forest management: Looking beyond non-timber forest products. In M. Ruiz-Perez and J. E. M. Arnold, eds., *Current issues in non-timber forest products research,* 103–118. Bogor, Indonesia: CIFOR.

Padoch, C. and M. Pinedo-Vasquez. 1999. Concurrent activities and invisible technologies: An example of timber management in Amazônia. In D. A. Posey, ed., *Human impacts on the Amazon: The role of traditional ecological knowledge in conservation and development,* 102–117. New York: Columbia University Press.

Pereira, V. F. G., R. G. Congalton, and D. J. Zarin. 2002. Spatial and temporal analysis of a tidal floodplain landscape: Amapá, Brazil—Using geographic information systems and remote sensing. *Photogrammetric Engineering & Remote Sensing* 68: 463–472.

Pinedo-Vasquez, M. 1995. *Human impact on várzea ecosystems in the Napo-Amazon, Peru.* Doctoral dissertation, Yale University, New Haven, Conn.

Pinedo-Vasquez, M. and F. Rabelo. 2002. Sustainable management of an Amazonian forest for timber production: A myth or reality? In H. Brookfield, C. Padoch, H. Parsons, and M. Stocking, eds., *Cultivating biodiversity: Understanding, analyzing, and using agricultural diversity,* 186–193. London: United Nations University Press.

Pinedo-Vasquez, M., D. Zarin, K. Coffey, C. Padoch, and F. Rabelo. 2001. Post-boom timber production in Amazônia. *Human Ecology* 29: 219–239.

Prance, G. T. 1979. Notes on the vegetation of Amazônia III. The terminology of Amazônian forest types subject to inundation. *Brittonia* 31: 26–38.

Putz, F. E. 2000. Economics of home grown forestry. *Ecological Economics* 32: 9–14.

Roosevelt, A. C. 1999. Twelve thousand years of human–environment interaction in the Amazon floodplain. In C. Padoch, M. Ayres, M. Pinedo-Vasquez, and A. Henderson, eds., *Várzea: Diversity, development and conservation of Amazonia's whitewater floodplains*, 371–391. New York: The New York Botanical Garden Press.

Sears, R. R., C. Padoch, and M. Pinedo-Vasquez. In press. Amazon forestry transformed: Integrating knowledge for smallholder timber management in eastern Brazil. In G. Martin, ed., *Innovative wisdom*. San Francisco, Calif.: Earthscan.

Silva, J. N. M. 1989. *The behavior of the tropical rain forest of the Brazilian Amazon after logging*. Doctoral dissertation, University of Oxford, U.K.

Uhl, C., P. Barreto, A. Veríssimo, E. Vidal, P. Amaral, A. C. Barros, C. Souza, J. Johns, and J. Gerwing. 1997. Natural resource management in the Brazilian Amazon. *BioScience* 47: 160–168.

Zarin, D. J. 1999. Spatial heterogeneity and temporal variability of some Amazônian floodplain soils. In C. Padoch, M. Ayres, M. Pinedo-Vasquez, and A. Henderson, eds., *Várzea: Diversity, development, and conservation in Amazonia's whitewater floodplains*, 313–321. New York: The New York Botanical Garden Press.

Zarin, D. J., V. F. G. Pereira, H. Raffles, F. G. Rabelo, M. Pinedo-Vasquez, and R. G. Congalton. 2001. Landscape change in tidal floodplains near the mouth of the Amazon River. *Forest Ecology and Management* 154: 383–393.

PART III

Working Forest Paradoxes

Chapter 15

NEOTROPICAL WORKING FORESTS

FOR WHAT AND FOR WHOM?

Janaki R. R. Alavalapati and Daniel J. Zarin

With nearly 1 billion ha of natural forests, Latin America accounts for about 25 percent of the world's forests and half of all remaining tropical forests. For many indigenous groups, local communities, and governments, working forests are major sources of livelihood and economic growth. Deforestation and forest degradation rates of these working forests are alarming. The average annual deforestation rate in the continent is about 7.5 million ha, or 0.8 percent (Keipi 1999); rates of forest degradation by wildfires and uncontrolled logging are even higher (Cochrane 2003). Keipi (1999) noted that growing population pressure, rural poverty, limited environmental awareness, inappropriate land tenures and timber concessions, ineffective institutions, perverse economic policies, and macroeconomic forces are largely responsible for forest degradation and deforestation.

Keipi (1999) suggests several measures to reduce rates of deforestation and forest degradation in Latin America. These measures include improving the competitiveness of forestry operations relative to alternative agricultural practices, restructuring forest concessions to ensure best management practices and to attract long-term investment, working with regional and international partners to develop forest-friendly trade policies, and recognizing the rights and needs of people who live in and around forests. The first steps in pursuing these measures effectively will be a clear understanding about public preferences for forest use, tradeoffs and complementarities associated with multiple uses, conflicts arising between heterogeneous user groups, and the efficiency and equity aspects of management alternatives. In this chapter we discuss the complexities involved in making management decisions for neotropical working forests.

WORKING FORESTS: FOR WHAT?

Working forests produce a variety of goods and services including timber, recreational opportunities, water, forage, and environmental services such as clean air and biodiversity. The first question that arises in the management of working forests is, What should be produced? Should management efforts focus on timber or nontimber forest products and services, or both? The answer to this question is simple if we want to optimize only one output. However, in many instances we want to produce more than one output. With multiple outputs, three general scenarios are possible (table 15.1): the outputs are unambiguously complementary, the outputs are inversely proportional (figure 15.1), or the relationship between the outputs is ambiguous, nonlinear, or poorly understood.

For the second scenario, the number of choices on the timber versus nontimber product production frontier is infinite. Each choice results in a unique level of timber and nontimber output (e.g., T1–NT1 and T2–NT2). In this straightforward case, monetary criteria can help us select the optimal combination of timber and nontimber forest products. But even here, spatial, temporal, and technological variables influence production frontiers in a substantial way. Therefore an optimal combination of timber and nontimber forest products in one region may be suboptimal in another region. In the more complex case of the third scenario, the production relationship may vary greatly depending on the specific ecological context, and the tradeoffs may be characterized by thresholds and other nonlinearities. The same theoretical approach

Table 15.1

Three General Scenarios for Multiple Outputs from Neotropical Working Forests

Scenario	Example	Scale
Unambiguously complementary	Old-growth forest carbon storage and biodiversity	Landscape
Inversely proportional	Management of a species for timber or nontimber forest product	Stand
Ambiguous, nonlinear, poorly understood	Biodiversity and timber harvesting	Management unit

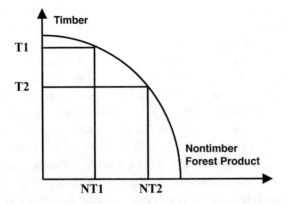

Figure 15.1 Stand-level production relationship between timber and nontimber forest products from a single species.

illustrated for the second scenario applies, but more information is needed for its effective implementation.

WORKING FORESTS: FOR WHOM?

Some of the principal stakeholders in working forests include indigenous and local communities, private companies, and nongovernmental organizations (NGOs). Drawing on de Camino (1999), we summarize the interests of various stakeholders, their positions, and their possible actions with respect to conservation of working forests, albeit in simplified, generalized terms.

Many indigenous and local community groups prefer to control traditional lands with limited intervention from outside communities. Toward this objective they may conserve or exploit primary forests in their territories. They are likely to work for demarcation of traditional lands and extractive reserves and for recognition of their customary and usufruct rights (see chapter 7).

Conservation-oriented NGOs prefer to gain protection status for the majority of land areas with forest cover, protect biological corridors, and maintain biodiversity. They may advocate capturing the forests' value through environmental service payments and sharing the opportunity costs of conservation with the international community (see chapter 16). In pursuing these interests, they attempt to establish national and international biodiversity strategies and land use plans and try to develop market mechanisms to realize income from environmental services. NGOs with the primary objectives of protecting human rights or indigenous cultures may have interests and actions that are consistent with those of indigenous and local community groups.

The primary objective of concessionaires is to maximize profits from logging and other value-added activities. Toward this objective they want areas with the most valuable timber species and greatest productive potential for timber production. Furthermore, they support less restrictive and secure timber concessions and acceptance of forest investment as collateral (Hardner and Rice 1999), with limits on usufruct rights of other users. Toward these goals, private logging companies lobby for policy actions that can accommodate increased production to meet domestic and external demand for forest products and demarcate areas for timber production (see chapter 3).

Other stakeholders include the general public and government agencies with the responsibility to regulate forest use on behalf of the general public. Stakeholder power is fluid, varying from place to place and changing over time. In one region, private companies may have great power to influence forest policies, whereas in other regions community groups may have the dominant influence on policy actions. Coalitions are common among user groups to produce policy actions that further their collective advantage, thereby distorting efficiency and equity. Although some stakeholders pursue democratic principles to resolve conflicts and make decisions, principles such as "one-person, one-vote" and "majority rule" often create huge distortions in decision making.

Let us say, for example, we have a referendum at a national scale placing a ban on commercial logging to protect biodiversity. Passage of such a measure may not be fair because the opportunity costs of this policy would fall solely on groups who are heavily dependent on the forest economy, whereas the benefits of biodiversity protection would accrue to all other groups. Timber-dependent forest stakeholders may strongly oppose such a referendum, but a one-person, one-vote approach does not recognize the preference intensity of these minority groups, whether they are corporations or rural communities. Developing mutually beneficial goals and building consensus in working forests obviously is a challenging task.

MANAGEMENT CHALLENGES

Working forests produce a variety of goods and services with varying degrees of joint consumption and excludability. At one extreme, some goods are amenable only for individual consumption and to exclude others from consuming the resource (e.g., privately owned timber and livestock). At the other extreme are goods that can be enjoyed by many at a level that is the same for all (e.g., watershed protection), and it is difficult to exclude others from enjoying these public goods. In between these two extremes are toll goods (e.g., timber concessions) and common pool goods (e.g., community forests and community access to hunt animals and collect nontimber products).

With no exclusive rights, individuals have limited motivation to produce public goods and common pool goods at optimum levels. People know that once public goods are in place they cannot be excluded from enjoying them even if they did not contribute to their production (free-riders). With respect to common pool goods, individuals often are motivated to overexploit in anticipation of similar behavior by others ("the tragedy of the commons," Hardin 1968). Government agencies and communities often attempt to fix these problems by setting user fees and creating specific institutions to regulate the behavior of stakeholders (Poteete and Ostrom 2002).

Selecting an optimal management strategy is a challenge. To keep the discussion simple, let us group activities such as selective felling, reduced-impact logging, and forest certification into strategy 1 (S1) and more intensive and uncontrolled logging as strategy 2 (S2). The production frontiers of these two strategies are different because of the variation in the choice of technologies. Figure 15.2 indicates that more nontimber forest products can be produced under S1, whereas more timber can be produced using S2. Each strategy may have a specific distribution of costs and benefits among the stakeholders.

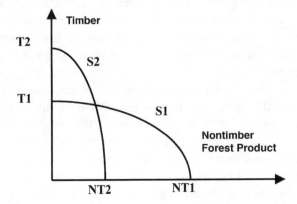

Figure 15.2 Management strategies and their impact on production possibility frontiers as illustrated in figure 15.1.

ASSESSMENT CHALLENGES

Following Clawson (1975) and Cubbage et al. (1993), we describe a multidisciplinary framework comprising five components—biophysical feasibility, ecological sustainability, economic efficiency, sociocultural acceptability, and operational practicality—and its potentials and limitations for addressing the issues. Discussion of any forest management strategy that is not physically and biologically feasible is moot. Can we increase timber production through intensive silvicultural practices? Can we ensure biodiversity protection or water and air quality along with timber production? Does natural forest regeneration increase or decrease under reduced-impact logging? Diverse perceptions, uncertainty, and risk make assessment of biological feasibility complex and challenging.

First, we will discuss why it is critical to ensure ecological sustainability. There is no single or simple answer. Some user groups contend that it is our moral responsibility to pass our collective ecological heritage on to future generations. Groups that embrace a biocentric or ecocentric philosophy posit that human beings have no right to drive other species to the brink of extinction. Those who adhere to Aldo Leopold's land ethic argue that each species is a thread in the complex web of ecosystems, and ensuring its sustainability is vital for effective functioning of ecosystems. Environmental economists point out that intrinsic, existence, and environmental values associated with ecosystems justify ecological sustainability. Furthermore, in most cases we do not have full information about the value of these ecosystems and the risk associated with their disappearance. Ciriacy-Wantrup (1968), who coined the term "safe minimum standard," urged its adoption to allow for the risk and uncertainty associated with resource use such that actions do not result in irreversible environmental damage. In the conservation of a plant or animal species, a safe minimum standard may be defined in terms of maintaining a certain stock or in terms of protecting a certain area of natural habitat.

Economic efficiency involves allocating scarce resources (e.g., labor, capital, or land) between competing demands using monetary value as the common denominator. The opportunity cost of resources generally is used as a guiding principle to make resource allocation decisions. For example, the opportunity cost of practicing forestry on a piece of land is the foregone benefits of not using it for the most financially attractive alternative, such as agriculture. Net present values (NPVS), benefit–cost ratios (BCRS), and internal rates of return (IRRS) are the major decision criteria. According to these criteria, management alternatives that result in the highest NPV, BCR, or IRR are preferred to their rivals. Approaches that maximize the possible output with a given amount of input or minimize the cost of production for a given level of output are commonly used in determining these criteria. Although economic efficiency is a commonly used measure in making resource allocation decisions, several cautions are in order in the context of working forests.

First of all, the decision criteria involve discounting future benefits and costs associated with each alternative to reflect that a dollar today is worth more than a dollar tomorrow. With greater discount rates, forestry projects with greater benefits in the short run and higher costs in the future will be favored over projects with lower benefits in the short run and lower costs in the future. As a result, higher discount rates make conservation practices, such as forest reserves and biodiversity conservation measures, less attractive relative to intensive logging, mining, or agricultural practices. However, there is no consensus on the use of a discount factor. The private sector typically argues for the use of market interest rates as a discount factor, whereas the public sector favors the use of lower discount rates to justify projects with long-term benefits. If future generations are considered into this equation, this issue becomes more complicated. For the current generation, a dollar today may be more valuable than a dollar tomorrow, but for an imaginary future generation representative, a dollar in the future may be more valuable than a dollar today. Issues such as irreversibility and uncertainty associated with future events also pose challenges in choosing the discount factor.

Second, the perspective on economic efficiency of a private entrepreneur is different from that of a rural community or social planner or policymaker. Private entrepreneurs such as owners of timber companies typically do not incorporate external costs and benefits of their actions into their decision making. For example, the costs of reservoir sedimentation or biodiversity loss that may be associated with logging do not affect profits, so there is little incentive for companies to consider them in production decisions. Communities, as well as responsible social planners and policymakers, must consider these external costs and benefits in making their decisions. Accordingly, if timber companies have to account for external costs, their profit margins will be reduced. On the other hand, if opportunities exist to internalize external benefits (e.g., carbon credits), forestry may become more profitable (see chapter 13). Either way, internalizing externalities would narrow the gap between private and social efficiency.

Third, private entrepreneurs typically do not consider the tradeoff impacts of their decisions because each business is small relative to the size of the overall economy. However, certain macroeconomic policies affect many entrepreneurs and companies in a region and thus influence the overall sector of the region. For example, agricultural subsidies increase the profitability of agricultural production relative to forestry and tend to cause expansion in the agriculture sector and contraction of the forest sector. Including tradeoff impacts is critical in assessing the economic efficiency of decision alternatives (Alavalapati et al. 1998, Das and Alavalapati 2003).

Fourth, economic efficiency assumes the "trickle-down" principle. Subscribers to this principle argue that once wealth is generated following the principles of efficiency, even without consideration of distributional concerns, it will still trickle down eventually into the hands of the masses. Governments can facilitate this process through tax policies and public expenditures; it also happens when wealthier groups start buying additional goods and services. The evidence to support this principle is mixed and is very limited in developing countries.

Equity, or the distribution of benefits and costs associated with each management or policy alternative, influences the social acceptability of those alternatives. Some management alternatives may be biologically feasible, ecologically sustainable, and economically efficient but fail to pass the test of social acceptability. A good example is protected area management in which local communities are denied access to the resources previously open to them. Berlik et al. (2002) point out that forest management strategies often fail because of their limited social acceptability (see also chapters 7 and 8). Many welfare and social justice principles can be applied to assess equity aspects of management alternatives:

- The Pareto principle, which stipulates that in response to a policy change anyone can be better off but no one should be worse off, can be used as a basis for policy choice. It is elegant in terms of protecting individuals from becoming worse off as a result of policy change, but it strongly favors the status quo. Very few policies qualify according to this principle because some people may become worse off in response to any policy alternative.
- The compensation principle suggests that if gainers from a policy change can compensate losers and still be left with benefits, that change can be considered. In the absence of actual compensation, it may be difficult to muster the support of local communities for protected areas management, for example. Even if compensation is allowed, its adequate determination may be impossible in situations such as relocation of communities in response to a forest management strategy.

- Rawls (in Peterson 2001) suggests two principles of justice: Each person is to have an equal right to the basic liberties compatible with a similar system of liberty for all, and an equal distribution of social primary goods is favored unless an unequal distribution is to the advantage of the least favored. This means that basic liberties are not to be infringed upon in the name of increased efficiency, and no amount of overall gains is acceptable if they come at the expense of socially disadvantaged groups.
- Nozick's principles provide valuable insights into many property rights issues that plague Latin America. He suggests that individuals can come to possess property in two ways: initial acquisition and trade or exchange. According to Nozick (1974), "just acquisition" of property can occur when one uses personal labor to take possession of something that is not already owned by someone else; then, one can use it, sell it, bequeath it, offer it in barter, and so on (Peterson 2001). This suggests that indigenous and other traditional rural communities in working forests have exclusive rights to their forest resources, and government economic development policies should not violate these rights. Furthermore, according to Rawls (1972), if those communities are viewed as socially disadvantaged groups, then any amount of economic and ecological gains of conserving forests is not acceptable if they come at the expense of indigenous groups.

Depending on the weight national governments place on equity and justice principles, social acceptability criteria can influence choices of forest management alternatives.

CONCLUSION

Success in formulating biologically sound, economically profitable, and socially acceptable policies does not necessarily result in their successful implementation. Limited resources often impede implementation. Proposed policy changes may be so large and indivisible that they are challenging to implement in an incremental fashion. Limited research capabilities and training opportunities often prevent user groups from adopting effective management strategies. Managers who have been trained to discharge certain duties may not be able to undertake new responsibilities. Commonly called "trained incapacities," this situation is a serious problem in many neotropical working forest contexts. For example, professionals trained with an emphasis on custodial aspects of public lands may have less capacity to enlist community participation in management. On the contrary, they may view community participation as a threat to their custodial power. In addition, resource-rich forest industry groups, agencies responsible for implementing government policies, and policymakers traditionally have supported each other's actions for their mutual advantage by developing an "iron triangle" to oppose implementation of policies that could have negative impacts on the profitability of private industry. The growing influence of NGOs and local communities on government agencies and policy makers has begun to weaken the triangle.

Ideally we would like to have management alternatives that are biologically feasible, ecologically sustainable, economically efficient, socially acceptable, and operationally feasible. In reality, very few alternatives pass all of these tests, and it is difficult to prioritize these criteria. Tradeoffs and complementarities between them are context specific, and explicitly identifying those tradeoffs and complementarities is essential for both honest exchange of views and good decision making.

REFERENCES

Alavalapati, J. R. R., W. L. Adamowicz, and W. A. White. 1998. A comparison of economic impact assessment methods: The case of forestry developments in Alberta. *Canadian Journal of Forest Research* 28: 711–719.

Berlik, M. M., D. B. Kittredge, and D. R. Foster. 2002. *The illusion of preservation: A global environmental argument for the local production of natural resources.* Harvard Forest Paper no. 26. Cambridge, Mass: Harvard University Press.

Ciriacy-Wantrup, S. V. 1968. *Resource conservation: Economics and policies.* Berkeley: University of California Press.

Clawson, M. 1975. *Forests for whom and for what?* Baltimore, Md.: The John Hopkins University Press.

Cochrane, M. 2003. Fire science for rainforests. *Nature* 421: 913–919.

Cubbage, F. W., J. O'Laughlin, and C. S. Bullock III. 1993. *Forest resource policy.* New York: Wiley.

Das, G. and J. R. R. Alavalapati. 2003. Trade mediated biotechnology transfer and its effective absorption: An application to the U.S. forestry sector. *Technological Forecasting and Social Change: An International Journal* 70(6): 545–562.

de Camino, R. 1999. Sustainable management of natural forests: Actors and policies. In K. Keipi, ed., *Forest resource policy in Latin America,* 93–109. Washington, D.C.: Inter-American Development Bank.

Hardin, G. 1968. The tragedy of commons. *Science* 162: 1243–1248.

Hardner, J. J. and R. Rice. 1999. Rethinking forest concession policies. In K. Keipi, ed., *Forest resource policy in Latin America,* 161–193. Washington, D.C.: Inter-American Development Bank.

Keipi, K. 1999. *Forest resource policy in Latin America.* Washington, D.C.: Inter-American Development Bank.

Nozick, R. 1974. *Anarchy, state and utopia*. New York: Basic Books.

Peterson, E. W. F. 2001. *The political economy of agricultural, natural resource, and environmental policy analysis*. Ames: Iowa State University Press.

Poteete, A. and E. Ostrom. 2002. *An institutional approach to the study of forest resources*. Bloomington: International Forestry Resources and Institutions Research Program, Indiana University.

Rawls, J. 1972. *A theory of justice*. Cambridge: Harvard University Press.

Chapter 16

ON DEFYING NATURE'S END

Gustavo A. B. da Fonseca, Aaron Bruner, Russell A. Mittermeier, Keith Alger, Claude Gascon, and Richard E. Rice

Thirteen thousand years ago, North America underwent a major extinction spasm that completely changed the character of its fauna in a period of less than 3000 years. Magnificent mammals, including ground sloths, giant elk, mastodonts, and saber-toothed tigers, disappeared in the blink of an eye in geological time. Although the exact cause of this transformation is still debated, there is increasing evidence that it was induced directly and indirectly by the progressive occupation of the American continent by humans (Alroy 2001, Dayton 2001, Flannery 2001).

Today, some of the earth's last remaining biodiversity hotspots appear headed for a similar cataclysm caused by widespread loss of native habitat, particularly in the species-rich tropics (Myers et al. 2000). Even where forests still remain, in many areas inadequate protection has resulted in the elimination of most medium and large-bodied wildlife species, resulting in the empty forest syndrome (Redford 1992). This phenomenon is in effect the second phase of the human-induced biosimplification of natural ecosystems initiated during the Pleistocene. This time, however, humans have the power to eliminate a far broader spectrum of species, not just large game, and to destroy entire biological communities.

Fortunately, scientists studying these changes have accumulated enough information to provide strong predictions of what can be expected if we do not intervene. Recent analyses suggest that in the next five years, for example, Mesoamerica (Mexico to Panama) is likely to lose 10 percent of its remaining natural vegetation, with the resulting extinction of at least twenty-two vertebrate species and ninety-three plant species (Brooks et al. 2002). Even the major tropical wilderness areas (Myers et al. 2000, Mittermeier et al. 2003), which, unlike the hotspots, still retain 70 percent or more of their native vegetation cover, are rapidly changing with the advancement of agriculture frontiers. Anticipated loss of habitat in these areas will put a far greater number of species at risk of extinction (Pimm and Raven 2000).

Awareness of this impending crisis gives us early warning that if we do not act, it will soon be too late; the question is what actions are necessary. The challenges faced by conservationists in the past offer some important lessons. Despite widespread pressure, parks and reserves have shown themselves to be the only areas where the full complement of biodiversity persists in contexts of serious threats. On the other hand, ecological and economic dynamics have also made it clear that the status quo approach to conservation, highly site-specific and largely reactive, is barely holding the line in a sort of environmental trench warfare and is not adequate to protect biodiversity in the long run. Despite increased conservation efforts, many critical areas are still lost each year.

If we are to avert a crisis, there is an urgent need to both drastically increase the scale of conservation work and, equally important, adjust our strategies to address large-scale ecological, social, and economic realities. This chapter describes some of the principal results arising from a broad portfolio of scientific investigation conducted by the Center for Applied Biodiversity Science (CABS) at Conservation International (CI), which has functioned as a strategic research unit closely linked to CI's needs in the field since its creation in 1999. The strategy presented here, similar to those being developed by many conservation organizations worldwide, begins with the need for strict definition of biodiversity conservation priorities, followed by focused action at both site and regional scales, seeking to achieve concrete, measurable, and time-bound conservation outcomes.

WHERE TO WORK: SETTING BIOLOGICAL PRIORITIES

The world is far too big and resources too limited for conservationists to be active everywhere. Setting priorities for investment and action therefore is vital. Biodiversity loss is arguably the only major global environmental problem that is truly irreversible, and facing this challenge entails immediate and targeted action.

If we are to minimize loss of biodiversity, as measured at the level of species, identifying areas with concentrations of endemic (restricted

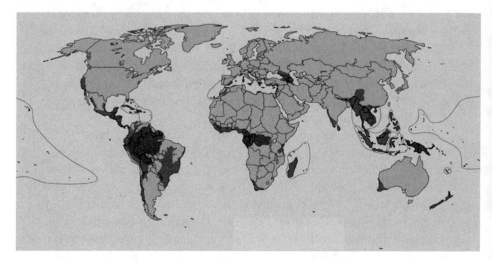

Figure 16.1 Original extent of the global biodiversity hotspots and major tropical wilderness areas. (For color reproduction and explanation see Plate 4.)

range) plants and animals becomes paramount. A number of regions stand out globally as centers of terrestrial species richness and endemism. A pioneering approach to identifying these regions is represented by the global biodiversity hotspots, areas featuring exceptional concentrations of endemic species and experiencing exceptionally rapid habitat loss. Myers (1988, 1990) was the first to highlight the value of these few terrestrial habitats that account for a significant portion of the earth's biodiversity, represented by endemic species.

A recent reanalysis of this framework (Mittermeier et al. 1998, 1999, Myers et al. 2000, CI) defined twenty-five hotspots (figure 16.1), currently covering only 1.4 percent of the land surface of the earth, which provide the only remaining habitat for an estimated 44 percent of all species of vascular plants and 35 percent of all of mammals, birds, reptiles, and amphibians. All of the hotspots have already lost more than 70 percent of their original vegetation. Many species in the hotspots are also extremely vulnerable, with diminished populations, highly fragmented habitat, and pressures from numerous sources. Since 1800, close to 80 percent of all bird species that have gone extinct were lost from the biodiversity hotspots (Myers et al. 2000).

A complementary approach to priority setting is to select regions that are exceptionally species rich but still largely intact. These regions offer the opportunity to protect large, nearly pristine areas and intact faunal assemblages, a strategy that may prove vital in the long term. The biological importance of the three major tropical wilderness areas (MTWAS) (figure 16.1) has been recognized by a range of groups for more than a decade. Covering only 4.8 percent of the earth's land surface, they provide the only habitat for more than 14 percent of the world's vascular plant species and more than 7 percent of all nonfish vertebrate species (Mittermeier et al. 2003). A recent reanalysis of important wilderness areas, considering thirty-seven regions in a range of ecosystems, suggests that at least two new wilderness areas should be considered highest priority for conservation (Mittermeier et al. 1995, 2003).

Cumulatively, the hotspots and the three MTWAS contain, as endemics, almost 59 percent of the world's vascular plants and just over 42 percent of the world's nonfish vertebrates in just over 6 percent of the land surface. With the addition of the two new high-biodiversity wilderness areas, the hotspots and wilderness areas contain an even greater share of the world's biodiversity. Focusing on these two types of areas, representing extremes of extinction threat and intact functioning ecosystems, offers an unparalleled opportunity to save great numbers of species by concentrating conservation activities on a geographically limited area.

The identification of a global priority agenda is a critical first step in achieving much-needed consensus on priority areas. To a large extent, the results of different approaches to setting priorities at a global scale, led by different conservation organizations, are beginning to converge (Fonseca et al. 2000). Moving to finer scales, where specific regions and sites can be selected for action, is the next challenge, one that can be accomplished only with detailed, spatially explicit, species-level data. Progress is being made on this front as well: A number of research groups and organizations are collaborating in compiling such data and making them available to the global conservation community (Brooks et al. 2001). These data make it possible for the first time to identify with precision where we need to work to protect specific species.

SITE CONSERVATION TOOLS

Species conservation objectives are made more manageable by defining geographic focus areas. But once we decide where to work, the challenge becomes how to do effective conservation there. In this section, we discuss conservation tools for protecting specific areas. We review evidence on the effectiveness of two main categories of conservation tools—protected areas and sustainable development projects—and draw conclusions for what strategies are likely to be most effective in the future. We also present a new conservation tool, conservation concessions, which aims to address some of the difficulties encountered by conservation work to date. In the following section, we present conservation corridors as a means to combine site conservation tools into an integrated strategy at a scale sufficient to address ecological and economic needs.

Beginning with the model of Yellowstone National Park in the United States, established in 1872, the creation of protected areas to restrict direct use of biological resources became the predominant strategy to ensure the persistence of representative samples of native habitat and their associated biodiversity in many parts of the world. Other forms of protected areas, such as game reserves and national forests, also sought to prohibit public use of specific resources (in these cases, large game species and timber, respectively). In the last two decades, however, protection through reserves and activities traditionally associated with parks, such as border demarcation and enforcement, have been criticized as both inappropriate and ineffective in many cases (IUCN et al. 1991, Brown and Wyckoff-Baird 1992, Ghmire and Pimbert 1997, Wilshusen et al. 2002). Furthermore, many groups have come to view the often-stated goal of placing 10 percent of national territory in protected areas as a limit to the acceptable amount of protection rather than an important short-term objective (Soulé and Sanjayan 1998, Schwartzman et al. 2000).

These criticisms have combined with the appealing possibility of jointly promoting conservation and development to bring about a major change in conservation strategies. A large portion of conservation effort is now dedicated to promoting, often as a direct substitute to parks, the vague concept of sustainable development (IUCN et al. 1991). Instead of seeking to separate areas for conservation from areas for resource use, sustainable development attempts to integrate them in the same place by promoting types and intensities of use that are profitable but compatible with conservation goals. This strategy is based on an appealing premise: Successful sustainable development–based conservation projects should create a win–win situation in which relevant stakeholders benefit from, and therefore try to promote, conservation. Sustainable development therefore can ideally create a situation in which pressure on natural resources decreases, constituencies for conservation increase, and effective conservation becomes possible in a range of difficult contexts.

What does recent experience tell us about these strategies? In regard to parks, there is evidence of both successful areas and those that have become heavily degraded. It is also clear that in many cases park management is far from ideal. Studies detail myriad problems such as Ghana's "empty" forests (Oates 1999), oil spills in parks in Ecuador (van Schaik et al. 1997), and illegal logging and clearing of Indonesia's parks (EIA and Telepak Indonesia 1999). In a review of rainforest parks across the tropics, van Schaik et al. (1997:64) write, "Protected nature reserves are in a state of crisis. A number of tropical parks have already been degraded almost beyond redemption; others face severe threats of many kinds with little capacity to resist. The final bulwark erected to shield tropical nature from extinction is collapsing." They go on to detail numerous cases of degradation from causes such as illegal hunting, grazing, logging, and land clearing. More fundamentally, there is a widespread perception that traditional parks cannot protect the resources within their borders against ever-increasing human pressures.

In contrast, ample evidence suggests that protected areas have had a significant impact even with low levels of investment. In large areas across Latin America that are completely cleared, parks often stand out as the only remaining natural habitat (Dourojeanni 1999). Even highly degraded parks often harbor the last remaining species in otherwise devastated ecosystems (van Schaik et al. 1997). A growing body of literature from various disciplines offers convincing support for parks. Statistical analyses have found strong protective effects of parks in Belize and Mexico (Chomitz and Gray 1996, Deininger and Minten 1997). A study in Costa Rica, using satellite imagery, similarly found that whereas the country as a whole lost approximately 10 percent of its remaining forest between 1987 and 1997, national parks lost only 0.4 percent (CCT and CIEDES 1998). A regional study in Costa Rica found similar trends over a twenty-year period starting in 1975 (Sanchez-Azofeifa et al. 1999).

A study of twenty-two tropical countries (Bruner et al. 2001) attempted to quantify effectiveness in parks under high levels of threat. They used a sample of ninety-three parks to assess effectiveness by both calculating land clearing over time and comparing the condition of parks with the condition of their surroundings. They found that 83 percent of the parks in the sample experienced no net clearing since they were established (median age twenty-one years) and that a full 40 percent permitted the regeneration of native vegetation on land that was cleared at the time of park establishment. Only 17 percent had a net loss of native vegetation to land clearing. In comparing parks with their surroundings, although they found instances of serious degradation, most often from hunting, overall the parks were in significantly better condition than their surrounding areas for all impacts tested (land clearing, logging, hunting, grazing, and fire). These findings suggest that the perception that parks cannot resist high levels of pressure is inaccurate and that, on the contrary, with modest support parks can be highly effective.

Finally, challenging another common claim, the rate of creation of new protected areas has not slowed in recent years (WCPA 1999), demonstrating that opportunities still exist and may even be expanding to create and support more protected areas in key ecosystems around the world. A wealth of data from countries including Brazil (Ayres et al. 1997) and India (Kutti and Kothari 2001) indicate a burst of creation of additional parks and reserves in the last decade.

What about the track record of sustainable development? A look at the effects on biodiversity conservation of a range of sustainable development projects suggests that the reality has not lived up to original expectations. For instance, despite years of effort and hundreds of millions of dollars spent to support sustainable forest management (SFM), there is still very little natural forest in the tropics actually under SFM. As of 2001, the Forest Stewardship Council had certified only 2 million ha of natural forest in the tropics (FSC 2001). In broader terms, the International Tropical Timber Organization (ITTO) notes that "while policy successes have been many and awareness . . . of the need for sustainable forest management is growing, the review of progress (Poore and Chiew 2000) reports far less evidence of the implementation of good management in the forest itself" (ITTO 2002:3).

A number of fundamental limitations are likely to continue to keep SFM from being more widely adopted in the future. Most importantly, it is generally less profitable than conventional logging (Rice et al. 2001). Efforts to increase the profitability of SFM, such as certification, improvement of access, or increasing security of land tenure, are unlikely to change this dynamic, either because they are expensive or because they typically increase the profitability of conventional logging as well and therefore fail to make sustainable management a relatively attractive land use. Even in forests that are well managed for timber, biodiversity conservation is far from guaranteed and actually entails additional investments, making SFM even less economically profitable (Rice et al. 2001). In the institutional context described by a recent ITTO report (Poore and Chiew 2000), in which only one producer country in Latin America (Guyana) even has the capacity to manage its forests sustainably, profitability will play the deciding role for most producers.

The presence of sustainable forestry can also make conservation more difficult. Logging itself, even under SFM, can cause significant direct ecological damage. Also, if timber supply is sustainable, access must remain permanent. Preventing illegal activities, such as hunting and agricultural clearing, therefore becomes more difficult, not easier, under SFM, because of increased road and transport access (Auzel and Wilkie 2000). Loggers themselves often cause significant damage through hunting and other illegal activities (Dourojeanni 1999). Finally, logging of any kind can increase the susceptibility of forests to fire (Holdsworth and Uhl 1997, Nepstad et al. 1999).

Related limitations also exist for conserving areas via other types of sustainable development projects, such as sustainable harvest and marketing of nontimber forest products, development of nondestructive means of income generation (e.g., beekeeping), and organic or low-impact agriculture. Some of the most important of these limitations are inadequate market value, difficulty in marketing many forest products, and limited markets for green agricultural products. These factors make it difficult in many cases for sustainably harvested forest resources to generate sufficient income to compete with land conversion and also mean that the majority of agricultural production will not be able to take advantage of the demand for green products (Dourojeanni 1999, Hardner and Rice 2002).

Finally, even where projects succeed in creating profitable enterprises, conservation has been promoted largely as only a byproduct of development activities. Abundant literature suggests that the result of this strategy has been that most sustainable development projects have failed to shift people's behaviors toward helping to conserve biodiversity (Robinson 1993, Simpson 1995, Kramer et al. 1997, Southgate 1998). Indeed, reviews of integrated conservation and development programs have found that sustainable development as a standalone conservation strategy has been widely unsuccessful (CIFOR et al. 1999, Terborgh 1999, Wells et al. 1999).

These limitations suggest that substituting sustainable use schemes for protected areas is unlikely to result in effective species conservation and that support for protected areas should be the top priority for conservation funds. On the other hand, ensuring that production supports conservation goals in key areas and that conservation and development are mutually reinforcing remains a fundamental goal: Well-designed development-based conservation projects have an important role to play supporting protected areas in this context. Among other key needs, these projects can provide connectivity across fragmented landscapes, local benefits, and increased support for conservation.

In this context, it is important to consider a number of innovative conservation tools that seek to address some of the fundamental limitations of sustainable use projects to date while still providing a means for biodiversity conservation to become economically competitive. We present one here: conservation concessions. Under a conservation concession agreement, national authorities or local resource users agree to protect natural ecosystems in exchange for a steady stream of structured compensation from conservationists or other investors. In its simplest form, a conservation concession might be modeled after a timber concession, whereby a logging company pays the government for the right to extract timber from an area of public forestlands. Rather than log the concession area, the conservation investor would pay the government for the right to preserve the forest intact. The international community has long demonstrated a willingness to pay for conservation; currently at least half a billion dollars is spent annually on tropical biodiversity conservation. Conservation concessions seek to create a direct mechanism to channel this willingness to pay into conservation outcomes and to provide an alternative opportunity for countries to capitalize on vast tracts of forest or other areas of high conservation value (Hardner and Rice 2002).

Efforts to establish conservation concessions have met with success in a number of countries. In July 2002, CI obtained a timber sale agreement from the government of Guyana to establish a conservation concession that will protect approximately 80,000 ha of pristine forest. In April 2001, the Indonesian Minister of Forestry issued a public declaration in support of conservation concessions. In Peru, the government recently approved new regulations for its Forest and Wildlife Law that for the first time enable conservation bidders to compete for the land use rights of its 67.6-million-ha forest estate. In late July 2001, the country's first conservation concession under this law, an area of approximately 135,000 ha., was granted to the Asociación para la Conservación de la Cuenca Amazónica, a Peruvian nongovernmental organization.

Conservation concessions have the potential to address a number of the limitations of sustainable use. Among the most important of these is that rather than promoting conservation indirectly, conservation concessions seek to directly promote conservation by providing concession payments contingent on the concession area meeting clearly defined and measurable biodiversity conservation objectives. Furthermore, the incentive provided by conservation concessions does not depend on often unreliable profits from resource extraction; instead, conservation concessions seek to make payments from endowed funds to provide a stable, long-term source of financing.

Through these mechanisms, conservation concessions can bring a clear market value to the protection of important areas. In the long term, the goal is to create a functional market in which direct investment in biodiversity conservation becomes a competitive land use in key areas. A critical role for concession projects will be directly replacing destructive and often only marginally profitable land uses with a steady stream of economic benefits *from conservation*. At an even broader scale, direct protection may have the potential to become the basis of entire local economies in critical biodiversity areas by making use of conservation concessions and a number of other resource- and employment-generating activities, including enforcement activities, research, ecotourism, watershed values, carbon sequestration, and training and education opportunities.

THE LIMITS OF SITE-BASED ACTION: BRINGING CONSERVATION TO THE LANDSCAPE SCALE

If parks can work for species conservation and there are serious limitations to sustainable development as a substitute, then it appears that conservation must come primarily from setting resources aside from human use while enabling a supporting role for sustainable use projects. Still, many critical biodiversity areas are located in regions where economic development needs are a reality, and park creation may not be a viable option because of population, social, or political pressures. Even where parks exist, many are too small to maintain ecological processes and allow global change dynamics. In particular, changes driven by human-induced global warming may cause such serious shifts in habitat locations that protected areas that do not contain an altitudinal gradient may lose all suitable habitat for the species they are designed to protect (Peters and Lovejoy 1992, Hannah et al. 2002). Finally, with millions of people living in poverty, highly indebted governments, excessive and growing levels of consumption in developed countries, and world population expected to increase by another 3 billion in the next fifty years (United Nations 1998), development needs and pressures on protected areas are only expected to increase (figure 16.2). In this context , the aim of reconciling poverty alleviation with conservation objectives seems largely unattainable at the site scale, particularly when dealing with small and fragmented parks.

To face these challenges, we must find a way to implement conservation strategies that address development needs but still put effective conservation tools in place at a scale commensurate with ecological processes. A key issue in finding the solution to this challenge is scale.

Traditionally, conservationists have focused only on individual pieces of the landscape. We believe that past efforts to combine conservation

Figure 16.2 Hard edge around the Adolpho Ducke Forest Reserve, Manaus, Brazil. Photograph taken in 2000. (For color reproduction see Plate 5.)

and development objectives in this context have often failed because the planning and implementation scales were geographically so limited that they placed conservation and development goals in direct competition with each other, resulting in frequent conflict and mutual loss. In reality, biologically important landscapes often are highly varied, with a wide range of actors, ecosystem types, and economic activities. Embracing all land uses by broadening the focus of conservation planning to the landscape level greatly increases opportunities to coordinate and promote conservation and development goals together, addressing both ecological and economic dynamics.

We call conservation planning units at this scale landscape-level biodiversity corridors, a concept first articulated in the connection with a major project designed to stimulate the creation of additional protected areas in the Brazilian Amazon and the Atlantic Forest, financed by the Brazilian government and the World Bank's Pilot Project to Conserve the Brazilian Rain Forest (Ayres et al. 1997). Landscape corridors are distinct from biological corridors in that their purpose is not simply to permit demographic and genetic flow of animal and plant populations. A landscape corridor is a biologically and strategically defined subregional space selected as a unit for large-scale conservation planning and implementation purposes in which conservation action can be reconciled with inevitable economic development, in this case freed from the constraints of competing land use claims over very small areas. Within landscape corridors, planners can seek to place critical biodiversity areas under strict protection, important areas can be allocated to economic development, and others with mixed goals can be defined. A landscape corridor therefore comprises a network of parks, reserves, and other areas of less intensive use whose management is integrated in the landscape matrix to ensure the survival of the largest possible spectrum of species while avoiding direct conflict with economic development needs.

Using landscape-level corridors as planning units can accomplish what planning at the scale of individual parks and buffer zones cannot: the optimum allocation of resources to conserve biodiversity at the least economic cost to society. Furthermore, planning at this scale enables conservation planning to address long-term trends and changes in ecological and economic dynamics. Large landscape-level corridors can even go a step further in designing mosaics that are mutually beneficial to both conservation and development goals (e.g., protected areas to conserve watersheds and tourism resources and compatible development to promote species movement between protected areas or to provide important buffers).

Corridor planning in Brazil's Atlantic Forest is a useful example of how the corridor strategy can work in practice. The Atlantic Forest is among the top five hotspots in the world. With only 7.5 percent of its original forest cover remaining, it is home to 11,000 endemic plant species and is among the top areas in the world in numbers of arboreal plants, reaching 454 species in a single hectare (Thomas et al. 1998). The area is also densely populated by more than 60 percent of the entire Brazilian human population. Only 2.7 percent of original forest is in protected areas, far too little to conserve its vast diversity of species.

Because the Atlantic Forest is highly fragmented, populations of plants and animals are highly vulnerable and isolated. The few parks and reserves that existed up to the mid-1990s were being progressively encroached, and opportunities for expanding the reserve network were perceived as diminishing or nonexistent. In this context, a site-by-site conservation strategy was not viable for long-term species protection. For species to persist, it was necessary to maintain and restore connectivity across the landscape. In the heavily populated context of the Atlantic Forest, this required both core zones of protection and mosaics of multiple land uses in a managed landscape to allow populations to move between proximate, intact forest blocks (Ayres et al. 1997) while addressing existing socioeconomic needs. Thus to design a functional mosaic of

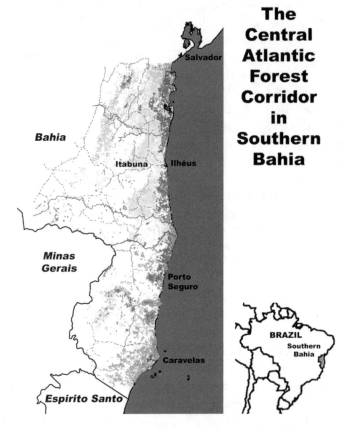

Figure 16.3 Southern Bahia portion of the central Atlantic Forest corridor. (For color reproduction and explanation see Plate 6.)

land uses (figure 16.3) corridor planning took account of a number of major socioeconomic and biological factors, including land ownership and major uses, the location of remaining forest, the location of key species, the location of current and proposed roads, and land values.

Priority actions under the corridor plan were first to consolidate existing protected areas and to create new ones, thereby forming critical corridor nuclei. These nuclei also needed to be supported by links across private properties that provided economic incentives for key private land owners to shift to compatible land uses. In the case of the Atlantic Forest, these uses included shade cocoa and the creation of private reserves. The final corridor design, spanning more than 50,000 km², includes conservation nuclei and linkages and areas for both high- and low-intensity economic activities, creating a plan that is increasingly being met with

Figure 16.4 Hypothetical land uses in a portion of a conservation corridor in the Brazilian Atlantic Forest. (For color reproduction and explanation see Plate 7.)

broad public approval (CABS 2000; figure 16.4). A multistakeholder management committee to oversee the implementation of corridor-scale activities is now operational, orienting the investment of financial resources from the World Bank and the Brazilian government.

Several important lessons can be drawn from work in the Atlantic Forest and other corridor projects to date. First, the value of biodiversity (both market and nonmarket) often is not recognized in local economies; planning at a regional scale can provide a format for ensuring that these values are considered. Second, there are always trade-offs in conservation planning. Given limited funding and competing interests, conservation of some areas must take priority over others. Finally, corridors, like all other conservation strategies, are no "silver bullet"; they simply increase the scope for cooperation and grant some breathing room to promote both conservation and development objectives without attempting to put them both in the same place. Experience suggests that there will be winners and losers in almost every possible outcome, even those that are optimal for society as a whole. What corridors offer is an opportunity to more effectively design combinations of site conservation tools and integrate them with development plans.

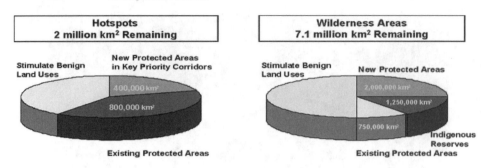

Figure 16.5 A plan of action for the hotspots and major tropical wilderness areas.

DEFYING NATURE'S END: A PRACTICAL PLAN OF ACTION

As part of a major effort to transform these ideas into a concrete plan of action, in August 2000 more than 50 scientists and seventeen private sector representatives met in California at a conference titled "Defying Nature's End: A Practical Agenda for Saving Life on the Planet." The objective was to pull together current scientific thinking to develop a plan for the fundamental components of a conservation strategy to save the most threatened portion of global biodiversity (Pimm 2001, http://www.defyingnaturesend.org). The conference concluded that acting rapidly and strategically in key places in the tropics, particularly targeting habitat protection in the global biodiversity hotspots and the major tropical wilderness areas, could have a major impact in stemming many looming extinction events (Pimm and Raven 2000, Brooks et al. 2002).

For the hotspots, the agenda calls for a focus on 60 percent of the remaining intact habitat by improving management of 800,000 km^2 of existing protected areas and by bringing an additional 400,000 km^2 of land under protection. For the wilderness areas the agenda is to focus on 55 percent of the remaining intact habitat to more than double the area under park protection in addition to improving management of existing protected areas and indigenous reserves (figure 16.5). In contrast to the hotspots, a significant portion of remaining natural habitat in wilderness areas is under indigenous control. For instance, more than 24 percent of the Brazilian Amazon has been demarcated for indigenous tribes (Ricardo 2001). Some tribes, such as the Kayapo of southern Pará, are doing a remarkable job of resisting encroachment from agriculture and cattle ranching, but over time these efforts alone may not suffice. If resources can be secured so that these lands are better managed in perpetuity and incorporate biodiversity objectives that can be pursued by indigenous

Figure 16.6 Landsat 7 image mosaic showing anthropogenic pressure around the Kayapo Indigenous Area in the southeastern Brazilian Amazon. (For color reproduction and explanation see Plate 8.)

peoples themselves, the wilderness areas agenda will be greatly strengthened. Finally, in both hotspots and wilderness areas, direct protection must be complemented by additional investments to bring more compatible land use schemes to critical parts of the remainder of the landscape matrix (figure 16.6).

Participants at "Defying Nature's End" also estimated the cost of implementing the direct protection components of this strategy. These included placing additional land under protection via land acquisition or compensation, managing new protected areas in the long term, and improving management in existing protected areas. Data used for these estimates included published figures (e.g., James et al. 1999b) and unpublished data on the cost of acquisition, compensation, and management in specific sites. For the hotspots, needs were estimated at $24 billion above current expenditure ($6 billion of private investment leveraging an additional $18 billion). For the wilderness areas, needs were estimated at $4 billion above current expenditure ($1 billion leveraging $3 billion). Taken together, an estimated one-time investment of $28 billion could take the world a long way toward conserving biodiversity (Pimm 2001, supplementary material).

CONCLUSION

Over the last few years conservation biologists, conservation economists, landscape planners, and conservation practitioners have been arriving at the consensus that several of the earth's most altered ecosystems are headed for catastrophes, the most noticeable consequence being species loss. Nonetheless, the analyses conducted at the "Defying Nature's End" conference were optimistic: Participants concluded that avoiding major extinctions in key areas is possible if we act urgently and at a scale commensurate with threats and ecological needs. Furthermore, the necessary actions are affordable: If funds are well spent, protecting a significant portion of the earth's biodiversity is within reach (James et al. 1999a).

The strategy emerging from "Defying Nature's End" for meeting this challenge was straightforward. Based on the conclusion that protected areas are the most effective tool we have to protect biodiversity at the site level, parks and reserves were proposed as the centerpiece of a conservation strategy. This will mean that the priority use of conservation funds should be to bring more area under protection and improve management of existing protected areas. Because working at the protected area scale is necessary but insufficient, conservation planning must also be increased in scale. Corridor-level planning offers a context in which conservation and development goals can both be promoted and become mutually reinforcing. In this context, there is an important supporting role for low-impact agricultural production, sustainable development projects, and new tools such as conservation concessions. Participants concluded that if we scale up conservation activities along these lines, focused on the most critical areas, we still have a real opportunity to save much of the earth's biodiversity.

REFERENCES

Alroy, J. 2001. A multispecies overkill simulation of the end-Pleistocene megafaunal mass extinction. *Science* 292: 1893–1896.

Auzel, P. and D. S. Wilkie. 2000. Wildlife use in northern Congo: Hunting in a commercial logging concession. In J. G. Robinson and E. L. Bennett, eds., *Hunting for sustainability in tropical forests*, 413–426. New York: Columbia University Press.

Ayres, J. M., G. A. B. da Fonseca, A. B. Rylands, H. L. Queiroz, L. P. Pinto, D. Masterson, and R. Cavalcanti. 1997. *Abordagens inovadoras para conservação da biodiversidade do Brasil: Os corredores ecológicos das florestas neotropicais do Brasil*. Brasília, Brazil: Programa Piloto para a Proteção das Florestas Neotropicais, Projecto Parques e Reservas. Ministério do Meio Ambiente, Recursos Hídricos e da Amazônia Legal (MMA), Instituo Brasilerio do Meio Ambiente e dos Recursos Naturais Renováveis (Ibama).

Brooks, T., A. Balmford, N. Burgess, J. Fjeldsa, L. A. Hansen, J. Moore, C. Rahbek, and P. Williams. 2001. Toward a blueprint for conservation in Africa. *BioScience* 51: 613–624.

Brooks, T. M., R. A. Mittermeier, C. G. Mittermeier, G. A. B. da Fonseca, A. B. Rylands, W. R. Konstant, P. Flick, J. Pilgrim, S. Oldfield, G. Magin, and C. Hilton-Taylor. 2002. Habitat loss and extinctions in the hotspots of biodiversity. *Conservation Biology* 16: 909–923.

Brown, M. and B. Wyckoff-Baird. 1992. *Designing integrated conservation and development projects*. Washington, D.C.: Biodiversity Support Program.

Bruner, A. G., R. E. Gullison, R. E. Rice, and G. A. B. da Fonseca. 2001. Effectiveness of parks in protecting tropical biodiversity. *Science* 291: 125–128.

CABS (Center for Applied Biodiversity Science). 2000. *Designing sustainable landscapes: The Brazilian Atlantic Forest*. Washington, D.C.: Conservation International.

CCT and CIEDES (Centro Cientifico Tropical and Centro de Investigaciones en Desarollo Sostenible). 1998. *Estudio de cobertural forestal actual (1996/97) y de cambio de cobertura para el período entre 1986/87 y 1996/97 para Costa Rica*. Paper presented to Fondo Nacional de Financiamiento Forestal (FONAFIFO).

Chomitz, K. M. and D. A. Gray. 1996. Roads, land use, and deforestation: A spatial model applied to Belize. *World Bank Economic Review* 10: 487–512.

CIFOR, UNESCO, and UNESCO World Heritage Centre. 1999. *World heritage forests: The world heritage convention as a mechanism for conserving tropical forest biodiversity*. CIFOR Ad Hoc Publication. Bogor, Indonesia: CIFOR, UNESCO, and UNESCO WHC.

Dayton, L. 2001. Mass extinctions pinned on Ice Age hunters. *Science* 292: 1819.

Deininger, K. and B. Minten. 1997. *Determinants of forest cover and the economics of protection: An application to Mexico*. Washington, D.C.: World Bank.

Dourojeanni, M. J. 1999. *The future of the Latin American natural forests*. Environmental Division Working Paper. Washington, D.C.: InterAmerican Development Bank.

EIA (Environmental Investigation Agency) and Telepak Indonesia. 1999. *The final cut: Illegal logging in Indonesia's orangutan parks*. London: Emmerson Press. Online: http://www.eia-international.org/Campaigns/Forests/Indonesia/FinalCut/.4/29/2002.

Flannery, T. 2001. *The eternal frontier: An ecological history of North America and its peoples*. New York: Atlantic Monthly Press.

Fonseca, G. A. B., A. Balmford, C. Bibby, L. Boitani, F. Corsi, T. Brooks, C. Gascon, S. Olivieri, R. Mittermeier, N. Burges, E. Dinerstein, D. Olson, L. Hannah, J. Lovett, D. Moyer, C. Rahbek, S. Stuart, and P. Williams. 2000. Following Africa's lead in setting priorities. *Nature* 405: 393–394.

FSC (Forest Stewardship Council). 2001. *Forests certified by FSC-accredited certification bodies*. Forest Stewardship Council Document no. 5.3.3. Online: http://fscoax.org.

Ghmire, K. B. and M. P. Pimbert, eds. 1997. *Social change and conservation: Environmental politics and impacts of national parks and protected areas.* London: Earthscan.

Hannah, L., G. F. Midgley, T. Lovejoy, W. J. Bond, M. Bush, J. C. Lovett, D. Scott, and F. I. Woodward. 2002. Conservation of biodiversity in a changing climate. *Conservation Biology* 16: 264–268.

Hardner, J. and R. Rice. 2002. Rethinking green consumerism. *Scientific American* 286: 89–95.

Holdsworth, A. and C. Uhl. 1997. Fire in Amazonian selectively logged rain forest and the potential for fire reduction. *Ecological Applications* 7: 713–725.

ITTO (International Tropical Timber Organization). 2002. *Assessing progress towards sustainable forest management in the tropics.* Online: http://www.itto.or.jp/inside/measuring_up/download/e.pdf.8/12/2002.

IUCN, UNEP, and WWF. 1991. *Caring for the earth: A strategy for sustainable living.* Gland, Switzerland: IUCN, UNEP, and WWF.

James, A. N., K. J. Gaston, and A Balmford. 1999a. Balancing the earth's accounts. *Nature* 401: 323–324.

James, A. N., M. J. B. Green, and J. R. Paine. 1999b. *Global review of protected area budgets and staff.* Cambridge, U.K.: WCMC.

Kramer, R., C. van Schaik, and J. Johnson, eds. 1997. *Last stand: Protected areas and the defense of tropical biodiversity.* Oxford, U.K.: Oxford University Press.

Kutti, R. and A. Kothari. 2001. *Protected areas in India: A profile.* Pune, India: Kalpavriksh.

Mittermeier, R. A., C. G. Mittermeier, T. M. Brooks, J. D. Pilgrim, W. R. Konstant, G. A. B. da Fonseca, and C. Kornos. 1995. Wilderness and biodiversity conservation. *Proceedings of the National Academy of Sciences* 100(18): 10309–10313.

Mittermeier, R. A., C. G. Mittermeier, P. R. Gil, J. Pilgrim, W. R. Konstant, T. Brooks, and G. da Fonseca. 2003. *Wilderness: Earth's last wild places.* Washington, D.C.: Conservation International.

Mittermeier, R. A., N. Myers, P. Robles Gil, and C. G. Mittermeier. 1999. *Hotspots.* Mexico City: Cemex.

Mittermeier, R. A., N. Myers, J. B. Thomsen, G. A. B. da Fonseca, and S. Olivieri. 1998. Biodiversity hotspots and major tropical wilderness areas: Approaches to setting conservation priorities. *Conservation Biology* 12: 516–520.

Myers, N. 1988. Threatened biotas: "Hotspots" in tropical forests. *Environmentalist* 8: 187–208.

Myers, N. 1990. The biodiversity challenge: Expanded hot-spots analysis. *Environmentalist* 10: 243–256.

Myers N., R. A. Mittermeier, C. G. Mittermeier, G. A. B. da Fonseca, and J. Kent. 2000. Biodiversity hotspots for conservation priorities. *Nature* 403: 853–858.

Nepstad, D. C., A. Verssimo, A. Alencar, C. Nobre, E. Lima, P. Lefebvre, P. Schlesinger, C. Potter, P. Moutinho, E. Mendoza, M. Cochrane, and V. Brooks. 1999. Large-scale impoverishment of Amazonian forests by logging and fire. *Nature* 398: 505–508.

Oates, J. F. 1999. *Myth and reality in the rainforest: How conservation strategies are failing in West Africa.* Berkeley: University of California Press.

Peters, R. L. and T. L. Lovejoy, eds. 1992. *Global warming and biological diversity.* New Haven, Conn.: Yale University Press.

Pimm, S. L. 2001. Can we defy nature's end? *Science* 293: 2207–2208.

Pimm, S. L. and P. Raven. 2000. Extinction by numbers. *Nature* 403: 843–845.

Poore, D. and T. H. Chiew. 2000. *Review of progress towards the year 2000 objective.* Lima, Peru: ITTO. Online: http://www.itto.or.jp/inside/report.html#review. 8/12/2002.

Redford, K. H. 1992. The empty forest. *BioScience* 42: 412–422.

Rice, R. E., C. Sugal, S. M. Ratay, and G. A. B. da Fonseca. 2001. *Sustainable forest management: A review of conventional wisdom.* Advances in Biodiversity Science no. 3. Washington, D.C.: Conservation International.

Ricardo, F. 2001. Sobreposições entre unidades de conservação (UCs) federais, estaduias, terras indígenas, terras militares e reservas garimpeiras na Amazônia legal. In A. Veríssimo, A. Moreira, D. Sawyer, I. dos Santos, L. P. Pinto, and J. P. R. Capobianco, eds., *Biodiversidade na Amazônia Brasileira: Avaliação e ações prioritárias para a conservação, uso sustentável e repartição de benefícios,* 1–5. Estação Liberdade, São Paulo: Instituto Socioambiental.

Robinson, J. G. 1993. The limits to caring: Sustainable living and the loss of biodiversity. *Conservation Biology* 7: 20–28.

Sanchez-Azofeifa, G. A., C. Quesada-Mateo, P. Gonzalez-Quesada, S. Dayanandan, and K. S. Bawa. 1999. Protected areas and conservation of biodiversity in the tropics. *Conservation Biology* 13: 407–411.

Schwartzman, S., D. Nepstad, and A. Moreira. 2000. Rethinking tropical forest conservation: Perils in parks. *Conservation Biology* 14: 1351–1357.

Simpson, R. D. 1995. *Why integrated conservation and development projects may achieve neither goal.* Discussion Paper no. 95-20. Washington, D.C.: Resources for the Future.

Soulé, M. E. and M. A. Sanjayan. 1998. Conservation targets: Do they help? *Science* 279: 2060–2061.

Southgate, D. 1998. *Tropical forest conservation: An economic assessment of alternatives in Latin America.* Oxford, U.K.: Oxford University Press.

Terborgh, J. 1999. *Requiem for nature.* Washington, D.C.: Island Press.

Thomas, W. W., A. M. V. Carvalho, A. M. A. Amorim, J. Garrison, and A. L. Arbelaez. 1998. Plant endemism in two forests in southern Bahia, Brazil. *Biodiversity and Conservation* 7: 311–322.

United Nations. 1998. *World population projections to 2150.* New York: United Nations.

van Schaik, C. P., J. Terborgh, and B. Dugelby. 1997. The silent crisis: The state of rainforest nature preserves. In R. Kramer, C. van Schaik, and J. Johnson, eds., *Last stand: Protected areas and the defense of tropical biodiversity,* 64–89. Oxford, U.K.: Oxford University Press.

WCPA (World Commission on Protected Areas), World Conservation Union. 1999. *Parks for biodiversity: Policy guidance based on experience in ACP countries.* Brussels: IUCN.

Wells, M., S. Guggenheim, A. Khan, W. Wardojo, and P. Jepson. 1999. *Investing in biodiversity: A review of Indonesia's integrated conservation and development projects.* Washington, D.C.: World Bank.

Wilshusen, P., S. R. Brechin, C. Fortwangler, and P. C. West. 2002. Reinventing a square wheel: A critique of a resurgent "protection paradigm" in international biodiversity conservation. *Society & Natural Resources: An International Journal* 15: 17–40.

Chapter 17

SELECTIVE LOGGING, FOREST FRAGMENTATION, AND FIRE DISTURBANCE

IMPLICATIONS OF INTERACTION AND SYNERGY

Mark A. Cochrane, David L. Skole, Eraldo A. T. Matricardi, Christopher Barber, and Walter Chomentowski

Deforestation in the tropics has been a major concern for several decades. Human conversion of ecosystems to agricultural use has generally entailed the felling and burning of ever-increasing tracts of forest. However, the tropics have been increasingly drawn into the global market as their regional economies have developed. Consequently, as external markets for wood and nontimber forest products expand, the wood products that can be derived from standing forests are becoming more valuable. Working forests and agroforestry are beginning to compete with other agricultural systems as economically viable human uses of the available land. This valuation of standing forests may prove to be a boon for the conservation of these rich ecosystems. To the extent that they become stable, economically productive components of the landscape, working forests will be preserved and nurtured instead of simply being used as brief transitional states on the path to deforestation.

To provide long-term conservation value and economic production, working forests must be managed sustainably. Typically, the issue of sustainability is framed in the context of the impacts caused by logging operations and the viability of continued timber production (see chapter 8). However, to achieve sustainable forestry in the tropics it will be necessary to look beyond simple cutting cycles and silvicultural treatments to the larger context of the landscape matrix in which these forest remnants exist and the disturbances to which they are exposed. Although such disturbances are manifold, including everything from global and regional climate change to the effects of hunting and habitat change on pollinators and seed dispersers, this chapter focuses on the conservation challenges posed by the interactions and possible synergy between forest fragmentation, selective logging, and forest fire.

THE CASE OF THE BRAZILIAN AMAZON

The Brazilian Amazon contains more than a third of the world's tropical forests. These forests play a vital role in water and carbon cycles and regional and global climate. Amazonian forests may support the richest collection of biodiversity in the world (Schneider et al. 2000). Tropical timber production is expected to increase in response to the growing domestic and international demand for Amazonian wood. With its vast timber stocks and expanding infrastructure (Laurance et al. 2001), the Amazon is well positioned to dominate the tropical timber trade in the twenty-first century (Uhl et al. 1997). Long-term conservation of biodiversity and natural resources will entail the establishment of sustainably managed production forests as a vital complement to fully protected parks (Frumhoff 1995, Gascon et al. 2000, Schneider et al. 2000).

The Brazilian government is committed to developing a new forest policy based on well-managed production within an expanded system of national forests (Veríssimo and Cochrane 2003). At present, national forests in Brazil make up less than 2 percent of the Amazon Basin (80,000 km^2). Even if all these forests were used for sustainable production, they could provide no more than 11 percent of the demand for Amazonian timber. To satisfy the expected demand for timber, approximately 700,000 km^2 (14 percent) of Brazil's Amazonian forests must be brought into well-managed production (Veríssimo et al. 2002). The Ministry of Environment is establishing 50 million ha of new national forests in the Brazilian Amazon (see chapter 7). The government has also announced plans to protect biodiversity by making 10 percent of the Amazon into fully protected parks and biological reserves (Veríssimo et al. 2002).

Although the initiative of the Brazilian government is laudable, at present, typical, unmanaged frontier logging operations catalyze deforestation by opening roads into unoccupied government lands and protected areas that are subsequently colonized by ranchers and farmers (Veríssimo et al. 1995). Thus the exhaustion of timber stocks in older frontier areas is resulting in a chaotic migration of loggers to new areas such as western Pará and southern Amazonas.

LANDSCAPE FRAGMENTATION AND LAND COVER CHANGE

Working forests, if established and sustainably managed, will still exist within the larger framework of a human-dominated landscape with a mosaic of different land covers and land uses. Deforestation, whether for agriculture or infrastructure development (e.g., roads), results in forest fragmentation. New forest edges are formed, and remnant forests become increasingly disturbed. Skole and Tucker (1993) estimated that by 1988 fragmentation and its associated edge effects (e.g., wind exposure, excessive drying, invasive species) had affected an area of forest 150 percent the size of what had been deforested.

Forest fragmentation exposes the remaining forests to increasing levels of disturbance along edges. Within the forest, this can result in biomass collapse and increased mortality out to at least 100 m (Laurance et al. 1997, 2000). Light penetration through the fractured canopy and increased levels of woody debris (Nascimento and Laurance 2002), can make these forests more susceptible to fire. With respect to fire risk, every meter of exposed forest is a potential avenue for fire entrance into the forest. Therefore, as a region develops and the forest becomes more fragmented, the risk of forest fire increases because there is more fire-susceptible edge that is being exposed to more fire more frequently.

Two locations in the eastern Amazon illustrate the importance of fragmentation and edge formation for a region's forests. Paragominas is an older frontier that was first settled in the mid- to late 1960s and is dominated by large ranching and logging interests. Tailândia is a newer frontier area that was created as a settlement project by the Brazilian government (Instituto Nacional de Colonização e Reforma Agrária) for small landholdings. The pattern of fragmentation differs in both locations, but the end result is the same. In both regions more than 50 percent of the remaining forests exists within 300 m of a forest edge. Fire regularly penetrates the forests of both sites for more than a kilometer, and almost all remaining forests in these areas are affected (Cochrane 2001).

Land cover change is also exacerbating the fire problem within the tropics, mainly through the increasing prevalence of flammable ecosystems (e.g., pastures) and the connectivity between them. In the past, agricultural plots and pastures existed as islands of easily flammable vegetation in a sea of largely fire-immune forest. However, as a region develops, its forest remnants become increasingly fragmented and surrounded by large areas of easily flammable grasses. The connectivity of these flammable ecosystems results in a greater chance of each fire escaping into adjacent lands, directly increasing the economic damages caused by fire while increasing the total area of forest exposed to fire.

SELECTIVE LOGGING

The effects of unmanaged selective logging include increased fire susceptibility (Holdsworth and Uhl 1997), damage to nearby trees and soils (Veríssimo et al. 1992, Johns et al. 1996), increased risk of local species extirpation (Martini et al. 1994), and carbon emissions (Houghton 1995). Many forests are revisited several times as loggers return to harvest additional tree species that become lucrative when regional timber markets develop (Uhl et al. 1997, Schneider et al. 2000). These forests become very degraded, and 40–50 percent of the canopy cover may be removed during logging operations (Uhl and Vieira 1989, Veríssimo et al. 1992). Therefore, instead of fires being contained by the very moist and dense foliage of an intact forest, easily flammable logged forests, with their heavy fuel loads and porous canopies, further link the region's agricultural lands and expose more forests to potential fire events. Whereas an intact forest may still resist fire encroachment, even after more than a month without rain, selectively logged forests may become flammable in as few as six days without rain (Uhl and Kauffman 1990). Once logged or burned, a forest is extremely prone to recurrent fires (Cochrane and Schulze 1999).

As early as 1985 there were warnings that forest fires were resulting from a disturbing synergism between cattle ranching and selective logging (Uhl and Buschbacher 1985). The accuracy of those warnings has been shown in subsequent studies (Uhl and Kauffman 1990, Holdsworth and Uhl 1997, Cochrane and Schulze 1999, Cochrane et al. 1999). Selective logging increases the fire susceptibility of forests for several years or even decades, with logged forests also burning more severely because of their heavy fuel loads (Siegert et al. 2001). To the extent that reduced-impact logging (RIL) techniques are used in working forests, these negative effects should be mitigated. However, there has been no quantification of the benefits of RIL in reducing fire susceptibility or severity in the tropics.

Burning has been observed in large areas of previously logged forests in Southeast Asia and Central and South America (UNEP 2002). For Brazil, the importance of the link between fire and logging is evident in the juxtaposition of fire-prone logged forests and fire-maintained lands. Most of the Amazon's logging centers (Nepstad et al. 1999b) and the more than 3 million ha of existing logged forests (Matricardi et al. 2001) are within the fire-dominated "Arc of Deforestation" (Cochrane et al. 1999). If a system of working forests is to be established within the purview of existing infrastructure (sawmills, roads, energy, human resources) then it must take fire into account.

THE FIRE DYNAMIC

Beyond issues of scale, it is worrisome that forest fires can initiate a positive feedback of increasing fire susceptibility (Cochrane and Schulze 1999), increasing fuel loads and increasing fire severity (Cochrane and Schulze 1998, Cochrane et al. 1999). The resultant change in the fire regime can lead to the complete destruction of the standing forest and extensive invasion of pyrophytic vegetation (Cochrane and Schulze 1999).

The growing importance of uncontrolled forest fire is obvious. In both Mato Grosso and southern Pará, the area of standing forest affected by accidental forest fires in 1995 exceeded the area that was deforested that year (Nepstad et al. 1999a). The fire dynamic in tropical forests is largely a function of location. Historically, fire was an exceedingly rare event in most tropical forests (Cochrane 2000). Now however, forests that are adjacent to fire-maintained pastures and agricultural lands are at high risk from fire (Cochrane 2001). Under the proper climatic conditions, even large tracts of undisturbed forests can burn. Such was the case in Roraima, Brazil, in 1997 and 1998, when fires burned an area of 3.8–4.1 million ha, of which 1.1–1.4 million ha was intact primary forest (Barbosa and Fearnside 1999). Although the El Niño–initiated drought made these forests highly flammable, the fires were ignited by the region's rapidly growing population of rural residents.

The new fire dynamic for many tropical forests is one of frequent fire incursions and increasing fire severity. The first fire in a closed-canopy forest is unimpressive. Except for treefall gaps and other areas of unusual fuel structure, the fire spreads as a thin, slowly creeping ribbon of flames a few decimeters high (Cochrane and Schulze 1998). Over much of the burned area, the fire will consume little besides leaf litter. The fireline may move only 100–150 m a day but can keep burning this way for days, weeks, or months (Schindele et al. 1989, UNDAC 1998, Cochrane et al. 1999). If the weather is cool or a light rain falls, fires may not burn at all. However, large fuels, such as fallen logs, can smolder and reignite fires for weeks. Many areas will reburn one or more times as falling leaves continue to cover the ground (Schindele et al. 1989, Cochrane et al. 1999). The density of large fuels (fallen boles, crowns, and large branches) is an important determinant of reignition probability. Logged forest stands are more likely to sustain fires over extended time periods and to reburn within a single season than undisturbed forests that have lower densities of coarse fuels (Cochrane and Schulze 1999).

The slow advance of tropical fires makes them deadly. The size of the flames is not the most important factor; it is the amount of time that they are in contact with the base of the tree that determines the damage that they cause. In the Amazon, most trees have very thin bark and therefore are highly susceptible to fire damage (Uhl and Kauffman 1990). Bark thickness increases with tree diameter, which explains why smaller trees experience greater mortality from these fires (Woods 1989, Uhl and Kauffman 1990); however, there is evidence that convoluted buttress roots, bark texture, and color may also affect tree survival (Kauffman and Uhl 1990).

If the forest reburns within a few years of the initial fire, the fires will be more severe. In recurrent fires, flame lengths, flame depths, spread rates, residence times, and fireline intensities are all significantly higher. In forests that reburn, large trees have little survival advantage over smaller trees because the changes in fire behavior overwhelm the defenses of even the largest, thickest-barked trees. In other words, whereas the first fire kills mostly small trees, the second fire is just as likely to kill a large tree as a small one (Cochrane et al. 1999).

Fires in selectively logged forests act similarly to those in intact forests except that the first fire may be very intense because of the large amount of slash fuels left over from logging operations (Uhl and Kauffman 1990). In logged forests that burn, there may be no survival advantage for larger-diameter, thicker-bark trees in an initial fire (Kauffman 1991), as has been reported in other tropical forests (Woods 1989, Cochrane and Schulze 1999). Therefore, even a single fire in a logged forest highly degrades the site and makes it much more vulnerable to recurrent fires.

SYNERGY OF DISTURBANCE

Landscape fragmentation and land cover change interact synergistically to expose more of the forest to fire and consequently raise the risk of unintended fires occurring across the entire landscape (Cochrane 2001, Cochrane and Laurance 2002). Consider the range of anthropogenic disturbances in a tropical forest, which includes agricultural deforestation, logging, fire, and fragmentation-induced edge effects. Selective logging degrades forests, resulting in local drying of these sites. Fire probability in logged sites is increased by the actions of farmers who enter logged forests to clear new lands for agriculture (Veríssimo et al. 1995). In addition, the use of fire to maintain existing cleared lands increases the probability of devastating fires escaping into nearby logged forests (Cochrane et al. 1999, Nepstad et al. 1999b). The risk of a fire externality in the landscape-level farming system tends to push farmers to adopt fire-resistant pastures, a land use strategy that minimizes fire losses, which are large in long-term investments such as agroforestry, thus greatly influencing the future trajectory of land use change in a region.

Land use and land cover change (in the tropics and elsewhere) arises by virtue of complex interactions, leads to unexpected feedbacks, and broadcasts ecological impact beyond the boundaries of direct human use of the land. Therefore, the future integrity and sustainability of working forests remain in doubt, even if they are protected from outright deforestation. Without an integrated view of disturbance, in which forest management incorporates the interactions and possible synergies of different land uses, conservation of tropical forests will be difficult or impossible in some regions. To the extent that working forests are interwoven with fire-maintained and fire-prone land covers, they will be threatened by accidental fire. Therefore, the utility and conservation value of working forests may depend more on managing the surrounding land uses than the actual logging operations.

QUANTIFYING THE EFFECTS OF SELECTIVE LOGGING, FOREST FRAGMENTATION, AND FIRE IN MATO GROSSO

Traditional land cover mapping results in the designation of general types of land cover (e.g., forest, pasture) and implies that they are discrete and homogeneous. This masks the fact that gradients exist for important biophysical attributes and that boundaries between classes are not abrupt, either between different natural covers or between natural and disturbed covers. In terms of working forests, alteration within forests through extraction (e.g., selective logging) or degradation (e.g., fire, fragmentation effects) can be critically important for determining the future potential for human use of the affected forest's natural capital.

The potential of changed land cover to alter the impression of an area is illustrated by the region of Sinope in Mato Grosso, Brazil (Landsat ETM+ path/row 226/68). Sinope is the largest logging center in the Amazon. Sawmills in the region have processed timber from hundreds of thousands of hectares of forest in the last decade. The landscape is a combination of large ranches, agricultural lands, and forests. As such it is an ideal place to investigate the interaction between the various land uses and explore the potential for working forests to be established in this important logging region.

The following results stem from investigation of a subsample of the Sinope region (16,819 km^2). In the study area, 4547 km^2 was deforested by 1999. Therefore, under traditional measures of land cover, the region would be considered to have been 27 percent deforested. In other words, the forest cover would be considered to be reasonably intact.

With 73 percent forest cover, the hypothetical establishment of a system of working forests to support the region's logging seems possible. In fact, issues of private ownership, infrastructure, and access would significantly complicate matters. For this argument, however, only issues of forest condition are considered. Based on the analysis of satellite imagery, using established methods for detecting selective logging (Matricardi et al. 2001), forest burning (Cochrane and Souza 1998), and fragmentation (Cochrane and Laurance 2002), it is possible to quantify these overlooked forest disturbances and investigate their spatial relationship across the landscape (Cochrane 2001).

Of the remaining forests (12,272 km^2), at least 2599 km^2 was logged between 1992 and 1999, with nearly 500 km^2 being logged multiple times. Furthermore, 958 km^2 of the remaining forests was subjected to forest fires in the first eight months of 1999 alone. Edge effects can be variously estimated as 1149 km^2 affected by biomass collapse (Laurance et al. 1997) or 2882 km^2 suffering elevated mortality of large trees (Laurance et al. 2000). Amazonian forests with similar climates and land use have been shown to have altered fire regimes extending more than 2 km from forest edges (Cochrane 2001, Cochrane and Laurance 2002). The existing configuration of forest remnants near Sinope implies that, even using a conservative estimate of 1 km for edge-related fires, 6359 km^2 of the remaining forests is likely to have altered fire regimes.

Combining all of the disturbance factors and controlling for superposition to avoid double counting indicates that 68 percent of the remaining forests have altered disturbance regimes. Although these forests may not show up in deforestation estimates, they are not primary forests and are degraded from the standpoint of conservation or sustainable use. Looking at the landscape in conjunction with deforestation indicates that 77 percent of the landscape has altered land cover, not just the 27 percent apparent from traditionally applied land cover measures. This is a conservative estimate especially as regards selective logging because the analysis was based on only three available satellite images (741 km^2 in 1992, 665 km^2 in 1996, and 1679 km^2 in 1999). Obviously, the region's forests have already been profoundly affected by human disturbance.

As can be seen in figure 17.1, fire disturbance is predominantly an edge effect, but one that extends for kilometers into the forest. Burned forests predominate near deforested edges where fire use is common, but forest fires away from forest edges are evident. The relationship to distance from forest edges is nonlinear but striking. Within the first 1500 m from deforested edges, corresponding to 97 percent of all forest burning, the relationship is highly significant ($p < .001$) and explains 92 percent of the observations (logarithmic regression). Similar results were found

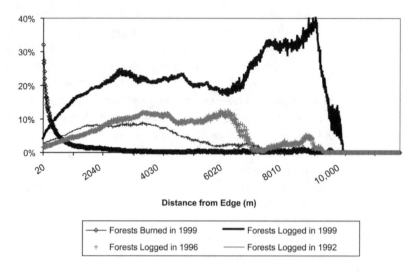

Figure 17.1 Percentage of existing forest subjected to either fire (1999) or logging (1992, 1996, 1999) as a function of distance from deforested edges in Mato Grosso, Brazil (path/row 226/68).

in eastern Pará for fires over a decade (Cochrane 2001, Cochrane and Laurance 2002).

In comparison, selective logging penetrates to the deepest reaches of the forest (figure 17.1). It is important to recognize that the majority of forests are within 1 km (51 percent) of edges, with less than 5 percent of the remaining forests more than 5 km from an edge. Logging activity penetrated deeper into the remaining forests in each successive time period and affected a greater percentage of the forest. Logging in 1992, 1996, and 1999 and fire in 1999 have disturbed an average of 30 percent of all forests out to 9 km from forest edges, or effectively 30 percent of all remaining forests (figure 17.2).

The specific interaction between selective logging and fire is an important factor to consider. Selective logging has been indicated as a causative factor in allowing fire to enter tropical forests (Uhl and Buschbacher 1985). Logging increases fire susceptibility and fuel loads in these forests (Uhl and Kauffman 1990, Holdsworth and Uhl 1997) and also increases the damage severity when fires do occur (Schindele et al. 1989). The chance of logged forests burning can remain higher than that of undamaged forests for decades (Siegert et al. 2001). However, when we look at the spatial interplay between fire and logging in Mato Grosso (figure 17.3), some interesting matters come to light. First, logging does not

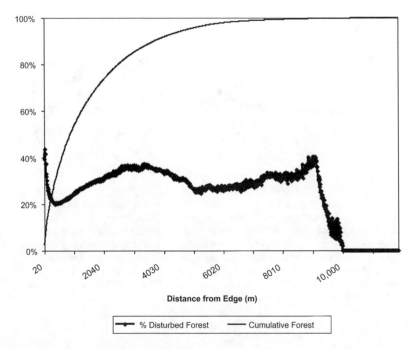

Figure 17.2 Percentage of forest disturbed by combined effects of fire (1999) and logging (1992–1999) as a function of distance from deforested edges near Sinope in Mato Grosso, Brazil. The cumulative percentage of existing forest is also shown, illustrating that the majority of forests are within a few kilometers of an edge.

seem to be a strong causative factor in allowing fires to enter the forest edges. Near edges, it appears that the forests are equally likely to burn regardless of the occurrence of logging. This is probably because edge effects, such as biomass collapse (Laurance et al. 1997) and microclimate changes (e.g., wind and light penetration), along forest borders make them as susceptible to fire as selective logging does, not because selective logging has no effect on fire susceptibility. In fact, the net effect of selective logging in all years and locations was to increase the likelihood of a forest burning in 1999 by 49.3 percent.

Spatially, the effect of selective logging on fire occurrence was more pronounced with distance from the edge, such that forests 1.6–2.4 km from an edge were more than three times more likely to have burned in 1999 if they had been logged in 1992 (figure 17.3). Apparently, the main effect of logging, in terms of fire occurrence, is to facilitate deeper penetration of the fires into the remaining forests. The average distance of fire

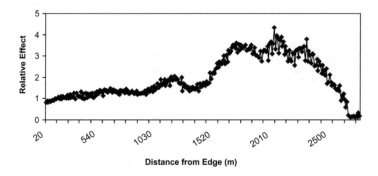

Figure 17.3 Example of forest burning in logged forests near Sinope, Mato Grosso, Brazil. The graph shows the effect of logged forests on the probability of fire occurrence in forests that were subjected to selective logging in 1992. By comparing fire occurrence in all forests at a given distance from deforested edges with fire occurrence in logged forests at those same distances, values for the relative effect of logging are produced. A value of 1 indicates no effect, values less than 1 show a negative effect, and values greater than 1 indicate a positive effect. Logging increased the risk of fire occurrence by more than 300% at 2 km from edges but had little or no effect near edges.

penetration in unlogged forests was 240 m, whereas the average fire penetration distance in logged forest was 700 m. Increased fire penetration results from both faster-spreading edge-related fires and greater numbers of non–edge-related fires (Cochrane 2001). Edge-related fires spread faster in selectively logged forests because of the drier, more fuel-laden conditions. Non–edge-related fires in logged forests often result from increased human access along logging roads (e.g., loggers, hunters) and may be accidental or intentional.

The combined effects of fragmentation, fire, and selective logging have substantially affected the study region's remaining forests. Despite a forest cover of 73 percent, the disturbance regime changes in the majority of the remaining forests indicates reduced viability of these areas for either production or conservation purposes. The interaction between logging and fire, combined with the synergy of fragmentation and fire (Cochrane 2001, Cochrane and Laurance 2002), will result in significant challenges for any timber management plan.

CONCLUSION

Thousands of square kilometers of tropical forests are being logged each year (Nepstad et al. 1999b, Barber and Schweithelm 2000, Matricardi et al.

2001, Siegert et al. 2001). Without proper management, typical logging practices amount to resource mining that will yield an all-too-familiar boom-and-bust economy that can quickly impoverish a region or country's forest resources. Much thought and research have gone into determining ways to preserve the production capacity of tropical forests while conserving much of their biodiversity. Establishing extensive sustainable working forests may be one way to do this. In fact, the Brazilian government is working under this presumption and is establishing 50 million ha of working forests in the Amazon (Veríssimo and Cochrane 2003).

The problems of conserving sustainable working forests in the tropics are substantial and go beyond issues of deforestation, cutting cycles, and silvicultural treatments. As the analyses of Mato Grosso show, selectively logged forests are more susceptible to fire, having been nearly 50 percent more likely to burn in 1999. Furthermore, fire penetration in logged forests on average was nearly three times more extensive in these forests than in unlogged forests. The access created by logging roads in selectively logged forests also leads to an increase in human access to the forest and in forest burning distance from the forest edge. In the study region and across the tropics, fragmentation, logging, and fire damage have combined to create a vast pool of tropical forests that are neither intact nor completely destroyed but may have 10–80 percent reduced on-site live biomass and carbon storage (Uhl et al. 1997, Cochrane and Schulze 1999). Fire risk is a function not only of a forest's susceptibility to burning but also of the expected fire severity. Fire severity in degraded forests is much worse than that in undisturbed forests (Cochrane et al. 1999).

The reality of human-dominated tropical landscapes is that there is no longer a question of whether forests will burn but only when and how severely. Land use and climate change are interacting to create unprecedented stresses on Amazonian forests (Laurance and Williamson 2001), and the situation described here can be expected to worsen. Without fundamental changes in land management practices, the synergy between land use and land cover changes will allow fires to affect vast reaches of tropical forest, degrading and eroding forest remnants (Gascon et al. 2000, Cochrane and Laurance 2002) and accelerating predicted levels of species extinctions (Pimm and Raven 2000). In terms of total annual area affected, forest fires are quickly overtaking slash-and-burn deforestation as the primary disturbance factor in tropical forests.

Fires are not randomly spread through the landscape but are mediated by human land use and the condition of the remaining forests. By their nature, working forests will increase both access to and damage of forests, both of which increase the likelihood of fire. If working forests are to be managed sustainably, then the entire landscape matrix, including the people living in it, must be managed in a coordinated way so as to break the synergy of disturbances caused by the interaction of current fire use, forest fragmentation, and selective logging. Without such efforts, and despite the best intentions and forest management plans, working forests in anthropogenic landscapes will be short-lived enterprises that accelerate the impoverishment of tropical forests.

REFERENCES

Barber, C. V. and J. Schweithelm. 2000. *Trial by fire: Forest fire and forestry policy in Indonesia's era of crisis and reform.* Washington, D.C.: World Resources Institute.

Barbosa, R. I. and P. M. Fearnside. 1999. Incendios na Amazonia Brasileira: Estimativa da emissão de gases do efeito estufa pela queima de diferentes ecossistemas de Roraima na passagem do evento Ël Niño (1997/98). *Acta Amazonica* 29: 513–534.

Cochrane, M. A. 2000. Forest fire, deforestation and landcover change in the Brazilian Amazon. In L. F. Neuenschwander, K. C. Ryan, G. E. Gollberg, and J. D. Greer, eds., *Proceedings from the Joint Fire Science Conference and Workshop, June 15–17, 1999, "Crossing the millennium: Integrating spatial technologies and ecological principles for a new age in fire management,"* Vol. 1, 170–176. Moscow, Idaho: University of Idaho and the International Association of Wildland Fire.

Cochrane, M. A. 2001. Synergistic interactions between habitat fragmentation and fire in evergreen tropical forests. *Conservation Biology* 15: 1515–1521.

Cochrane, M. A., A. Alencar, M. D. Schulze, C. M. Souza Jr., D. C. Nepstad, P. Lefebvre, and E. Davidson. 1999. Positive feedbacks in the fire dynamic of closed canopy tropical forests. *Science* 284: 1832–1835.

Cochrane, M. A. and W. F. Laurance. 2002. Fire as a large-scale edge effect in Amazonian forests. *Journal of Tropical Ecology* 18: 311–325.

Cochrane, M. A. and M. D. Schulze. 1998. Forest fires in the Brazilian Amazon. *Conservation Biology* 12: 948–950.

Cochrane, M. A. and M. D. Schulze. 1999. Fire as a recurrent event in tropical forests of the eastern Amazon: Effects on forest structure, biomass, and species composition. *Biotropica* 31: 2–16.

Cochrane, M. A. and C. M. Souza Jr. 1998. Linear mixture model classification of burned forests in the eastern Amazon. *International Journal of Remote Sensing* 19: 3433–3440.

Frumhoff, P. C. 1995. Conserving wildlife in tropical forests managed for timber. *BioScience* 45: 456–464.

Gascon, C., G. B. Williamson, and G. A. B. da Fonseca. 2000. Receding edges and vanishing fragments. *Science* 288: 1356–1358.

Holdsworth, A. R. and C. Uhl. 1997. Fire in Amazonian selectively logged rain forest and the potential for fire reduction. *Ecological Applications* 7: 713–725.

Houghton, R. A. 1995. Land-use change and the carbon-cycle. *Global Change Biology* 1: 275–287.

Johns, J. S., P. Barreto, and C. Uhl. 1996. Logging damage in planned and un-planned logging operations in the eastern Amazon. *Forest Ecology and Management* 89: 59–77.

Kauffman, J. B. 1991. Survival by sprouting following fire in tropical forests of the eastern Amazon. *Biotropica* 23: 219–224.

Kauffman, J. B. and C. Uhl. 1990. Interactions of anthropogenic activities, fire and rainforests in the Amazon basin. In J. G. Goldammer, ed., *Fire in the tropical biota,* 117–134. Berlin: Springer-Verlag.

Laurance, W. F., M. A. Cochrane, S. Bergen, P. M. Fearnside, P. Delamônica, C. Barber, S. d'Angelo, and T. Fernandes. 2001. The future of the Brazilian Amazon: Development trends and deforestation. *Science* 291: 438–439.

Laurance, W. F., P. Delamonica, S. G. Laurance, H. Vasconcelos, and T. E. Lovejoy. 2000. Rainforest fragmentation kills big trees. *Nature* 404: 836.

Laurance, W. F., S. G. Laurance, L. V. Ferreira, J. Rankin-de Merona, C. Gascon, and T. E. Lovejoy. 1997. Biomass collapse in Amazonian forest fragments. *Science* 278: 1117–1118.

Laurance, W. F. and B. Williamson. 2001. Positive feedbacks among forest fragmentation, drought, and climate change in the Amazon. *Conservation Biology* 15: 1529–1535.

Martini, A., N. Rosa, and C. Uhl. 1994. An attempt to predict which Amazonian tree species may be threatened by logging activities. *Environmental Conservation* 21: 152–162.

Matricardi, E. A. T., D. L. Skole, W. Chomentowski, and M. A. Cochrane. 2001. *Multi-temporal detection and measurement of selective logging in the Brazilian Amazon using Landsat data.* Document no. CGCEO/RA03–01. East Lansing: Michigan State University.

Nascimento, H. E. M. and W. F. Laurance. 2002. Total aboveground biomass in central Amazonian rainforests: A landscape-scale study. *Forest Ecology and Management* 168: 311–321.

Nepstad, D. C., A. G. Moreira, and A. A. Alencar. 1999a. *Flames in the rain forest: Origins, impacts, and alternatives to Amazonian fire.* Brasília, Brazil: The Pilot Program to Conserve the Brazilian Rain Forest, Brasilia, World Bank.

Nepstad D.C., A. Veríssimo, A. Alencar, C. Nobre, E. Lima, P. Lefebvre, P. Schlesinger, C. Potter, P. Moutinho, E. Mendoza, M. A. Cochrane, and V. Brooks. 1999b. Large-scale impoverishment of Amazonian forests by logging and fire. *Nature* 398: 505–508.

Pimm, S. L. and P. Raven. 2000. Extinction by the numbers. *Nature* 403: 843–845.

Schindele, W., W. Thoma, and K. Panzer. 1989. *The forest fire in East Kalimantan. Part I: The fire, the effects, the damage and technical solutions.* FR-Report no. 5. Eschborn, Germany: Deutsche Gesellschaft für Technische Zusammenarbeit.

Schneider, R., E. Arima, A. Veríssimo, P. Barreto, and C. Souza Jr. 2000. *Amazônia sustentável: limitantes e oportunidades para o desenvolvimento rural.* Série Parcerias. no. 1, Brasília, Brazil: Banco Mundial & Imazon.

Siegert, F., G. Rueker, A. Hinrichs, and A. A. Hoffman. 2001. Increased damage from fires in logged forests during droughts caused by El Niño. *Nature* 414: 437–440.

Skole, D. and C. J. Tucker. 1993. Tropical deforestation and habitat fragmentation in the Amazon: Satellite data from 1978 to 1988. *Science* 260: 1905–1910.

Uhl, C., P. Barreto, A. Veríssimo, E. Vidal, P. Amaral, A. C. Barros, C. Souza, J. Johns, and J. Gerwing. 1997. Natural resource management in the Brazilian Amazon. *BioScience* 47: 160–168.

Uhl, C. and R. Buschbacher. 1985. A disturbing synergism between cattle ranch burning practices and selective tree harvesting in the eastern Amazon. *Biotropica* 17: 265–268.

Uhl, C. and J. B. Kauffman. 1990. Deforestation, fire susceptibility, and potential tree responses to fire in the eastern Amazon. *Ecology* 71: 437–449.

Uhl, C. and I. C. G. Vieira. 1989. Ecological impacts of selective logging in the Brazilian Amazon: A case study from the Paragominas region of the state of Pará. *Biotropica* 21: 98–106.

UNDAC (United Nations Disaster Assessment Coordination). 1998. *Brasil, incendios no estado de Roraima, Agosto 1997–Abril 1998*. United Nations, unpublished report.

UNEP (United Nations Environment Programme). 2002. *Spreading like wildfire: Tropical forest fires in Latin America and the Caribbean: Prevention, assessment and early warning*. Mexico City: UNEP.

Veríssimo, A., P. Barreto, M. Mattos, R. Tarifa, and C. Uhl. 1992. Logging impacts and prospects for sustainable forest management in an old Amazonian frontier: The case of Paragominas. *Forest Ecology and Management* 55: 169–199.

Veríssimo, A., P. Barreto, R. Tarifa, and C. Uhl. 1995. Extraction of a high-value natural source from Amazon: The case of mahogany. *Forest Ecology and Management* 72: 39–60.

Veríssimo, A. and M. A. Cochrane. 2003. Fostering sustainable forestry and conservation in the Amazon. *Science* 299: 1843–1843.

Veríssimo, A., M. A. Cochrane, C. Souza Jr., and R. Salomão. 2002. Priority areas for establishing national forests in the Brazilian Amazon. *Conservation Ecology* 6: 4. Online: http://www.consecol.org/vol6/iss1/art4.

Woods, P. 1989. Effects of logging, drought, and fire on structure and composition of tropical forests in Sabah, Malaysia. *Biotropica* 21: 290–298.

Chapter 18

LIMITED OR UNLIMITED WANTS IN THE PRESENCE OF LIMITED MEANS?

THE ROLE OF SATIATION IN DEFORESTATION

Arild Angelsen and Martin K. Luckert

There is a widespread policy belief that one of the strategies needed to conserve forest lands is intensified use. This applies both to intensified use of adjacent agricultural land through provision of improved agricultural technologies (including agroforestry) and to new technologies, intensified use, and better prices of forest products. The integrated conservation and development programs (ICDPs) have been based on this assumption (e.g., Newmark 2000). The reasoning is that if more agricultural or forest products are produced through intensified efforts in some areas, then other areas of forests may be set aside and conserved. An underlying assumption of this approach seems to be that people have a set level of needs, and if we can meet those needs on a smaller piece of land, then people will not want to harvest forest products from conserved forests.

In contrast to these ideas, recent work by Angelsen and Kaimowitz (2001) suggests that new agricultural technologies and intensified production may accelerate deforestation by making the conversion of forests more profitable. Increased returns from intensification can also be used to hire more labor and capital to increase deforestation. Furthermore, the increased returns from intensification may also lure more people into an area, thereby increasing the demand on forest resources. Similar arguments can be made for forest harvesting technologies.

In addition to being affected by supply side factors, forest use is also affected by demand side factors. That is, peoples' preferences, which form the basis for market demands, can also influence how many trees will be cut. Unlike conservationists, economists typically assume that wants are unlimited. Therefore the classic textbook definition of scarcity in the field of economics is "unlimited wants in the presence of limited means" (e.g., Lipsey and Steiner 1981). Economists generally assume that it is not wants (i.e., demand side considerations) but means (i.e., supply side considerations) that limit our consumption.

Countering the unlimited wants assumption is the concept of satiation: that wants are limited. However, in the economics literature this concept has not been given much attention and is viewed as a rare exception in the theory of consumption in economics textbooks (e.g., Varian 1993). Nonetheless, the potential for satiation has been considered by some economists (e.g., Stryker 1976, Dvorak 1992) who have modeled rural households as "full-belly" farmers. The concept in these studies is that households seek to reach some basic subsistence level and then become satiated and substitute leisure for consumption. The policy implications for these different assumptions are far reaching (Angelsen 1999).

In this chapter we investigate the question of satiation by considering whether people have limited or unlimited wants in the presence of limited means. Assumptions about satiation or full-belly behavior are part of a surprising number of current debates on natural resource management in poor countries, and we first briefly review some of them. Next, we investigate some concepts of satiation in the context of developed and developing economies. Then we consider evidence from two case studies from Zimbabwe and Indonesia to see whether we can find evidence of satiation. We conclude with suggestions for further research regarding satiation and forest conservation.

IMPROVED AGRICULTURAL YIELDS AND DEFORESTATION

One widely held belief is that better agricultural technologies and agricultural intensification will take the pressure off forests: If yield doubles, a farm household can meet its subsistence needs from just half the land. This logic underlies many policy interventions intended to save tropical forests, such as agroforestry programs. For example, Sanchez (1990:378) claims, "For every hectare put into these sustainable soil management technologies by farmers, five to ten hectares per year of tropical rainforests will be saved from the shifting cultivator's ax, because of their higher productivity."

The Alternatives to Slash and Burn (ASB) program in the early 1990s was based on that assumption, but later research findings by ASB seriously question this logic:

> It is naïve to expect that productivity increases necessarily slow forest conversion or improve the environment. Indeed

quite the opposite is possible, since increased productivity of forest-derived land uses also increases the opportunity costs of conserving natural forests. These increased returns to investment can spur an inflow of migrants or attract large-scale land developers and thereby accelerate deforestation. (Tomich et al. 2001:242)

More generally, Angelsen and Kaimowitz (2001:9) argue that "trade-offs and win–lose between forest conservation and technological progress in agriculture in areas near forest appear to be the rule rather than the exception."

IMPROVED FOREST MANAGEMENT

The belief that intensification of forest management will take pressure off natural forest has many similarities to the agricultural technology and intensification debate. Increasing the timber yields by more intensive management allows us to meet a given market demand from a smaller forest area, leaving more natural forest unexploited.

Various measures have been promoted under the umbrella of sustainable forest management (SFM), including reduced-impact logging, greater efficiency in logging and processing, and use of lesser-known species. However, the results of these efforts have been disappointing. One reason is the reluctance of timber companies to adopt SFM as long as the alternatives are more profitable. Furthermore, as noted by Rice et al. (2001:3), "most policies aimed at increasing the profitability of SFM . . . also increase the profitability of conventional logging and therefore fail to make SFM a relatively more attractive land use."

ICDPS

As the development community increasingly identified links between conservation, poverty, and development, ICDPs have emerged since the early 1980s as a dominant approach to biodiversity (forest) conservation. The approach has several components, but as noted by Brandon (2001:419), "promoting local social and economic development adjacent to protected area boundaries has been the most common ICDP strategy." Development outside the protected areas is supposed to take the pressure off the core areas.

Although they still hold a dominant position, increasing evidence also points to the disappointing performance of ICDPs (Brandon et al. 1998). One reason is that the approach was based on a false assumption "that raising living standards will inevitably result in conservation" (Newmark and Hough 2000:689). In his review of the disappointing performance of these programs in Africa, Newmark questions whether species in protected areas would be helped by improvements in local living standards. ICDP activities, such as agricultural intensification programs, can provide both the incentives and the means for local encroachment into the core areas.

Despite such observations, modern explanations of the underlying causes of these conservation and development conundrums, at first glance, seem rare. However, there is a long history of debates regarding "the noble savage" that may shed further light on the limited wants hypothesis.

"NOBLE SAVAGES"

Underlying the limited wants hypotheses might be the idea of the noble savage, an eighteenth-century idea by Enlightenment philosopher Rousseau that informs the ideologies of many anthropologists and environmental nongovernmental organizations. Ecologically noble savages include traditional forest users who live close to a subsistence level of material consumption and manage forests as part of cosmologies that stress ecological balance. Accumulations of wealth and material greed are foreign to these populations. The noble savage thesis has been questioned by many authors, such as Alvard (1993) and Redford and Stearman (1993). Some have even labeled this thesis "sentimental rubbish" (Leach 1971, in Ellen 1993:126). One fundamental question is whether the observed behavior of aboriginal peoples, sometimes called noble, should be interpreted to reflect their preferences, culture, or conservation logic or whether this behavior should be interpreted as a reflection of their constrained opportunities. For example, does the avoidance of accumulation of physical wealth among nomads reflect their limited wants or simply the cost of carrying a lot of physical goods to their next site? Thus at the core of this debate are the same questions that we ask in this chapter. Is it limited wants or limited means that govern behavior? Although having limited material wants may be noble, being poor because of limited means involves being deprived.

CONCEPTS OF SATIATION

To begin delving into concepts of satiation, we ask what factors prevent infinite consumption. In the economics literature, the answers are fairly straightforward. Two general phenomena constrain our consumption.

First, there is the concept of increasing marginal costs of production. This supply side concept deals with means of producing goods and services that are consumed on the demand side. Increasing marginal costs of production means that as more and more of something is produced, the cost of producing an additional unit increases. Thus as consumption increases, costs of meeting those wants also increase. For example, in fuelwood gathering, costs of collecting an additional headload of wood may increase as more is consumed, as people are forced to walk further and further. In essence these increasing costs may protect some resources if the costs of extraction become prohibitive. Thus inaccessibility is among the most effective ways of protecting forests. This example assumes that the woodland resource cannot produce fuelwood as fast as people collect it. Introducing new technology (i.e., faster-growing tree species) could change this situation. Therefore quickly increasing marginal costs, which may be present in the short run, can be modified for longer-term supplies where technological innovation improves resource flows.

Second, there is the concept of diminishing marginal utility from consumption. This demand side concept deals with the benefits (utility) that people derive as they consume greater amounts of a good. Diminishing marginal utility from consumption means that as more and more of something is consumed, the benefits of consuming an additional unit decrease. For example, when a tree full of fruit ripens in the forest, the utility that a person derives from eating the first fruit is generally assumed to be greater than the utility derived from eating the tenth one (assuming that the fruit is large relative to the consumer's belly).

At first glance, the concept of diminishing marginal utility may seem to be at odds with the concept of unlimited wants. However, diminishing marginal utility is thought to apply only to the consumption of a particular good, not to total consumption (i.e., all goods consumed). That is, we may face some type of satiation when it comes to consuming fruit, but fruit is only one source of utility. When we consider the many goods and services from which people derive utility, as marginal utility begins to diminish with respect to one good or service, we switch to other things to consume, such as fuelwood, better clothes, or a television. Thus wants may appear to be unlimited even in the presence of diminishing marginal utility. If our fruit-eating consumer can start selling the fruits after his belly is full, he gets cash, and the market transforms the fruits into other commodities. He therefore escapes the diminishing marginal utility of fruits and starts satisfying other needs and wants.

The concepts of increasing marginal costs of production and diminishing marginal utility from consumption were first articulated in the context of developed economies. In developing economies, a number of circumstances may be different. For example, in subsistence households, producers and consumers often are the same people. Therefore the distinctions between supply and demand side phenomena become blurred. As we shall see later, it could be difficult to tell whether consumption is being limited by wants or means.

A further characteristic of subsistence economies is that markets for inputs into production and markets for consumption of products may be small or nonexistent. In terms of producing goods for consumption, this means that increasing marginal costs may be difficult to avoid if inputs cannot be purchased. For example, if labor markets are small, then a household may be limited to its household labor pool, causing labor allocations to become more and more costly as the pool reaches its limits. Similarly, with small product markets, satiation could begin to limit wants in the context of very few choices beyond individual consumption for the goods and services that the household produces.[1] The interest in picking fruit quickly stops if they cannot be sold. Empirical evidence along these lines indicates that the availability of consumer goods increases the agricultural elasticity of supply. That is, farmers respond more readily with increased production in response to price increases as more consumer goods are available (Sadoulet and de Janvry 1995:90).

In developed economies, consumption may be limited by people's ethical concerns over gaps between the rich and the poor or by personal, sometimes religious connections to natural resources. In subsistence economies, with potentially closer-knit communities and closer ties to the land, these factors could be stronger, playing a larger role in limiting consumption than in developed economies.

Here we need to be careful to distinguish between different roles that norms can play in limiting consumption. First, in cases where these ethics are strong, individual preferences (i.e., limited wants) could curtail consumption. We then consider "norms as internalized rules of conduct" (Baland and Platteau 1996:119). This might correspond to the "noble savage" view of traditional societies as inherently conservationist. Second, there might be informal rules that enforce satiation behavior. For example, wealth accumulation can be seen as a sign of greed. Or there may be restrictions that specify that some natural resources may be harvested only for personal use, not for commercial sale. Or there may be redistributive mechanisms that discourage extra efforts (e.g., food production above the subsistence level should be shared with your kin, not sold in the market to buy other commodities).[2] In these cases, the rule structure that prohibits the transfer of goods to others is inhibiting supply decisions and could be interpreted as limiting means. Strictly speaking, if a person willingly supports an institutional control on consumption, then limited wants would be the source of curtailed consumption. However, if a person's preferences did not coincide with the institutional control on consumption, but the person was nonetheless willing to abide by it, then means would be limiting the person from pursuing his or her wants.

These considerations suggest that either demand side factors (i.e., preferences or wants) or supply side factors (i.e., costs or means) could limit consumption. Furthermore, it may be very difficult to distinguish which factors are limiting in subsistence economies where producers consume their own products. This distinction is not merely an academic question; it is at the root of predicting impacts of increasing levels of development on forests. Consider a new road presenting new market opportunities for fruits. If demand side factors are limiting consumption and supply side factors are not, then further development may be slowed and may curtail further consumption. Under this scenario, producing more forest (or agricultural) products with intensified management could allow some forests to be saved. However, if supply side factors are limiting consumption and demand side factors are not, then increased development through intensification may increase the exploitation of forests. If demand and supply factors are limiting consumption, then the results of further development could be ambiguous, depending on which factors were more limiting.

These possibilities leave us with the difficult task of trying to assess empirical cases and speculating about whether supply or demand side factors are responsible for resulting behavior. Although we have not designed a study to attempt to separate these factors, we investigate two different cases here that provide some evidence.

Case 1: Farmer Labor Allocations in Zimbabwe

As part of a household livelihood study in Zimbabwe, Campbell et al. (2002) collected detailed seasonal information about how male, female, and child members of households spend their time. At this semiarid study site, conditions for agricultural production are poor, with sporadic rains and nutrient-poor soils. Furthermore, geography and a lack of transportation infrastructure limit access to markets for produce. There is pervasive poverty in the study areas, with 70 percent of the households falling under the food poverty line and 90 percent falling below the consumption poverty line.[3] Despite the fact that labor is a crucial input in most productive activities, employment is rare. Among the people in this area, we find close ethical connections with natural resources and highly developed institutional structures for regulating resource use (Mandondo et al. in preparation). In this supply-constrained environment, and with close ethical connections to natural resources, one might expect local people to behave as full-belly farmers.

With the data collected by Campbell et al. (2002), it is possible to investigate whether household members behave as full-belly farmers. One test used was to see whether time spent on leisure and sleeping varied significantly between quarters. If people really do become satiated, one would expect them to spend more time at leisure and sleep during the dry season, when agricultural tasks are minimal, than during the wet season, when agricultural tasks are most demanding. However, such evidence would be a necessary but not sufficient condition to support a satiation hypothesis. Full-belly behavior could also be caused by a lack of opportunities to increase welfare beyond satisfying hunger. Although results do show statistically higher amounts of leisure and sleeping during the dry season, differences in mean values are fairly minor (i.e., generally less than one hour per day). Accordingly, results do not strongly support the proposition that households behave as full-belly farmers. That is, despite the potential for production to be curtailed by a lack of opportunities or satiation, households are active in seeking to increase consumption year-round. One could argue that farmers continue to work to increase consumption because their bellies are never really full.

Another test used as part of this study was to see whether there are significant differences in wages between quarters. If labor markets are functioning and labor is in higher demand during the wet season, we would expect to see higher wages during this season. Results showed that although there are significant differences between quarters, the highest-wage quarter corresponds with the higher sleep and leisure quarters. Accordingly, seasonal differences in wages do not support concepts of full-belly farmers.

A final test was conducted by looking at partial correlations of time spent between alternative livelihood activities. If there were no slack periods of labor, one would expect to see negative partial correlations between activities because undertaking one activity would displace another. In contrast, if there were periods of slack labor, after farmers had full bellies, we would expect to see a lack of correlation, indicating that more of one activity could be undertaken without sacrificing another. Results indicated that most activities were negatively correlated, implying an absence of slack labor available. The few cases that had positive correlations were largely associated with sleep, implying that some activities may necessitate more sleep than others.

In short, despite conditions that could provide evidence of full-belly behavior, we find quite the opposite in the semiarid regions of Zimbabwe. Despite severe supply side constraints and close ethical ties to resources, households seem to be constantly trying to increase consumption. This strategy seems to be pursued through a variety of activities that make use of labor resources throughout the year.

Case 2: Deforestation and Rubber in Riau, Indonesia

The second case is from a lowland rainforest area of the Seberida district in Riau province, Sumatra. An extensive survey of about 200 households in seven villages was done in 1991–1992 and 1998–1999. We use results from the second survey to attempt to shed light on the issue of satiation. Angelsen (1995) reports on the main findings of the first survey and describes the area. The study area is made up of traditional Malay and Talang Mamak communities, as opposed to the transmigrant villages that now comprise more than half the population of the district. Other key actors are logging companies (since the early 1970s), spontaneous migrants, and, more recently, oil palm plantations and small-scale logging and sawmills.

Since the mid-1980s there has been extensive planting of smallholder rubber. Typically, a family clears 1–2 ha of secondary forest and plants rice and other food crops for one season before rubber is planted. The rice yield is low, and the primary motivation is rubber production. Besides the rubber outputs, planting perennials is also a way to secure property rights over the land. This aspect has become increasingly important as land has become scarcer in recent years.

The data from the 1998–1999 survey were analyzed to see which factors influence forest clearing (Rye Blæstad 2002). The satiation hypothesis suggests that higher income and wealth (proxied by rubber land holdings) would lead to less forest clearing. This is closely linked to a poverty hypothesis, suggesting that poverty forces farmers to clear forests.

A simple comparison of income groups (quintiles) suggests a weak negative correlation between income and forest clearing: In the lowest 20 percent income group, 45 percent opened a swidden field in the forest the last two years, whereas 36 percent did for the top quintile. In the regression analysis, however, the income variable is not significant.

Forest clearing is also positively but weakly correlated with rubber holdings; that is, those who have large holdings (6 ha or more) are more likely to clear additional forest. But again, the coefficient did not prove statistically significant in the regression analysis.

A much clearer picture emerges for forest products. Nontimber forest products (NTFPs) are most important for the poorest households, constituting about 10 percent of the income of the two bottom quintiles but only 3 percent for the top 20 percent. However, for timber harvesting income the picture is turned upside down: None in the lowest quintile had timber income, whereas timber harvesting made up 38 percent of the income for the top quintile. For timber harvesting, the link between forest use and income was the opposite of what a satiation hypothesis suggests: People with more income consume more.

How should these seemingly contradictory results be interpreted? There is no clear evidence of satiation. The analysis does not find any general pattern of forest clearing and forest product harvesting diminishing with higher income and more rubber gardens. What are the key factors? First, age of the household is important, with young households clearing significantly more than the old. Second, forest access and access to wage, business, and timber income are also key factors in forest clearing. Third, the sharp difference between NTFP and timber income occurs because timber harvesting entails access to capital and political connections, whereas NTFP harvesting is labor intensive and open access and tends to be an "employer of last resort." Generally, we believe that to understand and predict farmers' response to new opportunities, it is much more relevant to focus on farmers' access to various inputs—family labor, capital (cash, credit), and political power giving access to valuable resources—than vague concepts of satiation or full-belly preferences.

Improved infrastructure, large projects and influx of migrants, higher income through the rubber boom, and the general pace of development (including televisions in every village) have created a more consumer-oriented society in the district. A farmer told one of us that a major reason for living for a few months on the swidden field (guarding and weeding the rice field) was to avoid pressure to buy more and more things.

CONCLUSION

Distinguishing between supply and demand side factors that influence consumption is crucial. Demand side factors relate to preferences and concepts of satiation that, if present, could limit consumption of forest products and agricultural land and accompanying deforestation in the face of development initiatives. However, if supply side factors are limiting consumption, then alleviating these constraints with development activities could lead to increased deforestation.

Results from two case studies indicate that it may be difficult to find evidence of satiation. Despite supply side constraints and ethical concerns for natural resources, people appear to be driven by desires to increase consumption. Therefore, among the peoples investigated in these case studies, we would predict that if development reduces constraints on supply, then development will not necessarily reduce pressures on natural resources as people become satiated. Instead, relaxing supply constraints is likely to increase pressures.

Upon reflection, these conclusions should not be too surprising. At its core, much of the ecological literature is based on concepts of optimization in which evolutionary mechanisms allow plants and animals to increasingly get more from their environments. Do we expect any less of humans? Why, then, do we assume that they may be satiated and not be continuously driven to have more? Perhaps the response is that we *do* expect more of humans: to voluntarily restrain consumption (i.e., practice satiation) for the benefit of themselves and their environments (Ehrlich and Ehrlich 2002). However, a number of factors may prevent the practice of voluntary satiation.

First, it may be much easier to contemplate the potential for satiation in developed countries with higher wealth levels than among the poor in developing countries. We have discussed the concept of a full-belly farmer, but how full must a belly be before it is really full? If we interpret various indicators of poverty as representing a full belly, then we still have vast numbers of people who lack them. Can we expect to see satiation anytime soon given the level of welfare at which we are starting?

The literature on income and subjective well-being (SWB), as summarized by Offer (2000), is relevant to this discussion. SWB is closely linked to income at low-income levels, but "overall happiness" is fairly constant over time in developed countries. This might support those who claim that money does not make you happy and suggests that people may become satiated with wealth. But those who fall behind a gradually increasing norm for material living standards also state that they have low levels of SWB. In other words, the relative position of a person's wealth in society seems to be important to SWB.

Second, our discussion is also relevant to recent research on the environmental Kuznets curve. It is hypothesized that as income (wealth) levels increase, environmental degradation will eventually level out and decrease, following an inverted *U*-shaped pattern. It has also been hypothesized that such a relationship exists at the household level (Bulte and van Soest 2001). However, satiation is not generally believed to be the cause of reduced environmental damage along the Kuznets curve. Rather, it is hypothesized that a number of other factors, such as reductions in fertility rates and evolving institutions and policies, which are positively correlated with wealth, may lead to reduced resource degradation (Magnani 2001). Furthermore, observations of consumption levels in developed countries do not lead us to believe that satiation necessarily increases with wealth. However, the types of goods and services desired seem to change markedly. For example, conservation often is thought to be a luxury of rich countries. This phenomenon could be another explanation for the shape of the environmental Kuznets curve. Given the seemingly insatiable wants of people at high wealth levels in developed countries, it seems unlikely that those below the poverty line would become satiated.

Finally, there is the ongoing collective action and free-rider problem of protecting environments. Why would any one person want to voluntarily constrain consumption unless he or she knew that others would follow suit? Although institutions have evolved to attempt to direct individual behavior toward social actions (Ostrom 2002), such rule structures may be difficult to enforce and support under conditions of poverty.

A number of agencies are building development programs consistent with a thesis of limited wants. This may turn out to be an unfortunate and ultimately dangerous strategy. The existence of satiation has not been well documented, and evidence suggests it may be difficult to find, especially in the context of developing country poverty. Accordingly, it may be time to restrategize some of our approaches, beginning with a reexamination of human behavior.

NOTES

1. Note that we do not mean to confuse satiation and deprivation in this example. Satiation occurs because the household has so much fruit that marginal utility declines and may become zero. That is, because the household members have more than they can consume, they become satiated. The absence of markets is a deprivation condition that can cause the household to reach a satiated state. That is, the household members become satiated because they are deprived of market access that would allow them to sell produce as the value to the household begins to decline.

2. If a person derives as much utility from sharing with kin as from obtaining more personal consumption, then sharing would not be a disincentive.

3. The food poverty line represents the income that meets basic nutritional needs, and the consumption poverty line includes basic food consumption and some allowance of housing, clothing, education, health, and transport.

REFERENCES

Alvard, M. S. 1993. Testing the "ecologically noble savage" hypothesis: Inter-specific prey choice by Piro hunters of Amazonian Peru. *Human Ecology* 21: 355–387.

Angelsen, A. 1995. Shifting cultivation and "deforestation": A study from Indonesia. *World Development* 23: 1713–1729.

Angelsen, A. 1999. Agricultural expansion and deforestation: Modeling the impact of population, market forces and property rights. *Journal of Development Economics* 58: 185–218.

Angelsen, A. and D. Kaimowitz, eds. 2001. *Agricultural technologies and tropical deforestation*. Wallingford, U.K.: CAB International.

Baland, J.-M. and J.-P. Platteau. 1996. *Halting natural resource degradation: Is there a role for local communities?* Oxford, U.K.: Oxford University Press.

Brandon, K. 2001. Moving beyond integrated conservation and development projects (ICDPs) to achieve biodiversity conservation. In D. R. Lee and C. Barrett, eds., *Tradeoffs or synergies? Agricultural intensification, economics development and the environment*, 417–432. Wallingford, U.K.: CABI Publishing.

Brandon, K., K. Redford, and S. Sanderson, eds. 1988. *Parks in peril: People, politics, and protected areas*. Covelo, Calif.: Island Press.

Bulte, E. H. and D. P. van Soest. 2001. Environmental degradation in developing countries: Households and the (reverse) environmental Kuznets curve. *Journal of Development Economics* 65: 225–235.

Campbell, B. M., S. Jeffrey, W. Kozanayi, M. Luckert, M. Mutamba, and C. Zindi. 2002. *Household livelihoods in semi-arid regions: Options and constraints*. Bogor, Indonesia: Center for International Forestry Research.

Dvorak, K. A. 1992. Resource management by West African farmers and the economics of shifting cultivation. *American Journal of Agricultural Economics* 74: 809–815.

Ehrlich, P. R. and A. E. Ehrlich. 2002. Population, development and human natures. *Environment and Development Economics* 7: 158–170.

Ellen, R. 1993. Rhetoric, practice and incentive in the face of the changing times: A case study in Nuaulu attitudes to conservation and deforestation. In K. Milton, ed., *Environmentalism: The view from anthropology*, 126–143. London: Routledge.

Lipsey, R. and P. O. Steiner. 1981 (6th ed.). *Economics*. New York: Harper & Row.

Magnani, E. 2001. The environmental Kuznets curve: Development path or policy result? *Environmental Modeling and Software* 16: 157–165.

Mandondo, A., B. Campbell, M. Luckert, N. Nemarundwe, W. de Jong, and W. Kozanayi. In preparation. *Transacting institutional change in contexts of complexity: Experiences from Chivi District in Zimbabwe.*

Newmark, W. D. 2000. Conserving wildlife in Africa: Integrated conservation and development projects and beyond. *BioScience.* Online: http://www.find-articles.com/cf_0/m1042/7_50/64262813/print.jhtml.

Newmark, W. D. and J. L. Hough. 2000. Conserving wildlife in Africa: Integrated conservation and development projects and beyond. *BioScience* 50: 582–592.

Offer, A. 2000. Economic welfare measurements and human well-being. *Discussion Papers in Economic and Social History* 34. Oxford, U.K.: University of Oxford.

Ostrom, E. 2002. The evolution of norms within institutions: Comments on Paul R. Ehrlich and Anne E. Ehrlich's population, development and human natures. *Environment and Development Economics* 7: 177–182.

Redford, K. H. and A. M. Stearman. 1993. Forest-dwelling native Amazonians and the conservation of biodiversity: Interests in common or in collision? *Conservation Biology* 7: 248–255.

Rice, R. E., C. A. Sugal, S. M. Ratay, and G. A. B. da Fonseca. 2001. *Sustainable forest management: A review of conventional wisdom.* Washington, D.C.: Center for Applied Biodiversity Science at Conservation International.

Rye Blæstad, K. 2002. *Poverty and forest interlinkages: A case study from Seberida district, Indonesia.* M.S. thesis, Department of Economics and Social Sciences, Agricultural University of Norway, Ås.

Sadoulet, E. and A. de Janvry. 1995. *Quantitative development policy.* Baltimore, Md.: Johns Hopkins University Press.

Sanchez, P. A. 1990. Deforestation reduction initiative: An imperative for world substantiality in the twenty-first century. In A. F. Bouwman, ed., *Soils and the greenhouse effect.* New York: Wiley.

Stryker, J. D. 1976. Population density, agricultural technique, and land utilization in a village economy. *American Economic Review.* 66: 347–358.

Tomich, T., M. van Noordwijk, S. Budidarsono, A. Gillison, T. Kusumanto, D. Murdiyarso, F. Stolle, and A. M. Fagi. 2001. Agricultural intensification, deforestation, and the environment: Assessing tradeoffs in Sumatra, Indonesia. In D. Lee and C. Barrett, eds., *Tradeoffs or synergies? Agricultural intensification, economic development, and the environment,* 221–244. Wallingford, U.K.: CABI Publishing.

Varian, H. R. 1993 (3rd ed.). *Intermediate microeconomic analysis.* New York: W.W. Norton.

Chapter 19

FROM STAPLE TO FASHION FOOD

SHIFTING CYCLES AND SHIFTING OPPORTUNITIES
IN THE DEVELOPMENT OF THE AÇAÍ PALM FRUIT
ECONOMY IN THE AMAZON ESTUARY

Eduardo S. Brondízio

There may be no better example of an economic prospect for overcoming underdevelopment in rural Amazonia than the case of the açaí palm fruit (*Euterpe oleracea* Mart.) production system. Emerging from the initiative of local producers to supply a growing demand for açaí fruit, using locally developed technology and knowledge with respect to forest management, açaí fruit production embodies the social and environmental principles that permeate the discourse of sustainable development for the Amazon region. At the same time, the formation of this production system poses important questions concerning the spread and duration of benefits resulting from booming tropical forest economies. To what extent are production and market opportunities diminished by a history of sociocultural prejudice, land tenure insecurity, and differential access to economic incentives, thus reproducing cycles of underdevelopment even under ideal market conditions?

The boom of açaí fruit consumption in the past three decades provides an example of the development and formation of a production system and the structure of its corresponding commodity chain as new participants appear, new product pathways and transformation industries emerge, and profitable opportunities change across different sectors of the economy. In this chapter, I refer to shifting cycles and shifting opportunities to discuss the shift in economic opportunities and returns in each development phase of a production system. Factors underlying access to economic opportunities are discussed at two levels. First, at a local level, economic returns of production reflect the land tenure condition of the producer, the level of access to appropriate crop areas, and level of access to markets (defined, for instance, by the need for intermediaries or brokers). Second, at the level of the production system, factors underlying access to processing, stock control, and transformation industries determine the economic benefits experienced across different sectors and the socioeconomic outcomes for regional development. Access to emerging sectors as a complex economic system evolves is also defined in part by the hierarchy of social classes and the sociocultural identity of participants. These considerations raise the age-old question about the distribution of short- and long-term benefits from booming economies characteristic of tropical forests (e.g., rubber, gold, logging).

The interpretation of agrarian economies and forest crops in the Amazon requires attention to historical and sociocultural perspectives underlying their insertion into wider markets. These interactions are analyzed in this chapter from three related perspectives, taking into account the historical development of the different evolutionary phases of the açaí fruit production system, the factors defining the expansion of açaí production and the type and scale of consumer and market demand, and the sociocultural and political context that shapes the organization of labor and the structure of production, commercialization, and transformation of the product. In this context, this chapter examines the progressive growth of the açaí fruit economy in regional and, more recently, national and international markets as a venue to discuss sociocultural and economic factors underlying rural development in the Amazon estuary, where açaí production is concentrated.

The study of the formation of any production system requires a chronological, historical perspective that takes into account the interactions between its socioeconomic, technological, and ecological bases in relation to production and commercialization. Along with manioc flour, açaí fruit has continuously provided a caloric base for the rural diet throughout the historical periods of the region, from floodplain chiefdoms to missionary occupation to the period of social transformation marked by directorate policies all the way to the boom and bust of the rubber economy (Wallace 1853). In recent decades, açaí production continues to increase in order to meet the increasing staple food demand prompted by low-income urban population growth after 1970 and an increasing external demand prompted by the emergence of a national and international "fashion food" market that began in the early 1990s.

The expansion of the açaí fruit economy occurs as a combination of both endogenous and exogenous factors associated with the region as a whole and in association with its consumption basis. These include rural outmigration and urban expansion since the 1970s, the organization and marketing strategies developed for the export of other Amazonian fruits in the 1980s, and the growth of the green product industry in the 1990s. The fad of açaí fruit consumption is driven by various claims relating to its healthful and invigorating qualities, rainforest conservation, respect for indigenous causes and products, and its representation as an icon of the sustainable development agenda proposing alternative forms of land use in the Amazon. Açaí fruit's secure position at the regional level as a staple food favorite and its national and international outlook have transformed açaí fruit into a symbol of cultural identity and regional pride for estuarine people in the states of Pará and Amapá, in particular.

The current açaí fruit production system has been shaped by the particular social and political structure resulting from the region's long history of extractivism and absentee land ownership (Brondízio and Siqueira 1997). Although the last thirty years of the açaí fruit economy have created a distinctive production structure that offers new opportunities to several segments of the population, including small-scale estuarine producers, this structure tends to reproduce historical inequalities that characterize the regional sociopolitical configuration, which is based on social hierarchy, sharecropping, dependency on intermediaries, unequal access to infrastructure, and differential economic return. In this context, as the market expands, new participants enter to take advantage of economic opportunities restricted to most regional producers.

As new participants enter the commodity chain, they tend to represent local producers in their condition of extractivists as insensitive to growing market opportunities. These representations further prevent local producers from taking advantage of new markets and economic incentives aimed at supporting new forms of regional development. Examples of entrepreneurial and development discourses emerging in the last few years of açaí expansion illustrate the sociocultural position of açaí producers in the regional economy. Whether they are portrayed as a "noble savage" or as the stereotypical extractivist *caboclo* in need of assistance from the economic and technological "helping hands" of entrepreneurial development, few acknowledge the success of local producers in developing, with no external assistance, an agroforestry technology that has resulted in the most important contemporary economic system of the Amazon estuary in the last thirty years. Indeed, the hands and technology of local riverine producers have made açaí a food source crucial to the region's urban areas (e.g., açaí is consumed twice as often as milk in the capital of Belém; Rogez 2000) and provided a supply that has allowed national and international expansion of a commodity that is

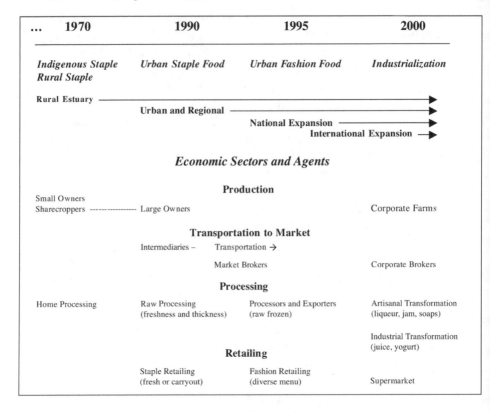

... 1970	1990	1995	2000
Indigenous Staple Rural Staple	*Urban Staple Food*	*Urban Fashion Food*	*Industrialization*

Rural Estuary ————————————————————————————►

Urban and Regional ——————————————————————►

National Expansion ——————————►

International Expansion —►

Economic Sectors and Agents

Production

Small Owners
Sharecroppers ---------------- Large Owners   Corporate Farms

Transportation to Market

Intermediaries –   Transportation →

Market Brokers   Corporate Brokers

Processing

Home Processing	Raw Processing (freshness and thickness)	Processors and Exporters (raw frozen)	Artisanal Transformation (liqueur, jam, soaps)

Industrial Transformation (juice, yogurt)

Retailing

	Staple Retailing (fresh or carryout)	Fashion Retailing (diverse menu)	Supermarket

Figure 19.1   Development of economic sectors in the açaí fruit economy.

seen by many as the key to achieving regional sustainable development. However, even the sustainable development discourse often reproduces cultural stereotypes that reinforce the region's vertical sociopolitical structure (Nugent 1993).

DEVELOPMENT OF PHASES OF THE AÇAÍ ECONOMY

For analytical purposes, the expansion of the açaí fruit economy can be divided into five main phases related to the progressive growth of its production, consumption, and position in the market (figure 19.1). In reality, these phases make up a continuum rather than separate stages. The indigenous staple phase represents the use of açaí resources by floodplain indigenous populations known to have occupied large areas of the estuary before European arrival and during the transition period after the first century and a half of European colonization (Roosevelt 1991). In a

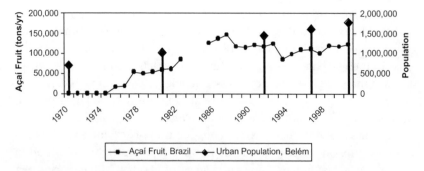

Figure 19.2 Açaí fruit production (1974–2000) and population growth in Belém and surrounding urban areas (1970–2000). Data were not available for 1983 and 1984. *Source:* IBGE
(1974–2001).

second phase, the use of açaí as a rural staple food spans a long period
starting in the seventeenth century, expanding during the directorate
and rubber periods, and continuing today by riverine occupants living in
isolated households and small communities and towns throughout the
estuary (Murrieta 1994, Siqueira 1997). These populations actually constitute the production basis of açaí fruit both then and now. The urban
staple food phase is characterized by a boom in consumption of açaí as
a staple food in large regional urban centers, particularly following post-
1970 population growth and coinciding with urban expansion of the region as a whole (figure 19.2). The urban fashion food phase began in the
late 1990s along with the popularization of other Amazonian fruits in
other regions of the country and, more recently, internationally. The energy value of açaí juice is an important health-based consideration for
teenagers and adults in urban areas throughout the country and abroad.
Finally, the industrialization phase is still emerging as açaí is becoming
widely visible and is incorporated into existing products of popular consumption such as yogurts, concentrated juices, energetic beverages, and
even beauty products such as shampoos and soaps. This phase can be
subdivided into a regional artisanal industry and, more significantly (in
economic terms), a multinational food production industry.

Açaí fruit consumption has two primary bases: a stable regional base
and a flexible, growing external market, which is still developing and fluc-
tuating as some areas experience bursts of consumption as a fashion food
while others settle into consolidated markets. Pará state, for instance, with
a production estimated between 300,000 and 500,000 tons of fruit per
year, is believed to consume two-thirds of this production internally (IBGE

1990–2001, Rogez 2000).[1] Reports indicate that consumption of açaí juice in Belém grew from 90,000 liters/day in the late 1980s to an estimated 400,000 liters/day in the late 1990s; this figure implies an estimated consumption of more than 60 liters/person per year. Families with the lowest level of income consume most of this food, which is bought fresh twice a day as a main meal staple, not a dessert. Poulet (1998) estimates daily consumption for the city of Macapá between 27,000 and 34,000 liters of fresh açaí processed by about 500 açaí stands (*amassadeiras de açaí*).

For the state of Pará as a whole, consumption of açaí juice varies widely depending on the region (higher in the estuary, lower in colonization settlement areas) but presents an average of about 27 liters/person per year. It is interesting to note that consumption in colonization areas of the Amazon, particularly in the state of Pará, is also growing at a steady pace; at least in part, the acceptance of açaí in these areas also stems from the popularity açaí has achieved elsewhere in the country.

Nationally, estimates indicate that from 1992 to 1996, exports to Rio de Janeiro jumped from 2 tons/month to more than 180 tons/month, and the total amount exported to other states (São Paulo, Goiás, Minas Gerais, and Rio Grande do Sul) reached 300 tons per month in 1996. It is estimated that by the end of the 1990s, the state of Pará was exporting almost 10,000 tons per year. Although export to foreign countries is still modest (less than 100 tons/year), it is increasing steadily and is expected to exceed 1000 tons per year after 2002 (Rogez 2000, IBGE 2001, Brondízio et al. 2002).

In the 1990s, along with other Amazonian fruits, açaí juice started to become known outside the region; in the case of açaí, it became known particularly among the active, young urban population as a "miraculous" source of energy. Exported mainly in the form of frozen pulp packages, açaí fruit was served first as smoothies (*suco de açaí*) or in bowls (*açaí na tijela*) in food huts on popular beaches in Rio de Janeiro. Soon, the açaí juice fever spread to gyms, shopping centers, and to a wide range of *lanchonetes* (sandwich shops); specialized açaí fruit stores emerged throughout Brazil with menus presenting dozens of variations of açaí preparations.

Until very recently, most Brazilians had heard the word *açaí* only in popular songs such as those from Paraense singer Fafá de Belém or popular singer Djavan. The media have played a crucial role in the fruit's rapid popularization. In the past few years, reference to *açaí* as a synonym of *energy* can be heard in any youth circle, on soap operas (e.g., on TV Globo), and on popular TV shows such as TV Globo's *Caceta & Planeta*. In this show an avid gym-going character drinks açaí juice as his strategic source of physical power. In this way, as new forms of consumption were becoming accepted outside Amazonia (as in the form of smoothies), a new cycle of the economy, a fashion food phase, was emerging with a new set of participants.

The recent expansion of açaí fruit juice, first to major national urban centers and later to Brazil as a whole, has been based on myriad new forms of consumption. Particularly, it involves the addition of guaraná syrup (a sweetener derived from *Paullinia enura*) that helps to cover açaí's peculiar taste for unfamiliar consumers. Other popular forms include smoothies with banana and other fruits and açaí–granola bowls. Interesting to note is that such forms of consumption are largely unacceptable in rural areas of the Amazon estuary. Actually, among riverine producers, there are food taboos related to the mixing of açaí juice and acidic fruits, which is said to provoke congestion strong enough to cause serious illness and, in some cases, even death. As frozen açaí reaches new markets, the process of thawing the pulp often leads to coagulation and acidification (souring), thereby making its flavor more difficult to accept. The addition of guaraná syrup and other fruits and the icy consistency of smoothies help to mitigate this problem. Besides, consumers of açaí juice in this form generally are unfamiliar with its fresh form. As a fashion food, açaí is known as a fruity blend and has nothing to do with the fresh, unsweetened pulp that is eaten with manioc flour to accompany beef, shrimp, fish, or even eggs during lunch or dinner among rural and urban Amazonian people (Strudwick and Sobel 1988, Murrieta 1994, Siqueira 1997).

The urban economic growth of açaí fruit has occurred in the context of other Amazonian fruits and their transformation industries. For instance, cupuaçu (*Theobroma grandiflora*), graviola (*Anona muricata*), and taperebá (*Spondias mombim*) were actually first in this progression, probably because of their flavors, which present a more palatable but still exotic flavor to non-Amazonians. Pioneers in this process were the Japanese communities in Tomé-Açu and Quatro-Bocas municipalities in the state of Pará. Emerging from the black pepper crisis in the 1960s, these producers started to emphasize agroforestry systems using tropical fruits, including non-Amazonian species such as acerola (*Malpighia grabla*). Of particular importance was the creation of a processing industry in the area, freezing methods, and a distribution network that opened the first pathways to popularize these fruits throughout Brazil, including representatives in São Paulo and other capitals. At the same time, other Amazonian cooperatives focused on exporting fruit pulp also emerged. The restaurant sector included several of these fruits on their menu. No less important was the informal introduction of açaí through the increasing number of Amazonians living elsewhere and, conversely, growing numbers of non-Amazonians living in this region.

Processed Pulp   **Artisanal Products**   **Industrial Products**

Figure 19.3   Examples of transformed açaí palm products.

More recently, the use of açaí fruit has been taken to a different level of industrial processing as its energy value and health qualities (e.g., thirty times the amount of anthocyanins found in red wine) have been promoted in advertisements. The yogurt industry was one of the first to jump in with a variety of flavor combinations. Similarly, pasteurized container versions of açaí juice sweetened with guaraná syrup and sport beverages were launched into the market. These industries are located mainly in southeastern and southern Brazil as part of dairy and fruit juice complexes. Today, these products are available in supermarkets throughout Brazil. Interestingly, most of them only slightly resemble the taste of açaí fruit as it is consumed in its place of origin (figure 19.3).

Açaí consumption still shows signs of a growing market. For instance, many stores in Rio and São Paulo that specialize in açaí products have stayed in business for more than five years. In the summer of 2002–2003, McDonald's included an açaí shake on their Brazilian menu. The state of Amapá has invested significantly in transformation industries of regional products, particularly new forms of Brazil nut products for export (oil, flour) but also açaí products such as soap, shampoo and conditioner, medicinal syrup, jams, and liqueurs. A new, international fashion food phase shows signs of emerging as commercialization of açaí juice has been reported in the United States (reports from California, Texas, Florida, and New York), Europe (England, France, and Scandinavian countries), and Australia. Although there is an enormous international potential, for instance in the ice cream and yogurt industries, this is a still a fledgling market. In fact, the ability of the industry to move from a fashion to an acquired consumption basis depends, at least in part, in adapting the taste and form of açaí fruit to culturally distinct markets. The incorporation of açaí fruit into industrial uses and transformation is key to maintaining and transforming the current fashion market into the assimilated consumption stage.

Recent examples of the expansion of açaí fruit internationally include feature articles in *Gourmet* magazine (July 2002) and the celebrity-centered magazine *InStyle* (April 2002), both in the United States. One of the key distributors of açaí pulp in the United States, Sambazon Inc., lists dozens of retail shops located throughout twelve states. As previously mentioned, the international industry has pursued a similar strategy that is working in Brazil, which is to focus on the health and energy claims of açaí and its conservation and indigenous culture linkages. Although often facing importation constraints regarding product safety, distributors have been able to grow by combining the health and green markets and focusing on the youth sectors, such as surfers, skaters, conservationists, and the health conscious.

A combination of a solid regional market (as a staple) and an emerging external market and transformation industries (as fashion) underlies an increasingly complex socioeconomic structure now in place.

INTENSIFICATION OF AÇAÍ AGROFORESTRY AND THE INVISIBILITY OF *CABOCLOS* AS AGRICULTURAL PRODUCERS

Historically, the açaí fruit production system has been considered to be a system of extraction, even in the wake of sixfold expansion of production from 1970 to 2000 (Brondízio and Siqueira 1997, Brondízio in press). To some extent, the extractivist label has not been dismissed but rather reinforced during the current boom of açaí fruit economy.

Explanations of land use intensification usually are based on conceptual models using parameters such as fallow cycle (Boserupian model) or variables based on factors of production, such as labor, energy, technology, and capital—the so-called input factors (Boserup 1965). Alternatively, output factors, such as the maintenance of productivity over time, often are used as a complementary measure of agropastoral intensification (for review see Brondízio and Siqueira 1997). However, these models are limited in their ability to explain agroforestry systems such as the açaí fruit case, where a clear distinction between the agricultural domain and the natural forest domain is not obvious.

Caboclo patterns of land use often are based on the coexistence of intensive and extensive activities that minimize risk while guaranteeing farm consolidation and expansion of market activities. Similarly, another element underlying our views of agricultural systems involves a subtle link between agronomic and aesthetic arrangements. Dominant views of productive agricultural systems include elements of field homogeneity and shape and the types and composition of plant species and crop varieties. It also includes particular patterns of land allocation representing domesticated, technologically driven production and a farmer's ability to keep areas "clean." These characteristics, usually borrowed from temperate areas, generally defy even the most productive farm lots in riverine Amazonia, such as açaí fruit production areas. The rigid boundaries drawn between different food production systems usually place forested areas (as in the case of agroforestry systems) in the "fallow," "unproductive," or, at best, "agroextractive" category.

The term *caboclo* has stimulated great discussion because of the stigma attached to it and discrepancies between academic and regional uses of the term (Parker 1985, Lima 1992, Nugent 1993, Brondízio and Siqueira 1997, Pace 1998). The regional connotations of the term refer to a lower social class made up of a technologically and economically backward population doomed to an extractive economy; historically, this has defined in several ways the interpretation of riverine *caboclos* as açaí fruit producers by reinforcing their position as extractivists. *Caboclos* have been repeatedly disregarded for their social and economic contribution to the region, a process similar to what Nugent (1993) has called "manufactured invisibility," in which *caboclos* are viewed as exhibiting a condition of "social pathology" that impedes regional development. In the current context of açaí fruit economy, this view tends to characterize producers as passive and depending on outside help to foster intensification of production and economic development (Brondízio and Siqueira 1997).

INVISIBLE INTENSIFICATION IN THE AÇAÍ ECONOMY

Açaí agroforestry management has been the focus of numerous studies in the Amazon estuary (Calzavara 1972, Anderson et al. 1985, Jardim and Anderson 1987, Anderson 1988, 1990, Anderson and Jardim 1989, Anderson and Ioris 1992, Brondízio et al. 1993, 1994, Moran et al. 1994, Brondízio et al. 2002). Contrary to a system based on extractivism, management and planting of açaí takes specialized agricultural and forestry labor to maintain and increase stand crop productivity. Different management and planting strategies transform these areas into açaí agroforestry, locally called *açaizais*. The term encompasses different intensities of management; tree, sapling, and seedling population densities and structure; and a diverse range of species composition. Encompassing a large range of management stages, the term *açaízal* refers in this work to açaí agroforestry. The three main means of açaí agroforestry development are management of native stands, planting of açaí stands after annual or biannual crops

Açaí Agroforestry

Figure 19.4   Management and planting of açai agroforestry.

(*roçado de várzea*), and combined management and planting in native stands. In simple terms, management of açaí stands can be understood on two different levels: the forest stand level and the plant level. On the forest stand level, thinning and weeding techniques are used. On the plant level, management focuses on pruning techniques (figure 19.4).

Stand thinning and selection control the density of individuals of all species competing with açaí palm, in addition to the balance between açaí basal area and other species. Propagation consists of planting and dispersing seedlings and seeds of açaí while introducing other economic species to the stand. Finally, pruning controls the selection of productive clumps and stems. In the case of pure planted stands (i.e., *roçado de várzea*), there is a need to include intercropping techniques between annual and perennial crops. These techniques demand intensive care of the crop site, including weeding, pest control, and pruning of other crops. Despite the modification of species composition, the managed areas largely retain the structural characteristics of the floodplain forest (e.g., basal area and biomass), but with an overwhelming concentration of individuals of economic value.

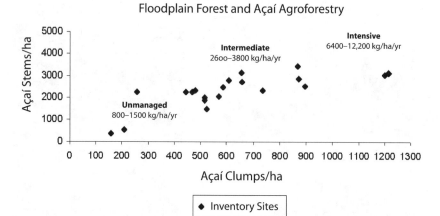

Figure 19.5 Açai palm stem and clump density, with inventory areas under different management regimes.

The production pattern resulting from different levels of forest management and planting clearly shows the level of direct intervention underlying açaí fruit production. Three basic levels of açaí agroforestry can be distinguished by variation in stem and clump density and are thus related to fruit yield and production (figure 19.5). The first, occurring in unmanaged sites, evidences an average of 250 clumps/ha. In this group production output averages around 1390 kg/ha per year, that is, an average of 116 fruit baskets/ha. The second, occurring in initially and intermediately managed sites, has an average of 600 to 730 clumps/ha. In this group, output production varies between 2600 and 3800 kg/ha per year, for an average of 269 fruit baskets/ha. Finally, the third level, characterized by more intensively managed sites, has an average of 890–1200 clumps/ha. In this group, production varies more widely from 6400 to 12,200 kg/ha per year, an average of 760 fruit baskets/ha (Brondízio 1996).

These data and measurements in experimental sites reported by Brondízio (1996) illustrate the variation in economic return of agricultural and forest products across the range of producers in the region. Net return per hectare varied from us$203.6/ha per year (unmanaged site) to us$2272.7/ha per year at the most productive site. However, within the same production class, such as the intermediate group, economic return varied from us$303.7/ha per year to us$669.8/ha per year as a function of the harvesting and selling period, which are closely related to land tenure.[2] In all cases, the economic return depends on harvesting schedules in relation to price fluctuations during the harvesting season. Based on our estimates, which integrate field inventories and Landsat TM data

(Brondízio et al. 1996), the area under intermediate and intensive açaí planting and management is the most important land use system in the region, surpassing other agropastoral production systems in economic and social importance.

Most claims of açaí production intensification tend to point to home gardens as the area that is managed intensively. However, a spatial perspective provides a different picture while highlighting the need to take into account the heterogeneity of floodplain areas in defining management levels (figure 19.6). Figures 19.4 and 19.6 show the potential

Figure 19.6   Spatial extent of intensive açaí agroforestry beyond house garden intensification, Ponta de Pedras region.

invisibility of this production system resulting from its forest characteristic and subtle differences between managed, planted, and unmanaged stands.

In summary, the limitations of intensification measures to evaluate the production system can be summarized as follows:

- Production technology is based on local management knowledge and presents low levels of input factors used to characterize intensity.
- The agroforestry structure can fit into both extremes (intensive or extensive) of Boserup's frequency model, depending on the definition of stages of production (besides being aesthetically different from other production systems).
- Spatial dimensions overlap areas of intensive, intermediate, and unmanaged areas, which allows expansion according to environmental conditions and household needs and possibilities.
- The multiple productivity dimensions of agroforestry areas (i.e., the "hidden harvest" of other fruits and raw material) tend to go unnoticed as economically relevant production.
- Floodplain cycles dictate cropping frequency more than the fallow period used in Boserupian models (see detail discussion in Brondízio 1996, Brondízio and Siqueira 1997).

ECONOMIC RETURN TO PRODUCERS: PRICE SIGNALS, LAND TENURE, AND HARVESTING SCHEDULE

Comparisons of the açaí price index and the agricultural and husbandry index for the state of Pará for the period between 1984 and 1995 are presented in figure 19.7. This figure shows a similar growth of both indices. This is an important parameter in the success of the açaí economy over the ten-year period presented. Using a ratio between the two indices. one observes that the açaí price index has followed and surpassed the inflation rates of most agropastoral products of the state (Brondízio 1996, Brondízio et al. 2002). Analyzing the evolution of this ratio, we can see that açaí producers had an incentive to grow açaí because its prices have kept up with those of other products and surpassed them at the beginning and end of the harvesting seasons. Another important point is the consistent market for the product in the last two decades, which shows signs of a well-structured production system. Production has increased sixfold in the past twenty years, based on management and planting rather than extraction from untapped sources. The increases in production and price maintenance have been followed by the emergence of a

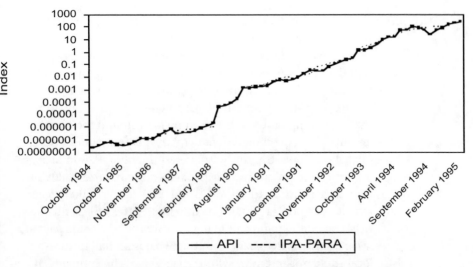

Figure 19.7 Açai price index (API) and the Fundação Getrilio Vargas index for agropastoral products, Pará State (IPA PARA) 1984–1995 (base 1994 = 100). *Source:* Adapted from Brondízio (1996).

socioeconomic organization around production, distribution, marketing, and processing, introducing a new class of regional producers and workers and, most significantly, new entrepreneurs in the processing and commercialization sectors. Emerging from a local rural economy, the açaí fruit industry is now functioning as a complex multilevel economic structure.

As previously suggested, for producers a key factor affecting economic return is related to one's land tenure condition because it underlies not only harvesting schedule (and thus response to price) but also commercialization. From a producer's perspective, several factors mediate the links between productivity, harvesting, and economic return. Daily and weekly distribution of harvesting throughout the season reflect the ability to market according to price signals and are the most important factor.[3] Similarly, the cost of transportation in relation to fruit price has a direct impact on return. Whereas the cost of transportation can hover around 10 percent of açaí prices at the beginning and at the end of the season, it can reach 25 percent or more at the season's peak, when the fruit price is lower (Brondízio et al. 2002). Whereas owners are free to wait for better prices, sharecroppers need to follow their landlords' schedules and decisions. In most estuarine municipalities, sharecroppers are the largest category of producers. They provide the bulk of açaí production, but they probably benefit least from its market growth.

THE DISCOURSE OF NEW PARTICIPANTS IN A BOOMING ECONOMY

In the Ilha de Marajó, an island twice the size of Wales at the mouth of the Amazon, . . . a food processing company is working with the local authorities to *persuade* the growing number of *ribeirinhos* (riverbank dwellers) to cultivate the açaí palms that grow abundantly in the swampy land around their wooden huts. . . . [A company representative] accompanies a state official on a boat trip to try to interest the *ribeirinhos* in *taking a short course* on cultivating the trees to maximize yields of fruit and palm hearts. "You could be earning 8,000 Reais (about US$4,000) a year from this plot," [the representative tells] . . . a father and son living nearby. The two smile *politely but disbelievingly—incredulous* that what is a small fortune by local standards might be within their grasp. The company already owns and tends its own plots of land on the island, but . . . [company representative] says he would rather leave the cultivation and processing to the locals and stick to being a distributor. (*The Economist,* May 10, 2001, emphasis added)

Entre as técnicas repassadas pela empresa aos pequenos produtores, como os de [localidade], está a poda de antigas palmeiras de açaí, que apresentam baixa produtividade e oferecem riscos aos trabalhadores no momento da colheita da fruta. . . . Integrados à natureza, eles conhecem a hora que a direção da maré do rio se altera e os perigos da floresta, como o de encontrar uma onça no momento da colheita, mas desconhecem técnicas agrícolas que permitem aumentar a produção de açaí, palmeira típica da região amazônica. . . . "Antes disso, o produtor só via o pé de açaí na hora da colheita," diz [responsavel de extensão para uma companhia]. (*Agrofolha, Folha de São Paulo,* February 29, 2000)

Among the techniques disseminated by the company to small producers . . . is *the pruning of old açaí stems* that present low productivity and are risky to workers during fruit harvesting. . . . Integrated with nature, they know the hour and direction of tides and the dangers of the forest, such as confronting a jaguar during harvesting, *but they do not know agricultural techniques that increase açaí production,* a palm typical of the Amazon region. . . . "Before now, *the producer would only see the açaí tree during harvesting,*" says [an extension agent for the company]. (Author's translation and added emphasis)

These are just two examples portraying companies in agriculture technology extension as a key element and producers as ignorant of opportunities and needing to learn about açaí management. The examples just cited are from well-known sources; the latter is a respected agropastoral news supplement of a leading Brazilian newspaper. It is important to note that some of these companies are actually working toward offering new opportunities for producers, but the way this discourse is presented gives several misguided impressions. They emphasize *açaizais* as "native forest" while stressing the need to teach *caboclos* to manage them in order to increase production. This allows companies to stress their role in preserving biodiversity, but it reinforces açaí producers as extractivists. There is a pattern of emphasizing the need to "persuade" local residents to engage in açaí production and that producers—usually portrayed as playing a passive economic role—disbelieve their potential return. Interestingly, the so-called rational management techniques presented by companies and aimed at increasing productivity not only have been learned and practiced for decades but were developed by the very people to whom the companies are offering technical assistance (Anderson et al. 1985, Jardim and Anderson 1987, Hiraoka 1994, Brondízio 1996, Brondízio and Siqueira 1997).

Most arguments also give the impression of a fledgling economy that these companies are nurturing and helping to grow. However, if one takes a closer look (see IBGE data, for instance), a very different picture emerges. The production of açaí fruit has reached the current level of performance entirely through the initiative and efforts of riverine *caboclos* and their management techniques. Companies are building on a production system that has been established at its current level for at least two decades. Both commercial enterprises and the state government tend to forget that açaí fruit has been a leader in state agropastoral production for years without any support or technological assistance from extension agencies. One has only to look at the level and role of açaí consumption in Belém and Macapá, among other important urban centers, to understand the economic scope of the açaí fruit economy. Regarding the claim that riverine producers currently use "native forest" as the basis of production, one can easily say that if the forests they are currently using were truly native forests, the state of Pará would be achieving no more than 30 percent of its current production of açaí fruit. Indeed, management figures presented in this work and elsewhere indicate that "native forest" (unmanaged floodplain forest) produces meager amounts of açaí compared with managed areas. Palm heart companies, many of which usually make claims such as those presented earlier, actually wiped out thousands of hectares of *açaizais* throughout the estuary; some of these exploited areas are now being called "native forest."

It is likely that today's açaí export economy would not even exist if riverine farmers had not been managing *açaizais* intensively for decades and were simply relying on "native" areas. The development discourses from the private and government sectors include both misinformation and lack of knowledge about the region and the production system, as well as a sociocultural prejudice typical of the regional elite against riverine *caboclos*. Though perhaps well intentioned and tapping into a green market that yields support loans and an attractive merchandising strategy, these discourses reproduce a sociocultural bias that fails to recognize riverine *caboclos* as the legitimate leaders of the current açaí fruit boom. This bias contributes to the perpetuation of a cycle of differential access to important economic opportunities, such as bank loans, under the guise of "promoting sustainable development." The ones who form the very foundation of the açaí fruit economy—the riverine açaí producers— are portrayed as economically insensitive and technologically impoverished, as well as both helpful and in need of help. In this way, an already golden business opportunity becomes a social and environmental cause, thus yielding further marketing revenues for industries that espouse "conscious consumption" and use the sustainable development discourse. As the international market opens and competition increases, it remains to be seen whether this type of discourse will continue at the cost of portraying riverine producers erroneously.

SHIFTING CYCLES AND SHIFTING OPPORTUNITIES: A CONCEPTUAL MODEL TO EXPLAIN SHIFTING ECONOMIC RETURNS IN DIFFERENT PHASES OF A TROPICAL AGRARIAN ECONOMY

Figure 19.8 presents a conceptual model for a process of shifting cycles and shifting opportunities, or the shift in economic opportunities and returns in each development phase of a production system. In the context of development cycles of the açaí fruit production system, economic returns have increased significantly during the regional staple food expansion of açaí consumption, when the production base was growing and producers could benefit more directly from daily and seasonal fluctuations in fruit supply. In the first two decades of expansion of the açaí fruit economy, demand exceeded supply for most of the production season. However, IBGE production data indicate similar levels of production since 1990; in this decade, producers have found lower prices for most of the main production season (from September to December), when açaí

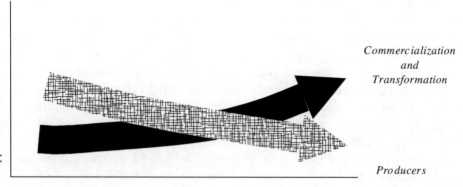

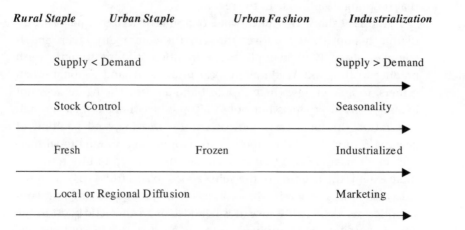

Figure 19.8 Conceptual model for shifting opportunities and economic returns in the açai fruit economy.

arrives from all corners of the estuary and the state of Maranhão. As the regional production base expanded (including to southern and western Amazonia), supply started to meet demand and even exceed it in particular seasonal periods. During this phase (e.g., the last ten years), profits shifted in favor of the processing and export sectors and, particularly, the transformation industry that controls storage and aggregation of value to derived products. While producers maintain a secure market, particularly in the northern region, profit opportunities narrow and harvesting decisions, negotiation with intermediaries and brokers, and transportation costs play a greater role in economic return for the producer. The bottleneck of infrastructure (on a basic level, storage and transportation, and at an advanced level, access to processing, industrial transformation, and retailing) constrains the participation of producers in the most profitable sectors of a booming economy based on the expansion of the national and international consumption bases. Producers in the estuarine region, though seeing some investments in pulp processing plants, are not taking full advantage of the profitable commercialization and transformation sectors but rather are staying with the raw material side of supply. Although the government is working with established industries, little has been done to build producer-controlled transformation industries and commercialization infrastructure. As described earlier, producers are "supported" in their position as extractivists who receive "help" from new participants, sometimes in the form of repackaged technology that has long been in use in the region.

Figure 19.9 shows the added value of açaí produced in 1 ha of the estuarine floodplain as it moves through the commodity chain and is commercialized in different places and in different forms, from the fresh product in the producers' lots to local rural towns and regional urban centers, to markets elsewhere in Brazil and abroad. The figure does not include derived products but only pulp products transformed through maceration (in some cases pasteurization), freezing, and addition of guaraná syrup.[4] From the producer to national and international markets, one hectare of açaí fruit may change in value up to fifty times. To some extent, the majority of the value added to açaí fruit is based on the fad value that is increasing promotion of the product to different consumption sectors. For instance, it is heralded as an energetic boost to the health conscious, as an antioxidant to the heart conscious, and as a sustainable development alternative to the environmentally conscious, making it an outstanding consumer product for the twenty-first century.

The prosperous Japanese community of Tomé-Açu offers an interesting contrast to and validation of this model. When they opened the market for Amazonian fruits in southern Brazil in the 1980s, their strategy was based on creating a processing industry in their area and distribution venues through their own cooperative. Two key differences can be noted: The role of their social organization in creating this infrastructure and the fact that they are respected as intensive producers and hard workers both helped to increase national and international support for their enterprise. The opposite can be said for riverine *caboclos,* whose attempts to establish collective forms of social organization have been historically undermined, for instance by forms of debt servitude and absentee land ownership; similarly, they continue to be seen as extractivists

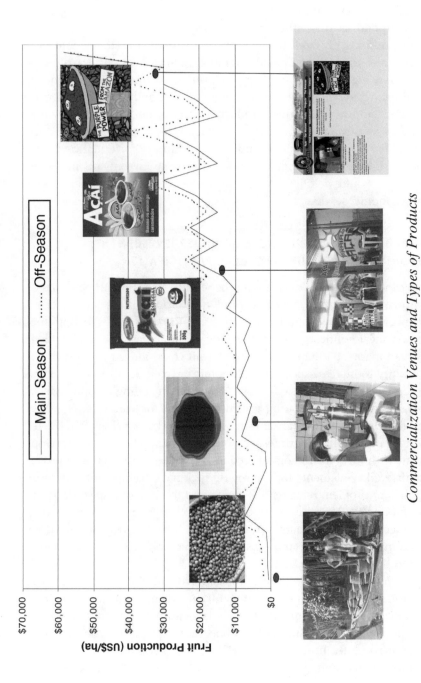

Figure 19.9 Adding value through the commodity chain for 1 ha equivalent of açaí fruit. Assumptions: Production is ~9000 kg/ha; average conversion of fruit to pulp is 1.9 kg/liter; prices are for the year 2000.

Commercialization Venues and Types of Products

taking advantage of "native forests," not as producers harvesting the products of their work. These are key underlying factors perpetuating regional underdevelopment and explaining their "inability" to engage in the high-end sectors of their production system.

In summary, the lack of infrastructure support for storage and processing and the lack of a broader agrarian policy to support transformation industries prevents riverine producers, and the region in general, from taking advantage of the booming national and international markets and industrializing their product. There has not been an economic phase as significant for the Amazon estuary as the current açaí fruit since the rubber economy;[5] this is a unique opportunity for estuarine towns and the population at large to call for large-scale investments in the region that would yield long-term improvements in their access to social and economic services.

OVERCOMING A VICIOUS CYCLE OF UNDERDEVELOPMENT: OPPORTUNITIES TO SUPPORT LOCAL PARTICIPATION

Estuarine towns and people are not benefiting from the full potential of a growing economy and will continue not to do so if the sociocultural, political, and infrastructure constraints are not addressed. Most producers and local politicians are enthusiastic about at least having the possibility of market participation, and açaí fruit could indeed provide an opportunity to increase social and economic development throughout the region. Yet regional socioeconomic indicators including income, education, infant mortality, youth prostitution, access to clean water, housing, and land tenure security are among several indices that show that the region is falling behind with respect to the basic aspects of social development. Although technological, economic, and infrastructure improvements are key elements for improving regional development, the most significant problem remains the stigma and the lack of respect for riverine producers. The açaí fruit economy is clearly the product of local knowledge of smallholders, but, conversely, it has helped reinforce their position as extractivists and subsistence forest dwellers who are insensitive to the regional market.

Regional improvements in agropastoral technology and processing are urgently needed but should be built on existing knowledge and carried out through the support of education and training, lines of credits, and storage and transformation cooperatives, among other services. Most importantly, however, political support is needed to overcome land tenure conflicts and provide access to credit incentives and basic infrastructure in order to develop commercialization infrastructure and high-end transformation industries that will generate jobs and increase the circulation of capital in the region.

There are several examples of promising developments, but they may not be adequate in the context (and scale) of the booming açaí fruit economy. Although some companies are locating their pulp processing plants in estuarine towns, it does not guarantee the participation of producers in high-revenue sectors, such as in distribution, commercialization, and transformation.

The initiative of Projeto Pobreza e Meio Ambiente na Amazônia (POEMA, an organization associated with the Federal University of Pará) in creating a type of "Amazonian stock market" and mediating direct commercialization between the production sector and international outlets shows promising results that, with support, could be reproduced throughout the region. Recently, POEMA reported the export of several tons of açaí pulp to Australia (Revista AgroAmazônia 2002 [http://www.revistaagroamazonia.com.br/index.htm]). The state of Amapá has been particularly aggressive in pursuing transformation industries and partnerships with international distributors in aggregating value to regional products. In the case of açaí fruit, the state has particularly promoted artisanal transformations that, though limited, may open opportunity for new industrial sectors to build partnerships with regional cooperatives.[6]

Infrastructure conditions, economic incentives, and support for social organization of the type that the new açaí fruit entrepreneurs are receiving from banks and government could help increase the share of the wealth generated by açaí fruit among local municipalities and riverine communities. Açaí producers are responsible for the palm fruit that has been transformed, through direct and indirect marketing, from a rural food item to an international fad, and they should be entitled to receive support to participate in its commercialization and transformation. This may help to break a continuous cycle of exporting the regional wealth—as raw material—at the expense of local labor and social development.

ACKNOWLEDGMENTS

This chapter benefits from long-term collaboration between numerous projects and research efforts by a large number of colleagues from Indiana University, Museu Paraense Emilio Goeldi, University of São Paulo, Embrapa-Cpatu, and Instituto Nacional de Pesquisas Espaciais since 1989. Research funds to colleagues and to the author include support from the National Science Foundation, Conselho Nacional de Desenvolvimento

Cientifico e Tecnologico, the National Aeronautics and Space Administration, the National Institute for the Study of Global Environmental Change, and the MacArthur Foundation. Most importantly, it benefits from the collaboration of açaí producers from Ponta de Pedras and other areas in the estuarine region and of friends and local institutions throughout these places. At Indiana University, enormous support from colleagues, staff, and students at the Anthropological Center for Training and Research on Global Environmental Change, the Department of Anthropology, and the Center for the Study of Institutions, Population and Environmental Change have been invaluable, particularly Amanda Evans, Patti Torp, Vonnie Peischl, and Sarah Mullin. I would like to acknowledge the invitation and motivation to write this chapter particularly from Daniel Zarin and Marianne Schmink. I would like to thank Andrea D. Siqueira, Michael Sauer, Thomas Ludwigs, and Ryan Adams for comments and suggestions and acknowledge the collaboration of Marcelo Brondízio Portela for his assistance and enthusiasm in visiting and interviewing a number of açaí shops in Sao Jose dos Campos and for his photos. The views expressed herein are the sole responsibility of the author.

NOTES

1. Estimates by IBGE actually are smaller than this figure; it is based on literature sources (Rogez 2000) and author estimates.

2. Economic return is related more to harvesting period than to total area production and productivity. One can compare data supporting this chapter with most of the figures presented in the literature. Jardim and Anderson (1987) calculated an average return (discounting cost of management) of US$235.2–371.5/ha/year for areas producing around 1158.8–1854.8 kg/ha/year. These figures are comparable to those for the unmanaged site. For an area producing around 2437.6 kg/ha/year, they estimate a return of US$504.6/ha/year, a figure comparable to that of some sites used in this research. Hiraoka's (1994) estimate of gross economic return was US$946/ha/year. This is a satisfactory estimate because it is intended to be an average return, thus placing it between those of intermediate and intensively managed sites. Muniz-Miret et al. (1996) found higher rates of return, particularly for sites managed less intensively, and point to strong variation in seasonal prices.

3. Owner–sharecropper relationships during the harvesting season are typified by a number of informal and formal rules in relation to harvesting periodicity and schedule, price, and transportation costs. It has become more common for owners to organize a general meeting with the sharecroppers to decide on these issues. Owners usually choose a starting date for harvesting that coincides with that of different sharecroppers working on the same property (Brondízio 1996).

4. Production cost is maintained at 30 percent throughout the chain. Research in this area is still in development, so this figure is merely illustrative;

published figures of production costs are still unavailable for new sectors entering this economy.

5. Some may argue that the logging boom after 1950s in parts of the estuary was equally important.

6. In my opinion, the most important contribution of the state of Amapá is the sociocultural valorization and acknowledgment of açaí producers (and others) to the state economy.

REFERENCES

Agrofolha. 2000. Açaí marajoara quer ganhar o mundo. Roberto Oliveira. *Agrofolha*, February 29, 2000, agricultural supplement.

Anderson, A. B. 1988. Use and management of native forests dominated by açaí palm (*Euterpe oleracea*) in the Amazon estuary. *Advances in Economic Botany* 6: 144–154.

Anderson, A. B., ed. 1990. *Alternatives to deforestation: Steps toward sustainable use of the Amazon rain forest*. New York: Columbia University Press.

Anderson, A. B., A. Gely, J. Sturdwick, G. L. Sobel, and M. das G. C. Purto. 1985. Um sistema agroforestal na várzea do estuário Amazônico (Ilha das Oncas, Municipio de Barcarena, Estado do Para). *Acta Amazônica* 15: 195–224.

Anderson, A. B and E. Ioris. 1992. The logic of extraction: Resource management and income generation by extractive producers in the Amazon estuary. In R. Kent and C. Padoch, eds., *Conservation of neotropical forests*, 175–199. New York: Columbia University Press.

Anderson, A. B. and M. A. G. Jardim. 1989. Costs and benefits of floodplain forest management by rural inhabitants in the Amazon estuary: A case study of açaí palm production. In J. O. Browder, ed., *Fragile lands of Latin America*, 114–129. Boulder, Colo.: Westview.

Boserup, E. 1965. *The conditions of agricultural growth: The economics of agrarian change under population pressure*. Chicago: Aldine.

Brondízio, E. S. 1996. *Forest farmers: Human and landscape ecology of* caboclo *populations in the Amazon estuary*. Ph.D. dissertation, Indiana University, Bloomington.

Brondízio, E. S. In press. Agricultural intensification, economic identity, and shared invisibility in Amazonian peasantry: *Caboclos* and colonists in comparative perspective. *Culture and Agriculture*.

Brondízio, E. S., E. F. Moran, P. Mausel, and Y. Wu. 1993. Dinamica na vegetacao do baixo Amazonas: Analise temporal do uso da terra integrando imagens Landsat TM, levantamentos florísticos, e etnograficos. *Anais do VII Simposio Brasileiro de Sensoriamento Remoto* 2: 38–46.

Brondízio, E., E. Moran, P. Mausel, and Y. Wu. 1994. Land use change in the Amazon estuary: Patterns of *caboclo* settlement and landscape management. *Human Ecology* 22: 249–278.

Brondízio, E. S., E. F. Moran, P. Mausel, and Y. Wu. 1996. Changes in land cover in the Amazon estuary: Integration of thematic mapper with botanical and historical data. *Photogrammetric Engineering and Remote Sensing* 62: 921–929.

Brondízio, E. S., C. Safar, and A. D. Siqueira. 2002. The urban market of açaí fruit (*Euterpe oleracea* Mart.) and rural land use change: Ethnographic insights into the role of price and land tenure constraining agricultural choices in the Amazon estuary. *Urban Ecosystems* 6: 67–97.

Brondízio, E. S. and A. D. Siqueira. 1997. From extractivists to forest farmers: Changing concepts of *caboclo* agroforestry in the Amazon estuary. *Research in Economic Anthropology* 18: 234–279.

Calzavara, B. B. G. 1972. As possibilidades do açaízeiro no estuario Amazonico. *Boletim Fundacao de Ciencias Agrarias do Pará* 5: 1–103.

The Economist. 2001. Managing the rainforests: Sustainable management could help to save the Amazonian rainforest without harming economic development. May 10, 2001. Online: http://www.economist.com.

Gourmet. 2002. Rainforest rarities. Vol. 62, July. Online: http://www.sambazon.com.

Hiraoka, M. 1994. The use and management of "Miriti" (*Mauritia flexuosa*): Palms among the ribeirinhos along the Amazon estuary. Paper presented at "Whitewater *Várzeas:* Diversity, Development and Conservation of Amazonian Floodplain," December 12–14, 1994, Macapa, Amapá, Brazil.

IBGE. 1974–2001. *Producao da extracao vegetal e da silvicultura.* Rio de Janeiro: Dept. Agropecuario, Diretoria de Pesquisas, Instituto Brasileiro de Geografia e Estatistica.

InStyle. 2002. Hip blips: What's on our radar this month. April. Online: http://www.sambazon.com.

Jardim, M. and A. Anderson. 1987. Manejo de populacoes nativas de açaízeiro no estuario Amazonico: Resultados preliminares. *Boletim de Pesquisa Florestal* 15: 1–18.

Lima, D. M. 1992. *History, social organization, identity and outsiders' social classification of the rural population of Amazonian region.* Unpublished Ph.D. dissertation, King's College, Cambridge, U.K.

Moran, E. F., P. Mausel, and E. S. Brondízio. 1994. Secondary succession and land use in the Amazon. *National Geographic Research & Exploration* 10: 456–476.

Muniz-Miret, N., R. Vamos, M. Hiraoka, F. Montagnini, and R. O. Mendelsohn. 1996. The economic value of managing the açaí palm (*Euterpe oleracea* Mart.) in the floodplains of the Amazon estuary, Pará, Brazil. *Forest Ecology and Management* 87: 163–173.

Murrieta, R. S. 1994. *Diet and subsistence: Changes in three caboclo populations on Marajo Island, Amazonia, Brazil.* Unpublished master's dissertation, University of Colorado, Boulder.

Nugent, S. 1993. *Amazonian caboclo society: An essay on invisibility and peasant economy.* Province, Oxford, U.K.: BERG.

Pace, R. 1998. *The struggle for Amazon Town: Gurupa revisited.* Boulder, Colo.: Lynne Rienner Publishers.

Parker, E. 1985. Caboclization: The transformation of the Amerindian in Amazonia, 1615–1800. *Studies in Third World Societies* 29: xvii–li.

Poulet, D. 1998. *Açaí: Estudo da cadeia produtiva, fruto e palmito.* Macapá, Brazil: Governo do Estado do Amapá.

Rogez, H. 2000. *Açaí: Preparo, composição e melhoramento da conservação.* Belém, Brazil: Editora da Universidade Federal do Pará.

Roosevelt, A. C. 1991. *Moundbuilders of the Amazon: The geophysical archeology on Marajo Island, Brazil.* San Diego, Calif.: Academic Press.

Siqueira, A. D. 1997. *The ecology of food and nutrition among caboclo populations in the Amazon estuary.* Ph.D. dissertation, Indiana University, Bloomington.

Strudwick, J. and G. L. Sobel. 1988. Uses of *Euterpe oleracea* in the Amazon estuary, Brazil. *Advances in Economic Botany* 6: 225–253.

Wallace, A. R. 1853. *Palm trees of the Amazon and their uses.* London: J. Van Voorst.

Chapter 20

THE HOMOGEOCENE IN PUERTO RICO

Ariel E. Lugo

Biologists fear the Homogeocene, the era when humans dominate the biosphere (McKinney and Lockwood 1999, Lockwood and McKinney 2001), because it signals a drastic reduction in biodiversity and a homogenized biota with little resemblance to the conditions we experience today (Putz 1997, 1998). Although there are differences of opinion on how human activity leads to species homogenization (Lugo 2001), there is agreement that human activity causes changes in species composition of forests. McKinney and Lockwood (1999) base their argument for global homogenization on a faster rate of extinction of rare species than the rate of invasion of globally common species. This results in a lower total number of species, a loss of endemic species, and a high proportion of weedy species. In equation form, they propose the following (numbers are percentages of all species):

$$-50 \text{ in extinction} + (2 \text{ invasive} + 29 \text{ expansion}$$
$$\text{of natives} + 1 \text{ domestic species}) = -18. \qquad (20.1)$$

We can test these notions of the Homogeocene and preview the future by examining places in the world where conditions today are what they are expected to be elsewhere in the future. One such place is Puerto Rico, a Caribbean island whose history and current conditions approach those expected of much of the world during the Homogeocene. The following attributes qualify Puerto Rico as a place where the Homogeocene is already the present:

- Its landscape has experienced an almost total deforestation with subsequent forest recovery (Birdsey and Weaver 1982).

- About 15 percent of the land is urbanized (López et al. 2001).
- Human density exceeds 450 people/km^2, with a standard of living and per capita energy consumption that are among the highest in Latin America.
- Alien species make up a significant fraction of the total species complement of the island's biodiversity (e.g., more than 20 percent of the flora).
- The economy depends mostly on outside subsidies for its food, energy, and goods (Scatena et al. 2002). This means that human activity is so intense that the island cannot support its basic needs without significant outside help. For example, almost 100 percent of the energy and food consumed on the island are imported.

Few places in the world have such intensity of human activity and high dependency on external anthropogenic inputs to maintain its economy. Moreover, the island has a mature flora with more than 100 million years of evolution (Graham 1996). Unlike young islands in the Pacific such as Hawaii (about 5 million years old), the long evolutionary history of Caribbean biota offers a measure of resistance to invasion by aliens. Human habitation over millennia influences the ecological context of Caribbean islands, but the indigenous people, their language, and their culture are all gone with the exception of a community of Caribbean Indians in Dominica. Today, Puerto Rican culture is a mixture of African, Spanish, and North American elements interacting in synergy, harmony, or conflict depending on the social circumstances.

My objective is to assess the degree to which expectations about the Homogeocene might occur as the intensity of human activity increases. I will examine this issue in the context of Puerto Rico.

HAS PUERTO RICO EXPERIENCED HOMOGENIZATION OF ITS FLORA?

Forest areas where pantropical species dominate or codominate stands have expanded in Puerto Rico, especially because small-seeded species colonize abandoned agriculture and pasture lands. However, the island has not experienced a sufficiently large extinction event (Brash 1984, Lugo 1988, Figueroa Colón 1996) to reduce the number of rare and endemic species. Presumably, the island avoided mass extinctions because agricultural clearing did not simultaneously extend over the entire landscape. Nevertheless, Puerto Rico lost 99 percent of its primary forests and at one time had only about 10 percent forest cover (including shade coffee, Murphy 1916), but only a small fraction of the species have gone extinct.

Summaries of flora and fauna from Puerto Rico show increases in the number of species of plants (Liogier and Martorell 1982), trees (Little et al. 1974, Francis and Liogier 1991), orchids (Ackerman 1992), ferns (Proctor 1989), birds (Brash 1984, Raffaele 1989), earthworms (Borges 1996), and ants (Torres and Snelling 1997). Instead of homogenization, in the sense that generalists cause native species extinctions, Puerto Rico experienced an increase in the total number of species in the island. Moreover, the number of species per unit area and the species diversity of forest stands dominated by alien species is similar to those of native forest stands (Aide et al. 1995, 2000).

Some alien species may even complement native flora through their ability to colonize new environments that humans create—environments that native species invade more slowly or cannot invade. For example, *Cecropia schreberiana,* a native colonizer, does not invade abandoned pastures (Brokaw 1998). In contrast, several alien species, such as *Syzygium jambos, Albizia procera, Prosopis juliflora,* and *Spathodea campanulata,* readily colonize pastures and reestablish forest conditions that allow native species to grow and then coexist with alien species in the resulting new forest ecosystems (Wadsworth and Birdsey 1985, Lugo et al. 1993, Lugo 1997, Parrotta and Turnbull 1997, Chinea 2002). Consequently, some alien species may decrease the extinction likelihood of native flora. An important question is, How many additional native species will eventually reestablish in stands that alien species currently dominate?

Homogenization of flora and fauna will occur—even in the absence of species extinctions—when humans or natural forces homogenize the conditions for plant growth, as plowing did in New England. Plowing changed the soil profile and favored certain species such as pitch pine, essentially homogenizing their distribution over the landscape (Motzkin et al. 1996, Fuller et al. 1998). This observation suggests an alternative definition of species homogenization, that is, the expansion of total land area where globally common species are locally abundant at the expense of the total area inhabited by globally rare endemic species.

Pantropical alien species will expand in proportion to the formation of suitable habitat (Cousens and Mortimer 1995), particularly when these habitats are not suitable for native species. Large areas of these habitats will cause local homogenization of flora. Furthermore, large areas that generalist species dominate, by homogenizing landscapes and regions, may result in ecologically vulnerable landscapes and regions, where a homogeneous forest cover is more vulnerable to natural disturbances, pests, and pathogens. However, if the new habitats are fragmented, dispersed, and small enough to sustain native species, their formation can enrich native flora and increase the variety of ecosystem types on the landscape. As long as growth conditions are diverse, natural processes guide the development of new forests, and their novel combinations of species maintain overall diversity (Lugo and Helmer in press).

WHAT IS THE STATUS OF THE HOMOGEOCENE BIOTA IN PUERTO RICO?

Human activity has resulted in dramatic changes of the landscape and biota of Puerto Rico over the past 500 years. Briefly, an essentially 100 percent forested island was converted to an almost 100 percent cover of agricultural systems in the early 1900s (Roberts 1942). This landscape is now urbanizing (15 percent), with 40 percent forest cover (López et al. 2001). Forest fragmentation was also dynamic, with periods of intense fragmentation (Lugo 2002). The degree of forest fragmentation in the 1990s was lower than in previous decades of the twentieth century, when forest cover was much lower (Lugo 2002). The forest area increase is part of an island-wide process of forest expansion and defragmentation after abandonment of agricultural lands (Rudel et al. 2000). The secondary forests that developed during this expansion, along with forests that fragmentation affected, include Puerto Rico's new forests. Alien species are among the dominant species in these postagricultural forest stands, and their dominance ranges from about 10 to about 50 percent, depending on the level of human influence.

The biota of Puerto Rico formed new ecosystems after the abandonment of a variety of land uses (Lugo and Helmer in press). These new forest ecosystems are regenerating naturally in Puerto Rico under many conditions, including

- Abandoned pastures (Aide et al. 1995, 1996, 2000, Chinea and Helmer 2003)
- Active and abandoned coffee plantations (Birdsey and Weaver 1982, Franco et al. 1997, Rivera and Aide 1998, Rudel et al. 2000, Marcano-Vega et al. 2002)
- Abandoned sugarcane, tobacco, and other crop lands (Thomlinson et al. 1996, Rudel et al. 2000, Chinea 2002)
- Abandoned subsistence agriculture (Molina Colón 1998)
- Abandoned human habitation (Molina Colón 1998)
- Abandoned roads, even those with pavement (Heyne 1999)

Structurally, these new forests are less developed than native forests, and their rates of aboveground biomass accumulation, tree growth per unit area, and soil carbon accumulation are slower (Silver et al. 2000). Many of the large trees in the new forests were protected by humans because they were useful, such as large mango trees. However, even after sixty to eighty years of succession, the number of trees with more than 70 cm diameter at breast height is lower in new forests throughout Puerto Rico than in mature native stands, and predicting the amount of time for predisturbance large size classes to appear is difficult. The species composition of new forests is different from those of native forests, and species turnover is faster (Aide et al. 1996). Nevertheless, thirty to sixty years after abandonment, the richness of tree species and the species diversity in new forests is similar to that of mature native forests. New forests contain a larger fraction of alien species and a lower fraction of endemic species than their native counterparts.

New forests occur in Puerto Rico because native species apparently cannot compete with alien species during early succession or cannot regenerate under the degraded conditions of abandoned agricultural lands (Zimmerman et al. 2000). Limited seed sources and the absence of dispersal agents may also inhibit native species establishment, thus leading to arrested succession (Wunderle 1997). New forests slowly rehabilitate soil conditions in these sites, reestablish a forest environment, and facilitate the reestablishment of native species (Wadsworth and Birdsey 1985). However, after sixty to eighty years of growth, alien species remain in stands, albeit in lower abundance, and continue to function as part of new ecosystems.

MATURE NEW FORESTS

A mature forest stand is one whose structural state variables (basal area, tree density, biomass) and processes (primary productivity, nutrient cycling) approach steady state values. The time needed for mature forest establishment after land abandonment probably is a function of the level of degradation (Aide et al. 1995, 2000, Silver et al. 2000) but could also derive from fragmentation-induced lack of seed sources. In some successions, trees do not regenerate unless planted. My focus is on succession on lands abandoned after agricultural use where alien species are capable of invading the damaged lands (Chinea 1992, Molina Colón 1998). However, even if alien species have advantages over natives on degraded lands, life history characteristics determine the success of species rather than their designation as alien (Aide et al. 2000, Zimmerman et al. 2000).

In all available examples from Puerto Rico, studies of forest succession document that mature forests develop sixty to eighty years after abandonment (figure 2 in Aide et al. 1996, figure 3 in Aide et al. 2000, figure

3 in Marcano-Vega et al. 2002, figure 2 in Silver et al. 2000, Molina Colón 1998). These forests develop different levels of species richness, basal area, biomass, and wood volume at maturity but retain alien species. *Syzygium jambos,* an alien species, invades mature native forest stands after disturbance and prevails in the recovered stands (Smith 1970, Figueroa Colón et al. 1984, Lugo 1992, Aide et al. 1996, 2000).

WORKING FORESTS IN THE HOMOGEOCENE

The Puerto Rico case study shows that dramatic change will occur in the biota of the Homogeocene. Regardless of the level of species extinctions, the establishment of alien plant and animal species resulted in the formation of new forest types with a different mix of species composition. Puerto Rico today has more types of forests and more species of plants and animals than it did in the past. However, the new forests that form after human abandonment of land have species diversity and species per unit area similar to that of undisturbed native forests, and they favor the reestablishment of native species in places where they otherwise could not grow. Studies of these forests show that their biotic activity is resulting in the recovery of forest biomass and soil structure, chemistry, and organic matter (Silver et al. 2000), and they have conservation value for ecotourism and other ecosystem services, including watershed protection and carbon sequestration. Thus new forests are working forests.

New forests are different from the native forests they replace because they grow on sites degraded by human activity. The differences in species composition and ecological attributes between new forests and native ones are the cost of land degradation. We need to learn about the processes of land rehabilitation that occur when new forests develop on abandoned lands. Of particular importance is nutrient cycling in relation to the reversal of soil degradation and the relationship of these processes to the regeneration of native species and diversification of forest stands. The 100-year experience in the development of new forest stands in Puerto Rico leaves no doubt that the path to recovery of vegetation and soils after human degradation is through new forests dominated by alien species. As human activity continues to increase the pressure on lands for products and services, working forests will be new forests.

A WORD OF CAUTION

I reported only on basic structural, functional, and compositional attributes of forests recovering from agricultural clearing in Puerto Rico. Much information on important structural, functional, and compositional characteristics is missing from this analysis. When new species invade a landscape, they have numerous postarrival impacts (Ewel et al. 1999), most of which we do not understand. In addition, we know that alien animal species can reduce native wildlife populations to the point of endangerment, especially when alien impacts combine with habitat loss and spread of alien diseases. A need exists for research on the long-term effects of the high density of alien species in this landscape. However, the Puerto Rico case study illustrates the complexity of response of the biota to human activity. The analysis cautions against broad generalizations and suggests that the biota are resilient and capable of sustaining species diversity at the landscape scale under intense human pressure.

ACKNOWLEDGMENTS

This study has been conducted in collaboration with the University of Puerto Rico (UPR). It is part of the U.S. Department of Agriculture (USDA) Forest Service contribution to the National Science Foundation Long-Term Ecological Research Program at the Luquillo Experimental Forest (Grant BSR-8811902 to the Institute for Tropical Ecosystem Studies of the UPR and the International Institute of Tropical Forestry, USDA Forest Service) and the National Aeronautics and Space Administration Institutional Research Award (Grant NAG8-1709, under UPR subcontract 00-CO-11120105-011). I thank G. Reyes, G. Sánchez, and M. Alayón for their help in manuscript preparation and S. Brown, B. Bryan, C. Domínguez Cristóbal, J. J. Ewel, G. González, E. Helmer, R. Ostertag, F. N. Scatena, J. M. Wunderle, and two anonymous reviewers for their review of the manuscript.

REFERENCES

Ackerman, J. D. 1992. *The orchids of Puerto Rico and the Virgin Islands.* Río Piedras: University of Puerto Rico Press.

Aide, T. M., J. K. Zimmerman, L. Herrera, M. Rosario, and M. Serrano. 1995. Forest recovery in abandoned tropical pastures in Puerto Rico. *Forest Ecology and Management* 77: 77–86.

Aide, T. M., J. K. Zimmerman, J. B. Pascarella, L. Rivera, and H. Marcano-Vega. 2000. Forest regeneration in a chronosequence of tropical abandoned pastures: Implications for restoration. *Restoration Ecology* 8: 328–338.

Aide, T. M., J. K. Zimmerman, M. Rosario, and H. Marcano. 1996. Forest recovery in abandoned cattle pastures along an elevational gradient in northeastern Puerto Rico. *Biotropica* 28: 537–548.

Birdsey, R. A. and P. L. Weaver. 1982. *The forest resources of Puerto Rico.* USDA Forest Service Resources Bulletin no. SO-85. New Orleans: Southern Forest Experiment Station.

Borges, S. 1996. The terrestrial oligochaetes of Puerto Rico. *Annals of the New York Academy of Sciences* 776: 239–248.

Brash, A. R. 1984. *Avifauna reflections of historical landscape ecology in Puerto Rico.* New Haven, Conn.: Tropical Resources Institute, Yale University.

Brokaw, N. V. L. 1998. *Cecropia schreberiana* in the Luquillo Mountains of Puerto Rico. *The Botanical Review* 64: 91–120.

Chinea, J. D. 1992. *Invasion dynamics of the exotic legume tree* Albizia procera *(Roxb.) Benth., in Puerto Rico.* Ph.D. dissertation, Cornell University, Ithaca, N.Y.

Chinea, J. D. 2002. Tropical forest succession on abandoned farms in the Humacao Municipality of eastern Puerto Rico. *Forest Ecology and Management* 167: 195–207.

Chinea, J. D. and E. H. Helmer. 2003. Diversity and composition of tropical secondary forests recovering from large-scale clearing: Results from the 1990 inventory in Puerto Rico. *Forest Ecology and Management* 180: 227–240.

Cousens, R. and M. Mortimer. 1995. *Dynamics of weed populations.* Cambridge, U.K.: Cambridge University Press.

Ewel, J. J., D. J. O'Dowd, J. Bergelson, C. C. Daehler, C. M. D'Antonio, L. D. Gómez, D. R. Gordon, R. J. Hobbs, A. Holt, K. R. Hooper, C. E. Hughes, M. LaHart, R. R. B. Leakey, W. G. Lee, L. L. Loope, D. H. Lorence, S. M. Louda, A. E. Lugo, P. B. McEvoy, D. M. Richardson, and P. M. Vitousek. 1999. Deliberate introductions of species: Research needs. *BioScience* 49: 619–630.

Figueroa Colón, J. 1996. Phytogeographical trends, centers of high species richness and endemism, and the question of species extinctions in the native flora of Puerto Rico. *Annals of the New York Academy of Sciences* 776: 89–102.

Figueroa Colón, J., L. Totti, A. E. Lugo, and R. O. Woodbury. 1984. *Structure and composition of moist coastal forests in Dorado, Puerto Rico.* Southern Forest Experiment Station Research Paper no. SO-202. New Orleans: USDA Forest Service.

Francis, J. K. and H. A. Liogier. 1991. *Naturalized exotic tree species in Puerto Rico.* USDA Forest Service General Technical Report no. SO-82. New Orleans: Southern Forest Experiment Station.

Franco, P. A., P. L. Weaver, and S. Eggen McIntosh. 1997. *Forest resources of Puerto Rico, 1990.* USDA Forest Service Resources Bulletin no. SRS-22. Asheville, N.C.: Southern Forest Experiment Station.

Fuller, J. L., D. R. Foster, J. S. McLachlan, and N. Drake. 1998. Impact of human activity on regional forest composition and dynamics in central New England. *Ecosystems* 1: 76–95.

Graham, A. 1996. Paleobotany of Puerto Rico: From Arthur Hollick's (1928) scientific survey paper to the present. *Annals of the New York Academy of Sciences* 776: 103–114.

Heyne, C. M. 1999. *Soil and vegetation recovery on abandoned paved roads in a humid tropical rain forest, Puerto Rico.* Master's thesis, University of Nevada, Las Vegas.

Liogier, A. and G. Martorell. 1982. *Flora of Puerto Rico and adjacent islands: A systematic synopsis.* Río Piedras: University of Puerto Rico Press.

Little, E. L., R. O. Woodbury, and F. H. Wadsworth. 1974. *Trees of Puerto Rico and the Virgin Islands,* Vol. 2. Washington, D.C.: USDA Forest Service Agriculture Handbook 449.

Lockwood, J. L. and M. L. McKinney. 2001. *Biotic homogenization.* New York: Kluwer Academic/Plenum.

López, M. T. del, T. M. Aide, and J. R. Thomlinson. 2001. Urban expansion and the loss of prime agricultural lands in Puerto Rico. *Ambio* 30: 49–54.

Lugo, A. E. 1988. Estimating reductions in the diversity of tropical forest species. In E. O. Wilson and F. M. Peter, eds., *Biodiversity,* 58–70. Washington, D.C.: National Academy Press.

Lugo, A. E. 1992. Comparison of tropical tree plantations with secondary forests of similar age. *Ecological Monographs* 62: 1–41.

Lugo, A. E. 1997. The apparent paradox of re-establishing species richness on degraded lands with tree monocultures. *Forest Ecology and Management* 99: 9–19.

Lugo, A. E. 2001. El manejo de la biodiversidad en el siglo XXI. *Interciencia* 26: 2–10.

Lugo, A. E. 2002. Can we manage tropical landscapes? An answer from the Caribbean perspective. *Landscape Ecology* 17: 601–615.

Lugo, A. E. and E. Helmer. In press. Emerging forests on abandoned land: Puerto Rico's new forests. *Forest Ecology and Management.*

Lugo, A. E., J. A. Parrotta, and S. Brown. 1993. Loss of species caused by tropical deforestation and their recovery through management. *Ambio* 22: 106–109.

Marcano-Vega, H., T. M. Aide, and D. Báez. 2002. Forest regeneration in abandoned coffee plantations and pastures in the Cordillera Central of Puerto Rico. *Plant Ecology* 161: 75–87.

McKinney, M. L. and J. L. Lockwood. 1999. Biotic homogenization: A few winners replacing many losers in the next mass extinction. *Trends in Ecology and Evolution* 14: 450–452.

Molina Colón, S. 1998. *Long-term recovery of a Caribbean dry forest after abandonment of different land-uses in Guánica, Puerto Rico.* Ph.D. dissertation, University of Puerto Rico, Río Pedras.

Motzkin, G., D. R. Foster, A. Allen, J. Harrod, and R. Boone. 1996. Controlling site to evaluate history: Vegetation patterns of a New England sand plain. *Ecological Monographs* 66: 345–365.

Murphy, L. S. 1916. *Forests of Puerto Rico: Past, present and future and their physical and economic environment.* USDA Bulletin no. 354. Washington, D.C.: U.S. Government Printing Office.

Parrotta, J. A. and J. W. Turnbull, eds. 1997. Catalyzing native forest regeneration on degraded tropical lands. *Forest Ecology and Management* 99: 1–290.

Proctor, G. R. 1989. Ferns of Puerto Rico and the Virgin Islands. *Memoirs of the New York Botanical Gardens* 53: 1–389.

Putz, F. E. 1997. Florida's forests in the year 2020 and deeper into the Homogeocene. *Journal of the Public Interest Environmental Conference* 1: 91–97.

Putz, F. E. 1998. Halt the Homogeocene, a frightening future filled with too few species. *The Palmetto* 18: 7–10.

Raffaele, H. A. 1989. *A guide to the birds of Puerto Rico and the Virgin Islands.* Princeton, N.J.: Princeton University Press.

Rivera, L. W. and T. M. Aide. 1998. Forest recovery in the karst region of Puerto Rico. *Forest Ecology and Management* 108: 63–75.

Roberts, R. C. 1942. *Soil survey of Puerto Rico.* USDA Series 1936, no. 8. Washington, D.C.: U.S. Government Printing Office.

Rudel, T. K., M. Pérez Lugo, and H. Zichal. 2000. When fields revert to forest: Development and spontaneous reforestation in post-war Puerto Rico. *Professional Geographer* 52: 186–397.

Scatena, F. N., S. J. Doherty, H. T. Odum, and P. Kharecha. 2002. *An EMERGY evaluation of Puerto Rico and the Luquillo Experimental Forest.* General Technical Report no. IITF-GTR-9. Río Piedras, Puerto Rico: USDA Forest Service, International Institute of Tropical Forestry.

Silver, W. L., R. Ostertag, and A. E. Lugo. 2000. The potential for carbon sequestration through reforestation of abandoned tropical agricultural pasture lands. *Restoration Ecology* 8: 394–407.

Smith, R. F. 1970. The vegetation structure of a Puerto Rican rain forest before and after short-term gamma irradiation. In H. T. Odum and R. F. Pigeon, eds., *A tropical rain forest.* Chapter D-3. Springfield, Va.: National Technical Information Services.

Thomlinson, J. R., M. I. Serrano, T. del M. López, T. M. Aide, and J. K. Zimmerman. 1996. Land-use dynamics in a post-agricultural Puerto Rican landscape (1936–1988). *Biotropica* 28: 525–536.

Torres, J. A. and R. R. Snelling. 1997. Biogeography of Puerto Rican ants: A nonequilibrium case? *Biodiversity and Conservation* 6: 1103–1121.

Wadsworth, F. H. and R. A Birdsey. 1985. A new look at the forests of Puerto Rico. *Turrialba* 35: 11–17.

Wunderle, J. M. Jr. 1997. The role of animal seed dispersal in accelerating native forest regeneration on degraded tropical lands. *Forest Ecology and Management* 99: 223–235.

Zimmerman, J. K., J. B. Pascarella, and T. M. Aide. 2000. Barriers to forest regeneration in an abandoned pasture in Puerto Rico. *Restoration Ecology* 8: 350–360.

PART IV

Envisioning a Future for Sustainable Tropical Forest Management

CONVENTIONAL WISDOM ABOUT SUSTAINABLE FOREST MANAGEMENT AND A PRO-POOR FOREST AGENDA

David Kaimowitz

Conventional wisdom is a funny thing. We hear some ideas so many times that they end up seeming almost self-evident. This is particularly common when those ideas make a certain amount of intuitive sense. With understandable complacency, we often fail to ask ourselves about the evidence for this conventional wisdom.

The previous statement definitely applies to the case of the conventional wisdom about sustainable forest management in tropical countries. Many people in the forestry community have repeated the same ideas for so long that everyone simply assumes they are true, but they may not be. I suggest we need to think about them more critically, especially when this conventional wisdom is used to justify giving control over public forests to small groups of wealthy people rather than the large numbers of communities and smallholders that might otherwise benefit from them.

Many policies designed to promote sustainable forest management have failed to achieve that goal and are unlikely to do so. In the meantime, they end up giving access to public forests, which belong to the entire nation, to large companies rather than to poor people. The point is neither that sustainable forest management is impossible nor that large logging companies are bad. Rather that we should rethink policies that generally lead to discrimination against poor people, smallholders, and local communities in the name of sustainable forest management (Stone and D'Andrea 2001).

Much of the conventional wisdom about appropriate policies for promoting sustainable tropical forest management revolves around the following six recommendations (Repetto and Gillis 1988, World Bank 1992):

- Remove trade barriers that lower timber prices.
- Auction concessions and increase stumpage fees.
- Promote more efficient technologies to avoid waste.
- Require management plans prepared by foresters.
- Use performance bonds or similar mechanisms to guarantee high-quality management.
- Provide long-term tenure security to large-scale forest concessions.

At first glance these recommendations seem to make sense. But is there any evidence that such policies promote sustainable forest management?

The underlying logic behind these six basic ideas is the following. Companies that have secure tenure will manage their forests with a long-term perspective. They will stop mining the resource for short-term gain and start thinking about the second, third, and fourth rotations. Higher timber prices resulting from the removal of trade barriers, competitive bidding for forest concessions, and increased stumpage fees will lead to fewer trees being logged. More efficient technologies will have the same effect because if companies use trees more efficiently they will not have to use so many of them, which will save forests. Formal management plans will allow companies to manage their forests sustainably. To make sure companies follow those plans, they must be regulated. Performance bonds can ensure that they follow those regulations. If all these things are true, then the six proposed policies should help us achieve sustainable forest management.

Although not always stated explicitly, the conventional wisdom implies forests are best left in the hands of large companies. Furthermore, the proposed policies are to a large extent suitable only for large companies. For example, most small farmers and local communities cannot afford to hire professional foresters to prepare management plans. In most parts of the world, the only small farmers or communities that have prepared management plans did so with external financial support; unfortunately, once the projects ended, so did the communities' abilities to prepare management plans. With only a few exceptions, including some Mexican forest *ejidos,* it is difficult to imagine where most small farmers or communities might get the money to hire professional foresters to prepare management plans for them.

In any case, the thirty- or forty-year cutting cycles with annual cutting blocks that most management plans (and forestry laws) demand require larger areas than smallholders typically possess. Furthermore, serious regulatory efforts based on examining how individual management plans are implemented on the ground are nearly impossible if you have large numbers of scattered and dispersed small-scale producers, as applies to most situations involving smallholder and community forestry. Also, small producers and communities tend to use less efficient technologies than large companies. Not too many smallholders are likely to bid for blocks of forest at auctions or put up million-dollar performance bonds (Karsenty 2000). If we accept the conventional wisdom, then, it appears that communities, smallholders, and indigenous people are not the most likely groups to achieve sustainable forest management.

But the conventional wisdom is flawed on several accounts. First, secure tenure is neither a necessary nor a sufficient condition for sustainable forest management. Second, in many situations more efficient production is as likely to increase pressure on forests as to reduce it. Third, in addition to encouraging companies to use timber more efficiently, higher timber prices are likely to increase demand for logs, promoting increased supply (i.e., more logging). Fourth, just because one prepares a formal management plan does not necessarily ensure that one will actually manage forests sustainably. Fifth, serious regulation of large companies or small companies is not realistic in most tropical countries for the foreseeable future, and systems that ultimately rely on national governments regulating effectively are likely to fail.

FLAW #1: SECURE TENURE WILL FACILITATE BETTER MANAGEMENT

Except for a small fraction of companies that sell certified forest products to niche markets, managing natural tropical forests sustainably is rarely as financially profitable as rapid and uncontrolled logging (Pearce et al. 2002). In some cases it is profitable to adopt specific reduced-impact logging practices, but sustainable forest management as an overall package is rarely the most financially attractive option.

Under most circumstances, then, companies practice sustainable forest management in natural tropical forests only if regulators make them do so. Those regulators may be either government agencies or private certifiers. If it is more profitable for the companies to comply with the regulations than not to, they will do so whether or not they have long-term tenure. If it is not, they probably will not.

Giving companies long-term tenure is not likely to significantly affect their decisions about what management practices to implement because most large industrial companies significantly discount the future. As a result, revenue that might come twenty or thirty years from now is not going to have a major impact on their decisions about what technologies or practices to adopt. Companies with ten, twenty, forty, or a thousand years of tenure will do exactly the same thing (Boscolo and Vincent 1998).

With serious regulation, sustainable forest management can be achieved without secure tenure. Without serious regulation, sustainable forest management cannot be achieved, even with secure tenure (Walker and Smith 1999).

The main effect of giving large companies long-term tenure over public forests is to perpetuate their monopolistic control over large areas of forests that should be used for the public interest. Recently in Indonesia a number of well-intentioned policy analysts lobbied the government to give large companies long-term tenure security over their forest concessions. Doing that would have guaranteed that indigenous people and local communities with legitimate claims to large parts of these forests would never get access to them because the companies would already have legally binding documents giving them exclusive rights to the forest. Similar issues have arisen in recent years in Bolivia. In many cases long-term forest concessions simply perpetuate government handouts to large companies.

FLAW #2: INCREASED EFFICIENCY WILL DECREASE PRESSURE ON FORESTS

It sounds nice when we say that less waste means more forests. But what does less waste actually mean in practice? Sometimes it implies recycling paper and other products, which in principle could lead to less pressure on forest resources. Putting recycled paper on the market depresses the price of paper, which would make it less profitable to log natural forests to produce pulp.

Often, however, the story is the opposite. More efficient technologies usually increase the profitability of logging, which may encourage more logging both by making it more profitable compared with other possible investments and by providing the capital to finance the expansion.

More efficient wood processing technologies often allow the profitable use of smaller-diameter timber and species that previously had no commercial value. The changes can make it financially viable to log where it was not previously profitable to do so and to reenter and log areas that previously were of little commercial interest. Such changes are likely to put more pressure on forests, not reduce it. The history of forestry over the last two hundred years demonstrates that as technology has improved, more and more forest has become profitable to log (Sayer et al. 1997, Vincent 1998). For example, many Indonesian ply-wood mills now use wood more "efficiently" than in the past. Now they can profitably process 20- or 30-cm logs as opposed to the 40- to 50-cm logs they used in the past. This change has not led to sustainable man-agement. It simply means that they can now go back and profitably reen-ter areas that have only small-diameter timber (Barr 2001).

FLAW #3: HIGHER TIMBER PRICES WILL STIMULATE MORE SUSTAINABLE FOREST MANAGEMENT

Convention wisdom has it that higher timber prices are likely to result in better management of natural forests in the tropics. Nevertheless, none of the publications that promote this idea provide empirical evi-dence to support it. Instead, substantial evidence suggests that higher timber prices lead to greater logging in natural forests (Barbier et al. 1995, von Amsberg 1994). As long as unsustainable logging remains more profitable than sustainable forest management, higher timber prices will lead to more logging, not to sustainable forest management. It is worth noting that higher timber prices do not change the relative profitability of unsustainable forest management and sustainable forest management.

Why does conventional wisdom not suggest that if we have higher-priced logs, we will get more logging and that will lead to greater pres-sure on the forests? There are two reasons. The first is related to the effi-ciency idea discussed earlier. Proponents of this conventional wisdom argue that higher-priced timber will stimulate the use of more efficient technologies, and that will lead to less pressure on forests. They are right that higher timber prices are likely to encourage the adoption of more ef-ficient technologies. Unfortunately, as noted earlier, that will not neces-sarily lead to less pressure on forests.

The second argument is that higher prices will lead to more sustain-able forest management because they will make companies more con-cerned about the second, third, and fourth rotations because the value of timber produced in the future will be higher. Conceptually that makes a lot of sense. In practice, however, given the high discount rates of most companies operating in the tropics, they are likely to have little com-mitment beyond the first rotation even if timber prices rise substantially above their current levels (Karsenty 2000). Any simple exercise with a fi-nancial spreadsheet and discount rates higher than 2 or 3 percent is like-ly to confirm this conclusion.

FLAW #4: IF COMPANIES FOLLOWED THEIR FORMAL MANAGEMENT PLANS, SUSTAINABILITY WOULD BE GUARANTEED

It makes an awful lot of sense for companies to think through how they are going to manage their forests and put that down on paper. They should seriously consider where to locate their skid trails, do inventories to plan their logging, and adopt other similar practices. But most management plans professional foresters are approving in the tropics are unlikely to lead to sustainable forest management. In most cases, their main emphasis is on not logging trees smaller than some minimum diameter, on the flawed assumption that if you take out only the largest logs, the ecosystem will be able to maintain a commercially viable, sustainable level of timber production over time (Putz et al. 2000, Sist and Nguyen 2002). Most tropical forest management plans do not fully consider the regeneration ecology of the species involved, in terms of either their need for light or their pollination or seed dispersal needs (Fredericksen 1998, Sheil and Van Heist 2000).

A large number of requirements have crept into management plans and associated government regulations over time that have no scientific basis. It is more a question of tradition or conventional wisdom than of scientific forest management. Most regulations and management plans also focus too much on carrying out specific operations rather than on achieving specific outcomes in terms of sustainable forest management. And these management plans often have very optimistic allowable annual cuts because the companies argue that they need to have high allowable annual cuts to make a profit. A forester's signature is on the bottom of a piece of paper is no guarantee of sustainability.

FLAW #5: GOVERNMENT REGULATORS CAN ENSURE THAT COMPANIES FOLLOW THEIR FOREST MANAGEMENT PLANS

Even when the management plans make ecological sense, they are extremely difficult to enforce. It is easy to force a company to do its paperwork. It is much harder to make sure that it actually does something out in the middle of the forest, particularly if what one wants it to do is not its most profitable option. Undoubtedly certain aspects of well-constructed management plans make sense in terms of profitability, so companies are reasonably likely to take them on, particularly if they get a little push. For example, enlightened self-interest might lead companies to adopt specific reduced-impact logging practices whether or not they had a government-sanctioned management plan. But companies are unlikely to undertake sustainable forest management in the full sense of the term without substantial monitoring and high penalties to get them to do the things that are not profitable. Most tropical countries lack both the resources and the political will for that sort of monitoring and regulating.

Performance bonds are increasingly being touted as an effective means of forcing companies to adhere to their formally approved management plans. Nevertheless, in the few countries of the world where these have been tried—such as the performance bond system in the Philippines and the reforestation fund in Indonesia—they have been dismal failures. Governments have generally lacked the political will to implement performance bonds as theory suggests they should be implemented. Furthermore, it has proven difficult to set a level for the performance bonds that is high enough to determine company behavior but low enough not to greatly discourage forestry sector investments.

CONCLUSION

Most of the conventional wisdom about sustainable forest management in the tropics favors large companies. But around the world, large companies have not used forests more sustainably and less destructively than smallholders, local communities, or indigenous people. Smallholders, communities, and indigenous people do not necessarily have a conservation ethic (although some do), and they do not necessarily manage their forests sustainably. But there is little evidence that on average they have performed worse than the large companies. Throughout the tropics it is far easier to find cases of sustainable small-scale timber production than to find cases of large-scale commercial companies that are practicing what one could really consider sustainable forest management. Despite that reality, however, much of the sustainable forest management by smallholders, communities, and indigenous people is actually illegal, and existing laws sanction many of the unsustainable practices of large companies.

A very interesting workshop was held in Cochabamba, Bolivia, a few years ago during which the United Nations Food and Agriculture Organization Forest, Trees, and Peoples Project (FTPP) presented a number of cases in which indigenous people, local communities, and small farmers in Bolivia were engaged in sustainable forest management. I made the point there that if the government officials and donor agencies present at that workshop were in any way consistent, they would try to get the people who had just presented their sustainable forest management experiences arrested because they were all systematically engaged in activities considered illegal under the Bolivian forestry laws that the government officials and donors had helped produce. As I pointed out, not everyone who manages their forest has a formal management plan, whereas many companies have formal management plans but do not manage their forests.

Most logging on government-owned forests, which today constitute about 80 percent of all the forests in the world, involves some type of subsidy. Governments give loggers access to the resources in those forests for less than their true value. Why should a few wealthy individuals and companies get access to those resources rather than the millions of poor and marginalized people living in forests or on forest margins? Industrial loggers are at least as likely to destroy the forest as smallholders, communities, and indigenous people, and that is unlikely to change any time soon. Large-scale industrial logging can and should be improved and made more sustainable. But it is high time to give poor people greater access to public forest resources.

REFERENCES

Barbier, E. B., N. Bockstael, J. C. Burgess, and I. Strand. 1995. The linkages between timber trade and tropical deforestation: Indonesia. *The World Economy* 18: 411–42.

Barr, C. 2001. *Banking on sustainability: Structural adjustment and forestry reform in post-Suharto Indonesia.* Bogor, Indonesia: Center for International Forestry Research and Macroeconomics for Sustainable Development Program Office, World Wide Fund for Nature.

Boscolo, M. and J. R. Vincent. 1998. Promoting better logging practices in tropical forests: A simulation analysis of alternative regulations. *World Bank Working Paper Series* 1971.

Fredericksen, T. S. 1998. Limitations of low-intensity selective and selection logging for sustainable tropical forestry. *Commonwealth Forestry Review* 77: 262–266.

Karsenty, A. 2000. *Economic instruments for tropical forests: The Congo Basin case.* London: Center for International Forestry Research, Centre de Coopération Internationale en Recherche Agronomique pour le Développement, and International Institute for Environment and Development.

Pearce, D., F. E. Putz, and J. Vanclay. 2002. Sustainable forestry: Panacea or pipedream? *Forest Ecology and Management* 172: 229–247.

Putz, F. E., K. H. Redford, J. G. Robinson, R. Fimbel, and G. M. Blate. 2000. Biodiversity conservation in the context of tropical forest management. *Conservation Biology* 15: 7–20.

Repetto, R. and M. Gillis. 1988. *Public policies and the misuse of forest resources.* Cambridge, U.K.: Cambridge University Press.

Sayer, J., J. K. Vanclay, and N. Byron. 1997. Technologies for sustainable forest management: Challenges for the 21st century. *Commonwealth Forestry Review* 76: 162–170.

Sheil, D., and M. Van Heist. 2000. Ecology for tropical forest management. *International Forestry Review* 2: 261–270.

Sist, P. and N. Nguyen. 2002. Logging damage and the subsequent dynamics of a dipterocarp forest in East Kalimantan (1990–1996). *Forest Ecology and Management* 165: 85–103.

Stone, R. D. and C. D. D'Andrea. 2001. *Tropical forests and the human spirit.* Berkeley: University of California Press.

Vincent, J. R. 1998. Discussion on Barbier's article. In M. Palo and J. Uusivuori, eds., *World forests, society and environment,* 118–120. Dordrecht, the Netherlands: Kluwer Academic Publishers.

von Amsberg, J. 1994. Economic parameters of deforestation. World Bank Policy Research Working Paper no. 1350. Washington, D.C.: World Bank.

Walker, R. T. and T. E. Smith. 1999. Tropical deforestation and forest management under the system of concession logging: A decision theoretic analysis. *Journal of Regional Science* 33: 387–419.

World Bank. 1992. *World development report.* New York: Oxford University Press.

Chapter 22

GOVERNING THE AMAZON TIMBER INDUSTRY

Daniel Nepstad, Ane Alencar, Ana Cristina Barros, Eirivelthon Lima, Elsa Mendoza, Claudia Azevedo Ramos, and Paul Lefebvre

The Amazon is the world's largest reserve of tropical timber (Uhl et al. 1997). Each year, approximately 2000 wood mills process 30 million m³ of timber harvested from 10,000–15,000 km² of forest (Veríssimo and Lima 1998, Nepstad et al. 1999b). And yet the Amazon timber industry is in its infancy. Most of the old-growth forests of Amazonia are not yet accessible, protected from loggers' chainsaws by high transport costs. The "passive protection" of these forests will be lost in coming years, however, as all-weather roads are paved into the core of the Amazon forest (Nepstad et al. 2000, 2001, Carvalho et al. 2001, Laurance et al. 2001). An expansion of export-oriented timber harvesting from the Amazon will also be motivated by exhaustion of the current principal source of tropical hardwoods, Southeast Asia (Uhl et al. 1997). The prospect of governing the Amazon timber industry takes on greater urgency in this context of imminent transformation.

One goal of governance is to defend the public's interests in Amazon forests. These interests range from the harvest of game, nuts, and oils by forest residents, to the stabilization of regional rainfall regimes, to the role of the forest as home to nearly one-third of the planet's species. These interests are manifested primarily among the people of the Amazon but also extend to the Amazon countries generally and to the planet.

Our analysis is based on the assumption that timber is the one of the most important Amazon commodities in the design of a forest-based development pathway that provides social and economic prosperity indefinitely, without crippling the ecological processes that sustain life in the region (Uhl et al. 1997, Schneider et al. 2000). We measure progress to-

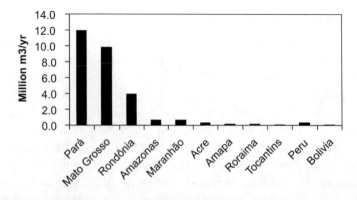

Figure 22.1 Roundwood production in the states of the Brazilian Amazon and in leading non-Brazilian Amazon countries. *Sources:* Brazilian data, Veríssimo et al. (2002c), Nepstad et al. (1999b); Bolivian data, F. Merry (unpublished data 2002); Peruvian data, D. Nepstad and E. Mendonza (unpublished data 2001).

ward governance using two criteria: maximization of social and economic benefits of the timber industry and minimization of ecological damage. The industry's 250,000 direct jobs and $2.5 billion in annual revenue are one measure of the social benefits of the timber industry and are often cited as the rationale for broad government support of the timber industry (Veríssimo et al. 2002a, 2002b, 2002c, Lima et al. 2002, Lentini et al. 2003). But beyond mostly seasonal employment opportunities shoveling sawdust and pushing planks through planers, the timber industry has the potential to improve the livelihoods of low-income rural Amazon populations in more dignified, long-lasting ways by contributing to on-farm infrastructure and the income of rural farm communities. The timber industry can provide an initial injection of capital and a perpetual flow of income to rural farms through fairly negotiated timber sales, careful harvest procedures, and investments in forest management planning and infrastructure.

The Amazon logging industry is concentrated in Brazil, which is the focus of our analysis. Approximately 2 percent of Amazon roundwood production occurs outside Brazil (figure 22.1). This pattern could change in the future as the network of all-weather highways expands into the western Amazon and across the Andes and as timber supplies in the Brazilian Amazon are depleted.

THE ECONOMIC LOGIC OF LOGGING

The Amazon timber industry is best understood in the context of the economic logic of logging companies. The cost of transporting tree trunk sections weighing up to ten tons across remote forest landscapes places a premium on accessibility. The first waves of timber exploitation in the Amazon followed the rivers, where logs were floated out of the forest and down the river to sawmills (Barros and Uhl 1995). The paving of all-weather roads across the upland, interfluvial forests of the Amazon, beginning in the 1960s with the paving of the Belém–Brasília highway, provided access to immense, unexploited forests with high timber volumes (by Amazon standards). These upland *terra firme* forests became the target of a timber industry explosion beginning in the 1980s, provoked in part by the depletion of the timber stocks in Brazil's Atlantic Coastal Forest (Uhl et al. 1997). Most of the Amazon's 2000 wood mills are concentrated in logging districts located on the region's all-weather highways through *terra firme* forests (figure 22.2a).

High transportation costs of tree trunks, market access, and timber stocks determine the species and volumes that are harvested from forests and the strategies for marketing sawn timber (Stone 1998). Close to sawmills and markets, it is profitable to harvest tree species of very low market value. The largest markets for Amazonian timber are in Brazil, in the northeast and industrial south (Smeraldi and Veríssimo 1999). Approximately 80 percent of the timber produced in Amazonia is consumed in these diversified markets. The large logging centers in eastern Amazonia (along the Belém–Brasília highway), Mato Grosso, and Rondônia, arose primarily in response to the proximity of these Brazilian markets. The influence of market access on species and volumes harvested is illustrated by the Paragominas logging center, located on the Belém–Brasilia highway, with easy access to ports in Belém and consumers in the northeast and south of Brazil. In its heyday, the Paragominas timber industry harvested a total of 2.5 million m³/year of more than 100 tree species, at intensities of up to 40 m³/ha (Veríssimo et al. 1995, Nepstad et al. 1999b).

The large timber stocks in central and western Amazonia, far from all-weather highways or navigable rivers, are isolated from Brazilian markets because of low accessibility. They are also cut off from most of the urban centers of Peru and Bolivia—far smaller consumers of timber than the Brazilian timber markets—by the Andes Mountains.

The small volume of timber that is exported from the Amazon to international markets in Europe, Asia, and the United States is mostly of a

(a)

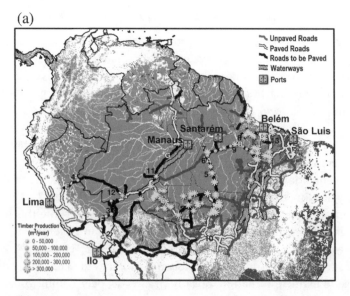

(b)

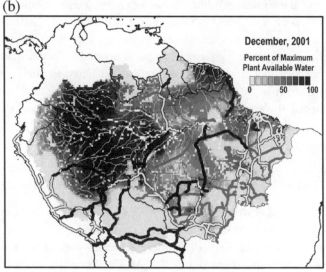

Figure 22.2 **(a)** The network of major roads, associated logging centers, ports, and planned waterways in the Amazon. These roads include the Cuiabá–Santarem highway (A), the Transamazon Highway (B), the Manaus–Boa Vista highway, recently paved (C), the trans-Andean highways (E, F), and the Humaitá–Manaus highway (G). Cities mentioned in the text include Cuzco (1), Puno (2), Puerto Maldonado (3), Pucallpa (4), Novo Progresso (5), Trairão (6), Itaituba (7), Vitória (8), Altamira (9), Cuiabá (10), Humaitá (11), Rio Branco (12), and Paragominas (13). **(b)** Soil water depletion in the forests of Amazonia at the beginning of the 2001–2002 El Niño. Depletion below 30% is associated with high fire risk (Nepstad et al. in press). The logging industry is concentrated in areas of high seasonal drought and low rainfall during El Niños and often leads to accidental forest fire. *Sources:* Roundwood volumes are from Nepstad et al. (1999b) and Veríssimo and Lima (1998), updated through expeditions conducted along A, B, and E in 2000 and 2001 (D. Nepstad, A. Alencar, and E. Mendonza, unpublished data).

few high-value species, the most prominent of which is mahogany (*Swietenia macrophylla*). Unlike low-value species, mahogany can be profitably extracted throughout its range across southern Amazonia, even if extraction entails blazing hundreds of miles of truck trails through the forest (Veríssimo et al. 1995, Grogan 2001). The largest remaining stocks of mahogany are in the indigenous reserves of Pará state and southwestern Amazonia. Mahogany is one of the few species that can be profitably transported across the Andes on unpaved highways. Rapid harvest rates and poor regeneration after harvest have drawn international attention to mahogany, leading to its recent listing as an endangered species by the Convention on International Trade in Endangered Species. Before this listing, mahogany extraction was prohibited by the Brazilian government, a ban that was recently extended for five months (*O Liberal*, February 14, 2003). Other species, such as ipê (*Tabebuia serratifolia*), may actually be more vulnerable to extinction than mahogany (J. Zweede, pers. comm. 2002).

Loggers, like wildcat goldminers, prosper through high-speed extraction of the resource. Wood is viewed as a nonrenewable, extractive resource. Speedy extraction allows the logger to acquire more of the resource than competing loggers and to build up timber stocks that can be sawn through the wet season when extraction halts. In the race to remove logs from forests, careful planning of tree felling and road networks goes by the wayside, and a far larger number of trees are damaged or destroyed through harvest activities than is necessary (Barreto et al. 1998, Holmes et al. 2002).

THE INDUSTRY IN TRANSITION: NEW ROADS IN THE RAINFOREST

The Amazon timber industry is undergoing a dramatic transition as all-weather roads are paved into the region's core. The Brazilian government has begun to pave the first all-weather access to the giant interfluvial forests of central Amazonia (figure 22.2a). The Peruvian government is improving the highways across the Andes, and corridors to ocean ports have already been completed to the Caribbean and through Bolivia to the Pacific (figure 22.2a). One of the economic driving forces behind this road expansion is the substantial savings that would accrue to the soybean industry through improved access to Amazon ports. These savings would equal $70 million for today's level of soybean production in central Brazil and greater savings as soy production increases in the future (Nepstad et al. 2000, 2001, 2002a, Carvalho et al. 2001, Fearnside 2001). But a second economic driver for road paving through central Amazonia is timber. As timber stocks in eastern and southern Amazonia are depleted, the stocks that are closest to the markets in southern and northeastern Brazil are located along the BR-163 highway in southwestern Pará state, the Transamazon Highway, and the BR-319 highway from Porto Velho to Manaus (figure 22.2a).

Road paving is rapidly increasing the area of forest lands and the number of tree species per area that can be profitably harvested, as the logic of logging is played out on an expanding stage. In 2000 and 2001, we conducted expeditions along three of the major highways that are being paved to assess the impacts of paving on the people, economies, and ecosystems of each corridor. We interviewed supervisors of twenty-four logging companies to assess the response of the timber industry to paving. These expeditions included the 1600-km Cuiabá–Santarém highway, the 1200-km Transamazon Highway (from Novo Repartimento to Itaituba), and the 1800-km highway from Rio Branco, Acre, across the Andes to Puno and Ilo (figure 22.2a). Our findings paint a very consistent picture of the future of the timber industry. In Brazil, much of the forest land—perhaps most of it—along these highways has already been high-graded for mahogany and other value species such as cedar (*Cedrella odorata*) and freijó (*Cordia goeldiana*) with minor structural impacts on these forests. But with improved road access and the depletion of timber stocks in forests along the Amazon's eastern and southeastern flank, many new species are becoming profitable to harvest for sale in Brazil's domestic timber market, and the ecological damage associated with logging is growing proportionally. The towns in regions of abundant timber that are closest to these domestic markets are booming with new sawmills. Novo Progresso, in southern Pará (figure 22.2a), for example, had 3 sawmills in 1997, 60 in 2000, and more than 120 in 2001, even though it is still separated from the national paved road grid by 200 km of dirt road that becomes almost impassable during the seven-month rainy season. The logging industry that supplies the Brazilian timber market will move north along BR-163 and west along the Transamazon while remaining timber stocks along the Belém–Brasília highway, along PA-150 in northern Mato Grosso, and along BR-364 (in Rondônia) are depleted. Paving of the trans-Andean highways will increase logging pressure on forests of the Andean east slope, although the size of this expansion may be much slower than that in the eastern Amazon because of the small size of the Peruvian domestic timber markets.

The export timber industry is also burgeoning because of improved road conditions but in different places. River ports in Vitória (north of Altamira on the Xingu River), Itaituba (on the Cuiaba–Santarém highway), Itacoatiara (near Manaus), and the ocean port in Lima shape the spatial distribution of export-oriented timber harvest (figure 22.2a). With paving of BR-163, the Santarém port will replace the Itaituba port, and export-oriented logging will extend down to Novo Progresso and along the entire length of the Transamazon Highway. The road connecting Humaitá and Manaus (BR-319) will be a less important source of timber for the international market because it passes through a region of low timber volumes and because it probably will be the last of the main highways to be paved. Road paving will also make several medium-value timber species profitable to harvest and export from an expanding area of forest land, thereby increasing the forest damage associated with export-oriented logging.

The influence of road paving on the type of logging that is practiced is illustrated by the Pucallpa–Cuzco highway. Before paving, the Pucallpa timber industry, like Puerto Maldonado today, shipped primarily mahogany across the Andes for export from Lima (figure 22.2a). After paving, this industry grew to supply fifteen Amazon timber species to the Peruvian markets in Cuzco and Lima (D. Nepstad and E. Mendoza, unpublished data 2001).

LOGGING AND ECOLOGICAL IMPOVERISHMENT

Perhaps the greatest ecological threat posed by the expanding Amazon timber industry is large-scale, fire-mediated displacement of Amazon high forests by repeatedly burned, degraded forests. Timber harvest favors this displacement by increasing forest susceptibility to the fires that escape from agricultural lands. This threat is greatest where high-intensity (high volume per area) timber harvest, seasonal drought, and fire-dependent agricultural systems converge (Nepstad et al. 1999a, Alencar et al. in press), and is occurring today in eastern and southeastern Amazonia, along the Belém–Brasília highway, and in northern Mato Grosso. As the logging and agricultural frontiers move north along the Cuiabá–Santarém highway and west along the Transamazon Highway, the fire-driven impoverishment of forests may follow. Seasonal drought is severe in this region, particularly during El Niños (figure 22.2b).

The magnitude of the threat is illustrated by the severe El Niño of 1997 and 1998, during which an estimated 40,000 km^2 of forest—three-fourths of the area of Costa Rica—caught fire in the Brazilian Amazon (Diaz et al. 2002). Most of the forest that burned had been previously logged. With an expanded logging and agricultural frontier, forest fire could transform many of the forests of eastern and southeastern Amazonia into increasingly fire-prone, degraded forests.

How does logging increase the flammability of tropical forests? Throughout the tropics, most of the forests that are being logged experience annual dry seasons of several months, during which the amount of water leaving the forest as water vapor (via evapotranspiration) is greater than the amount of water entering the forest as rainfall (Nepstad et al. 1999b, Whitmore 1985). Logging operations are much more efficient during the dry season, especially in areas of clay soils, where heavy machinery can become mired when it rains. In their natural state, these seasonally dry forests have low susceptibility to the fires that threaten them from neighboring agricultural lands. The dense leaf canopies of intact forests, dozens of meters above the ground, prevent all but a small fraction of solar radiation from reaching the forest floor beneath the continuous canopy. Because little sunlight penetrates into the forest interior, temperatures remain low and relative humidity of the air remains high. Even as moisture is depleted from the soil surface, tree and liana root systems extending more than 10 m deep into the soil continue to absorb water, allowing the leaf canopy to remain green and active and the forest interior to remain moist and cool, with low susceptibility to fire (Nepstad et al. 1994, 2002b, Jipp et al. 1998).

Logging perforates the canopy of the forest, allowing large amounts of sunlight to penetrate the forest interior. Logging also introduces fuel to the forest floor. Intensive logging in eastern Amazonia (30–40 m³/ha harvested) reduces canopy cover from 95 percent to 50 percent and increases the amount of organic fuel on the forest floor from 60 tons/ha in natural forest to 180 tons/ha after logging (Uhl and Vieira 1989, Uhl and Kauffman 1990). As a result of these changes, the treefall gaps created by logging operations can catch fire within two weeks of a dry season rain event, whereas the dark, moist understory of the intact forest needs months of consecutive rainless days before ignition is possible (Uhl and Buschbacher 1985, Uhl and Kaufman 1990, Cochrane and Schulze 1999, Nepstad et al. 1999a). The effect of logging on forest flammability therefore is proportional to the intensity of the harvest. With increased intensity, more of the forest is converted into very flammable gaps, and the probability of a fire moving through the forest, from one gap to another, increases.

Once burned, the probability of a forest burning again increases in a positive feedback cycle. The trees that are killed by fire gradually fall to the ground, further exposing the forest floor to the drying action of the sun as they deposit large amounts of new fuels (branches and wood) on the forest floor (Nepstad et al. 1995, Cochrane and Schulze 1999, Cochrane et al. 1999). Some logged forests in eastern Amazonia have burned more than 7 times in less than twenty years and have been transformed into severely degraded, fire-prone forests, dominated by low-statured woody plants, forbs, and grasses (Cochrane and Schulze 1999). This risk of "savannization" is highest in the eastern and southern Amazon, where severe droughts are associated with El Niños (figure 22.2b).

Reduced-impact logging (RIL), in which the forest is inventoried before harvest, trees to be harvested are mapped, lianas tying these trees to their neighbors are cut, and the locations of skid trails are planned, can greatly reduce the ecological damage associated with logging (Johns et al. 1996, Barreto et al. 1998). Because a larger portion of the forest canopy is left intact, there is less heating of the forest interior, and a smaller amount of fuel is introduced to the forest floor. The susceptibility of forests to fire is much lower after RIL than after traditional logging (Holdsworth and Uhl 1997). Interestingly, the profitability of RIL is similar to that of traditional harvest operations because a higher proportion of the trees that are felled are found by the skid crews (Barreto et al. 1998, Holmes et al. 2002).

Beyond its influence on forest flammability, logging causes a range of more subtle effects on tropical forests, including soil damage from skidding and yarding operations, changes in the species composition of plant and animal communities, and changes in the genetic structure of plant and animal populations. These effects vary greatly depending on the intensity of timber harvest, the logging practices used, and the scale at which the effects are measured (reviewed by Putz et al. 2000). In one of the few studies of logging effects on forest animals in the Amazon, Azevedo-Ramos et al. (unpublished data 2001) and Kalif et al. (2001) compared the composition of reptile, mammal, bird, and ant communities in 100-ha blocks of forest that had undergone conventional logging (26 m^3/ha harvested), RIL (23 m^3/ha harvested), and no logging in an eastern Amazon forest. Both types of logging dramatically reduced the richness of native forest animals relative to the unlogged forest control. The loss of native animal species associated with logging varied from 17 to 26 percent after conventional logging (17 percent for reptiles, 18 percent for mammals, 24 percent for birds, and 26 percent for ants) and from 17 to 24 percent after RIL (17 percent for reptiles, 18 percent for mammals, 19 percent for ants, and 24 percent for birds). Despite this reduction in native species, overall animal species richness remained similar across the three forest treatments because of the appearance of new animal species not encountered in the intact forest control. Further study is needed to understand the rate at which nonforest animals disappear from logged forests and the rate at which the full assemblage of forest animal species is reestablished. However, it is clear that even if the loss of animal species associated with logging is persistent, the effects of logging on forest biodiversity is minor compared with the major competing land uses in the Amazon, namely cattle pasture and shifting cultivation.

MISSING SOCIOECONOMIC BENEFITS

The economically marginalized rural populations of Amazonia—the six million smallholders, folk societies (*caboclos, ribeirinhos*), and indigenous groups—occupy approximately one-third of the region's forests but capture only a tiny share of the wealth generated by the timber industry. The weight of wood shapes the economic logic of logging and also excludes the rural poor from direct involvement in the industry; the heavy machinery that is needed to transport tree trunks to sawmills is too expensive for most of these people. Some rural entrepreneurs find a way to acquire chainsaws or rudimentary trucks (Uhl et al. 1991, Guimarães and Uhl 1997) that allow them to derive greater monetary benefits from the timber industry, but the smallholders and indigenous groups of Amazonia generally act as sources of raw material and unskilled labor to the industry, selling the trees on their land to logging operations and working in harvest and milling operations. They can also derive indirect benefits when the timber operations improve the roads that link remote farms and villages with urban centers and give rides to hitchhiking farmers, schoolchildren, and the sick.

These benefits are not trivial. Quick cash for the sale of forest trees is an important source of income to smallholders and indigenous groups, whose main source of revenue often is the sale of manioc flour for less than $500 per year per family. Opportunities for wage labor are scarce in much of rural Amazonia, and the timber industry directly employs approximately 250,000 laborers in sawmills and harvesting operations (Veríssimo and Lima 1998, Veríssimo et al. 2002c, Lima et al. 2002, Lentini et al. 2003). This enormous socioeconomic benefit often is cited as a major rationale for developing public policies that support industrial logging in the Amazon (Veríssimo et al. 2002a, 2002b). And the links with schools, health clinics, and markets that can be provided by logging roads and logging trucks can be, quite literally, the difference between life and death for some isolated farm families.

The socioeconomic benefits of the timber industry to date fall far below the potential benefits, however. Jobs in timber companies are predominantly seasonal, with lay-offs driven by rainy-season depletion of timber yard stocks. Working conditions often are harsh, with clay and wood dust suspended in the air, causing respiratory ailments for mill workers and their families. There is little safety equipment, and accidents are common. The remote location and absence of effective government regulatory agencies can also open the door to violations of human rights in both mill and harvest operations, with child labor, excessive working hours, and inadequate working conditions (Rohter 2002).

The greatest potential benefit of the timber industry to the rural poor is largely unrealized. As the owners or controllers of vast forest resources, the smallholder farmers, folk societies, and indigenous groups of Amazonia could receive a perpetual flow of income from the management and sale of their timber resources while conserving the nontimber resources and ecological services provided by their forests. Indeed, several pilot experiments demonstrate the role that wood can play in improving rural livelihoods in the region. In the wake of the timber boom–bust cycle in the Amazon estuary, *caboclo* families who gained knowledge and skills in the timber industry during this cycle began to manage their secondary forests and logged forests for the sale of high-grade timber (Pinedo-Vasquez et al. 2001). Similarly, *caboclo* communities of the Tapajós–Arapiuns Extractive Reserve have increased their income through the sale of rustic furniture that they make from fallen timber on their land that is removed below the rate at which it is produced (see chapter 11). And the Xikrin Indians, of Pará state, were awarded government approval of their mahogany management plan. At least thirteen other community-based forestry initiatives are under way in the Brazilian Amazon (Amaral and Amaral 2000, Muchagata and Amaral Neto 2001). But as in similar projects in Peru and Bolivia (Smith and Wray 1996), the inexperience of rural communities in commercial enterprise has presented an important impediment to the success of these initiatives. Most of the community-based forestry initiatives in Amazonia have excluded the logging companies that have the expertise and machinery to harvest and process tree trunks and then struggled to develop this capacity among the communities themselves (Melo et al. 2001, Muchagata and Amaral Neto 2001, Cunha 2002; see chapter 11). Most significantly, a successful model for transferring more benefits from the timber industry to smallholder farmers of government settlement projects—the largest and fastest-growing population of rural poor in Amazonia—is conspicuously absent.

SYNERGIES BETWEEN SMALLHOLDERS AND LOGGERS

Smallholder farmers and logging companies have formed alliances across the Amazon because of the mutual benefits associated with harvesting timber from the forests of government agricultural settlement projects.

The potential magnitude of such alliances in shaping forest use in Amazonia is very large. Since 1995, the federal government of Brazil has settled 210,000 families on 190,000 km^2 of land (INCRA 2001). In typical settlement projects, each farm family receives 100 ha of land in 400- by 2500-m parcels that are arranged in fishbone patterns, side by side along secondary access roads. Each family can convert up to 20 percent of the land in their parcel to agriculture and cattle pastures (according to the Brazilian Codigo Florestal and its current Medida Provisoria) and is permitted to sell the timber before clearing the forest. Timber can also be sold from the property's legal forest reserve if a management plan is prepared and approved by the Brazilian Government Institute for the Environment and Renewable Resources (IBAMA), the federal environmental regulation agency.

There are three major benefits to the timber industry of agricultural settlement projects. They provide timber at low or nonexistent stumpage fees. The forests are easily accessible because of the settlement's road network (although road repairs often are necessary). And smallholders can legalize timber removal from their land by licensing their deforestation, thereby legalizing the timber mill's production system, as discussed later in this chapter. In turn, smallholders can receive benefits from the logging industry through the sale of timber from their land, through improvements in their road network, and through the transportation provided by logging companies.

Currently, the flow of these benefits is skewed toward the timber industry, however. Most smallholder farmers have little experience or power in negotiating fair harvest agreements with logging companies and usually are cut off from government agencies that might enforce fair trade arrangements. Payments for harvested trees often are never made (M. Campos, pers. comm. 2002, based on interviews along the Transamazon Highway). The prices that are negotiated can be a small fraction of the stumpage payments made to more powerful landholders (Mattos et al. 1992). Farmers also have little control over harvest operations. Located far from towns and isolated even from neighbors, smallholder farmers have little power to influence the tree felling and extraction techniques used and volumes harvested by the logging crews that enter their land with heavy machinery to take away choice tree trunks. The road improvements made by the logging company and the transportation provided by logging vehicles are ephemeral benefits. With the completion of the harvest, the smallholders are left, once again, to seek local government support to maintain their secondary roads. With an annual cost of approximately $1400/km, road maintenance is rarely provided by local governments. The *municípios* (counties) of Trairão and Novo Progresso, for example, have 500 and 700 km of secondary road, which would cost 60 and 70 percent, respectively, of these local governments' annual operating budgets to maintain. Finally, after a harvest operation, a farmer's forest is far more vulnerable to forest fire and often ignites when slash-and-burn fires escape beyond their intended boundaries. Accidental forest fires damage the forest and reduce its potential for hunting and for gathering of nontimber forest products such as lianas, medicinal plants, oils, nuts, fruits, and resins (Nepstad et al. 1999a). In sum, against the benefits that flow to smallholders from the logging industry must be weighed the unnecessary damages done to the forests on which they depend, the unnecessarily low stumpage fees that are paid to these farmers, and the short duration of the transportation benefit.

Important real-life experiments demonstrate the potential for moving beyond the current skewed relationship between loggers and farmers toward one of equal exchange. In response to invitations from farmers of agricultural settlement projects, a small logging company (Manejo Florestal e Prestação de Serviço [MAFLOPS], Forest Management and Services) operating close to the city of Santarém has put in practice a replicable model of fair exchange that provides each farm family with legal title to their land, a network of roads, a property-level forest management plan, and an average of $1430[1] for the sale of a portion of their timber to MAFLOPS. Thus far, six communities with a total forest area of 32,000 ha have entered into accords with MAFLOPS, acquiring government-approved forest management plans in the process.

In the first year of the four-year contract, MAFLOPS determines the legal limits of each property and prepares a *memório descritivo*, the legal document that describes the boundaries, areas of permanent forest reserve (including stream margins and slopes, as stipulated by the forest code), and areas destined for clearing as the basis of land titles. This document is registered with the federal colonization agency (Instituto Nacional de Colonização e Reforma Agrária [INCRA]). Within thirty days of submission, the landholder receives a certificate of legal title to his or her land. INCRA expedites the titling of farmers who are working with MAFLOPS as part of a larger accord in which the company makes roads to the community, as required by law. In conducting these property surveys, MAFLOPS discusses with the farmers of each colonization project the physical arrangement of its properties that can best provide each property with access to both surface water and feeder roads. During this structuring of the farm settlement, overlap between neighboring properties is common, leading the farm community to expel some of its members.

Property legalization is the key step in financing the development of the settlement's road network using timber. Once farmers have acquired their certificate of land title, they are allowed to request a permit to harvest the timber from the land that they will clear for agriculture in the subsequent year. MAFLOPS requests these permits on behalf of the farmers, then harvests and sells the timber, using the proceeds to cover the costs of feeder road construction. Road construction in agricultural settlements is the responsibility of the federal government. INCRA is obligated to provide $3700/km of feeder road and $860/km of minor property-level road for new agricultural settlements, although these funds often are not available when roads must be constructed. MAFLOPS uses this money, when it is available, to purchase gravel to make the feeder roads more durable.

During the first year of the contract, a 100 percent forest inventory is also conducted of each individual property, mapping the position, identity, size, condition, and market value of every tree with a diameter of at least 35 cm and indicating the preharvest treatments and harvest strategy. This inventory is presented to each family as part of their property-level forest management plan. No money is exchanged between MAFLOPS and the community in the first year.

In the subsequent three years, MAFLOPS harvests timber according to the forest management plans, paying families $2.90/m³ of roundwood harvested from the property. Forty-five timber species are harvested at an average intensity of 13 m³/ha. This harvest intensity is low in part because hollow trees and seed trees are left standing. Each family receives $600–3100 for the sale of their timber during this period and is left with additional timber to sell in the future. Much of the interproperty variation in timber harvest is associated with the variable occurrence of liana forests, which have little timber volume. Revenues from timber sales provide capital to smallholders that can be used to establish agricultural systems that provide higher income on smaller areas of land than traditional slash-and-burn agriculture. For example, MAFLOPS recommends to farmers that they pool a portion of their timber revenues to purchase small farm machines (tractors, rice processors) that would enable them to shift to mechanized agriculture, which is far more productive and profitable than slash-and-burn. The company also encourages the communities to commercialize nontimber forest products. One community decided to sell the oil of the andiroba seed, netting revenues of $55/tree each year. Some farmers also reported investments in coffee and cacau trees. Some of the communities have asked MAFLOPS to construct high-quality houses and buildings using the money provided by INCRA for this purpose ($750/family).

Several challenges remain to be addressed in the MAFLOPS accords. For example, the risk that farm families will transform their forests into cattle pastures continues to be high in the partner communities, despite the greater awareness that these families have of the commercial value of their forests. After the initial timber harvest, the flow of forest-based income to farm families declines sharply as their supply of marketable trees dwindles. As new species come into local markets, the sale of trees can continue at a low level. But thirty to forty years may be needed before the forest has regrown sufficiently to provide a second round of cutting, which is well beyond the economic planning horizons of most Amazon smallholders. Such long-term investments in forest management may be more acceptable to smallholders than to industrial timber firms because the former have lower opportunity costs on their investments of labor and time (Putz 2000).

The farmers may emerge from this experience more likely to conserve their forests and more likely to respect the forest code that requires that 80 percent of each property be maintained in forest. The families gain experience in a marketing their timber, which defends them against exploitation by logging companies in the future. MAFLOPS hires members of each community to work in its forest inventory and timber extraction crews, and this local expertise may increase the chances that the community will conserve and manage its forest resources.

What is the prospect of replicating the MAFLOPS experience widely across the Amazon? Experience in other parts of the world demonstrates that company–community forestry partnerships work best with government support and when communities have strong claims on their forests (Mayers and Vermeulen 2002). Perhaps the greatest barrier is one of social capital. We simply do not know how many logging companies are interested in or capable of entering into accords of this kind with honesty and a commitment to fair negotiations. But in regions such as the Transamazon Highway, where a 50-km-wide corridor of agricultural settlements will soon gain easier access to Brazilian timber markets through road paving, grassroots organizations such as the Movimento pelo Desenvolvimento da Transamazonica e Xingu could play a prominent role in overseeing the accords between loggers and farmers. An important step would be to build the capacity of the Transamazon Highway's existing agricultural cooperatives to represent farm communities in timber negotiations. Rural extension programs could also disseminate broadly the skills for negotiating timber deals and for monitoring their implementation. As new timber species become economically viable to harvest along this corridor, groups of farmers could work with loggers to develop forest management plans and fair harvest agreements. The policy challenge is to identify an efficient regulatory framework for forcing logging companies to deal fairly with smallholders.

In addition to the direct social benefits to the rural pool that this system provides, it could also provide a source of timber large enough to sustain the entire industry for many years. If a sufficient number of landholders are successful in maintaining forest on 80 percent of their land after the initial round of timber extraction, then privately owned forests could become a long-term source of timber. With sufficient numbers of agricultural communities and landholders of medium-sized properties defending and managing their forests as they intensify agricultural production on small portions of their properties, the timber industry would gain an important source of legal timber for the indefinite future. The 190,000 km^2 of agricultural settlements that have been created since 1996 could supply the industry with approximately eight years of timber. There are 450,000 km^2 of forest still standing within 50 km of the region's paved highways (some of which has already been logged). This accessible forest area will double as additional roads are paved (Nepstad et al. 2001). A central goal of forest policy should be to ensure that most of this forest is brought into a polycyclic management regime to provide a perpetual flow of benefits to both landholders and the timber industry.

PUBLIC FORESTS

One of the most ambitious new policies designed to regulate the Amazon timber industry is the Politica Nacional de Florestas (National Forest Policy) of Brazil's environment ministry (Ministério de Meio Ambiente 2002, Veríssimo et al. 2002a). This policy is based on the premise that the timber industry is a crucial source of employment and revenues for Amazon society that is constrained by a lack of available forest land to harvest. Large areas of uninhabited forest that are close enough to transport networks to permit economically viable timber extraction and that do not overlap existing forest reserves are targeted for the creation of 50 million ha of national forest by the year 2010 (from a current area of 8 million ha) (Veríssimo et al. 2002a, 2002b). In this expanded network of public forests, concessions will be opened up to bidding from the timber industry, and timber companies will be granted the right to harvest timber from these concessions. The area of forest concessions is planned to reach 28 million ha by 2010. The proposal would address the problem of illegal logging by regulating the industry in public forests.

Although the goals of this new policy are laudable, some of its basic assumptions break down under closer scrutiny. The most important assumption—that the timber industry should be directed away from the active agricultural frontiers—is the most perplexing. The rationale for this assumption is that it is too difficult for the timber industry to acquire the large forest holdings that are necessary to carry out forest management in the active agricultural frontier and that the industry therefore should be given big blocks of forest in an expanded national forest system. But if the goal of governance is to maximize social and economic benefits while avoiding ecological damages, then the industry should be forced to derive much its timber from the forests that are controlled or owned by the rural poor. The leaders of the Amazon timber industry with whom we have talked confirm that the industry could be supplied with timber from private land if land titling were streamlined in young frontier regions.[2] And the MAFLOPS system demonstrates that timber companies can foster the long-term management of privately owned forests on private lands without owning them. Ecologically, this is also a far more positive focus for the timber industry. As proposed, Brazil's National Forest Policy directs the industry toward the forests that have suffered the least disturbance from humans instead of to the forests that are already being used. Even RIL impoverishes tropical forests (Putz et al. 2000) and should be avoided in the region's wilderness forest lands. Another premise of the National Forest Policy—that the government can regulate the timber industry's use of forests best by owning these forests—has little empirical evidence to support it (Repetto and Gillis 1988, Barbier et al. 1994, Contreras-Hermosilla and Rios 2002).

The Brazilian Amazon's first concession experience illustrates some of the constraints on concession-based forestry and warns against grandiose claims of benefits from shifting the industry to concessions. Negotiations for the first and only concession, which is located in the Tapajós National Forest, near Santarém, began in 1988 and were finally completed for a 3000-ha forest tract in 2000. A single company competed for this concession. Part of the delay in closing this deal was caused by the prolonged but crucial negotiations with the communities of farmers and *caboclos* who live in the Tapajós National Forest and who saw few future benefits of the concession accruing to them. Some of these communities have decided to withdraw from the national forest through a boundary redefinition, and others are now benefiting from the fruits of their negotiations in the form of projects that are helping them commercialize nontimber forest products, such as andiroba.

Brazil's proposed shift to concession-based forestry is best viewed as an important pilot experiment in governing the Amazon timber industry. The prospect of multiplying the area of forest timber concessions from 3000 ha to 25 million ha without first knowing how well this system will work is clearly ill-advised. However, this is not to say that the government should not move forward with the expansion of the national forest system. National forests could be the most effective way to expand the region's network of forest reserves, even if they are never turned over to the timber industry through concessions. National forest designations may best be used to restrict the advance of the agricultural and logging frontiers into large, intact forest tracts that are under imminent threat from loggers and land speculators, such as the Terra do Meio, located south of the Transamazon Highway. National forests may be more acceptable than biological reserves to local Amazon governments who are concerned more about jobs and revenue than about forest conservation because they allow economic activities.

CERTIFICATION AND DEVELOPMENT RIGHTS

Certification of forest management has also been heralded as a mechanism by which the demands of socially and environmentally conscious timber consumers can act as a positive market force favoring sustainable production systems. The number of sawmills with certified logging operations has grown slowly, however, totaling six out of approximately 2000 mills operating in the region. The reasons for this slow rate of expansion are not fully understood but certainly include the high cost of certification and the meager premium consumers pay for certified wood. This second factor is exacerbated by the large quantity of illegal timber that enters the Brazilian timber market, driving prices down. Certified producers may simply find it difficult to compete in the largely unregulated Amazon industry but may flourish if illegal logging is brought under control.

Conservation International (CI) has championed the purchase of development rights as a way of conserving land that would have otherwise been logged (Gullison et al. 2001). In the first example of this strategy, logging rights were purchased from timber companies in Guyana by investors looking for projects with high conservation impact. The purchase allowed CI to set aside this forest for biodiversity conservation. This approach could play an important role in conserving forests that are particularly valuable because of the plant and animal species that they support. But in Brazil, areas of high conservation value have already been excluded from the forests that are targeted for concessions (Veríssimo et al. 2002a, 2002b). It is also not clear whether conservation buyouts could reduce the overall area of forest that is affected by logging because companies will simply go elsewhere to find their timber. Moreover, the cost of this approach does not end when the development rights are purchased because defending land is expensive on the Amazon frontier (Schneider 1994). As the Guyana forest becomes economically viable to log, further investments will be needed to protect the forest from squatters and illegal loggers. Conservation buyouts are best viewed as an important pilot experiment in the governance of the Amazon timber industry.

These and other market-based approaches to the governance of the Amazon timber industry are important experiments whose ultimate success, like that of Brazil's new forest policy, will depend on successful enforcement of forest regulations throughout the Amazon. All market-based approaches to the conservation of natural resources depend on a functioning regulatory framework in which the legitimate ownership and control of property are recognized and defended, environmental regulations are enforced, and social and environmental investors are confident that their investments will not be swamped by illegal activities.

CHEATERS PROSPER

Cheating is the most insidious element of the logger's logic in the Amazon. As long as logging companies can flout government regulations designed to defend public interests in the region's forest resources, the prospect of governing the industry will remain dim. All strategies that are being advanced to govern the timber industry are based on the premise that government regulations can be enforced. The emerging partnerships between timber companies and the rural poor will expand only if government can efficiently provide land titles and enforcement of fair trade principles within these relationships. Brazil's new public forest approach to governance assumes that it can keep illegal loggers out of these forests, that it can force concessionaires to comply with their contracts, and that it can control the illegal logging taking place outside public forests that floods the market with inexpensive timber. Similarly, certified timber production systems will flourish and expand only if they are protected from competition presented by the cheaper logging operations of cheaters through successful enforcement of forest legislation.

Compliance with government regulations designed to control where and how timber is extracted from Amazon forests is low because it reduces the profits of logging companies and because enforcement is still inefficient. In Brazil, logging is legal only in forests that have been licensed for clearing in preparation for agriculture and in forests for which the government has approved a management plan. Both forms of legalization involve the transaction costs of the legalization process. In addition, licensed clearcuts (which require legal land titles) often are in short supply on logging frontiers, and management plans are costly. Enforcement depends on proving that timber sitting in a stock yard or carried on a truck came from a managed forest or a licensed deforestation.

From the perspective of logging criminals, the profitability of cheating depends on the cost of complying with the regulation that is being avoided, the chance of getting caught, and the fines (or imprisonment) that follow. For many years, the chance of being fined or imprisoned for an environmental crime was very low in Brazil. But with the enactment of the environmental crime legislation of 1998, the federal environmental regulatory agency (IBAMA) was given the power to levy fines and put environmental criminals in jail, greatly reducing the impunity of the timber industry. Today, the temptation to ignore forest legislation or engage in false compliance through bribing or document falsification is greatest in remote, young logging frontiers, where government enforcement capacity is weakest. Small clandestine operations often try to avoid enforcement agents altogether by moving their log-laden trucks along roads and highways at night, when enforcement agents do not work. Their mills are small and therefore are less likely to be visited by agents. Larger companies are more inclined to seek false compliance through bribing or false documentation. A commonly used technique of false compliance is to inflate the timber volumes that are assigned to areas of licensed deforestation, therefore providing *cobertura* (coverage) of the illegal timber that is carried on trucks or stored in timber yards. Another common approach is to simply falsify the Autorização de Transporte de Produtos Florestais (ATPF, Authorization for the Transport of Forest Products), the legal document that specifies the volumes and species of timber that the company can legally harvest.

Information about illegality is difficult to obtain in the Amazon. Of twenty-four mill operators we interviewed along the Cuiabá–Santarém highway, the Transamazon Highway, and the Trans-Andean highway in 2000 and 2001 (figure 22.2a), only one admitted to cheating. He purchased timber from clandestine timber harvesting operations for many years, bribing IBAMA officials to overlook his lack of ATPF coverage of the timber stored in his yard. When he decided to legalize his mill through the development of a government-approved management plan for a 3000-ha tract of forest, enforcement agents were displeased and threatened him at gunpoint. When bribes become an important source of income for enforcement agents in remote forest frontiers, it can become more dangerous to abide by the law than to cheat.

Smeraldi (2002) reports that the Amazon timber industry has shifted to a pattern of "predatory legality" in recent years, in which farmers and ranchers provide most of the legal coverage of the timber industry through licensed deforestation of their private lands. Timber, they argue, creates a perverse incentive for deforestation. This trend can also be interpreted in a different way. It is inevitable that the agricultural frontier will expand, and it is appropriate that timber is harvested from future agricultural lands to avoid wastage. The problem, then, is when timber volumes are exaggerated on ATPFs to provide coverage for illegal logging or when timber sales lead to deforestation of land that is not appropriate for agriculture. If the total area of agricultural land is allowed to climb from 15 percent (currently) to 20 percent while the remaining 80 percent is maintained under various levels of protection (Nepstad et al. 2002a), then deforestation could supply total industry timber needs for nearly twenty years. More prudently, timber from licensed deforestation represents a mechanism for buying time as the network of managed forests on private lands and in indigenous and extractive reserves expands and comes into a second rotation over the next thirty to forty years.

ENFORCEMENT

According to optimal penalty theory, governments should invest in the enforcement of environmental regulations up to the level at which the marginal costs of further enforcement are equal to the marginal social benefits of this added enforcement (Becker 1968). In this sense, current investments in enforcement of forest regulations clearly are suboptimal in the Amazon. Illegality is the major obstacle to the region's most promising innovations in governance of the Amazon timber industry. Large increases in enforcement efforts will be needed to increase the likelihood that logging criminals will be caught, building on the remarkable progress in enforcement that has been made in recent years (Nepstad et al. 2002a).

Although a thorough review of enforcement options in the Amazon is beyond the scope of this chapter, we highlight one enforcement option that has received little attention in the region. Private enforcement is emerging as one of the most important tools in environmental regulation. Nongovernmental organizations and watchdog groups are valuable sources of information about the illegal activities of environmental criminals and of government enforcement agents (Tietenberg 1996, Cohen 2000), and the Amazon is no different. Farmers' organizations often denounce illegal logging activities to IBAMA, and illegal loggers take revenge through death threats and assassinations. Along the Cuiabá–Santarém highway, we are aware of at least three leaders of farm organizations who have received death threats for denouncing illegal logging activities. One of these farmers was found murdered, with both of his legs broken, in July 2002.

Government interventions could increase the effectiveness of these private enforcement efforts. First, smallholders, folk societies (*caboclos* and *ribeirinhos*), and indigenous groups need to realize greater benefits from the timber industry. In other words, as the economically marginalized populations who occupy at least 30 percent of rural Amazonia begin to view their forests as the source of a perpetual flow of benefits, illegal activities that threaten these benefits—both on their land and in forest reserves—become less acceptable. Greater benefits will flow to these rural populations from the timber industry only through concerted efforts to foster—and enforce—honest business relationships characterized by fair exchange. If the social and environmental commitments of the timber industry are generally weak, as history suggests, then government must develop means of forcing these commitments on the industry, just as it has forced on the industry the need to find legal coverage for timber harvesting. Simultaneously, nongovernmental organizations that are supporting community forestry projects should try to involve logging companies as partners in their projects in addition to building community capacity to engage in commercial enterprise. Rural education and extension efforts must expand to include training of community members to negotiate fair timber deals (Mattos et al. 1992). Streamlined certification efforts should target emerging partnerships between farmers and loggers, finding ways to make certification affordable to such small-scale logging operations, perhaps through certification of groups of landholders.

Private enforcement also must include direct support to informers. Death threats must be answered rapidly with police protection and investigations. Reports of illegal logging must be investigated rapidly by enforcement agents who live outside the target area and therefore are less likely to be part of the illegal logging circle. It should be simple and safe to report environmental criminals.

CONCLUSION

Brazil has made important strides toward governing the Amazon timber industry. Several experiments are under way that provide promising components of an overall strategy to defend public interests in the enormous timber resources of the Amazon. Loggers even in remote forest regions are aware of forest policies and the risk of fees, equipment confiscation, and imprisonment associated with illegal logging. But recent policy trends seem to be in the wrong direction. The strategy has been to look beyond the inhabited forests of the Amazon to eventually push the timber industry into a public forest management regime in forests that have the lowest level of human disturbance, thereby missing an important opportunity to bring greater social and economic benefits to the region's most economically marginalized rural people. The farmers, folk societies, and indigenous groups living in the forests that line the region's roads and waterways could receive a steady flow of income from the forest industry as they provide, in exchange, a sustainable source of timber. To realize the potential of this missing component of the Amazon timber strategy, government and nongovernmental efforts to promote synergistic, fair relationships between the rural poor and logging companies must expand and be supported through the integration of environmental and agrarian reform policies.

ACKNOWLEDGMENTS

This chapter was supported by a grant from the U.S. Agency for International Development to the Woods Hole Research Center and by the Brazilian Large-Scale Biosphere Atmosphere Experiment through a grant from the National Aeronautics and Space Administration. Jack Putz, Sergio Rivero, Anthony Anderson, Daniel Zarin, and an anonymous reviewer provided valuable input to an earlier version of the manuscript.

NOTES

1. The exchange rate in February 2003, was 3.5 reais/US$1 and artificially high. The values we present in dollars therefore are underestimates.

2. For example, the president of the Amazon wood exporters' association (Associaçáo das Industrias Exportadoras de Madeiras do Estado do Pará), Roberto Puppo.

REFERENCES

Alencar, A., L. Solórzano, and D. Nepstad. In press. Modeling forest understory fire in an eastern Amazon landscape. *Ecological Applications*.

Amaral, P. and M. Amaral. 2000. *Manejo florestal comunitário na Amazônia Brasileira: Situaçao atual, desafios e perspectivas*. Brasília: Instituto Internacional de Educaçao do Brasil.

Barbier, E. B., J. C. Burgess, J. Bishop, and B. Aylward. 1994. *The economics of the tropical timber trade*. London: Earthscan.

Barreto, P., P. Amaral, E. Vidal, and C. Uhl. 1998. Costs and benefits of forest management for timber production in eastern Amazonia. *Forest Ecology and Management* 108: 9–26.

Barros, A. C. and C. Uhl. 1995. Logging along the Amazon River and estuary: Patterns, problems and potential. *Forest Ecology and Management* 77: 87–105.

Becker, G. S. 1968. Crime and punishment: An economic approach. *Journal of Political Economics* 76: 169.

Carvalho, G. O., A. C. Barros, P. R. S. Moutinho, and D. C. Nepstad. 2001. Sensitive development could protect Amazonia instead of destroying it. *Nature* 409: 131.

Cochrane, M. A., A. Alencar, M. D. Schulze, C. M. Souza Jr., D. C. Nepstad, P. A. Lefebvre, and E. A. Davidson. 1999. Positive feedbacks in the fire dynamic of closed canopy tropical forests. *Science* 284: 1832–1835.

Cochrane, M. A. and M. D. Schulze. 1999. Fire as a recurrent event in tropical forests of the eastern Amazon: Effects on forest structure, biomass, and species composition. *Biotropica* 31: 2–16.

Cohen, M. A. 2000. Empirical research on the deterrent effect of environmental monitoring and enforcement. *Environmental Law Report* 30: 10245–10252.

Contreras-Hermosilla, A. and M. T. V. Rios. 2002. Social, environmental and economic dimensions of forest policy reforms in Bolivia. Washington, D.C.: Forest Trends; Bogor, Indonesia: Center for International Forestry Research.

Cunha, L. H. 2002. *Analise institucional do manejo comunitária de recursos naturais na Amazônia*. Doctoral dissertation, Universidade Federal do Pará, Nucleo de Altos Estudos Amazônicos, Belém, Brazil.

Diaz, M. del C. V., D. Nepstad, M. J. C. Mendonça, R. M. Seroa, A. A. Alencar, J. C. Gomes, and R. A. Ortiz. 2002. *O prejuizo oculto do fogo: Custos econômicos das queimadas e dos incêndios florestais da Amazônia*. Belém, Brazil: Instituto de Pesquisa Ambiental da Amazônia e Instituto de Pesquisa Econômico Aplicado (www.ipam.org.br).

Fearnside, P. M. 2001. Soybean cultivation as a threat to the environment in Brazil. *Environmental Conservation* 28: 23–38.

Grogan, J. E. 2001. *Bigleaf mahogany (Swietenia macrophylla King) in southeast Pará, Brazil: A life history study with management guidelines for sustained production from natural forests*. Doctoral dissertation, Yale University, School of Forestry and Environmental Studies, New Haven, Conn..

Guimarães, A. L. and C. Uhl. 1997. Rural transport in eastern Amazonia: Limitations, options and opportunities. *Journal of Rural Studies* 13: 429–440.

Gullison, R. E., M. Melnyk, and C. Wong. 2001. Logging off: Mechanisms to stop or prevent logging in forests of high conservation value. Cambridge, Mass.: UCS Publications. Online: www.ucsusa.org/index.html.

Holdsworth, A. R. and C. Uhl. 1997. Fire in Amazonian selectively logged rain forest and the potential for fire reduction. *Ecological Applications* 7: 713–725.

Holmes, T. P., G. M. Blate, J. C. Zweede, R. Pereira Jr., P. Barreto, F. Boltz, and R. Bauch. 2002. Financial and ecological indicators of reduced impact logging performance in the eastern Amazon. *Forest Ecology & Management* 163: 93–110.

INCRA. 2001. Instituto Nacional de Colonização Rural e Reforma Agrária (www.incra.gov.br).

Jipp, P., D. C. Nepstad, K. Cassel, and C. J. R. d. Carvalho. 1998. Deep soil moisture storage and transpiration in forests and pastures of seasonally-dry Amazonia. *Climatic Change* 39: 395–412.

Johns, J., P. Barreto, and C. Uhl. 1996. Logging damage in planned and unplanned logging operations and its implications for sustainable timber production in the eastern Amazon. *Forest Ecology and Management* 89: 59–77.

Kalif, K., S. A. O. Malcher, C. Azevedos-Ramos, and P. Moutinho. 2001. The effect of logging on the ground-foraging ant community in eastern Amazonia. *Studies of Neotropical Fauna and Environment* 36: 215–219.

Laurance, W., M. Cochrane, S. Bergen, P. Fearnside, P. Delamônica, C. Barber, S. D'Angelo, and T. Fernandes. 2001. The future of the Brazilian Amazon. *Science* 291: 438–439.

Lentini, M., A. Veríssimo, and L. Sobral. 2003. Falós florestais da Amazonia. Belém, Brazil: Imazon.

Lima, E., M. Lentini, and A. Veríssimo. 2002. *Polos madeireiros do Estado do Mato Grosso*. Belém, Brazil: Imazon (www.imazon.org.br).

Mattos, M. M. d., D.C. Nepstad, and I. C. G. Vieira. 1992. *Cartilha para agricultores e extensionistas sobre mapeamento de áreas, cubagem de madeira e inventário florestal [Handbook for farmers and extension specialists on land mapping, timber volume measurement, and forest inventory]*. Woods Hole, Mass: Woods Hole Research Center.

Mayers, J. and S. Vermeulen. 2002. *Company–community forestry partnerships: From raw deals to mutual gains?* London: International Institute of Environment and Development.

Melo, R. de A., C. G. S. Rocha, and M. C. dos Santos. 2001. Um aporte metodológico à pesquisa-ação como mecanismo potencializador da regulação do uso dos recursos floresais. O caso das comunidades Ribeirinhas do Baixo Rio Xingu, Brasil. In A. Simões, L. M. S. Silva, P. F. da S. Martins, and C. Castellanet, eds., *Agricultura familiar: Métodos e experiências de pesquisa-desenvolvimento*, 205–228. Belém, Brazil: NEAF/CAP/UFPa: GRET.

Ministério de Meio Ambiente. 2002. *Política Nacional de Florestas*. Online: www.mma.gov.br.

Muchagata, M. and M. Amaral Neto. 2001. Tem barulho na mata: Perspectives para o manejo comunitário de florestas em uma região de fronteira. In A. Simões, L. M. S. Silva, P. F. da S. Martins, and C. Castellanet, eds., *Agricultura familiar: Métodos e experiências de pesquisa-desenvolvimento*, 89–103. Belém, Brazil: NEAF/CAP/UFPa: GRET.

Nepstad, D. C., J. P. Capobianco, A. C. Barros, G. O. Carvalho, P. R. d. S. Moutinho, U. Lopes, and P. A. Lefebvre. 2000. *Avança Brasil: Os custos ambientais para a Amazônia*. Belém, Brazil: Instituto de Pesquisa Ambiental da Amazônia e Instituto Socio-Ambiental. Online: www.ipam.org.br.

Nepstad, D.C., C. J. R. d. Carvalho, E. A. Davidson, P. Jipp, P. A. Lefebvre, G. H. d. Negreiros, E. D. da Silva, T. A. Stone, S. E. Trumbore, and S. Vieira. 1994. The role of deep roots in the hydrological and carbon cycles of Amazonian forests and pastures. *Nature* 372: 666–669.

Nepstad, D. C., G. O. Carvalho, A. C. Barros, A. Alencar, J. P. Capobianco, J. Bishop, P. Moutinho, P. A. Lefebvre, U. L. Silva, and E. Prins. 2001. Road paving, fire regime feedbacks, and the future of Amazon forests. *Forest Ecology and Management* 154: 395–407.

Nepstad, D. C., P. Jipp, P. Moutinho, G. Negreiros, and S. Vieira. 1995. Forest recovery following pasture abandonment in Amazônia: Canopy seasonality, fire resistance and ants. In D. Rapport, C. L. Caudet, and P. Calow, eds., *Evaluating and monitoring the health of large-scale ecosystems,* 333–349. Berlin: NATO ASI Series, Springer-Verlag.

Nepstad, D., P. Lefebvre, U. Silva Jr., J. Tomasella, L. Solórzano, P. Schlesinger, and D. Ray. In press. Amazon drought and its implication for forest flammability and tree growth: A basin-wide analysis. *Global Change Biology.*

Nepstad, D., D. McGrath, A. C. Barros, A. Alencar, M. Santilli, and M. C. Vera. 2002a. Frontier governance in Amazonia. *Science* 295: 629–630.

Nepstad, D. C., A. G. Moreira, and A. Alencar. 1999a. *Flames in the rain forest: Origins, impacts and alternatives to Amazonian fire.* Brasília, Brazil: The Pilot Program to Conserve the Brazilian Rain Forest, World Bank.

Nepstad, D., P. Moutinho, M. B. Dias-Filho, E. Davidson, G. Cardino, D. Markewitz, and R. Figueiredo. 2002b. The effect of partial throughfall exclusion on canopy processes and biogeochemistry of an Amazon forest. *Journal of Geophysical Research* 107(53):1–18.

Nepstad, D. C., A. Veríssimo, A. Alencar, C. A. Nobre, E. Lima, P. A. Lefebvre, P. Schlesinger, C. Potter, P. R. d. S. Moutinho, E. Mendoza, M. A. Cochrane, and V. Brooks. 1999b. Large-scale impoverishment of Amazonian forests by logging and fire. *Nature* 398: 505–508.

O *Liberal.* 2003. Exploração de mogno continua proibida por mais cinco meses. February 14, p. 1.

Pinedo-Vasquez, M., D. J. Zarin, K. Coffey, C. Padoch, and F. Rabelo. 2001. Post-boom logging in Amazonia. *Human Ecology* 29: 219–239.

Putz, F. E. 2000. Economics of home-grown forestry. *Ecological Economics* 32: 9–14.

Putz, F. E., K. H. Redford, J. G. Robinson, R. Fimbel, and G. M. Blate. 2000. *Biodiversity conservation in the context of tropical forest management.* Biodiversity Series—Impact Studies Paper no. 75. Washington, D.C.: World Bank.

Repetto, R. and M. Gillis, eds. 1988. *Public Policies and the Misuse of Forest Resources.* Cambridge, U.K.: Cambridge University Press.

Rohter, L. 2002. Brazil's prized exports rely on slaves and scorched land. *New York Times,* March 25, p. A1.

Schneider, R. R. 1994. *Government and the economy on the Amazon frontier.* World Bank Environment Paper no. 11. Washington, D.C.: World Bank.

Schneider, R. R., E. Arima, A. Veríssimo, P. Barreto, and C. Souza Jr. 2000. *O setor florestal na Amazônia: Oportunidades para uma economia sustentável.* Série Parcerias no. 01. Brasília, Brasil: World Bank.

Smeraldi, R. 2002. *Ilegalidade predatorio.* Predatoria, Brazil: Amigos da Terra.

Smeraldi, R. and A. Veríssimo. 1999. *Acertando o alvo: Consumo de madeira no mercado interno brasileiro e promoção da certificação florestal.* São Paulo, Brazil: Amigos da Terra, Imaflora e Imazon.

Smith, R. C. and N. Wray. 1996. *Amazonia: Economia indigena y mercado—Los desafios del desarrollo autonomo.* Quito, Ecuador: COICA and Oxfam America.

Stone, S. W. 1998. Using a geographic information system for applied policy analysis: The case of logging in the eastern Amazon. *Ecological Economics* 27: 43–61.

Tietenberg, T. 1996. *Private enforcement of environmental regulations in Latin America and the Caribbean: An effective instrument for environmental management?* Washington, D.C.: Inter-American Development Bank.

Uhl, C., P. Barreto, A. Veríssimo, E. Vidal, P. Amaral, A. C. Barros, C. J. Souza, J. Johns, and J. J. Gerwing. 1997. Natural resource management in the Brazilian Amazon. *BioScience* 47: 160–168.

Uhl, C. and R. Buschbacher. 1985. A disturbing synergism between cattle ranching burning practices and selective tree harvesting in the eastern Amazon. *Biotropica* 17: 265–268.

Uhl, C. and J. B. Kauffman. 1990. Deforestation, fire susceptibility and potential tree responses to fire in the eastern Amazon *Ecology* 71: 437–449.

Uhl, C., A. Veríssimo, M. M. d. Mattos, Z. Brandino, and I. C. G. Vieira. 1991. Social, economic, and ecological consequences of selective logging in an Amazon frontier: The case of Tailândia. *Forest Ecology and Management* 46: 243–273.

Uhl, C. and I. C. G. Vieira. 1989. Ecological impacts of selective logging in the Brazilian Amazon. *Biotropica* 21: 98–106.

Veríssimo, A., P. Barreto, R. Tarifa, and C. Uhl. 1995. Extraction of a high-value natural resource from Amazonia: The case of mahogany. *Forest Ecology and Management* 72: 39–60.

Veríssimo, A., M. A. Cochrane, and C. Souza Jr. 2002a. National forests in the Amazon. *Science* 297: 1478.

Veríssimo, A., M. A. Cochrane, C. Souza Jr., and R. Salomao. 2002b. Priority areas for establishing national forest in the Brazilian Amazon. *Conservation Ecology* 6. Online: www.consecol.org/vol6/Iss1/art4.

Veríssimo, A., and E. Lima. 1998. *Pólos de exploração madeireira na Amazônia.* Belém, Brazil: Imazon. Online: www.imazon.org.br.

Veríssimo, A., E. Lima, and M. Lentini. 2002c. *Polos madeireiros do estado do Pará.* Belém, Brazil: Imazon. Online: www.imazon.org.br.

Whitmore, T. C. 1985. *Tropical forests of the Far East.* Oxford, U.K.: Oxford Press.

Index